Arms, Yen & Power

Arms, Yen & Power
The Japanese Dilemma

John K. Emmerson
Foreword by Edwin O. Reischauer

DUNELLEN

New York

© 1971 by the Dunellen Publishing Company, Inc.
145 East 52nd Street
New York, New York 10022

International Standard Book Number 0-8424-0057-5

Library of Congress Catalogue Card Number 70-168683

Printed in the United States of America.

This book was researched and written under a grant from the
Georgetown University Center for Strategic and International
Studies, Washington, D.C. The Center is a private nonprofit
organization that seeks to advance the understanding of international policy issues. The Center does not take a position
on any policy issue, and the views expressed in works it
sponsors are those of the individual author.

To Dorothy

Contents

List of Tables

Foreword

Japan recently has been pronounced a "giant" or even a "superpower." But it has remained a strangely invisible giant or superpower—at least to Americans. We tend to look straight past Japan or through it to countries and problems that seem more clear-cut and therefore easier to focus on.

This situation is not new. Our trade with Japan began to exceed our trade with China close to a century ago, but Americans remained fascinated with the "open door" to a Chinese trade that never materialized. We were obsessed with the "China problem," when the real problem was the adjustment of the international system to a rapidly rising Japan, which found most of the world locked up inside the empires of earlier aggressors and a temptingly weak China next door.

The war that resulted from the failure of Japan and the international system to mesh peacefully did focus attention on Japan for a few years, but then once again it seemed to sink out of sight. Americans became obsessed with a new "China problem," seen as our "loss" of a China that had never been ours to lose, the disappearance of a "sister Republic" that had never been more than a military dictatorship, and the containment of a force that was not expanding but that reacted explosively to the pressures of containment. We fought one terrible war in Korea, made all the more tragic for having probably been avoidable. We became mired in an even more horrible war, which certainly was needless. These wars and the continuing question of the recognition of China and its admission into the United Nations have so absorbed our attention that once again we have failed to see that the big questions for the future of Asia all revolve around Japan.

Japan today, even in relative terms, is much stronger economically than when its army and navy spread devastation a quarter of the way around the globe, from the mid-Pacific to

Burma. It soon will be producing as much wealth as China, India, and all the other lands of East and South Asia combined. Virtually every country in the Far East finds Japan either its first- or its second-largest trading partner. The economic future of the whole area depends heavily on Japanese trade, investment, and aid. Our own trans-Pacific economic contacts are overwhelmingly with Japan. It is not only the fastest-rising but also the most global economic power in the world. Already it is number three, behind only ourselves and the Soviet Union, and catching up fast. But at the same time, its own economy remains curiously isolated behind jealously maintained barriers to foreign economic penetration. How, indeed, will this burgeoning economic colossus fit into a world growing much more slowly?

Vast economic strength and superb organizational skills give the Japanese great potentialities for military power and international political influence. So far, they have quite wisely preferred not to move in these directions and have concentrated only on economic growth. The people remain determinedly pacifistic and uninclined to play the game of international politics. They feel little threat to their security—perhaps because of the security treaty with the United States, but some would say in spite of it.

This is the way things have been for the past two decades; but there is now a great ferment under way in Japan, and no one can be sure what it will produce. There is an uneasy feeling among the Japanese that, as the world's third-greatest economic power, Japan should play a concomitant role in other fields. There is much talk of "autonomous defense." Despite strong economic and cultural ties with the United States, most Japanese wish to see a diminution of the defense relationship, if not its immediate severance. There is a great desire to feel free of the American shadow. Attitudes are also in flux toward Japan's closer neighbors—Korea, Taiwan, China, the Soviet Union, and the troubled nations of Southeast Asia.

The next few years will probably be a time of decision for the Japanese, and the decisions they make will undoubtedly have a profound impact not just on East Asia but on the world. A re-armed Japan, especially one with nuclear weapons, would greatly change the world situation. A "neutralist" Japan, whether armed or not, would produce a far different East Asia than a Japan that sees the United States as a "partner." Much depends on how the

Japanese conceive of their relationship to the world economy and what they see as their role in the economic development of Asia.

Thus, once again the great question is how a rapidly rising Japan fits into the world. But the problem is complex and not sharply focused. Japanese attitudes seem murky—even contradictory. It is hard to grasp what is at stake and how it will be decided.

It is for this reason that John Emmerson's present volume is so important. He forces us to look at the future of Japan as perhaps the most important factor in the future of Asia. He lays out the confused, interlocking problems in all their complexities. He looks at these from a variety of angles, helping to reveal their vague but portentous shapes. He brings to his task a clarity of vision that derives from a lifetime of intimate contact with Japan and acute observation of its problems. I have known him well during most of this period and have always found his knowledge impressive and his balance of judgment admirable. He, no more than anyone else, can be sure what will happen. But he shows with great clarity what could, and why, and what this might mean for all of us.

Edwin O. Reischauer

Belmont, Massachusetts
March, 1971

Acknowledgments

So many people, knowingly or not, have contributed in one way or another to the making of this book that no adequate expression of appreciation can ever be made. There are, however, several debts which I wish to acknowledge.

Professor Robert E. Ward of the Department of Political Science at the University of Michigan first suggested that I write this book, then patiently prodded me along, read tirelessly through my drafts and gave me the benefit of his sensitive and intelligent criticism.

Much of my research and travel in Asia was made possible by the Center for Strategic and International Studies of Georgetown University which took an early interest in the project. The former Executive Director, David Abshire, and his successor, Ambassador John M. Steeves, together with their experienced staffs, accorded me the encouragement, professional advice, and continuous counsel so sorely needed by an ex-Foreign Service Officer venturing into a new and untried enterprise.

In Japan many friends, both in and out of government, talked with me, provided me with material, and suggested sources and approaches. To name one, I should name all, and space forbids. Each will know who he or she is and I hope will accept my thanks.

Expecially deserving of my gratitude are my many Foreign Service friends and former colleagues, expecially in the Embassy in Tokyo, but also in American Embassies in the capitals of East and Southeast Asia visited by me in 1968 and 1969. Their friendly cooperation and expert knowledge of the countries where they served were invaluable to me.

Two individuals in Japan merit special mention. One is Mr. Raymond Aka of the Embassy who was particularly helpful to me; the other is Miss Yachie Takashima of the Japan Defense Agency, whose courteous assistance contributed much to my working arrangements in Tokyo.

Many friends, specialists in their respective fields, read and commented on portions of the manuscript; others answered queries and contributed useful data and advice. To all of these I am grateful.

Obviously I alone am responsible for errors which remain.

I was fortunate during the writing of the book to enjoy the excellent facilities of the Hoover Institution on War, Revolution, and Peace at Stanford University, whose outstanding East Asian collections are of unique value.

Arms, Yen & Power

We are now engaged in the task of building a new Japan, a Japan we hope can make a unique contribution to this world. In the history of mankind, countries which have become economically powerful have always been fated eventually to become military great powers as well. The new Japan challenges this commonly accepted rule of history. Japan does not want to hang on to the outdated concept that economic great powers must necessarily become military great powers. Nor do we want to adopt the philosophy that in order to become a great power, we must possess nuclear arms.

—Nakasone Yasuhiro, Director General of the Japan Defense Agency, in a speech to the National Press Club, Washington, D.C., September 10, 1970.

Introduction

In the second half of the twentieth century, Asia has been the scene of America's deepest frustrations. The Soviet Union, our rival superpower, with all of its threats and its atomic arsenals, has never brought us the prolonged and maddening agony we have known in Asia. Once we stared Khrushchev down in the Cuban missile crisis, we accepted peaceful coexistence and, assuming neither of us wanted world war, believed we could tolerate a balance of terror while keeping our guard up and waiting for the chance to find together some ways to lower the tension.

In Asia it was different. Watching "our" China being devoured by Communists was a searing experience to which we reacted with self-flagellation which has hardly ceased to this day. In Europe, NATO gave us confidence and no call ever came to meet an aggressor. The 175 Soviet divisions, charted on top-secret intelligence maps as poised to march across Western Europe in a great invasion, somehow never moved. But in June 1950, the North Koreans did march; and when the war was over three years later, 157,000 Americans were dead and wounded and Korea was divided at an armed border. Seventeen years later, 62,000 Americans were still in South Korea with the Park Chung Hee government reacting in panic at the first news of planned force reductions.

Ironically, the same Geneva conference of 1954 was called to solve the problems of both Korea and Indochina—for us, one war ending and another, if we had only known it, about to begin. For years the arguments will rage about how we got into war in Vietnam, what we were fighting for, why we bombed the North, and why we stayed so long. This is not the place to discuss Indochina. The Vietnam War, however, has long been a fact of life in Asia and no Asian nation, including Japan, has escaped its effect.

3

In these turbulent postwar years, while revolutions were working themselves out in China, while wars were being fought in Korea and Southeast Asia, while Sukarno rose and fell in Indonesia and his country turned in a new direction, the Japanese with one mind and heart were building a nation whose Gross National Product by 1970 would be third in the world and would be advancing rapidly.

In contrast to the American pain over China and our baffling crusade in Southeast Asia, the American postwar experience with Japan has been generally a happy one. The Occupation was a constructive effort and subsequent relations have developed a partnership which both nations have recognized as essential to security and stability in Pacific Asia. Turning from our frustrations in other parts of Asia, we see Japan as the hope for the future. This stable, economically powerful democracy is destined to become the leader of Asia, we say; and as we reduce our troops in Asia we contemplate the kind of stabilizing force the Japanese can be. But can we shed our frustrations so easily? Will the Japanese respond? Why don't they act faster? And why do they shut their economic doors to us while getting rich on trade? Will they assume defense responsibilities in the area? If they do, what will the other Asians think? If they don't, what will we think? What do we expect of Japan and what does Japan expect of us? How will Japan react toward China? Will these neighbors become friends or enemies, and how will the balance of power in Asia be affected?

My purpose in this book is to discuss some of these problems. First let me say that the book is not a history, although modern problems can hardly be explained without referring to the past. Neither is it a survey of Japan today, although to describe contemporary policies and actions one must sketch in some of their background. It is not a study of Japan's international relations, which are global, since the focus is on East Asia and the United States.

In the first chapter I have attempted to set the stage, to describe briefly Japan's present economic status and political situation, to seek the reasons for Japan's success, and to identify the problems which face the country in the decade of the 1970's. In the succeeding chapters I have explored four themes integrally related to each other and representing priority interests for Japan in foreign affairs. These are: (1) the Japanese-American relationship, (2) security, (3) relations with Asian neighbors, and (4) certain decisions for the 1970's.

Japan's relationship with the United States since World War II has been so dominant, economically, politically, and militarily, that it is no wonder the Japanese have become somewhat restive under this overwhelming influence and therefore seek greater "independence" in the present age. The Japanese-American relationship is inseparable from the security and the Okinawa problems, and American policies and influence have often intruded upon Japan's relations with her Asian neighbors. The reader will meet the American element throughout the treatment of these subjects and will find in the next to the last chapter a separate discussion of the problems of security and economics in the Japanese-American relationship.

Security is the most important and the most controversial issue for Japan. From the Occupation period it has been intimately involved with Americans and with American policy. The problem of Japan's security also affects future Japanese policies toward near neighbors and those in Southeast Asia. To understand the inhibitions, conflicts, and judgments which impinge upon the current, evolving policies and actions related to the defense of Japan, some appreciation of past history is required. This is the purpose of the chapters on the security treaties and the Self-Defense Forces.

The problem of Okinawa is both a Japanese-American issue and a security problem and is intimately related to Japan's developing relationships in Asia. The time agreed for reversion, 1972, is the next critical date already marked on Japan's international calendar.

The interaction of four powers, the United States, the Soviet Union, Communist China and Japan, will be crucial to the future of East Asia. We therefore look first at Japan's relations with the two Communist neighbors, mainland China and the U.S.S.R. Here economic, political, and defense interests are intermingled. Moscow and Peking view Japan with apprehension; yet, motivated by economic self-interest and by competition which seeks advantage over a rival who is also an enemy, they woo her. In these chapters we shall glance at the historical origins of Japan's relationships with China and with Russia, then examine present-day attitudes, problems, prospects, and dangers.

After the United States and the giant Communist neighbors, the two nations most important to Japan are her former colonies, Korea and Taiwan. This importance was formally recognized in the agreements reached by President Nixon and Prime Minister Sato in November 1969, which declared that the security of South Korea was "essential" and the security of the Taiwan area "important" to the security of Japan. The significance of Japan's economic and political interests in the Republics of Korea (ROK) and of China (ROC) has long been evident. Future Japanese policy toward mainland China must consider the problem of Taiwan, and policies toward the ROK will be formulated with due regard for the uncertainty of what North Korea might do.

The next and natural sphere of interest for Japan is Southeast Asia. Here we look at countries which knew invasion and occupation by imperial Japan but now are engaged in a speedily climbing trade bringing massive distribution of industrial and consumer goods pouring from Japan's inexhaustible factories. Southeast Asians receive this Japanese invasion, which includes the ever-enlarging presence of Japanese businessmen and entrepreneurs, with some uneasiness. To some, the Japanese in Southeast Asia seek economic domination instead of territorial control as in the past. Others see a future armed Japan reverting to the militarism of old. Security, economics, and politics invariably become mixed, with demands for aid increasing.

Finally, the later chapters are devoted to decisions of the 1970's, to those policies which will affect the security of Japan and relations with the countries of Asia and with the United States. First and of supreme importance will be the nuclear decision, which Japan may take in the 1970's or which she may postpone to a time beyond this decade. The state of technology, the usefulness of nuclear energy for Japan, and the problems of weapons construction are relevant to capability, but the decision will be political. A decision by Japan to build the bomb would be far-reaching. Unless taken in response to some sudden and cataclysmic change in the world situation, it would seriously affect relations with the United States and the Asian countries whose relations with Japan are discussed in this book. A Japanese decision to "go nuclear" would not be a "Pearl Harbor" decision; it would be based on the most meticulous assessment of the consequences and of Japan's best national interests.

Some decisions of the greatest consequence for Japan will be made by the United States. Asians are not yet sure of the true meaning of the Nixon doctrine, of how far and how fast the American presence in East Asia will be reduced. Japanese faith in the American word has in some degree been eroded, and, unfortunately, the quarrels about economic questions have worsened the atmosphere. Succeeding Japanese Governments will watch American actions intently and will decide policy according to their judgments of Japanese national interests.

The final chapter looks at Japanese policy in the 1970's and speculates on its content and direction, how it might fit into the framework of Asia, the likelihood and nature of leadership, and the conflict or compatibility which could characterize the Japanese relationship with the United States.

Part 1

The Setting

1 Japan Enters the 1970's

Economic Success

The Japanese Empire in 1940 extended from the northernmost Kurile Islands to the southern tip of Formosa, embraced Korea and Manchuria, controlled much of China, and included the fortified mandated islands in the mid-Pacific. Population throughout the Empire was described in the propaganda slogans of the day as the "one hundred million with one heart," suggesting unanimous support for Japan's destiny in bringing a "New Order" to East Asia. Thirty years later, Japan on its four main islands was smaller in area than California but had five times the population, 103 million in 1970—already more people than lived in all of the old Empire. This new Japan was again a leading trading partner of the countries of East and Southeast Asia and had expanding economic interests throughout the world. Today no Japanese wishes to recall the "New Order in East Asia" or to repeat the failures of the past. The postwar period has brought phenomenal economic success. As George Ball has written: "Compared with this island nation's progress, the German 'economic miracle' appears as apprentice magic." [1]

Japan's Gross National Product was estimated at $200 billion in 1970 and is expected to double by 1975. This was about half the estimated Soviet GNP and one fifth of the trillion-dollar GNP of the United States. Japan's growth rate averaged more than 13 percent in the three years 1967 through 1969 and was expected by some economists to continue to rise at an average annual rate of more than 12 percent from 1970 through 1975. However, at the end of November 1970, the Keidanren (Federation of Economic Organizations) predicted a slowing down in 1971, to 10.7 percent in real terms owing to a slackening in the rate of increase of exports and investments in plants and facilities. [2]

Whether or not this happens by 1971, at least by the second half of the decade it is reasonable to expect the growth rate to begin to fall off. Some experts look for Japan to pass both the Soviet Union and the United States by the end of the century. Still one cannot ignore the very serious problems which will confront Japan's leaders as the century wanes. The demands on the Government for expenditures to develop technology, improve the character of life, including education, environment, welfare and urban development, and the requirements of defense and foreign aid, will impose burdens which Japan has largely escaped thus far. Additionally, the export drive may meet increasing resistance and, with the labor shortage, may contribute to slowing the rate of Japan's up-to-now phenomenal growth.

Japan's economy has been built principally on the home market, rather than on exports, notwithstanding the fact that foreign trade is essential to Japan's industrial life. The percentage of exports to GNP has been consistently smaller than in any industrial country except the United States.[3] In 1969, exports amounted to only 8 percent of the GNP ($16 billion out of $200 billion). Lacking essential raw materials (coking coal, iron, oil, cotton, wool), Japan depends upon imports to feed her industrial machine and must in turn export to pay for imports.

In 1935 a writer could observe: "Today a powerful stream of Japanese manufacturers is flooding the markets of the world."[4] Thirty-five years later the stream was again powerful and was constantly and rapidly swelling, Japan's share of the world's exports had risen from 4.8 percent in 1965 to 6.9 percent in 1970 and was expected to pass 10 percent by 1975. Export growth in 1969 was 23 percent and the surplus over imports $3.7 billion. The export total is forecast by one economic researcher to reach $41 billion by 1975.[5]

In the 1970's Japan's economic interests would be global, although with major emphasis on Pacific countries. A third of her trade has been with the United States and a quarter with East and Southeast Asia. Of the remainder with the rest of the world, the Middle East was prominent for its supply of oil. For the future, prospects point toward growing trade with the Soviet Union and Communist China (now about 5 percent of the total) and the likelihood that the never-ending search for raw materials will open new channels for Japanese trade elsewhere.

By the end of 1968, 2,600 private investments had been approved, in accordance with the Foreign Exchange and Foreign Trade Supervision Laws, for a total of nearly two billion dollars in ninety countries. Half of this amount had been committed in the years 1966-1968, and in 1968 alone investments amounted to $552 million. The favored area was North America with 30 percent of the total; Latin America followed with 21 percent; Southeast Asia was third with 18 percent. Sixty percent of the investments was equally divided between manufacturing (principally lumber, pulp, and textiles) and mining. The remainder was in business ventures of various kinds.[6]

In comparison with other advanced countries, Japanese direct investments were still relatively small; they were 15 percent of exports in 1968, about the same percentage as that of West Germany but hardly in the same class as the 190 percent of the United States. In terms of world shares, Japan's was the smallest, 1.9 percent, contrasting with 61 percent for the United States, 18 percent for Great Britian, and 2.8 percent for West Germany.[7]

The smooth running of the Japanese economic machine and the leaping growth rate could not have been possible without a stable political situation during the postwar period.

Political Stability

If the Japanese economy is to continue its uninterrupted rise through the rest of the century, the continuation of political stability must be assumed. The signs are favorable.

The Liberal Democratic Party (LDP)

The continuity of Japanese postwar politics has been carried on by the Liberal Democratic Party, formed in 1955 by the merger of two parties, the Liberals and the Democrats, who in turn were the inheritors of the leading parties of the prewar period. Except for a brief period in 1947 and 1948 when coalition Governments were headed by a Socialist (Katayama Tetsu) and a Democrat (Ashida Hitoshi) respectively, Japanese Governments since the war have been controlled by the same political grouping. Struggles for power have occurred among the factions within the LDP and its predecessors and, in one sense, these have been more important than battles between the parties. With little chance of capturing the Government, the opposition parties tended toward irresponsibility in their actions and policies and in their parliamentary conduct have been more obstructive than constructive.

Yoshida Shigeru, who quickly emerged in the Occupation as a diplomat who knew how to deal with foreigners and a politician with impeccable anti-war credentials (he had suffered house arrest during the war), was Prime Minister five times in the period of years stretching from May 1946 to December 1954. He left his indelible stamp on the LDP and on Japanese governmental leadership. The succession to the prime ministership, the "Yoshida Line" as it was called, was set forth by him and thus far has been followed scrupulously: Kishi, Ikeda, Sato. Fukuda Takeo, Minister of Finance in the 1970 Sato Cabinet, was rumored as next in the Yoshida Line, and it remained to be seen whether the Line would be broken at the end of Sato's fourth term.

The LDP won the largest number of seats in the history of any party, 302 out of 486, in the House of Representatives elections in December 1969. This victory encouraged Prime Minister Sato, who had returned from Washington in November with the promise of Okinawa for 1972, and who later in 1970 ran successfully for an unprecedented fourth term as president of the LDP and thus continued as Prime Minister.

The LDP, which forms one element in the triumvirate said to rule Japan—Party, Big Business, and Bureaucracy—has, in spite of its victories, been receiving weakening support. In the previous lower house elections (January 1967), the party took 48.8 percent of the popular vote; in the 1969 elections, this percentage dropped to 47.6. There were various reasons. Traditionally the LDP wins support from rural areas and with the migration to the cities, the farm vote decreases. As it is, the Japanese electoral system gives the rural population over-representation at the expense of the cities. To many voters, particularly the younger ones, the LDP has become a party of "tired, old politicians" and it inspires little enthusiasm. In contrast, the *Komeito* (Clean Government Party), at least in 1967 and 1969, drew away LDP support by its fresh appeal and insistence on probity in government. In addition, the rising cost of living and the difficulties of housing, overcrowding, and unhealthful environment were all beginning to impress the voter and to lead him to disappointment and frustration with the party in power.

14

On balance, however, the LDP's losses have not been of a dimension to threaten the party's continued dominance. Public opinion polls in late 1970 indicated about 50 percent popular support for the party.

The Japan Socialist Party (JSP)

The principal opposition party, the Japan Socialist Party, is in confused disarray after losing in the last three elections: four seats in the lower house elections of January 1967, eight for the upper house in July 1968, and finally a crushing fifty in the general elections of December 1969, reducing the party's representation in the House of Representatives from 140 to 90. The JSP's percentage of the popular vote declined from 27.89 to 21.44. Torn by factionalism and struggling to present a more attractive face to the public, the Socialists seemed paralyzed, unable either to unify themselves on a new program or to split and go separate ways. New defeats appear to lie ahead.

The JSP seems to have lost touch with its natural clientele. The labor unions, which were the traditional supporters of the party, not only with their votes but also with their pocketbooks, became much less dependable. The *Sohyo* (General Council of Trade Unions) found that its younger members were more interested in the economic benefits of trade unionism than in political action, which previously had received priority attention, and were not necessarily ardent supporters of the JSP. In a recent poll taken among members of the National Railway Workers Union, only 55 percent favored the JSP in contrast to 83 percent in a similar poll in 1967. [8]

Other explanations for the heavy Socialist defeat in 1969 were poor election strategy, inability to compete with the energetic *Komeito* and Communist Party, and failure to take a clear-cut stand on student violence.

However, the gaping flaw in the JSP was its hopeless split between right and left wings whose purposes and positions were so far apart that their coexistence in the same party seemed incredible. The traditional Socialist voter probably expressed his disgust with such a state of affairs by seeking a more comfortable home, either with the *Komeito* or the Democratic Socialists, if he were moderate in inclination, or, if left-wing, with the Communists. If none of these satisfied, he would refuse to vote. The abstention rate (31.49 percent) was the highest in the postwar period, except for the election of 1947. [9]

The *Komeito* or "Clean Government Party" and the Democratic Socialist Party (DSP) are two smaller parties which attempt to attract the "middle-of-the-road" voter.

The *Komeito* (Clean Government Party)

The *Komeito* was founded by the *Soka Gakkai* (Value Creation Society), an aggressive, proselytizing offshoot of the *Nichiren* Buddhist sect, and ran its first candidates for the House of Representatives in 1967. Two years later the *Komeito* increased its seats from 25 to 47 and doubled its percentage of the popular vote (from 5.4 percent to 10.9 percent).

The *Soka Gakkai*, with its persistent methods of winning members (*shaku-buku*, conversion by high-pressure salesmanship), its spectacular mass meetings, imperious discipline, and set hierarchy, reminiscent of Communist and Fascist organizations, led some observers, particularly foreigners, to see in it a future totalitarian threat to the Japanese State. However, the vagueness of the principles and policies of both parent organization and political party and the character of the leadership have not so far justified such alarms.

The party was politically on the make, adjusting its stands on domestic and foreign issues to win maximum support. *Soka Gakkai* upheld basic virtues which no one could reject and supplied one answer to many Japanese experiencing the restless postwar "spiritual vacuum." It preached international brotherhood and welcomed foreigners into its midst. At one time the organization claimed more than 7,000 members in Los Angeles, many of whom were former soldiers married to Japanese girls belonging to *Soka Gakkai*. The movement was a kind of "Moral Rearmament." It had a strong appeal to middle- and lower-income groups in a nation with a strong Buddhist tradition and appeared at a receptive moment in Japanese history.

In early 1970, *Komeito* officials were accused of trying to suppress the publication and distribution of an unfavorable book called *Soka Gakkai wo Kiru*, Literally "Cut Down the *Soka Gakkai*", but published in English as *I Denounce Soka Gakkai*. [10] The Japanese Communist Party, glorying in its role of defender of Japanese democracy, denounced both the Buddhist organization

16

and its political party for violating two of Japan's constitutional guarantees: separation of Church and State and freedom of speech and press. *Gakkai* leaders finally publicly admitted that the charges of trying to suppress the book were generally true.

The episode was the first challenge to the *Komeito* and brought the issues of religion and politics and freedom of the press sharply to focus. The party leadership was at first singularly inept in handling the problem and, in their confusion, lost respect from the public. Party officials then declared that they would cut all relationships with the *Soka Gakkai* and resign from the positions which they had held in the religious organization. In turn, those with high posts in the latter renounced their offices in the party.

Hatred of *Soka Gakkai*, always intense among other Buddhist sects, was fanned by these disclosures. The public image of the *Komeito* was seriously tarnished, and it remained to be seen whether the party's future growth would be affected. Its leaders recognized that to expand further, the party would have to recruit support, membership, and even candidates outside the folds of the *Soka Gakkai.* Many observers believed that this would be difficult and that the *Komeito* might therefore be approaching a plateau in membership and political influence. Of course much would also depend on the future progress of both the LDP and the JSP, from whose ranks the *Komeito* has in the past weaned away supporters.

The Democratic Socialist Party (DSP)

The Democratic Socialist Party was formed by the right wing of the Socialist Party, which split off in 1960. The party espouses moderate policies in both domestic and foreign affairs, but it has never captured the public imagination or been able to expand significantly its base of support. In the 1969 elections, the DSP won an additional seat—taking 31 as compared with the 30 it had controlled before.

The Japan Communist Party (JCP)

The Japan Communist Party, first organized in 1922, was totally suppressed for most of the prewar period; it began to function openly only after General MacArthur's civil rights directive of October 4, 1945 permitted freedom of political activity and ordered the release of political prisoners.

In the first years of the Occupation, the party gained adherents rapidly and in 1949 won 35 seats in the House of Representatives from nearly three million voters. In 1950, the then Cominform denounced the head of the party, Nosaka Sanzo, for trying to achieve power through parliamentary means and failing to take revolutionary action. The party bowed to Moscow's dictates, "took to the streets," was soon purged of its principal officers by General MacArthur because of its violent actions, and lost all House seats in the next election, with its popular vote reduced to less than a million.

Working its way back gradually to increased influence and representation in the Diet, the JCP broke first with the Soviet Communist Party over the nuclear test ban treaty and later with the Chinese Communist Party over questions of party policies and strategy. Internationally the party follows an "independent" line.

The JCP has in recent years sought popularity by opposing violence, appealing to middle-class virtues, affecting a benign posture, and advertising its dedication to the pursuit of power exclusively through parliamentary means. The policy has paid off. The party won 6.8 percent of the popular vote in the 1969 elections, an improvement of 2 percent over the percentage in 1967, and increased its seats held in the House of Representatives from five to fourteen. Together with seven seats in the House of Councillors, the JCP total reached 21 for both Houses, the highest since 1949.

Continued pursuit of the present successful policy of independent, non-violent, friendly action could, according to some observers, bring the JCP as many as forty seats in the next lower house elections.

Political Party Prospects

The leadership of Japan's left-wing movements by the JSP, the JCP, and the *Sohyo* (General Federation of Labor Unions) has been challenged by the radical, militant groups characterized as the "New Left." These include the anti-JCP factions of the student organizations, such as the "Red Army Faction," whose members highjacked a plane to North Korea. Opposed by both JCP and JSP, they were responsible for most of the violence which paralyzed Japan's universities and characterized the "demos" (demonstrations) and rallies taking place in 1969 to protest American bases, the Vietnam War, and the security treaty with the United States. The effectiveness of these groups was tested in the anti-security treaty movement of 1970—to have reached its climax in June. The young "wild ones" tossed their Molotov cocktails but met only hardened, experienced police and public resentment and fury. Disruptions will continue. But the militant elements lack mass support and even sympathy and face the continued attacks of both the Socialist and Communist Parties. They can hardly hope to influence decisively Japanese political life.

The LDP will probably control Japanese governments through the 1970's. The retention of comfortable LDP majorities in both houses of the Diet does not appear to be immediately threatened.

Conceivably the coming years could witness a coalescence of opposition parties potent and popular enough to challenge continued domination by the LDP. Such a party could be formed by a union of right-wing elements from the JSP, dissidents from the LDP, and most of the present members of the DSP. It would be moderate in ideology but slightly to the left of the LDP. The *Komeito*, to avoid isolation, might cooperate in such a coalition although it would not wish to abandon its identity. The difficulty in organizing such an assortment of political entities would be agreement on leadership. To split has always been easier than to unite, and each group would want to be the senior partner.

The Basic Elements of Japanese Success

Japan is economically strong and politically stable. How did this happen? Some elements in the success story stand out.

Geography. The moat of oceans surrounding Japan afforded both protection and a sense of identity and unity. Until 1945, Japan had never been invaded nor defeated in war.

Homogeneity. The Japanese are one in race and language. The only minority groups worthy of mention are the disappearing *Ainu* tribesmen of Hokkaido, the relatively small but continuing outcast *Eta* communities, and the Koreans resident in Japan. Some regional dialects and accents persist, but universal education and the mass media influence most Japanese to use the national language in its standard form. Freedom from serious problems of race and minorities is fortunate.

Climate. Japan is endowed with a generally temperate climate, but with variations from the heavy winters of Hokkaido to the semitropical areas of southern Kyushu. If climate and natural energy are related, the Japanese climate is an asset.

Education. Japan's educational tradition dates from the *terakoya* (temple schools) of the Tokugawa period (1603-1868). Today Japan boasts a 99 percent literacy rate and 99.9 percent of the eligible age group of children (6-14) pursue nine years of compulsory education. Of those completing this elementary course, 82.4 percent went on to high schools in 1969, an increase from 75.2 percent in 1967. Comparable percentages for the Soviet Union and for Great Britain in 1967 were 73 and 53.5 respectively. Of those eligible Japanese students (aged 18 to 21), 16.7 percent were enrolled in colleges and universities in 1969; percentages were 23.3 for men, 9.8 for women. These were increases over the percentages in 1967: 16.0, 22.8 (men) and 9.5 (women). In 1967, the American percentage of men and women college entrants combined was 46.6 percent of those eligible; in Great Britain the percentage was 12.6, in France, 13, and in West Germany, 8.7.[11]

Outside Infusions. Japan has profited by massive infusions of learning and technology from the outside. The first was the absorption of the literature and language of China from the fourth to seventh centuries, which endowed Japan with the essence of a rich culture to be adapted and developed in entirely indigenous and original ways. The second infusion came after two hundred years of self-imposed isolation and after Commodore Perry's "black ships" had forced the Tokugawa regime to open its doors to the world. Once this happened, the foreigner changed overnight from unwanted "barbarian" to sought-after mentor, and the youthful Japanese leaders of the period, bursting with energy and enthusiasm, set out deliberately to catch up with the Western world. The third infusion came at the end of World War II, when the foreign enemy became occupier and all-powerful ruler and a prostrate Japan had to face the task of recovery from a devastating war and the reconstruction of the nation. The Japanese were determined to profit from their erstwhile enemies, to make up for lost time by learning as rapidly as possible the technology they had missed and, in the process, to better the instruction.

The System. Japan's rapid industrialization after the opening of the country to the West owed much of its success to the close cooperation established then between the Government and private enterprise. This has continued. Government, Business, and

Bureaucracy work hand in hand, baffling the foreigner with what they do and how. This amazingly workable fusion of interests has inspired some Japanese to dub their politico-economic conglomerate "Japan, Inc." However described, the system works.

Loyalties. Japan, like America, has experienced youth in revolt. The trans-Pacific transfer of "hippies," "mod" clothes, long hair, and "happenings" has seemed instantaneous. And to older Japanese, with their Confucian concepts of family, the generation gap has appeared to be a chasm. But Japanese traditions still die hard, and the militant leaders of the snake-dancing *Zengakuren* are likely to return home to family rituals—an act which a rebelling American youth, rallying against the "generation gap," could never comprehend. What is more, the radical student militant, donning coat and tie after graduation, joins *Mitsui* or *Mitsubishi* and happily begins a lifetime of loyal service to the "company." His wild oats "demo" days behind him, and with a job and a wife, the "salary-man" begins to form his life around three loyalties: his family, his company, and his country. The company's interests become his interests; he will work hard, do his best, and the company will take care of him until retirement. He expects his semi-annual bonuses, his annual raises in salary; if competent, he rises rapidly in the business; if less so, he finds himself in duller and less exacting positions, but he is never fired. Seniority is security and whatever his job, his loyalty stays unshakeable. Even when his union calls a strike, its leaders thoughtfully arrange it at times least inconvenient for the company and for the public: private railway employees seem usually to strike between 2 and 6 A.M.! Some newer companies have rejected lifetime employment and hire and fire for merit alone, but they are still a small minority. Company loyalty is a strength of the Japanese industrial system. It has increased output and reduced labor troubles.

The Achievement Ethic. Japan is a nation of achievers. Lacking either ideology or religion as a potent motivating force, Japan has since the war held up for its people one national goal: economic growth. For each Japanese, the goal is achievement born out of competition. Life for a child can become an "examination hell" from the time he enters kindergarten (there are entrance exams for kindergarten) until he is ready for high school and finally, and worst of all, when he applies to a university. Often his mother—called the "Education Mamma"—goads her son to his achievements. She broods over his school work, monitors his activities, and guides his every step so that he passes the all-important, all-determining examination. (Activities of the "Education Mammas" can start early. The *Japan Times* on July 25, 1968 published an article headlined "Education Moms' Facing Stiff Fines," which related that two mothers were alleged to have bribed ten teachers to have their children admitted to a primary school.) The result will decide not only his school (and if his father went to Tokyo University the moral pressure on him to do likewise is intense) but his job, his wife, and his future life. In spite of modernized youth, many marriages taking place in Japan are still arranged by parents, in which case the education of the groom, his job prospects, or the kind of job he has are all determining factors in the selection of an attractive, intelligent wife from a good family. This choice very significantly influences his future social position and family life.

The single-minded concentration on preparing for examinations is carried into the job. It produces the aggressive salesman in Southeast Asia, the ambitious company manager plotting new markets to capture, and the astute ex.cutive seeking sources of raw materials. This focus on success is not alien to the American "go-getter" and "rags-to-riches" tradition, but Japanese competitiveness is more frenetic, more ruthless, and more resolute.

Savings. The Japanese are among the world's greatest savers. They saved 19.3 percent of their incomes in 1968 and are expected to step this up to 23.2 percent by 1975.[12] Continued economic growth will bring increased personal income, but the level of consumption will probably not rise at the same rate.

Economic Advantages in the Postwar Period. Several fortunate factors have materially boosted Japan's economic growth in the postwar period. First, Japan benefitted by having to start from scratch. War's destruction eliminated antiquated, obsolete industrial equipment. Producers could take advantage of the latest innovations, including automation, and leap-frog immediately to positions of strong competitive advantage. Second, American help, amounting to some $400 million per year in the years before the Korean War, gave Japan needed injections at a critical early period. American technology, obtained principally through licensing agreements, was invaluable at this crucial time. Third, the Korean War, with its extraordinary demands for large quantities of essential supplies, gave a sharp boost to the Japanese economic take-off. Finally, the unique chance to spend less that one percent of GNP on defense was a beneficent luxury no other industrial power could enjoy.

Political Advantages in the Postwar Period. The Occupation gave Japan certain advantages quickly and in large doses at the very beginning of the postwar period. Freedoms were guaranteed, a democratic Constitution enacted, and the social system thoroughly reformed. The country was not divided and was kept stable, and the Russians were not allowed to disrupt the Occupation by taking over a zone, as they wished. The Japanese found many faults in Occupation policy and reversed many American actions when they regained their independence. In retrospect, they found the Occupation not so bad. In a poll taken shortly before the 25th anniversary of the surrender, 74 percent of those queried believed that, on balance, more good than bad was done in the name of "democracy" after the end of the war. [13] This judgment by a people occupied by a conqueror for seven years, given twenty-five years after their defeat in war, must be a rare example in history.

Problems for the 1970's

In spite of good prospects for continued economic growth and political stability, Japan faces serious problems and competing demands for national resources in the decade of the 'seventies.

Population and Labor Supply. Japan's population is one of the best controlled in the world. Through family planning and legalized abortions, the population growth rate has been kept to an estimated 1.1 percent. The Population Division of the United Nations predicts a slight rise in the 1970-1975 period to 1.2 percent, returning to 1.1 percent from 1975 to 1980 and again decreasing after 1980 to 0.8 percent. [14] Total Japanese population is expected to increase from 103 million in 1970 to 110 million in 1975 and 116 million in 1980. The labor force will grow only modestly, and the age group between 15 and 24 will decrease from about 20 million in 1970 to less than 16 million in 1980. [15]

The labor shortage facing Japan's presently booming economy is one of the most serious problems for the nation in this decade. Unlike their colleagues in the United States who find a Ph.D. no longer a guaranteed ticket to a good job, Japanese high school and university graduates are courted eagerly by competing companies. Many may choose among several alluring offers.

Manufacturing concerns are finding it profitable and indeed necessary to build factories in countries which can offer cheaper and plentiful labor. This trend can only increase. Okinawa offers possibilities, as we shall see later; it is still uncertain to what extent Japanese industries will establish factories and utilize labor in Okinawa. Already Okinawans are being sought for employment in Japan, as was the case in the prewar period.

Wages. Wages in Japan are still lower than those in the United States. In 1968, the average monthly wage of a worker in industrial concerns with more than 30 employees was approximately $154; however, fringe benefits would make this considerably higher. [16] The steady rise of Japanese wages has reduced one of the special advantages which prewar Japanese exports enjoyed. Annual percentage increases averaged 11.8 percent between 1960 and 1970, and the prospects are that this average may rise to 15.7 percent in the period 1970-1975.[17]

Research and Development. As we shall explore in a later chapter, Japan in the postwar period has depended in a major way on technology imported from abroad, usually through licensing arrangements. Although Japanese firms are now themselves exporting technology, the inflow is still greater. Both government and industry recognize the need to devote more attention and money to R & D (present official and private budget allotments are far less than those of other industrial countries), and this is certain to happen in the future.

Agriculture. Japanese farmers number about 19 percent of the total labor force. This is less than half of the prewar percentage of farm labor but still well ahead of the United States figure, now only 5 percent. Farming plots are small and, although remarkable productivity increases have been achieved, maximum efficiency is impossible. As has been suggested, rice fields should be combined into larger units, with their care entrusted to a capable operator, thus freeing other landowners for jobs in factories.

The Government buys the entire rice crop and most of the wheat and barley crops at inflated prices from producers and sells them at lower prices to consumers. The objective is political, to win rural support for the Liberal Democratic Party. The results are enormous expenditures and warehouses bulging with rice, some of it accumulating for two or more years. According to Finance Ministry announcements published in the press, the system worked along the following lines in 1970. The Government was buying rice at $383 per ton and selling it at $347. In addition to making up this loss, the Government was obligated to pay farmers a total of $226 million to compensate them for reducing their rice acreage. The aim was to bring production down by one million tons. Actually, farmers had cut their planted paddy fields by 45 percent more than requested, thereby putting an extra 30 million dollars charge on the budget. The Government encourages the growing of high-quality rice by paying the farmers premiums if they succeed. These payments amounted to another $66 million. The total budget for rice control was calculated at $1.2 billion, or more than $14 for every Japanese taxpayer who was not a farmer. The problem is never-ending. A surplus of seven million tons was on hand in 1970, and yet another bumper crop of 14 million tons was expected.[18] Production was 14.4 million tons in 1968, compared with 12.4 million in 1965 and only 9.6 million in 1950.[19] Although the farmers have curtailed their acreage, they have at the same time increased their productivity and have been paid extra for both. The Government has only more costs and more rice!

Education. The continuing, violent student unrest in 1969, causing the closing of many of the nation's universities for extended periods, called public attention to the need for reforms in higher education. The motives for student riots were partially ideological, and the most disruptive actions were instigated by militant factions of the New Left student movement. At the same time, students in general were dissatisfied with the working of the university system, physical facilities which in many cases were medieval in character, methods of instruction, and the lack of faculty-student communication. These grievances became more acute as student enrollment grew.

More young people have indeed been entering high school and college each year. The percentage of eligible children in high schools was expected to rise from approximately 84 percent in 1970 (82.4 percent in 1969) to 96 percent in 1975. Those attending both junior and four-year colleges, estimated at 19 percent of the eligible age group in 1970, were predicted to advance to 24 percent in 1975.[20] However, the decline in school-age population will affect the actual numbers of students entering high school and college so that the problem will not be primarily excessive enrollment but rather the allocation of educational resources and the quality of education.

In 1969, a Commission was appointed by the Government to produce a plan for the reform of higher education. The Commission's interim report, published in 1970, recommended a drastic reorganization of the universities and colleges, dividing them into six categories, running from specialized and vocational colleges to graduate schools. According to Morito Tatsuo, chairman of the Commission, a former Minister of Education, and one of Japan's leading educators, the report proposed the creation of "open" universities to meet the social changes of the 1970's; he asserted that the university should be a social institution, not an ivory tower.[21]

It seemed doubtful that the specific recommendations of the Morito Commission would be put into effect. Some cynical Japanese regarded its appointment as more of a political gesture to respond to the public outcry over student violence than an attempt to solve Japan's problems in higher education. Still, after a year of quiet following the student turbulence of 1969, the mood seemed conducive to changes in the educational system. Reforms will probably be achieved, in good time and without fanfare.

Strong injections of funds will be required. Plant and equipment are woefully inadequate and teachers' salaries so meager that university professors, in order to support their families, must supplement their incomes with a variety of moonlighting activities. It has been estimated that an additional three or four percent of the national budget added to the present 12 percent allocated to education might easily be required to bring about the needed reforms.[22]

People's Livelihood

Finally there is the problem which the Japanese call "People's Livelihood" (*Kokumin Seikatsu*). Because of its overpowering nature, it merits special attention.

Very suddenly the Japanese realized they were "choking on their GNP." For years the belching smoke, the acrid fumes, and the uncontrolled gases had been ingested and ignored by a population dedicated to production. Finally, the noxious vapors penetrated. A people whose income had quadrupled in ten years began to think that life was more than that, more than "Work to produce." For the first time the question was asked: Produce—for what?

Japan's "problems of people's livelihood" had arisen largely from the rapid concentration of population in urban areas. From an agricultural country with only 18 percent of the people living in cities in 1920, the movement away from the farms brought 33 percent to the cities by 1935. The momentum accelerated after the war, to 56 percent by 1955, 68 percent in 1965, and to more than 70 percent by 1969. Some dispersal of industries to rural parts of the country and the already excessive overcrowding and unhealthful conditions in the cities may to some extent stem the migration in the future. [23]

Unfortunately there is no sign yet of any easing in the housing shortage which plagues the city dweller. In spite of efforts to build new housing complexes and high-rise apartments, to plan suburban developments, and to offer government assistance, one estimate of shortage in 1970 was 2.6 million units. [24]

Applicants for apartments offered for sale or lease by government Housing Authorities far outnumber the units available. For example, in Tokyo in 1969, 250,757 persons applied to rent 2,557 housing units, i.e., the number of applications is 98 times the number of available housing units. Also in 1969, 22,054 people throughout Japan applied to buy 2,500 apartments in housing developments. The demand for the same kind of housing in Tokyo brought 18 times more applicants than housing units available. [25]

Japanese living patterns have changed. Newlyweds, who in the past customarily lived with the husband's parents, now want a house or apartment of their own. Many housewives work, as in the United States. There are more bachelor workers than ever in the past. The family unit is smaller for all of these reasons, and there is a greater dependence on social services than in the past, when each Japanese could count on being cared for within the "family system."

The 1970 White Paper on People's Livelihood listed the four problem areas resulting from urban concentration: (1) community facilities for social welfare; (2) local roads; (3) motor traffic; and

(4) environment. Long-suffering, stoic, and willing to sacrifice to rebuild their country and make it prosperous, the Japanese only recently became aware of how lacking they were in amenities of life which people of many other advanced nations took for granted. The crowded cities have few parks, poor recreation facilities, inadequate public libraries, and insufficient schools, hospitals, and child-care centers.[26]

As for public parks and open space, the Construction Ministry set a standard of seven square yards per person. The national average is only 2.8 and cities fall far short of this. Tokyo, the largest city in the world, affords only slightly more than one square yard of public park space for each of its more that 11 million citizens.[27] A comparable figure for New York City, counting its population at 7.7 million and its 14,375 acres of parks, would be almost nine times that of Tokyo, 8.9 square yards per person.

Roads have not kept up with automobiles. Only 10 percent of the country's total highway mileage was paved in 1967, and this contrasted with three percent in 1960. By 1969, one out of every 24 Japanese had an automobile; in Tokyo, the concentration was greater: one for 14. This is still some distance from the American average of one car for two people, but progress is rapid!

The cities of Japan compete with the metropolitan centers of the world in traffic congestion, as any recent traveller in Japan can so feelingly testify. Most of these would agree that a survey would not be necessary to support the statement of ninety percent of Tokyo's drivers that traffic delays are a daily experience![28] For the near future only worsening congestion can be foreseen, given the constantly increasing automobile production and sales in Japan, the restricted area of the country, and the slowness and limitations of highway construction. Surprisingly, in spite of the *kami kaze* taxi drivers so well known to American visitors to Tokyo, Japan's death rate from traffic accidents is lower than that of the United States, 14 per 100,000 persons in 1968 as contrasted to 27 for the United States.[29]

The White Paper on People's Livelihood states starkly but poignantly:

> In the cities recently, both the green of Nature and the presence of birds of different kinds have diminished; the pollution of sea water and of the atmosphere has worsened. The destruction of cultural monuments and of the natural and historical environment has occurred.[30]

A study of the various polluting wastes being ejected into the atmosphere, largely by industrial plants, showed that in the city of Osaka alone, daily household waste amounted to about one and a half pounds per person, while industrial waste reached more than 330 pounds daily per person! A projection for the whole country concluded that amounts of waste in 1975 would grow two and a half times over those measured in 1967 and would reach the staggering total of 2.9 million tons per day.[31]

The threat to their environment has so shaken the Japanese that during 1970, the principal topic for discussion in newspapers, magazines, radio, television, and in the National Diet, was *kogai*, translated as "public nuisance," but a phrase with a much stronger connotation, better expressed by "public damage" or "public hurt."

As an American journalist wrote recently, discussing the ecological problem in Japan, "If all this sounds like the United States, it is because it is like the United States—but the suddenness and intensity with which it has occurred make it infinitely worse."[32] Suddenly the GNP, which had been the shining goal of the hundred million achievers, lost some of its allure, at least in the public eye, and the quality of life for the first time seemed more important.

A Policy Research Group within the Ministry of International Trade and Industry (MITI) made public in the fall of 1970 a doctrine totally unexpected from the Ministry with the reputation as the tough, ruthless driving force behind "Japan, Inc." Instead of exhorting production and more production, exports and more exports, the MITI document, most unbureaucratically, and reflecting the views of the younger officials who wrote it, urged a shift in emphasis from material affluence to considerations of leisure, environment, and the "meaningfulness of life." It radically suggested examining not just the volume of GNP but also its content. The report advocated an "open economic system" for Japan, a lowering of tariffs, and the abolition of import restrictions. Taking the cue from the "Kennedy Round" of a few years ago, the young MITI employees proposed a "Japan Round," to take the initiative in the formation of an effective international economic order.[33] Whether such—for MITI—revolutionary and far-reaching policies would be adopted by the Government remained to be seen. Such ideas emerging from the staid citadels of MITI showed how seriously the unprecedented problems of social structure and "public damage" had struck the conscience of some public servants.

Pollution has become so intolerable that local communities have risen to action. A recent example was the effort of the Japan Steel and Tube Corporation to build a new factory on reclaimed land in the crowded, industrial area between Tokyo and Yokohama. The prefectural government, cooperating with two local city governments, negotiated with the steel company for eighteen months. Finally, the company was allowed to construct the plant on the condition that the sulphur dioxide density in the air directly above the ground in the area of the plant be under 0.012 ppm (parts per million) by 1978 when equipment would be moved to the new factory. The company stated that at present no technology exists for producing this result. The company president was quoted as saying: "But we must keep the promise that we have made—a promise to eliminate environmental pollution resulting from the operation of our factory. If we do not do so, our company might be doomed."[34]

Other industrial concerns have had similar difficulties with protesting local residents. The vice-president of the Tokyo Electric Power Company was frank: "We must admit that we have not done enough to obtain the understanding of local residents by formulating effective measures to eliminate pollution."[35]

However belatedly, Japan has now by legislation engaged in the battle of the environment. On December 10, 1970, the House of Representatives, after a lively "anti-*kogai*" session, passed fourteen laws designed to fight pollution. One of them made the polluting of the environment a crime.[36] How rigidly the Government will enforce the laws, and how seriously they will be taken by the affected industries, remains to be seen. At least, however, a first step has been taken toward coping with Japan's most urgent and, literally, killing problem.

The Mood

For some time the mood in Japan was called "my-home-ism." This Japanified English phrase was apt in its succinct summation of the aims and desires of most Japanese during this period of history. It suggested the rewards of achievement, the better life which came to those who worked hard. This Japanese pursuit of happiness, led by the "salary man," grew out of increased income and more leisure time. Some years ago another phrase was coined, the "*rayzha boomu*" (leisure boom) to denote the new importance of this pleasant side of life. The feeling was communicated by the many "my" words which have enjoyed a prolonged fad in the Japanese language. The word for private car is "my-car," a popular magazine is called "My-Way," and a food manufacture advertises "My-Jam." The comforts, the gadgets, the conveniences, the new possessions, are all for "Me," the individual, and for enjoying.

Progress in Japan was measured by replacements of the "three national treasures." Every schoolboy knows that in the dim, shadowy past when the islands of Japan were conceived, three treasures were handed down as symbols of the imperial authority for "ages eternal": the mirror, the jewel, and the sword. A few years ago, the modern "treasures" became the electric refrigerator, the washing machine, and the television set. These were soon outdated as they became universally possessed. In 1970, ninety percent of all Japanese owned electric refrigerators and television sets; 91.4 percent had washing machines. [37] The treasures soon became the "three C's," the color television set, the "cooler" (air conditioner), and the car. These are less universally possessed: 26.3 percent with a color T.V., only 5.7 percent with a "room cooler," and 22.1 percent driving ther own automobiles. [38] More recently, the treasures changed again indicating continued rising expectations: the vacation cottage, central heating, and the electric cooking range. For these, no statistics seem yet to be available.

To some Japanese, "my-home-ism" connoted hedonism without responsibility. It was disparaged by Japanese leaders who believed a more serious national purpose should be instilled and nurtured in growing youth. This was the theme so often sounded by the contemporary novelist Mishima Yukio and expressed in the final "appeal" which he issued just before his ritualistic suicide in November 1970:

> We have seen Japan become intoxicated with economic prosperity, forget the fundamental principles of the nation, lose the national spirit, quibble over trifles without rectifying the fundamental basis, fall into time-serving hypocrisy, and drive itself with its own hands into a spiritual vacuum. [39]

My-home-ism was blamed for the attitude of many young workers whose trade union militancy had become lukewarm, who were more interested in better wages and a bigger bonus than in chanting political slogans and demonstrating for political causes. Both the Socialist Party and the Federation of Labor Unions suffered from this new attitude of the younger workers. "My-home-ism" bore an element of pacifism, but was not necessarily contradictory to nationalism or pride in country. Neither were loyalties to family, company, and country diluted by "my-home-ism." Nevertheless it expressed the mood of the country.

To the complacency which might have developed with "my-home-ism" came the shock of a fast-deteriorating environment and, suddenly, the quality of life in its spiritual sense was challenged. As in America, youth saw that the material pleasures of life gave less satisfaction than one first believed. So to "my-home-ism" was added a restlessness, a malaise, a searching for ill-defined and ill-understood goals. Unlike their American counterparts who could berate the Establishment for the inequities of an Indochina war in which they might have to serve, young Japanese could only look on the great economic achievements of their nation, enjoy transitory pleasures, and grope for an unknown role both for themselves and for their country.

The mood of the Japanese, a contradictory mixture of growing confidence, nationalism, "my-home-ism," and worry over the menace of *kogai*, may not make them eager to march out as "leaders" or "policemen" of Asia. Their mood may be more inward-looking than action-prone, more self-centered than poised for great outside challenges.

We have looked briefly at Japan's economy, politics, successes, problems, and present mood. Conditioned by these elements, Japanese leaders approach the future. As for any nation, survival is their prime concern. National security must be the most important foreign affair, since it depends upon relationships with other countries. Japan trades with the world but Japan is in Pacific Asia. Japan's crucial relationships are with the United States, with the close neighbors of East Asia, and with Southeast Asia, where economic and strategic interests mix.

But before examining these contemporary problems, let us look back in history to the ending of the war and pick up the threads of Japan's beginning security problem.

Notes

1. George W. Ball, *The Discipline of Power* (Boston: Little, Brown and Company, 1968), p. 184.

2. *Nihon Keizai*, November 27, 1970.

3. Peter F. Drucker, *The Age of Discontinuity* (New York: Harper & Row, 1968), p. 68

4. Guenther Stein, *Made in Japan* (London: Menthuen and Company, Ltd., 1935), p. 1.

5. Kanamori Hisao, Nihon Keizai Kenkyu Senta (The Japan Economic Research Center), *Keizai Taikoku "Nippon"* ("Nippon" the Great Economic Nation), (Tokyo: Nihon Keizai Shimbun-sha, March 28, 1970), p. 60.

6. Japan: Tsusho Sangyo Sho (Ministry of International Trade and Industry), *Tsusho Hakusho, Soron* (White Paper on Foreign Trade, General), (Tokyo: July 10, 1970), pp. 245-47.

7. *Ibid.*, p. 247.

8. Gerald F. Curtis, "The 1969 General Election in Japan," *Asian Survey*, Vol. X, No. 10, October 1970, p. 868.

9. *Ibid.*, p. 863.

10. Hirotatsu Fujiwara, *I Denounce Soka Gakkai* (Tokyo: Nisshin Hodo Co., 1970).

11. Japan: Ministry of Education, Minister's Cabinet, "International Comparison of Education Index, 1970."

12. "Consumption and Saving," *Fuji Bank Bulletin*, The Fuji Bank, Ltd., Tokyo, April 1970, p. 70.

13. Mainichi, August 15, 1970.

14. Statistics supplied by Population Division, United Nations Secretariat, United Nations, New York.

15. *Ibid.*

16. Japan: Office of Prime Minister, Bureau of Statistics, *Japan Statistical Yearbook 1969* (Tokyo: Japan Statistical Association, 1970), p. 394.

17. Kanamori, *op. cit.*, p. 11.

18. *Yomiuri,* English edition, September 23, 1970.

19. *Japan Statistical Yearbook 1969, op. cit.,* p. 114.

20. James William Morley, "Growth for What? The Issue of the 'Seventies," in Gerald L. Curtis, ed., *The American Assembly, Japanese-American Relations in the 1970's* (Washington, D.C.: Columbia Books, Inc., 1970), p. 78.

21. Morito Tatsuo, "Chu-Kyo-Shin no Daigaku Kaikaku Shian ni Tsuite" (Regarding the University Reform Proposal of the Central Education Investigating Commission), in *Seikai Josei* (World Situation), Tokyo, May 5, 1970, p.9.

22. Morley, *op. cit.*, p. 79.

23. Japan: Keizai Kikaku-sho (Economic Planning Board), *Kokumin Seikatsu Hakusho* (White Paper on People's Livelihood), 1970 edition (Tokyo: July 20, 1970), p. 32.

24. S. A. Wickremasinghe, "Japan's Instant Houses," *San Francisco Chronicle,* June 21, 1970.

25. White Paper on People's Livelihood 1970, *op. cit.*, p. 395.

26. *Ibid.*, p. 110.

27. *Ibid.*, p. 111.

28. *Ibid.*, p. 113.

29. *Japan Statistical Yearbook 1969, op. cit.*, p. 632.

30. White Paper on People's Livelihood 1970, *op. cit.*, p. 114.

31. *Ibid.*, p. 123.

32. John B. Oakes, "Can Japan Survive Its Own Success?" *New York Times*, November 30, 1970.

33. "International Trade and Industry Policy for the 1970's," drafted by MITI Policy Research Group, *Nihon Keizai,* October 11, 1970.

34. Sugiyama Kimikazu "Environmental Pollution," *Yomiuri,* English edition, September 23, 1970.

35. *Ibid.*

36. Takashi Oka, "Polluting a Crime in Japanese Bill," *New York Times*, December 11, 1970.

37. White Paper on People's Livelihood 1970, *op. cit.*, p. 444.

38. *Ibid.*, pp. 444-45.

39. "Appeal: *Tate no Kai* Commander Mishima Yukio," *Asahi*, November 26, 1970.

Part 2

Security

2

From Peace
to Police

Defeat and Occupation

The G.I. stood by his jeep. "Go to Yokohama? No, sir, not without sidearms!"

The day was September 9, 1945, a week after General Douglas MacArthur had accepted the surrender of Japan on board the battleship *Missouri*. The place was Yokosuka, the great Japanese naval base. Admiral Togo had been here once. Admiral Halsey was here now.

Well-armed, the G.I. driver set out with his passenger to find General MacArthur's temporary headquarters at the Grand Hotel in Yokohama. The streets were silent, empty. Occasionally a papered door would slide a tentative inch, an eye would peer quizzically. Again, more boldly, a face would appear. A child would look out. Along the way, someone waved. There was no sound but the sound of the jeep. There were no voices, no menacing gestures. But the children could not contain their curiosity and stared out at these strange figures who were coming to their country. The ashes and the rubble everywhere seemed to add to the quiet.

Probably nothing has ever happened like the meeting between Americans and Japanese during those first days after the war's end. Both sides expected the worst. The Japanese had been told that the conquerors would kill, rape, ravage, and loot; the Americans knew well of the flaming death crashes of *kami kaze* pilots, of atrocities in China and the South Seas, and of the glorification of sword and suicide in Japanese tradition.

The expected horrors did not happen. The Emperor had spoken on August 15, and as the meaning of his stilted language sank into their consciousness, the people were ready as he told them to "bear the unbearable," to "endure the unendurable." There had been plots to stop the surrender, and blood had flowed in suicides. But once the Emperor's voice had been heard, defeat was accepted and resistance to the Occupation was never conceived.

The defeat left its indelible imprint on those generations who experienced it. Only now, in a youth born after the war, is the mark of this searing national experience absent.

In the United States, government officials charged with planning for the post-surrender period had focused their thoughts on two objectives: how militarism could be eradicated from Japan and democratic processes instilled into its government. For most Americans, Tojo was the evil symbol of a force which had dominated the life of the Japanese nation, vandalized China, sought to rule and oppress Asia, and brought war to the United States at Pearl Harbor on "the day of infamy." Americans and their allies believed that after the total defeat of Japan, the transcendent task would be to destroy Japanese militarism and prevent it from ever rising again. Thus in the Initial Post-Surrender Policy Statement for Japan drafted in the State Department in the summer of 1945 and approved by the War and Navy Departments, the first objective was "to ensure that Japan will not again become a menace to the United States or to the peace and security of the world." Later at Potsdam on July 26, 1945, when President Truman, Prime Minister Churchill, and President Chiang Kai-shek communicated the first official allied appeal to Japan to surrender, they asserted that "there must be eliminated for all time the authority and influence of those who have deceived and misled the people of Japan into embarking on world conquest, for we insist that a new order of peace, security and justice will be impossible until irresponsible militarism is driven from the world." The Potsdam Proclamation announced further that points in Japanese territory would be occupied "until such a new order is established and until there is convincing proof that Japan's war-making power is destroyed" and "there has been established in accordance with the freely expressed will of the Japanese people a peacefully inclined and responsible government."[1]

The energies of the vast American Occupation apparatus were concentrated on the disarmament, demilitarization and democratization of Japan. Arms were destroyed; ceremonial Japanese swords were collected and distributed as souvenirs. The country's only cyclotron, evidence of Japan's probings into nuclear science, was smashed.

The resources of counter-intelligence were directed to ferreting out those individuals, "secret societies," and organizations deemed exponents of ultranationalism, militarism, and aggression. In the first, confused days of the Occupation, faced with the need to start a list of war criminals, someone asked an American Foreign Service Officer for the names of the Japanese Cabinet. The indictments, trials, executions, and imprisonment of war criminals followed. Of those imprisoned, all were released in due course, with little stigma suffered. One, Kishi Nobusuke, became Prime Minister and negotiated the revision of the security treaty with the United States in 1960. Another, Kaya Okinori, a member of the Tojo Cabinet, became Minister of Justice in the Ikeda government, 1963-1964.

The "purge" of leaders in military, political, and economic life removed 200,000 individuals from their positions, based on categories or according to such criteria as "tainted with war responsibility" or "are or may become anti-democratic." The *zaibatsu*, or industrial combines, were dissolved only to reform later but in a different mold, akin to the great American corporations. Law, education, religion, and land were fundamentally reformed.

One of the most significant Occupation accomplishments was the restoration of individual freedoms, all but extinguished in the prewar period. All restrictions on the freedom of communication as well as laws giving Government the control of press and radio were abolished. In fairness, it must be recorded that the Occupation itself exercised its own controls over press and radio and even censored classical *kabuki* plays. However, for the future, Japan was to be left with a heritage of free speech. The Civil Rights Directive of October 4, 1945, called the "Japanese Bill of Rights," guaranteed political, civil, and religious liberties and outlawed discrimination on grounds of race, nationality, creed, or political opinion. Those imprisoned for political crimes, including Communist leaders, some of whom had been incarcerated continuously for as long as eighteen years, were ordered released by October 10. Probably there are few examples in history of reforms so sudden, sweeping, comprehensive and, in the light of subsequent history, lasting.

The zeal in stamping out militarism was a little exaggerated. The mighty power of the American and allied occupying forces was not needed to exorcise a devil who was ceasing to exist even as the

Emperor spoke on August 15, 1945. The Japanese quickly turned against their military masters, whom they held responsible for the tragic disaster which had befallen them. So deep, so all-consuming became their hatred of war and the perpetrators of war that twenty-five years after their nation's surrender, pacifism still motivated the great majority of the Japanese people.

Yoshida Shigeru, who bore the delicate, difficult, and unenviable responsibility of leading the Government during the Occupation years, believed historians would judge the Occupation "a successful venture." He qualified this judgment, however, with the opinion that the task of reforming Japan had been carried out on the erroneous assumption that the Japanese were "an aggressive people of ultramilitaristic tradition to be castigated thoroughly in order to be refashioned into a peace-loving nation." "Moved by such a prejudice," he averred, "the Occupation vigorously condemned all the existing institutions—political, economic, and cultural—as an embodiment of the militarism which it sought to eradicate."[2]

Yoshida had a point. The Occupation gave to a prostrate nation a shock treatment which reverberated to the foundations of Japanese society and institutions. Many misjudgments, injustices, stupidities, and useless acts were committed. But as the Japanese recovered their vigor and their independence, they abolished, revised, replaced, or altered reforms imposed upon them which they judged unsuitable or unworkable. Yet, freedoms were gained and new directions plotted. Japan would never be the same again, and no Japanese would wish to return to the past.

Perhaps nothing reflected the spirit of the Occupation and the confusion pervading it as starkly as the forced birth of Japan's postwar Constitution. The story of how the new constitution came about is worth recounting in some detail both as a vignette of the times and because of its abiding relevance to Japan's security problem. The long shadow of the Constitution, and particularly of the controversial Article 9, continues to hover over Japanese security policies.

Revising the Constitution

It became clear early in the Occupation that the fundamental changes envisaged in the Japanese body politic could not be effected without revision of the Constitution. This charter, promulgated in 1889 by Emperor Meiji, established a parliamentary system under an absolute monarchy and set the framework for Japan's emergence as a modern state. The Constitution declared the Emperor to be "sacred and inviolable," vested sovereignty in him, and permitted a small group of oligarchs to exercise extraordinary power. Later, especially in the 1930's, the militarists achieved a dominating influence. The constitutional weakness of the Diet and the Cabinet made them ineffectual. The direct access to the throne granted to heads of the armed forces, as well as the rule that Army and Navy Ministers must be high-ranking active officers, permitted the usurpation of political power by the military. Futhermore, the Meiji Constitution, although including a chapter on "the rights and duties of subjects," limited all such rights by the proviso "unless according to law." Thus, as war began to consume national energies, political parties disappeared and a system was established which over the years approached a police state, yet to the end was neither fascism nor even totalitarianism but something uniquely "Japanese."

For the postwar future, it seemed clear that minimum reforms must include eliminating the political authority of the Emperor, strengthening the legislative institutions, and establishing civilian control of the military and guarantees of human rights. The Potsdam Proclamation had stipulated that obstacles to the revival and strengthening of democratic tendencies would be removed and "freedom of speech, of religion, and of thought, as well as respect for the fundamental human rights" would be established To write such reforms into the law of the land, a new constitution was required.

The United States, as the nation principally responsible for the Occupation of Japan, did not, however, wish to force Japan into a new mold which would be quickly thrown off once independence was regained. The Basic Initial Post-Surrender Directive, establishing the overall policy for the Occupation and sent to General MacArthur on November 3, 1945 by the Joint Chiefs of Staff, specifically stated that "it is not the responsibility of the Occupation forces to impose on Japan any form of government not supported by the freely expressed will of the people."[3]

Those Japanese in positions of influence as the Occupation began recognized that compliance with the Potsdam Proclamation would make inevitable fundamental revisions in Japan's governmental structure. Their principal fear was for the future of the imperial institution and the continuity of the state which it symbolized. There were opinions at the time, among Americans and more generally among the Allies, that the Emperor should be tried as a war criminal, deposed, or forced to abdicate. The anxiety in Japan over the position of the Emperor had been first revealed in the condition attached to acceptance of the Potsdam Proclamation, that the prerogatives of the Emperor as sovereign ruler should not be prejudiced. The answer sent by the Allies, while implying that the Emperor could remain, made no commitment for the future.

Prince Konoye Fumimaro, prewar Prime Minister who, in highly secret conversations with Ambassador Joseph C. Grew during the tense summer of 1941, had probed the possibilities of preventing war between Japan and the United States—including a proposed dramatic meeting with President Roosevelt on a battleship off Alaska—became a Minister of State in the cabinet of the first postwar Prime Minister, Prince Higashikuni. Konoye had first met General MacArthur early in the Occupation, on September 13. At his second meeting with MacArthur on October 4, Konoye was given, he thought, a mandate by the Supreme Commander to revise the Japanese Constitution. Also present at this meeting was Ambassador George Atcheson, Jr., at that time State Department Acting Political Advisor to the Supreme Commander for the Allied Powers (SCAP), with whom Konoye subsequently discussed constitutional reform.[4]

What MacArthur said to Konoye was reported differently by Konoye and by the Supreme Commander's Headquarters. Professor Takagi Yasaka, then professor of American constitutional law at Tokyo Imperial University and close friend of Prince Konoye, has written that "MacArthur virtually encouraged Konoye to take leadership, as a liberal statesman, in constitutional reform."[5] In another Japanese account, MacArthur is reported to have said to Konoye: "Today I have something very specific to tell you. You should bring together some liberal-minded people and revise the imperial Constitution. This must be done just as quickly as possible. This a unique service which you, Prince Konoye, can perform for your country. You know the world, you are a cosmopolitan, and you are young."[6] The Government Section of General Headquarters, headed by General MacArthur's close and trusted friend General Courtney Whitney and charged with general supervision over Japanese political institutions, wrote in its official report on "The Political Reorientation of Japan," that Konoye's assumption that MacArthur had charged him with the work of revising the Constitution was "unwarranted" and explained that Konoye was being spoken to "not only in the most general terms but merely as a responsible member of the Japanese Cabinet."[7]

Marquis Kido Koichi, Lord Keeper of the Privy Seal, a close adviser to the Emperor and a man who had played a prominent and courageous part in the difficult days before surrender, on October 8 discussed the problem of constitutional reform with Prince Konoye, the latter's prewar private secretary Ushiba Tomohiko, Professor Takagi, and Matsumoto Shigeharu, a well-known journalist and confidant of the Prince. According to his diary, Kido on October 9 had an opportunity to mention constitutional revision to Baron Shidehara Kijuro, who had been designated Prime Minister to replace outgoing Prince Higashikuni and was awaiting the investiture ceremonies. Shidehara's attitude was somewhat negative. Both he and Kido agreed that the objectives desired by the Americans could as well be achieved through the actual practice of government as by changing the formal charter. Both realized however, that this would never satisfy the Americans, who seemed intent upon liberalizing the Japanese Constitution in their own American way and "by their own hands." Shidehara thought resistance to them would be useless. The most important point, he believed, was that revision must originate with the Emperor and that, therefore, Prince Konoye, associated as he was with the Imperial Household, would be the logical person to make the study.[8]

The concern of the Konoye group indeed centered on revision "by imperial order" to preserve continuity with the Meiji Constitution and maintain the permanence of the imperial institution. Later Shidehara took the view that constitutional revision was the prerogative of the Cabinet. He told Kido, however, that he had no objection to a "study" being made by the Prince.[9] After Marquis Kido had obtained imperial sanction for the study, the Emperor on October 11 ordered Konoye, on the basis of the Potsdam Proclamation, to study the Constitution, determine whether it needed revision, and if so, make recommendations. This was Kido's interpretation of the Emperor's instructions. The Acting Political Adviser, George Atcheson, reported that Konoye had been attached by the Emperor to the Office of the Lord Keeper of the Privy Seal "for the purpose of undertaking studies leading to the thorough revision of the Constitution."[10]

Two days before his appointment by the Emperor, Prince Konoye, accompanied by Professor Takagi, had called on Atcheson to ask for advice and suggestions on the general subject of reform of the Constitution. Atcheson had anticipated the need for Washington guidance on the constitutional problem and had already wired the State Department on October 4 for instructions. As these had not arrived by the time of Konoye's call, he improvised his own "personal, unofficial" comment. He noted defects in the prewar Japanese constitutional system, the limitations on the legislative branch, lack of an effective "Bill of Rights," the undemocratic character of the House of Peers, the lack of judicial protection for people's rights, and the absence of controls over the War and Navy ministers. Konoye said the Emperor favored revision and that he, Konoye, would work for it. He hoped there could be further discussions and that Takagi might also call on Atcheson for this purpose.[11]

During the next several weeks a number of conversations were held with Takagi in the Political Adviser's office. The author, then a Foreign Service Officer assigned to Atcheson's Staff, had known Takagi before the war and met him several times during this period to discuss the constitutional problem. The American Constitution had been Takagi's life study, and he had long and deep associations with the United States. At the same time, he attached vital importance to the preservation of the imperial institution. He discussed very frankly the position of the Emperor, whether the Emperor should abdicate in favor of the Crown Prince, and how the historical continuity in Japan's existence as a nation could be sustained even while the essential democratic reforms were achieved.

The State Department, without undue haste, responded to Atcheson's telegram of October 4 with a reply sent from Washington on October 16. The telegram summarized the "attitude of departmental officers who had been giving consideration to this matter," concurred in the views Atcheson had expressed to Konoye, and expressed the hope that a full statement of the American views could be sent in the near future. The message suggested that the Japanese government should be responsible to an electorate based on wide representative suffrage and that the executive branch should derive authority from and be responsible to the electorate or to a fully representative legislative body. Constitutional safeguards were suggested for either of two alternatives: retention or abolition of the Emperor institution. The principle of civilian control over the military was enunciated in the statement that "any ministers for armed forces which may be permitted in the future should be civilian and all special privileges of direct access to throne by military should be eliminated." It is noteworthy that the Department instructions left open the question of the retention of the Emperor and assumed that in the future Japan would possess armed forces.[12]

Konoye's group, which included several experts on international and constitutional law in addition to Professor Takagi, continued to work during the rest of October and part of November. There were numerous conferences and exchanges between Takagi and members of the Political Adviser's Office. Takagi was particularly gratified that suggestions from the State Department included no demand for the abdication of the Emperor or abolition of the imperial system.[13]

According to the official report of the Government Section, General MacArthur in mid-October "pointedly advised" Prime Minister Shidehara that the reforms which Japan must undertake "will unquestionably involve a revision of the Constitution." Responding to this suggestion, Baron Shidehara appointed Dr. Matsumoto Joji as chairman of a committee responsible directly to the Cabinet, to draft a revised Constitution.[14]

On November 8, Atcheson informed the State Department that, with regard to discussions with Prince Konoye and his group, General MacArthur "has advised that we not associate ourselves in the matter further." As Atcheson explained, "General MacArthur feels that Konoye would make political capital out of further association and that, as the Japanese Government has been directed by the Supreme Commander through the Prime Minister to initiate a constitutional revision, none of us should be involved until the Japanese Government itself formally submits something on the matter."[15] The author was assigned the painful task of breaking the news to Professor Takagi and asking him to inform Prince Konoye.

Takagi later wrote that while criticism of Konoye's efforts from jurists, scholars, and political opponents had been growing, the withdrawl of SCAP support was the "most unexpected cut of all."[16] The Government Section, in its official record, claimed that "a curious confusion" had arisen in Prince Konoye's mind as a result of his meetings with MacArthur and Atcheson and that "the Supreme Commander was finally forced to clarify the situation with an express repudiation of Konoye's allegations"[17] that he had been entrusted with responsibility to draft a revision of the Constitution. Strangely enough, the Supreme Commander had permitted the "curious confusion" to continue for almost a month, during which time he was kept completely informed of all conversations held by the Political Adviser's Office with Konoye's associates and read the exchanges of telegrams with Washington.

MacArthur and General Whitney, Chief of the Government Section, clearly did not want the State Department involved in the Constitution-making process. MacArthur never held the Department in high esteem and had accepted a political adviser only reluctantly. The influence of the Political Adviser's Office, exiled across town from SCAP Headquarters, and its participation in the Occupation were deliberately circumscribed. George Atcheson wrote to Dean Acheson, then Under Secretary of State, on November 7: "It is obvious to us now that General MacArthur, or his Chief of Staff and other members of the Bataan Club who act as his Privy Council, or genro—wish if possible to keep the State Department out of this matter [the Constitution]."[18] General Whitney, who was to have direct responsibility for the Constitution, was a trusted member of the "Bataan Club" of MacArthur's war campaign associates.

After heeding MacArthur's dictum and cutting relations with Konoye and Takagi, Atcheson worried about the nature of the drafts the Japanese were preparing. The obsession of the Konoye group with preserving the imperial institution seemed to him to be so great as to compromise the emergence of a true democratic system. The Matsumoto committee had no contact with any Americans during the period of their deliberations. Takagi later wrote, "But as the course of events eventually revealed, just to the extent that the Matsumoto Committee refused to explore the American view of the revision, it was doomed to failure."[19] Atcheson on November 12 telegraphed the State Department that no British or American technicians were working with the Japanese on constitutional reform and that the discussions with Konoye and his associates by members of the Political Adviser's office were the nearest to any Japanese-American working arrangement and these had ceased.[20]

Atcheson suggested to the State Department that it issue a statement in Washington pointing out the essentials of a democratic system for Japan in order to bring some influence to bear on public opinion and those working on the revision. He stressed how important it was to influence any Japanese drafts before they received imperial sanction. As he pointed out in his letter to Under Secretary of State Acheson, "any attempt to cause correction of a draft once prepared with imperial sanction will meet with difficulties and will cause unfortunate political repercussions which can not help but militate against our long-term objectives." Atcheson recognized that a public statement by the Secretary of State would irritate General MacArthur, but he was ready to advise this step and, by so doing, show at least some degree of independence from the military. The general frustration which he and the members of his staff felt at the time came through in the almost despairing words of his letter which told the Secretary that without a certain independence from the chain of command "our job here would be almost completely empty." [21] The recommended statement was never issued.

Later, when he received the formal document promised by the State Department, "Reform of the Japanese Governmental System," Atcheson wrote to General MacArthur. He noted again that, since the conversations with Prince Konoye, no discussions of constitutional revision had taken place between American and Japanese officials at a working level. "There would seem real danger," he said, "if an effective liaison at this level is not reestablished, that the Japanese Government, working in ignorance of specific American desires and requirements, may arrive at an advanced stage in the preparation of a draft revision which fails signally to satisfy those desires and requirements." [22]

Konoye had not concluded his own activities. He presented his draft to the Emperor on November 22. On December 6, the Prince was indicted as a war criminal. He committed suicide on December 15. His efforts for constitutional revision were thus discredited.

The deliberations of the Matsumoto committee continued until first drafts had been prepared by late January, 1946. Although no recommended revision was ever formally submitted to the Supreme Commander, one purported draft plan appeared in the *Mainichi*, one of Japan's three leading newspapers, on February 1. On the same day, the Government Section informally received two documents, one labeled a "gist of the revision of the Constitution" and the other a "general explanation of the constitutional revision drafted by the Government."

It did not take long for the Government Section to decide that the Matsumoto revisions were totally unacceptable, since they did not establish the democratic reforms regarded as indispensable for a future Japanese government. On February 1, the same day on which the drafts were received by MacArthur's Headquarters, the Supreme Commander instructed General Whitney to prepare a detailed answer, rejecting the Matsumoto proposals. Two days later MacArthur changed his mind and directed Whitney and his Government Section to draft a new constitution. As guidance, he listed four points which he deemed essential: (1) preservation of the Emperor system with constitutional limitations; (2) renunciation of war and war-making; and (3) abolition of the feudal system, including the continuing rights of the peerage, except those of the Imperial Family, and of any governmental power of the nobility, and (4) patterning of the budget after the British system.[23]

The Government Section was literally isolated from the rest of SCAP Headquarters and in the deepest secrecy wrote the Japanese Constitution in six days, from February 4 to 10.

There were two reasons for haste. One was the first Japanese postwar elections, expected in April. On February 3, MacArthur decided that Japanese shilly-shallying had gone on long enough and with the elections only two months away, a draft must be presented to the public so that the elections would be considered a tacit plebiscite on the new Constitution.[24] A second reason was the imminent establishment of a Far Eastern Commission with power to pass on any proposed constitution. The conference of Foreign Ministers of the U.S.S.R., Great Britain, and the United States, meeting in Moscow in December 1945, had decided to replace the existing Far Eastern Advisory Commission with an eleven-nation Far Eastern Commission whose agreement would be required for "fundamental changes in the Japanese constitutional structure."* MacArthur had been bitterly opposed to the Moscow

---

* The agreement establishing the Far Eastern Commission and the Allied Council for Japan provided that the United States Government could issue "interim directives" to the Supreme Commander "whenever urgent matters arise not covered by policies already formulated by the Commission." However, this authority was limited by the statement which immediately followed: "provided that

Agreement; he foresaw with distaste and impatience the demands for jurisdiction, and the wrangling and the delays which would obtrude if the FEC—which would include a Soviet member—got its international hands on the making of a Japanese Constitution. Not suprisingly, he wired Washington on October 31 that the terms of reference of the FEC "are not acceptable." [25]

An ironic sidelight of history is that the members of the Far Eastern Advisory Commission, which had functioned since October without Soviet participation, had set out on December 26 on a six-week trip to Japan as guests of the American Government, flying to Honolulu and proceeding on the very comfortable "command ship," the USS Mt. McKinley. The members of this body, which was to reconstitute itself as the FEC upon return to Washington, with special prerogatives relating to constitutional revision, conferred, discussed, and saw the sights of a devastated Japan. In meetings with General Whitney and other officials of the Government Section, they specifically brought up the matter of the Constitution and were told that the "problem was strictly a matter for the Japanese to consider and that no work was being undertaken on it by SCAP." [26] By the time the FEAC returned to Washington on February 13, and well before the FEC first met on February 26, the American version of a new Japanese Constitution had been completed. Members of the Commission learned only on March 6 that a text of the proposed Constitution had been published in the Tokyo press and had already been personally approved by General MacArthur. Needless to say, displeasure and irritation were general among the members, who felt that their special duties and responsibilities had been ignored.

General Whitney showed the SCAP draft to Foreign Minister Yoshida, Dr. Matsumoto, and their associates on February 13. He announced that General MacArthur was determined to have a text published before the general election and that if no suitable and acceptable draft were forthcoming from the Japanese Government, the prepared outline by the Government Section would be presented directly to the Japanese people.

According to Whitney, Dr. Matsumoto sucked in his breath and

---

any directives dealing with fundamental changes in the Japanese constitutional structure or in the regime of control, or dealing with a change in the Japanese Government as a whole will be issued only following consultation and following the attainment of agreement in the Far Eastern Commission." *Political Reorientation of Japan,* II, Appendix A:10, p. 421.

Mr. Yoshida's face was a black cloud. The Americans waited in the garden of the Foreign Minister's residence for about an hour and then rejoined the Japanese. Whitney reports that he replied to the Japanese apologies for keeping him waiting by remarking, "Not at all, Mr. Shirasu. We have been enjoying your atomic sunshine."[27]

Shirasu Jiro, one of those accompanying Yoshida and Matsumoto, later wrote to Whitney that the destination aspired to by the Japanese and Americans was the same but that the routes were very different. "Your way is so American in the way that is straight and direct. Their way must be Japanese, in the way that is round-about, twisted, and narrow. Your way may be called an airway and their way a jeep way over the bumpy roads."[28]

By March 4, the Japanese presented a text based on the Government Section draft. The full text was published in Tokyo on March 6 and, with minor amendments made during futher discussions, including debates in the Diet and in the FEC in Washington, became the Constitution of Japan. It was promulgated on November 3, 1946, the birthday of Emperor Meiji, and went into effect six months later.

Many observers, both in Japan and the United States, predicted that this "made in USA" Constitution would be drastically revised or replaced once the Japanese regained independence. Significantly, this has not happened.

Looking back, one wonders whether the task of sculpturing a new constitution might not have been carried out a little more skillfully and diplomatically. As it was, American insistence on the direct literal approach clashed with the Japanese respect for forms, suggested by Shirasu's analogy of the devious, bumpy jeep road. More contacts between Japanese and Americans during the drafting process might have brought philosophies and points of view somewhat nearer and achieved in the end a result more "Japanese" and yet just as "democratic."

The "No-War" Article

Article 9 of the Japanese Constitution, the "no-war clause," is the key element in Japan's security problem. The text of the article follows:

Chapter II. Renunciation of War
Article 9. Aspiring sincerely to an international peace based on

justice and order the Japanese people forever renounce war as a sovereign right of the nation and the threat of force as means of settling international disputes.

In order to accomplish the aim of the preceding paragraph, land, sea, and air forces, as well as other war potential, will never be maintained. The right of belligerency of the State will not be recognized.

The true origin of Article 9 has never been irrefutably determined. The idea of renunciation of war seems first to have been discussed by Prime Minister Shidehara and General MacArthur at a meeting on January 24, 1946. No others were present and apparently no record of the conversation was made. The Prime Minister had come to thank the Supreme Commander for penicillin which Mac-Arthur had obtained for him. According to the General, Shidehara, after expressing thanks for the penicillin, proposed that the new Constitution contain an article renouncing war and the maintenance of any military establishment for all time. Japan would thus offer to the world proof of its intention to pursue a path of peace. According to one Japanese source, General MacArthur suddenly rose to his feet, took Shidehara's hands in his and with tears in his eyes exclaimed, "You are right!"[29]

On January 30, when MacArthur gave Whitney his "three points" for inclusion in the Constitution, the one referring to the renunciation of war read as follows:

War as a sovereign right of the nation is abolished. Japan renounces it as an instrumentality of settling its disputes and even for preserving its own security. It relies upon the higher ideals which are now stirring the world for its defense and protection.

No Japanese Army, Navy, or Air Force will ever be authorized and no rights of belligerency will ever be conferred upon any Japanese force.[30]

Thus, the SCAP draft which was handed to Matsumoto included the gist of what was to become the famous Article 9.

Prime Minister Yoshida was not so sure that the "no-war clause" was a Japanese idea. He states in his Memoirs, "It has been said by some that it was Baron Shidehara, the Prime Minister, who first proposed the clause. General MacArthur also seems to have testified to the same effect before the U.S. Senate on his return, but I have the impression that it was General MacArthur who suggested it to the Baron in some conversation between them, to which Baron Shidehara could very easily have replied with enthusiasm."[31]

51

Yoshida's belief is supported by the fact that the Matsumoto draft contained no provisions for renouncing war or prohibiting any armed forces. This draft was made available to MacArthur's Headquarters on February 1, more than a week after the interview in which Shidehara is supposed to have broached the idea to the General. If the Prime Minister had attached great importance to this principle, it seems likely it would have been included in the Cabinet committee's draft.

Article 9, later the center of so much controversy, was suprisingly not a focus of attention at the time the Constitution was being drafted. The Matsumoto documents had eliminated the words "Army" and "Navy," but provided for armed forces of a "very limited scope" once the Occupation ended. There seem to have been no discussions between members of the Government Section and Japanese authorities about the interpretation of Article 9 with respect to self-defense. Apparently the article was accepted without argument or opposition. Whitney says that the "no-war" article was "never once objected to in any form by the Japanese."[32] During Diet discussions an amendment by Ashida Hitoshi (later to become Prime Minister) was proposed and accepted. This added two phrases, one at the beginning of the first paragraph, "Aspiring sincerely to an international peace based on justice and order, . . ." and the other at the beginning of the second paragraph, "In order to accomplish the aim of the preceding paragraph. . . ."

At the time, Ashida apparently did not wish to pursue in the Diet the matter of Japan's ability to defend herself. Consequently he did not cite the reasons for his amendment. Only five years later did he explain that his intention was to ensure that Japan did not give up the legitimate, sovereign right of self-defense. By adding the restrictive phrase "to accomplish the aim of the preceding paragraph," maintenance and use of armed forces would be prohibited for the purpose of aggression (settling international disputes) but not for purposes of self-defense. Although Ashida was convinced that Article 9, qualified by his revision, clearly permitted the use of force for self-defense, in the election campaign of 1952 he energetically advocated revision of the Constitution and continued his support of revision until his death in 1959.[33]

It was generally assumed during the early period of the Occupation that the Constitution denied to Japan the right to rearm, even for self-defense. On March 6, 1946, when the draft Constitution was made public by the Japanese Government, MacArthur, in referring to Article 9, stated, "By this undertaking and commitment Japan surrenders rights inherent in her own sovereignty and renders her future security and very survival subject to the good faith and justice of the peace-loving peoples of the world."[34] The Japanese Government's position was set forth by Prime Minister Yoshida on June 26, 1946: "The provision of this draft concerning the renunciation of war does not directly deny the right of self-defense. However, since paragraph 2 of Article 9 does not recognize any military force whatsoever or the rights of belligerency of the state, both wars arising from the right of self-defense and the rights of belligerency have been renounced."[35]

It is remarkable that Japan's Constitution, called the "Peace Constitution" because of Article 9, but also labeled by many "made in USA," has not only survived the intervening years, but is still supported by the great majority of the Japanese people. The Government has come to maintain that Article 9 permits the right of self-defense and that the self-defense forces now in existence are constitutional. While the Supreme Court has so far avoided the issue of passing specifically on the constitutionality of the self-defense forces, it did in the Sunakawa case, on December 16, 1959, declare that Japan had not given up the right of self-defense:

> . . .this Article (Article 9) renounces the so-called war and prohibits the maintenance of the so-called war potential, but certainly there is nothing in it which would deny the right of self-defense inherent in our nation as a sovereign power. The pacifism advanced in our Constitution was never intended to mean defenselessness or non-resistance.[36]

The Impact of the Cold War

It was not long before world events began to impinge upon the Occupation of Japan. On March 12, 1947, President Truman delivered a message to a Special Joint Session of Congress which has been compared in importance to President Wilson's declaration of war against Germany on April 2, 1917.[37] In it he pronounced the words which created the "Truman Doctrine," a policy which in its basic conceptual outlines was to animate American endeavors in the world—beginning with aid to Greece and Turkey and continuing today in the jungles of Vietnam: "I believe that it must be the policy of the United States to support free peoples who are resisting attempted subjugation by armed minorities or by outside pressures."

In February 1948, Czechoslovakia fell to the Communists, and in June of that year the Berlin airlift was on. In April 1949, NATO was formed; and by October 1949, the Communists were in control of China. In December 1949, Mao Tse-tung signed in Moscow the Sino-Soviet friendship treaty which promised resistance against aggression from Japan or countries directly or indirectly associated with Japan in such aggression.

Meanwhile the Japanese Communist Party, whose leaders had emerged from prison in the early days of the Occupation praising the Supreme Commander who had released them, was pursuing a policy of "peaceful revolution," trying to become known as a "lovable Communist party." These tactics were not without some success. In the 1949 general elections, the Communist party won 10 percent of the vote and 35 seats in the House of Representatives. In the next elections three years later the JCP lost all of its seats and it was not until December 1969 that, again promoting the image of a "lovable party," it was able to break the two-digit barrier by securing 14 seats.

In this changed atmosphere, Occupation authorities turned their attention from rightists to leftists and began to worry more about Communist subversion than the resurgence of irresponsible militarism. The concept of the future Japan as a peaceful, pastoral "Switzerland of Asia" gave way to a new image in the minds of those responsible for policy toward Japan, the image of a strong Japan which could become a "bastion" against Communism in Asia.

In his New Year's message to the Japanese nation on January 1, 1950, General MacArthur spoke no more about the surrender of sovereign rights and Japan's dependence on the justice and faith of the peace-loving peoples of the world. Instead he emphasized that the Constitution had not taken from Japan the inherent right of self-defense.

In June the entire leadership of the Japanese Communist Party was purged by the Supreme Commander.

On Sunday, June 25, at 4 A.M. the North Koreans attacked across the 38th parallel. MacArthur's Far East Command would bear the brunt of defense. The focus of the Supreme Commander's attention from this time on necessarily shifted from the Japanese

Occupation to the Korean War. On June 30, MacArthur asked and was given authority to commit American ground troops to Korea; at the same time Washington reminded him that he "must regard the security of Japan as fundamental and basic policy."[38]

With American troops abandoning their Occupation posts for the battlefronts of Korea, it was natural that MacArthur, mindful of his responsibility for the security of Japan, should conclude that the Japanese ought to bear a greater share in the maintenance of order and stability in the home islands. On July 8, the Supreme Commander wrote to Prime Minister Yoshida directing the formation of a "National Police Reserve" to be made up of 75,000 men. Two days later the NPR was established by the Government of Japan as a supplement to local and provincial police forces and, without so saying, as the nucleus of a future military force.

Thus, less than five years after the Imperial Japanese Army, Navy, and Air Force had been destroyed in total defeat, and three years after the Constitution of Japan had solemnly renounced forever the maintenance of "land, sea, and air forces, as well as other war potential," the embryo of a new armed force appeared. Japan's "security problem" was about to begin.

Notes

1. Supreme Commander for Allied Powers, *Political Reorientation of Japan, September 1945 to September 1948,* Report of Government Section (2 vols., Washington, D.C.: U.S. Government Printing Office, 1949), II, Appendix A 3, p. 413. Hereafter referred to as *Pol. Reorient. of Japan.*

2. Yoshida Shigeru, *The Yoshida Memoirs* (Boston: Houghton Mifflin, 1962), pp. 287-88.

3. *Pol. Reorient. of Japan,* II, p. 429. The document which formed the basis for the Joint Chiefs' Directive of November 3, 1945 was drafted by the Far Eastern Subcommittee of the State-War-Navy Coordinating Committee (SWNCC), agreed to by the Departments concerned, transmitted to General MacArthur on August 29, 1945 and approved by President Truman on September 6. After transmission by the Joint Chiefs of Staff as a directive, it was later approved, with minor modifications, by the Far Eastern Commission on June 19, 1947. F.C. Jones, Hugh Borton and B.R. Pearn, *The Far East 1942-1946* (London: Oxford University Press, 1955), p. 318. For the text of the directive see *Pol. Reorient. of Japan,* II, pp. 428-39.

4. Atcheson, in reporting to the State Department a discussion with Konoye on October 9, referred only briefly to the October 4 meeting with MacArthur at which he was present and "at which the General told Konoye that Jap constitution must

be revised." U.S., Department of State, *Foreign Relations of the United States, 1945*, Vol. VI, The British Commonwealth, The Far East (Washington, D.C.: U.S. Government Printing Office, 1969), p. 739.

5. Takagi Yasaka, *Toward International Understanding* (Tokyo: Kenkyusha, 1954), p. 114.

6. Hosokawa Moritada, *Konoye Ko no Shogai* (Prince Konoye's Life) in *Konoye Nikki* (Konoye Diaries), (Tokyo: Kyodo Tsushinsha, 1968), p. 157.

7. *Pol. Reorient. of Japan*, *op. cit.*, I, p. 91, footnote. Konoye ceased having the rank of Minister without portfolio on October 9, after the resignation of Prince Higashikuni as Prime Minister on October 5.

8. *Kido Koichi Nikki* (Diaries of Kido Koichi), (2 vols., Tokyo: Tokyo Daigaku Shuppan Kai, 1966), II, p. 1241.

9. *Ibid.*, p. 1242.

10. *For. Relations of the U.S., 1945, op. cit.*, p. 750.

11. *Ibid.*, p. 739.

12. *Ibid.*, p. 757.

13. Takagi, *op. cit.*, p. 116.

14. *Pol. Reorient. of Japan, op. cit.*, I, p. 91.

15. *For. Relations of the U.S., i945, op. cit.*, p. 841.

16. Takagi, *op. cit.*, p. 116.

17. *Pol. Reorient. of Japan, op. cit.*, I, p. 91.

18. *For. Relations of the U.S., 1945, op. cit.*, pp. 837-38.

19. Takagi, *op. cit.*, p. 120.

20. *For. Relations of the U.S., 1945, op. cit.*, p. 849.

21. *Ibid.*, pp. 837-38.

22. *Ibid.*, pp. 883-84.

23. *Pol. Reorient. of Japan*, I, *op. cit.*, I, p. 102.

24. Major General Courtney Whitney, *MacArthur, His Rendezvous with History* (New York: Knopf, 1956), p. 248.

25. Douglas MacArthur, *Reminiscences* (New York: McGraw-Hill, 1964), p. 292. MacArthur states that he wired the "Secretary of State." In fact there was no direct communication between the Supreme Commander and the State Department.

MacArthur communicated only through the Joint Chiefs of Staff, who in turn relayed messages. Furthermore, the Political Adviser to SCAP, George Atcheson, had no means of sending messages directly to the State Department but had to transmit them through MacArthur's Headquarters and the JCS in Washington. This system contributed to the frustrations in both the State Department and the Political Adviser's Office in Tokyo in trying to carry out the State Department's normal responsibilities for policy in Japan.

26. F.C. Jones et al., *op. cit.*, p. 341.

27. Whitney, *op. cit.*, p. 251.

28. *Pol. Reorient. of Japan, op. cit.*, II, p. 624. The quotation is from a letter written by Shirasu Jiro to General Whitney on February 15, 1946.

29. Shimizu Nobu, *Kempo to Jieitai* (The Constitution and the Self-Defense Forces), (Tokyo: Asagumo Shimbun-sha, 1969), pp. 219-20.

30. *Pol. Reorient. of Japan, op. cit.*, I, p. 102.

31. Yoshida, *op. cit.*, p. 137.

32. Whitney, *op. cit.*, p. 258.

33. Mainichi Shimbun, *Jiminto Seiken no Anzen Hosho* (Security under a Liberal Democratic Party Government), (Tokyo: Mainichi, 1969), p. 243.

34. *Pol. Reorient. of Japan, op. cit.*, II, p. 657.

35. Theodore McNelly, "The Renunciation of War in the Japanese Constitution," *Political Science Quarterly*, Vol. LXXIII, No. 3 (September 1962), p. 370.

36. Supreme Court of Japan, *Judgment upon Case of the So-called "Sunakawa Case"* (Tokyo: General Secretariat of the Supreme Court, 1960) pp. 2-8. Published in English translation.

37. Louis J. Halle, *The Cold War as History* (New York: Harper & Row, 1967), p. 121.

38. Glenn D. Paige, *The Korean Decision, June 24-30, 1950* (New York: The Free Press, 1968), p. 260.

3 The American Alliance

A Peace Treaty

General MacArthur told the members of the Far Eastern Advisory Commission during their visit to Tokyo in January 1946, that a military occupation ought not to last more than three to five years. He also urged the Commission, even though it had no power to do so, to get to work quickly on the terms of a peace treaty for Japan.[1] Within the State Department, committees had already been considering postwar policies for Japan, but time dictated the priority of setting guidelines for the Occupation. During 1946 the United States Government, SCAP, and the Far Eastern Commission were largely concerned with reforms, economy, and the punitive aspects of the Occupation.

The first thoughts given to a peace treaty inevitably centered on mechanisms to prevent the revival of militarism and the repetition of aggressive adventures abroad. Secretary of State Byrnes had proposed a twenty-five-year disarmament and demilitarization treaty for Germany, and in June 1946, a similar treaty was drafted for Japan. The term was later extended to forty years. The parties to the agreement were to be the "four Great Powers," China, the United Kingdom, the Soviet Union, and the United States. The intent of the treaty was to insure that no armed forces would be maintained nor military equipment produced. All arms and ammunition, fissionable materials, naval vessels, aircraft "of all kinds," and military installations and bases were to be prohibited, and no factories, laboratories, research institutions, technical data, patents, or plans allowed for any military purpose. A Control Commission was to be established by the four signatory powers as soon as the Occupation ended to enforce the treaty provisions, carry out inspections, make investigations, and report to the contracting parties and to the United Nations.[2]

To read the provisions of this draft treaty twenty-five years after its publication is to evoke wonder and amazement that serious men could have imagined that such a system could ever be set up, let alone work. Yet to many officials at the time it seemed prudent, sensible, and even necessary. Secretary Byrnes, writing in June 1947, argued that the United States should propose such a forty-year pact at the Japanese peace conference. He commented that "both in the peace treaty and the demilitarization treaty we must look forward to a long period of involvement in Japanese affairs." Byrnes believed that treaties of the kind he had suggested would insure that neither Germany nor Japan would again threaten the peace of the world.[3]

The punitive spirit of the time is suggested by the fact that in those years the Far Eastern Commission was struggling with the insoluble problem of reparations and, at the same time, trying to decide what level of economic life should be permitted the Japanese and how Japanese industry should be controlled. In theory, the FEC would determine the future "peaceful needs" of Japan and how reparations could syphon off the surplus beyond those minimum needs. At one point it was agreed that the "peaceful needs" would be the Japanese standard of living of the period 1930-1934. By December 1945, Edwin W. Pauley had investigated the reparations problem and made a report to the President. He recommended that all steel-making capacity in Japan above 2.5 million tons per year should be made available in reparations. It would have been unbelievable if someone had predicted then that within twenty-five years (1970) Japan's steel-making capacity would be third in the world, approaching 100 million tons and that one company would be making more than ten times the minimum then projected for Japan's total "peaceful needs."

When each of the eleven member nations of the Far Eastern Commission put in a bid for a percentage share of the reparations, the total added up to 204.5 percent! In 1947 removals of some machinery and industrial equipment, called "advanced transfers," were carried out by China, the United Kingdom, the Netherlands, and the Philippines. However, no agreement on reparation shares was ever reached in the FEC, and by 1949 the United States had become more interested in the future economic viability of Japan than in punishing the nation by limiting its industry. On May 12, 1949, the United States representative read a statement to the members of the FEC that there would be no more reparations deliveries.[4]

Meanwhile State Department officials had been thinking about a treaty of peace. By early 1947 a first draft had been prepared in the Bureau of Far Eastern Affairs. This draft, written in the spirit of lingering anxiety over a resurgence of Japanese militarism, set up controls to guarantee that Japan would never again become a menace to peace and security. The safeguards—a carry-over from the Byrnes forty-year treaty—included a Council of Ambassadors representing the countries belonging to the FEC and a Commission of Inspection to see that demilitarization was continued. The purge was kept in effect by disqualifying certain categories of persons from holding public office, and war reparations were made a post-treaty obligation. Maintaining the reforms instituted by the Occupation was an imposed requirement. Drafters in the State Department recalled how quickly Germany had recovered from defeat in World War I and searched for effective controls which could be built into the treaty to prevent Japan from resuming a policy of warlike expansion.[5]

Hugh Borton, then chief of the Division of Japanese Affairs in the Department of State, was chairman of the drafting committee. He arrived in Japan on March 8, 1947, with a copy of the Department draft, which was sent by Political Adviser Atcheson to General MacArthur. Very likely this paper stimulated the Supreme Commander to think about a peace treaty for Japan; in any case, he expressed himself publicly on the subject very shortly thereafter. He began an interview with foreign press correspondents on March 19 with the statement: "The time is now approaching when we must talk peace with Japan." MacArthur described the three phases of the Occupation—military, political, and economic. He said that Japan had been demilitarized and the military phase of the Occupation terminated. The political phase, he felt, was approaching completion to the extent possible under occupation. Only the economic phase was difficult because of disagreement among the Allied Powers, and because it involved complex problems which the Occupation could not solve. MacArthur reiterated that "the world" should "at this time" initiate peace talks with Japan. He hastened to note that peace would not mean the removal of all guidance and controls.

Then the Supreme Commander raised the problem of Japan's defense: "Who is going to protect them?" He said one method would be to backtrack and permit a small military establishment, "but the Japanese are relying upon the advanced spirituality of the world to protect them against undue aggression. . . ." He proposed that the United Nations exercise control over Japan, since if the United Nations is ever to succeed, "this is the most favorable opportunity it ever had." Demilitarization was assumed. "I would not envision any military formations of any sort after the Peace Treaty. Bayonet control would be a mockery."[6]

In April, Borton discussed Japanese peace with MacArthur, who again expressed himself in favor of an early treaty. He recommended that a conference be held in Tokyo the same summer and that Occupation forces be withdrawn six months after the treaty was signed. MacArthur's views differed from the State Department draft on the concept of controls. He argued for a non-punitive treaty, unlike that of Versailles. The draft Borton brought to Tokyo was modified after his interview with MacArthur. However, the idea of controls, as exemplified in the Byrnes disarmament and demilitarization treaty, was strongly supported by most of the Allied Powers who would be directly involved in the peace-making process.[7]

The MacArthur proposal for a conference was accepted by Secretary of State Marshall, and invitations to meet in July were sent to the nations who formed the Far Eastern Commission. However, the reply of the Soviet Union was unresponsive, criticizing the American action for being unilateral and insisting that prior agreement among the four powers (China, the United Kingdom, the Soviet Union, and the United States) be reached before holding a general peace conference. The attitude of the Republic of China was also negative, and by the end of the year it became apparent that agreement could not rapidly or easily be achieved.[8]

Meanwhile, during 1947 political leaders in Tokyo had begun to plan for a peace treaty which would hasten the end of the Occupation and to think seriously about the future defense of Japan. Unofficial exchanges of views took place between Japanese and Americans, although ideas on how security should be ensured had not yet crystallized. Yoshida recalls that George Atcheson, who served as General MacArthur's deputy on the Allied Council for Japan as well as Political Adviser to SCAP, privately told members of the Foreign Office that one view in the Department of State was that Japan's safety should be guaranteed by the United Nations.

Foreign Office reaction was that if the structure of the United Nations were faultless this would be fine, but if not, Japan could effectively resist foreign aggression and maintain her independence only by having a link with another country.[9]

In June the Katayama Socialist-Democratic coalition government came into power and Ashida Hitoshi became Foreign Minister. According to Yoshida, on July 28 Ashida wrote letters to Ambassador Atcheson and to General Whitney, setting forth Japan's hopes for a peace treaty and touching particularly the security problem. The next day Whitney let it be known that the timing was "delicate" for Headquarters and he therefore could not accept the letter. Atcheson left almost immediately afterwards on a trip to the United States. His plane crashed en route and was lost at sea. Yoshida wrote that Atcheson was carrying the letter and that it disappeared with him. However, other opportunities were apparently seized to convey these Japanese ideas to the Allied Powers and through them to the Americans, including a visit to Japan of Australian Prime Minister Evatt to whom a similar memorandum was presented.

The Foreign Office was concerned that foreign troops would be stationed in Japan after the peace treaty for the purpose of enforcing its provisions, thus taking on the character of continuing occupation forces in thin disguise. However, American-Soviet relations were worsening. The United States was gradually beginning to perceive the importance of Japanese security and its role within the broader expanse of America's security interests.

According to Yoshida, Japanese thinking was beginning to shift from the concept of reliance on the United Nations to one of direct dependence on the United States and a concurrent buildup of national defense. Yoshida described an exchange of views on these subjects on September 3, 1947, by four leading Japanese politicians including former Prime Minister Shidehara and himself. He quotes Shidehara as saying, "As far as I am concerned, I cannot agree that we can expect much from membership in the United Nations. If Japan is attacked by a foreign country, I don't think we can expect any country to sacrifice its own soldiers in order to defend Japan. The United States may come to the aid of Japan, but if it does it will do so in its own interest and not just because there is a United Nations."[10]

Another effort was made on September 13 to communicate to authorities in the United States the ideas of the Japanese Government on the future problem of security. Ashida Hitoshi, then Foreign Minister, collaborated with Chief Cabinet Secretary Nishio Suehiro in writing a memorandum which was entrusted to General Robert Eichelberger, commander of the Eighth Army, then stationed in Japan, to carry personally to Washington. Yoshida describes the proposal, which in the main contained the principles later incorporated in the Japanese-American security treaty. The memorandum suggested that while Japan would be able to handle internal disturbances, the best method of guaranteeing independence in a time of increasing international tension would be to enter into a special agreement with the United States calling for defense against aggression from a third country and at the same time augmenting Japan's own land and sea police forces. The Japanese people would hope that the defense of their country would be guaranteed by the United States at least until the United Nations was able to carry out the functions specified in the Charter. The memorandum further suggested that the United States might station forces in the vicinity of Japan and in case of emergency be able to use bases in Japan. Even though the document did not specifically request the stationing of American military forces in Japan, its basic concept was identical with that of the Japanese-American security system later to be established.

Yoshida, who became Prime Minister a year later in October 1948, recalls that he agreed completely with the policy outlined in the Ashida memorandum and adopted it as his own without change. However, some time was to elapse before further progress would be made toward either a treaty of peace or a security pact.[11]

It is significant that more than four years before the San Francisco treaties were signed, responsible Japanese leaders viewed with remarkable realism the problems their country would have to face once the Occupation ended. They themselves rejected the unarmed neutrality and blind trust in the peace-loving peoples of the world so highly recommended to them by MacArthur in the early days of the Occupation. They concluded that there was no safe course for Japan other than dependence for protection upon the United States and upon some self-defense strength of their own. From 1947, Japanese Government leaders planned and hoped that the United States would take on the responsibility of protecting Japan. They were willing, if necessary, to pay the price of bases and facilities in return for this protection.

Change of Course: Demilitarization to Defense

The shift in policy from reform to recovery and from neutrality to security, was hastened by conditions within Japan, by pressures in the United States to end an expensive occupation, and by world events. As Japan in 1948 and 1949 began to show encouraging economic progress, the government in Washington and SCAP Headquarters in Tokyo turned increasingly to the problem of Japan's security after the Occupation. In spite of MacArthur's brave words about United Nations control and the "mockery"of an armed Japan, the thought was growing that a peace treaty could not leave an undefended Japan to rely solely on the "advanced spirituality" of the world.

George Kennan, then director of the State Department's Policy Planning Staff, worried over the situation in Japan, particularly because both General MacArthur and the State Department were urging an early peace treaty. He felt that a totally disarmed and demilitarized Japan, "semi-surrounded" as she was by military positions of the Soviet Union, would be dangerously vulnerable to Communist political pressures. He was alarmed that no one was planning for the defense of Japan in the post-treaty period.[12]

Before leaving on a mission to Tokyo in February 1948, Kennan suggested to Secretary of State Marshall that "Japan and the Philippines would eventually constitute the cornerstones of a Pacific security system adequate for the protection of our interests." He proposed that we "devise policies toward Japan which would assure the security of that country from Communist penetration and domination as well as from military attack by the Soviet Union and would permit Japan's economic potential to become once again an important force in the affairs of the area, conducive to peace and stability."[13]

Kennan was not sanguine about the success of his Japan trip, the objective of which was indeed to change the policies of the Occupation. As he noted, General MacArthur had a "violent prejudice against the State Department" and, when he heard of Kennan's visit, is supposed to have threatened, "I'll have him briefed until it comes out of his ears."

After an initial aloofness on MacArthur's part and several days of briefings, Kennan finally obtained an interview alone with the General and things went smoothly from then on. He felt that a general meeting of the minds had been reached with the Supreme

Commander. Kennan's anxieties that Japan at that time was in no condition to bear the responsibilities of independence were, in his mind, totally confirmed. He found that no one had any idea of rearming the Japanese and that SCAP reforms had created instability in Japanese life generally. He was particularly concerned over the threat of internal Communist subversion and infiltration, against which the Japanese had no defenses of their own and no way of preserving internal security. In Kennan's view, this was a much greater danger at that time than any likelihood of a Soviet or Chinese attack. He drew the conclusion that the vulnerability of Japanese society to this internal threat of a Communist takeover should be corrected and a much higher degree of stability established before Japan was left on her own.[14]

On his return to Washington, Kennan recommended, among other things, that SCAP control over the Japanese Government be relaxed, that no pressure be exerted to effect an early peace treaty, and that rentention of armed forces and bases in Japan be left for future decision—although we should "make up our minds that we were in Okinawa for a long time to come." Kennan further porposed strengthening the Japanese police establishment and adding a strong, efficient coast guard and maritime police force.[15]

In November 1948, the National Security Council took a decision, along the lines of the Kennan recommendations, which changed the direction and emphasis of the Occupation and recognized the importance of the security of Japan. Among other proposals, the NSC provided for the formation of a 150,000-man national police force.[16] MacArthur opposed this recommendation. It was not until July 1950, after South Korea had been invaded, that he asked the Prime Minister to establish a National Police Reserve of 75,000 men.

In 1949, NATO was formed, the Communists took China, and America lost the nuclear monopoly. How to defend Japan became an immediate question. American troops and bases in Japan acquired a new importance. Secretary of State Dean Acheson was later accused of having invited North Korean aggression by omitting South Korea from his definition of the American defense perimeter in Asia in his famous speech to the National Press Club on January 12, 1950. Whether or not the charge was justified, there could be no possible misunderstanding of American obligations toward Japan. Acheson spelled these out clearly in the same controversial speech:

the defeat and the disarmament of Japan have placed upon the United States the necessity of assuming the military defense of Japan so long as that is required, both in the interest of our security and in the interests of the security of the entire Pacific area and, in all honor, in the interest of Japanese security . . . . I can assure you that there is no intention of any sort of abandoning or weakening the defenses of Japan . . . that defense must and shall be maintained."[17]

Two Treaties: For Peace and for Security

Within the American Government there was no unanimity on how fast peace should be concluded, nor on what kind of security arrangement should be established. However, once John Foster Dulles was given the job of "managing" a peace treaty—a unique diplomatic experiment—the impetus to move ahead was strong. Dulles had urged Acheson: "Look at the Japanese Peace Treaty— the Department has been discussing it for four years without result. Why don't you give someone one year in which to get action, with the understanding that if he can't do it, he fails?"[18] Dulles made good on his own suggestion and opened negotiations to be conducted simultaneously on the peace treaty and on a separate security agreement. In less than a year and four months after Dulles got the assignment, both the peace treaty and the United States-Japan Security treaty were signed in San Francisco.

The stalemate in the negotiations to bring about a Japanese peace treaty conference was due to procedural objections by the Soviet Union and China. That the basic issue was security was recognized in both Tokyo and Washington. Rearmament for Japan was politically out of the question; it would be bitterly opposed both within Japan and by the nations who had so recently fought Japan. Unarmed neutrality could be safe only by the guarantee of the Soviet Union, and in these early years of the Cold War there was little trust in the good faith of the Soviet Union. The third alternative was the retention of foreign bases and forces in Japan—in essence, the proposal which Foreign Minister Ashida had sent to Washington in 1947. The choice was becoming clear: a treaty with all the Allies stipulating neutralization, or a treaty or separate security agreement to which neither the U.S.S.R. nor Communist China would adhere and which would permit the stationing of foreign forces, obviously American, for an indefinite period.

The subject was actively debated in Japan, particularly during the latter part of 1949. The Socialists supported unarmed neutrality, a position they have maintained to the present day. Others feared the adverse effects on Japan of Russian and Communist Chinese enmity in economic, political, and even possible military actions. Prime Minister Yoshida, who as we have seen, favored a security agreement with the United States, took the public position that the question of an overall or separate peace treaty was not one for Japan to decide and that a treaty with some countries would be better than a treaty with none.[19] On a later date Yoshida stated his position clearly. Writing in *Foreign Affairs* in January 1951 he said: ". . .I speak for myself, for my Government, and for a preponderant majority of the Japanese people in stating that Japan prefers a peace treaty with as many nations as possible to no peace at all."[20]

Meanwhile efforts continued within the United States Government to press toward peace with Japan. Dean Acheson, Secretary of State, said he had to reckon with four groups, the Communists, the Pentagon, our allies, and the former enemy, and that, of the four, the Communists gave the least trouble. He found the most obstinate resistance from the military, who were reluctant to give up the "secure status" of the Occupation for the uncertain results of a peace conference. Acheson comments that most officers in the State Department shared the view of John Allison, then director of the Office of Northeast Asian Affairs and much later Ambassador to Japan, that under the best of circumstances the chances were no more than even that Japan would continue the "liberal, democratic, and peaceful society" which the Occupation had aimed to establish. This view, he felt, underscored the "extreme hazard of delay" in concluding a peace treaty.[21]

George Kennan, however, thought there was danger in haste. He felt that, given adequate police forces and time to achieve domestic stability, Japan could be safely demilitarized and neutralized by international agreement, including that of the Soviet Union. The question of a future American military presence in Japan could, he believed, be used as a bargaining point in negotiations with the Russians. Unfortunately, however, in his view, a general understanding seemed to develop in the winter of 1949-1950 that, in addition to the peace treaty, a separate agreement would be concluded by the United States and Japan providing for American military bases in Japan. Kennan saw this as abandoning any chance to use the issue in seeking agreement from the Russians. He found official Washington at the time "impervious to any understanding of the possible effect of its own acts and policies on Soviet behavior beyond the rather primitive question as to whether what we did deterred or did not deter the Soviet government from its assumed desire to launch military attacks in every direction." In fact, Kennan surmised that the American decision to maintain military forces in Japan in the post-treaty period "probably had an important bearing on the Soviet decision to unleash the attack in Korea." He notes that he has seen no evidence that the possibility of such a connection "ever entered the mind of anyone in Washington except myself." [22]

Dean Acheson's comment on Kennan's statement is that the decision to proceed with the Japanese peace treaty was not taken until almost three months after the attack on South Korea and that "there never entered our minds the idea that unilateral concessions—to avoid pejorative terms—would change, by ameliorating, Soviet policy." [23]

Although no formal decisions on a Japanese peace treaty were made until well after the Korean War had begun, the Russians may have judged by the winter of 1949-50 that a separate security pact permitting American bases to be retained in post-treaty Japan was almost certain. As we have noted, since 1947 the Japanese themselves had proposed the conclusion of some kind of a defense arrangement with the United States. With the continuing deadlock over negotiations for a peace conference, including the obviously strong American and Allied opposition to according a veto to the Soviet Union, the alternative of proceeding to negotiate a peace treaty without the Communist countries, and to conclude at the same time a bilateral Japanese-American security agreement, appeared inevitable. These prospects were widely argued in Japan in 1949. Referring to prepartory talks on the treaty in 1949, Kennan has written:

> To what extent these discussions, and the American disposition they reflected, were a factor in the Communist decision to launch the attack in Korea is a question which still awaits exhaustive historical scrutiny. Certainly, they were not the only factor; but it would be surprising if they had had no effect at all on this decision. [24]

Kennan's argument appears plausible and, although difficult to prove, there could have been a connection between the decision to conclude a bilateral United States-Japan security treaty and the attack in Korea. Kennan has written recently that the Russians, aware that the United States would go ahead with a separate treaty without discussing with them the basic political questions involved, had no reason "to delay longer in pocketing whatever scraps of advantage to themselves lay loose around the table: and one of these scraps of advantage appeared to be South Korea, from which we had removed our forces."[25]

The question whether the neutralization and demilitarization of Japan could have been safely guaranteed through an overall peace treaty including the Soviet Union is more difficult to answer. A treaty signed by both the Soviet Union and Communist China would have contributed to a reduction of tensions in East Asia and have slowed the hostility then building between the Communist and non-Communist worlds. If serious negotiations with the Soviet Union looking toward the demilitarization and neutralization of Japan had been going on in late 1949 and early 1950, the invasion of South Korea might not have occurred. On the other hand, it is difficult to see, when one recalls the circumstances and atmosphere of that period, how the United States could then have successfully pursued such a policy. The national experiences of the postwar disillusionment with Stalin, of the Berlin blockade, and of the Communist conquest of China were still too vivid. Regardless of how farsighted and sensible an international guarantee of Japan's neutrality might theoretically have been, the confidence and trust necessary to achieve such a policy did not exist. Neither in Japan, in the United States, nor among our principal allies was there any faith in the word of the Soviet Union. We were seeking containment of the Soviet Union; we were not expecting cooperation. And to prolong the Occupation while waiting for Japan's stability to solidify might have produced the opposite effect, a rapidly growing restiveness which would have eroded the constructive accomplishments of the Occupation and actually weakened both the internal and external security of Japan.

The United States and Japan's Security

During 1950 a number of State Department officers put their minds to the study of Pacific security. Most agreed that some arrangements were needed to deter the Soviet threat and the new menace of Chinese Communism. Both Australia and New

Zealand were seeking closer military ties with the United States, and some form of guarantee for Korea, Formosa, the Philippines, and Southeast Asia seemed a natural consequence of the postwar situation. In the shock of the sudden attack in Korea, Communist thrusts were expected from any and all directions at any and all times. Organized defense mechanisms seemed urgent and compelling. A favorite concept was a "Pacific Pact." This idea had great appeal as an organization of Asian states for collective security, a kind of counterpart of NATO. Obviously, the quickest scrutiny of the eligible members of such a pact revealed a total absence of the first elements of any NATO-type structure. Either the grouping would be an all-white "club" of colonial and ex-colonial powers and become a target of Asian nationalism as well as Communism, or a mix of Asian weaklings and non-Asian "powers" whose so-called security could be neither mutual nor collective. Although the Pacific Pact idea died quietly, SEATO did emerge in its own corner of the Pacific—with some extensions—and history later bared the limitations of even this smaller assemblage of variegated members.

Inevitably Pacific security arrangements had to depend almost exclusively on the military power of the United States, and the only feasible structure turned out to be separate security treaties negotiated by the United States with Japan, South Korea, Taiwan, Australia and New Zealand, and the Philippines.

Dulles had no need to sell the Japanese Government on a bilateral security treaty with the United States. As we have seen, the Japanese had suggested such an arrangement as early as 1947. By the autumn of 1950 the Foreign Office already had a first draft. It declared that the maintenance of world peace required the "universal security" expressed in the United Nations Charter but that to meet the special threat in the Far East an American-Japanese security arrangement was needed as a supplement. The draft included three provisions: (1) if the United Nations determines that aggression against Japan has occurred, the United States will take necessary steps to stop it; (2) Japan has the right of self-defense and, in case of American military action to stop aggression committed against Japan, will accord all possible cooperation; (3) in case of an armed attack on Japan, both countries will invoke the right of self-defense under Article 51 of the United Nations Charter and without fail take whatever steps are necessary.[26]

As negotiations for a security treaty got under way, differences of view emerged. One issue was rearmament. Except for George Kennan, who continued to feel that we should use the demilitarization of Japan as a bargaining point with the Russians, opinion gained ground within the United States Government that Japan should rapidly assume responsibility for self-defense. Dulles argued for rearmament on his visit to Japan in June 1950, and met with Prime Minister Yoshida's strong protests.[27] An official of the Treaty Bureau of the Japanese Foreign Office at the time, Nishimura Kumao, describes a dramatic incident when, after a particularly heated discussion on the question of Japan's rearmament, Dulles and Yoshida called on MacArthur to ask his opinion. After each had outlined his position, the Supreme Commander exclaimed without hesitation, "The Japanese Prime Minister is right!" According to Nishimura, this ended the pressure for Japanese rearmament; he says the issue almost caused a breakdown and terms it a turning point in the negotiations.[28]

Another point of disagreement was the Japanese desire for a clear American commitment in the treaty to defend Japan. Such a commitment was included in the Foreign Office draft. The Americans would have preferred a mutual security treaty, but obviously a totally unarmed Japan could not assume defense responsibility toward another nation. The United States was reluctant to spell out a unilateral promise in the treaty text; for one thing, it was unnecessary since the presence of American troops on American bases would in itself obligate the United States to defend Japan in case of enemy attack. As Dulles wrote in *Foreign Affairs* at the time the treaty went into effect, ". . . the United States assumes no treaty obligation to maintain land, air and sea forces in and about Japan or to guarantee the security and independence of Japan, although this will be a practical result of the exercise by the United States of its right to station its forces in Japan."[29]

In the revised treaty of 1960 the United States assumed a specific obligation to defend Japan, but the arguments about the importance of American forces as "hostages" for Japan's security are still heard. As one Defense Agency official put it to the author in 1969, "American soldiers in Japan are our very precious guests!"

The first security treaty was negotiated during 1951 and signed September 8 at the Presidio in San Francisco at 5 o'clock in the afternoon, just five hours after the peace treaty ceremony had been concluded in the Opera House. Dean Acheson, John Foster Dulles, and Senators Wiley and Bridges signed for the United States; Yoshida Shigeru alone represented Japan; one member of his delegation belonged to a political party which refused to approve the security treaty. Just a week before, also in the Presidio, Secretary Acheson had signed the ANZUS agreement with representatives of Australia and New Zealand.

Unlike the peace treaty, the text of the security pact was kept secret until an hour before its signing. Thus prior public discussion was impossible, giving critics an excuse to allege later that the treaty had been forced on an impotent Japanese Government still under Occupation rule.

Several provisions are worth mentioning. First, the preamble recognized Japan's inherent right of self-defense and right to enter collective security arrangements. Second, the preamble expressed the willingness of the United States to maintain armed forces in Japan, in the expectation that Japan would increasingly assume responsibility for its own defense while avoiding armament which "could be an offensive threat or serve other than to promote peace and security in accordance with the purposes and principles of the United Nations Charter." Third, American forces in Japan could be used on request of the Japanese Government to quell internal riots instigated from outside the country.

These provisions provoked immediate and continuing controversy. The article permitting American intervention in internal disturbances, even though to occur only at the request of the Japanese Government, was widely regarded as a humiliating derogation of sovereignty as was the restriction on granting base rights. References to collective security, stationing of forces, and Japanese defense efforts drew charges of conflict with Article 9 of the Japanese Constitution and became elements in the constitutional controversy which has continued to the present day.

Also noted with dismay by the treaty's critics was the fact that it was open-ended, providing for expiration only when the parties determined that satisfactory United Nations or other collective security dispositions had come into force for maintaining peace and security in the Japan area.

An objection arose later which touched the sensitive question of sovereignty. The treaty put no restrictions on the use of American bases or military forces. This was another wrong to be righted when the day of revision came.

Foreign Office officials who worked on the treaty were disappointed in the final text. They had hoped for more highlighting of the grand principles of the United Nations Charter and for more specific expressions of harmony with the Japanese Constitution. Instead of a document with appeal to idealism, they found it a stark "troop-stationing treaty."[30]

The treaty was ratified in the Japanese Diet without difficulty and suprisingly well accepted at the time. A poll of September 13-14, 1951, showed 79.9 percent in favor of the pact.   However, dissatisfaction grew as the 1950's advanced. Revision in 1960 brought on the most serious crisis yet to occur in Japanese-American relations of the postwar period.[31]

Notes

1. U.S., Department of State, *The Far Eastern Commission, A Study in International Cooperation, 1945 to 1952*, Publication 5138, Far Eastern Series 60 (Washington, D.C.: U.S. Government Printing Office, 1953), p. 21.

2. U.S., Department of State, *Occupation of Japan, Policy and Progress*, Publication 2671, Far Eastern Series 17 (Washington, D.C.: U.S. Government Printing Office, undated), pp. 11-12. See appendix 15, p. 85 for text of Draft Treaty on the Disarmament and Demilitarization of Japan, June 21, 1946.

3. James F. Byrnes, *Speaking Frankly* (New York and London: Harper and Bros., 1947), pp. 225 and 311.

4. Dept. of State, *The Far Eastern Commission, op. cit.*, pp. 123-58.

5. Frederick S. Dunn, *Peace-Making and the Settlement with Japan* (Princeton: Princeton Univ. Press, 1963), pp. 57-59.

6. Supreme Commander for Allied Powers, *Political Reorientation of Japan, September 1945 to September 1948*, Report of Government Section (2 vols., Washington, D.C.: U.S. Government Printing Office, 1949), II, pp. 765-66.

7. Hugh Borton, *Japan's Modern Century* (2nd ed. rev.; New York: Ronald Press, 1970), p. 490, n. 20.

8. *Ibid.,* p. 480.

9. Yoshida Shigeru, *Kaiso Junen* (Reminiscences of Ten Years), (4 vols., Tokyo: Shinchosha, 1957, 1958), III, p. 111.

10. *Ibid.,* p. 113.

11. *Ibid.*, pp. 113-14.

12. George F. Kennan, *Memoirs 1925-1950* (Boston: Little, Brown, 1967), p. 376.

13. *Ibid.*, p. 381

14. *Ibid.*, pp. 382-90

15. *Ibid.*, pp. 391-92.

16. Dunn, *op. cit.*, p. 77.

17. U.S., Department of State, *Bulletin*, Vol. XXII, No. 551 (January 23, 1950), pp. 115-18.

18. John Robinson Beal, *John Foster Dulles: 1888-1959* (New York: Harper and Bros., 1957), p. 116.

19. Robert A. Fearey, *The Occupation of Japan, Second Phase: 1949-50* (New York: Macmillan, 1950), pp. 182-89.

20. Yoshida Shigeru, "Japan and the Crisis in Asia," *Foreign Affairs*, Vol. 29, No. 2 (January 1951). p. 175.

21. Dean Acheson, *Present at the Creation* (New York: W.W. Norton and Company, 1969), pp. 428-29.

22. Kennan, *op. cit.*, p. 395.

23. Acheson, *op. cit.*, p. 430.

24. George F. Kennan, "Japanese Security and American Policy," *Foreign Affairs*, Vol. 43, No. 1 (October 1964), p. 14.

25. Letter to the author from George F. Kennan, June 10, 1970.

26. Nishimura Kumao, "Nich-Bei Anzen Hosho Joyaku no Seiritsu Jijo" (Situation at the time of conclusion of the Japanese-American security treaty), in Nihon Kokusai Mondai Kenkyujo and Kajima Kenkyujo (Japan International Problems Research Institute and Kajima Research Institute), *Nihon no Anzen Hosho* (Japan's Security), (Tokyo: Kajima Institute, 1964) p. 210.

27. Yoshida, *op. cit.*, III, p. 116.

28. Nishimura, *op. cit.*, p. 210.

29. John Foster Dulles, "Security in the Pacific," *Foreign Affairs*, Vol. 30, No. 2 (January 1952), p. 179.

30. Nishimura, *op. cit.*, p. 211.

31. George R. Packard, III, *Protest in Tokyo* (Princeton: Princeton University Press, 1966), p. 12.

4 Umbrella, Bases, and 1970

The Treaty Revised

Independence came again to Japan on April 28, 1952, the effective date of the treaties of peace and security. MacArthur's "three- to five-year" Occupation had stretched to almost seven and, needless to say, its end was welcomed by the Japanese people. The Socialist and Communist parties, however, denounced both treaties, the peace treaty principally because it ignored the Soviet Union and Communist China, and the security pact because it was unconstitutional and tied Japan to the "imperialist" United States.

The end of foreign occupation and promising signs of economic recovery brought a slow return of self-confidence and with it a degree of irritation over the still strong military control held by the United States. A growing Left opposed the "treaty system" and stimulated propaganda attacks, agitation, and demonstrations.

The American Government, under the persistent strains and pressures of the Korean War, tried to get Japan to make greater defense efforts. After the Korean armistice in July 1953, a rearmed Japan took on an even greater appeal as a bulwark against future outbreaks of Communist aggression in the Northeast Asian area. The National Police Reserve was converted in August 1952 into the *Hoantai* (National Safety Force) and almost two years later, July 1, 1954, again changed to form the present *Jieitai* (Self-Defense Forces).

In October of 1953, negotiations began in Washington on a mutual Japanese-American defense assistance agreement. The Japanese rejected a suggestion that they build up an armed force of 350,000 men. Their objections included constitutional limitations, political and social difficulties, cost, and the conviction that they could not recruit that many men. The Japanese delegation also argued that since their troops could not constitutionally be sent overseas, manpower in the numbers proposed was unnecessary solely for the defense of the homeland.[1] Again in 1955, Americans tried to speed Japanese rearmament. Foreign Minister Shigemitsu visited Washington in August of that year to discuss with Secretary of State Dulles the reduction of United States forces stationed in Japan, an increased Japanese defense effort, and a possible revision of the security treaty. This time Dulles tried unsuccessfully to get Shigemitsu's agreement to a Japanese troop level of 300,000 men as a *quid pro quo* for American withdrawals.[2]

The Mutual Defense Assistance Agreement, signed on March 8, 1954, obliged Japan to assume increasing responsibility for her own defense. The agreement provided for the American military aid which in effect gave the Self-Defense Forces their healthy start in life and initiated the close relationship between the American and Japanese military establishments which so deeply influenced the subsequent development of the SDF.

While the Japanese Government was steadily nurturing its defense capability, although less rapidly and less effectively than the Americans wished, moves for treaty revision began to gather momentum. In June 1957, Prime Minister Kishi and President Eisenhower agreed that all American combat forces would be withdrawn from Japan and that a committee would be formed to study problems relating to the security treaty and consider "future adjustments in the relationships between the United States and Japan."[3] Revision came nearer when at another Japanese-American meeting in September 1958, Secretary Dulles and Foreign Minister Fujiyama decided that the then existing security arrangements would be reexamined *with a view to their readjustment.*[4]

Negotiations on revision of the treaty began in earnest in 1959 and were completed by January of 1960. Prime Minister Kishi and Secretary of State Christian Herter signed the new treaty in Washington on January 19, 1960.

The Crisis of 1960

The treaty crisis of 1960 was a watershed in Japan's postwar history. It brought the largest-scale riots to explode in Tokyo, including the death of a girl student, caused the cancellation of President Eisenhower's visit to Japan, and forced the fall of the Kishi Government. The causes were varied and complex. A basic one was the rise of nationalism, which translated itself into political forces lashing out at the parliamentary system. Thus the Diet, because of its prerogative of ratification of treaties, became the magnet for action. A foreign issue was involved, so those of the Communist Left whose first target was "American imperialism" could for once combine with Socialists and others of the Left who battled primarily against the "monopoly capitalism" symbolized by Kishi himself. To the swelling tide of Communists, Socialists, labor unions, leftist intellectuals, and Peoples Councils organized to defeat the treaty was added the explosive violence of the student *Zengakuren,* in the main responsible for the bloody assault of June 15 on the Diet. This was the climax. Kishi decided to ask the President not to come to Japan and then resigned as head of the Government.

The chain of events leading up to the crisis was long and complicated, and the movement opposing the treaty was more anti-Kishi than anti-American. Nevertheless the spark which set the fire was a military pact to be signed with the United States. Thus, the revised security treaty—far more advantageous for Japan that its predecessor—became a symbol and a rallying point for the diverse elements of the Left, who portrayed it as a betrayal of Japan's peace Constitution, the antithesis of a desired neutrality, and a dangerous lightning rod for war. Unfortunately, the majority Liberal Democratic Party, itself rent by factions which included strong opponents of Kishi, presented a less than persuasive case for the treaty. There was a notable failure by the LDP to overcome the general lack of enthusiasm for the principle of the "inherent right of individual or collective self-defense" repeated from the two treaties of 1951. Significantly, wariness and aloofness toward the concept of sharing responsibility for collective security have remained widely held Japanese attitudes to the present day.

The revised treaty received final, automatic approval of the Diet on June 19, a day to have been doubly celebrated to honor the Japanese-American alliance signified by the treaty and to welcome the first American President in office to visit Japan. But President Eisenhower was not to come, and four days later Kishi resigned. He was succeeded on July 15 by Ikeda Hayato, who immediately initiated his policy of the "low posture."

The crisis had ended, and its shock waves quickly subsided. Since their earliest contacts with the "land of the tycoons" (*tycoon*, meaning "great prince," was a title adopted by the *shoguns*, the real rulers of Tokugawa Japan, in their first contacts with foreign states), foreigners have found Japan a country of contradictions. Here again was a paradox. How could a country suddenly torn violently asunder and its governing processes paralyzed, just as suddenly settle quietly into "doubling the income," an Ikeda goal only too easily surpassed? Yet five months after Kishi's dramatic downfall, his Liberal Democratic Party won 13 new seats and 57.6 percent of the popular vote in elections to the House of Representatives. In the riots the Left had won a point, had dramatized Japan's defense dilemma, and had tested the postwar parliamentary system. Weaknesses had been revealed starkly to the world, but the system had survived. The conservative majority had reasserted its predominance, and Japan was on an even keel again. Graduates of the *Zengakuren* violence would find lucrative niches in Japan's booming industrial economy and look back on their experiences as "moments of glory." For most of the country, the next big event would be the Olympic Games of 1964 when Japan, having come through fire, would publicly and proudly come of age again before the world.

Meaning of the Treaty: Commitments and Limitations

Although the internal crisis abated, the Treaty of Mutual Cooperation and Security between the United States and Japan, ANPO for short, was only beginning a tumultuous life of its own. The revisions had met most of the complaints brought against the 1952 pact. The obligation of the United States to come to the defense of Japan was clearly stated although Japan, without the constitutional right to send forces overseas, could undertake no commitment to defend the United States. The clause allowing American forces to be used to quell internal disturbances was removed, as was the provision requiring the prior consent of the United States for Japan to grant bases and other military rights to third countries. The term of validity of the treaty was set at ten years with the proviso that at the end of that period, either party might give one year's advance notice of its intention to terminate the treaty. Separate from the treaty itself, an exchange of notes provided that major changes of deployment of American military forces into Japan, major changes in equipment, and the use of Japanese bases for combat operations to be undertaken from

Japan, should all be subject to prior consultation with the Japanese Government.

The key American defense commitment to Japan, often popularly called by the Japanese the "nuclear umbrella," is contained in Article V of the treaty:

> Each Party recognizes that an armed attack against either Party in the territories under the administration of Japan would be dangerous to its own peace and safety and declares that it would act to meet the common danger in accordance with its constitutional provisions and processes.

This provision differs markedly from those in the mutual defense pacts which the United States has signed with the Republic of Korea, Nationalist China, and the Philippines, or with Australia and New Zealand in the ANZUS treaty. In those agreements the parties undertake to act in instances of armed attack in territories belonging to either one or another of them. In the Philippine treaty, for example, both parties assume the obligation to act to meet the common danger in case of "an armed attack in the Pacific area on either of the Parties." Since the treaty with Japan applies explicitly only to those territories under the administration of Japan, Japan is not obliged to come to the aid of the United States, but only to defend herself. This is necessary because of Article 9, the "no-war" clause, of the Japanese Constitution.

Similarly, the treaty with Japan differs from those with other Pacific nations in its clause, "in accordance with its constitutional provisions and processes." The other treaties refer only to "processes." The insertion of the word "provisions" again recognizes the constitutional restrictions of Article 9.[5]

Because Japan has no obligation to defend the United States while the United States is committed to defend all Japanese territory, the treaty was criticized as being one-sided when it came before the United States Senate for ratification in 1960. Secretary of State Herter explained that Japan was according to the United States the use of valuable bases and facilities, not only for the purpose of defending Japan but for the maintenance of peace and security in the Far East. This was and remains the *quid pro quo.*

The American commitment to defend Japan has been reiterated in the intervening years. The Japanese were anxious that there be no misunderstanding about the readiness of the United States to use nuclear weapons, if necessary, should Japan be attacked. Consequently, considerable significance was attached in Japan to a statement included in the joint communique issued by President Johnson and Prime Minister Sato after their meetings in Washington on January 13, 1965: "The President reaffirmed the United States' determination to abide by its commitment under the treaty to defend Japan against any armed attack from the outside." The phrase "*any* armed attack" was understood in Japan to include attacks by nuclear weapons. The White Paper on Defense, issued October 20, 1970, reminded the Japanese people that "the United States bears the obligation of the defense of Japan" and quoted the statement in the 1965 Johnson-Sato communique. The White Paper also quoted a statement made by Secretary of Defense Laird in a conversation with Director General of Defense Nakasone in Washington on September 14, 1970, in which Laird "confirmed the readiness of the United States to use all types of weapons for the defense of Japan."[6]

The "Far East"

Since 1960 the two most controversial issues arising in Japan from the treaty have been its application to the "Far East," or the so-called "Far East clause," and the prior consultation system.[7]

What is the "Far East"? The use of this geographic term has stirred more debate and discussion in and out of the Diet than almost any other part of the treaty. The 1952 treaty authorized United States forces disposed in and about Japan to be "utilized to contribute to the maintenance of international peace and security of the Far East." Japan, however, shared neither responsibility nor obligation in this task. The revised treaty, however, expressed the *common* concern of *both* nations in the peace and security of the Far East, provided for consultations in case of threats to this peace and security and, as we have noted, established a system requiring the United States to consult Japan before taking certain actions involving forces stationed in Japan.

In analyzing how the treaty will function, the Japanese have defined several "areas." The first they call the "treaty area," which is where the treaty actually comes into operation and which, as specified in Article V, is confined to those "territories under the administration of Japan." A second is called the "stationing purpose area" and is more extensive since it includes those Far

Eastern territories where the United States has security responsibilities which might require deployment of American forces stationed in Japan. Another term, "consultation area" is also used to refer to the "Far East" as specified in Article IV of the treaty, which provides for consultation between the Japanese and American Governments in case of threats to the security of Japan or to international peace and security in the Far East.

Finally, there is the "operations area," which refers to the region within which and to which American forces stationed in Japan can be deployed. This area is far broader than the others; in fact, the Japanese Government has recognized that American forces may act outside of the Far East in cases of aggression or threats of aggression.[8] The United States would be obliged by the treaty to seek prior consultation should any combat missions be undertaken from bases in Japan and would have to be acting in exercise of the right of individual or collective self-defense in accordance with the charter of the United Nations.

Parliamentary arguments over the scope of the "Far East" were especially heated in 1959 and 1960. Interpretations were not always consistent, and for a time the Government shifted its ground to meet opposition attacks. Spokesmen first described the "Far East" as the area north of the Phillippines, around Japan, and including the coast of mainland China and Soviet Siberia. Later they excluded Chinese and Soviet territory.

In February 1960, the Japanese Government presented its "unified position," which defined the "Far East" as the area north of the Philippine islands and in and around Japan, territory under the control of the Republic of Korea and the Republic of China (Taiwan), the islands of Quemoy, Matsu, Takeshima, and the northern islands now occupied by the Soviet Union, Shikotan, the Habomais, Kunashiri and Etorofu.[9]

When pressed by questions about specific islands, Government representatives refused to say whether one or another particular island was part of the Far East or not. The scope of the Far East has remained vague, and controversy over it has continued.

There has been no attempt to reach a formal agreement between the United States and Japan on the scope of the Far East. Secretary Herter in testimony before the Senate Foreign Relations committee accepted the Japanese position; and when Senator Fulbright asked why the Soviet Union was not included, Herter replied that he thought it would be included, since the Japanese had referred to the "area north of the Phillippines." Foreign Minister Fujiyama later explained that there was no inconsistency between the American and Japanese positions, since Herter was talking about the United States' resisting aggression coming from the Soviet Union and not about the scope of the Far East. Fujiyama was making the distinction between the "stationing purpose area" and the "operations area"; Herter's testimony would suggest that he was not distinguishing between the two.[10]

The Treaty and the Vietnam War

The war in Southeast Asia made the security treaty a live issue in the Diet and before the Japanese public. The escalation of hostilities and the resulting increased use by United States forces of the military bases in both Japan and Okinawa focused public attention on the relationship of the treaty to the war, aroused fears of Japanese involvement, and thus sharpened the controversy over the treaty's scope. The period following the initial bombing of North Vietnam in 1965 marked a high point in Japanese tension over the consequences of expanding hostilities.

The Government recognized that the United States was entitled to use the bases to "maintain peace and security in the Far East" so long as the restrictions requiring prior consultation were observed. Vietnam was not part of the Far East, but it was within the "operations area" in which American military activities could be conducted. An official of the Foreign Office stated before a Diet committee in May 1965 that Vietnam was geographically in the general area of the Far East, that events there could affect the peace and security of the Far East, and that facilities in Japan could be used to achieve the objectives of the treaty. The Government recognized that the threat did not have to come from *within* the area designated as the Far East but since the war in Vietnam was a threat to peace and security in the Far East, resistance to it in every way except by sending combat forces, was permissible. Foreign Minister Shiina, in acknowledging that facilities in Japan could be used to help in the war, conceded that "Japan is not neutral in the Vietnam War."[11]

Critics of the treaty repeatedly attacked its Far East clause as sanctioning entanglements that would willy-nilly draw Japan into American conflicts in Asia. Some of those who favor striking the clause from the treaty accept the American guarantee and the use of bases for the security of Japan but reject the broader application to the preservation of peace and security in the Far East. Some Japanese fear these provisions may be regarded as a threat by the Soviet Union or China. This argument is buttressed by references to Soviet statements that the northern islands claimed by Japan would not be returned so long as American forces remained in Japan under the authority of the security pact. Among the more distinguished Japanese who have advocated the deletion from the treaty of all references to the Far East is Nishi Haruhiko, retired career diplomat and former ambassador to Great Britain. He has written and spoken against the treaty since 1959 and has called the "joint responsibility" which the treaty imposes on Japan and the United States an actual threat to peace in the Far East. He wrote that to prevent joint Japanese-American military action the treaty should never be activated.[12]

Although, as we shall see, American freedom to use Japanese bases is limited, the Japanese feared their own possible entanglement in war. As has been noted, in 1965 when the bombing of North Vietnam was at its height, genuine apprehension grew in Japan that the Vietnam War might flare into a conflict between China and the United States with unavoidable and sinister consequences for Japan. After the bombing ceased, peace talks opened in Paris, and the United States began obviously to move to end the war, these fears substantially diminished.

Nevertheless, Japanese continued to be uneasy over possible involuntary entanglement in the Far Eastern military strategy of the United States. To a public opinion poll taken in June 1969 which asked the subject of most dissatisfaction in the security treaty, the greatest number replied, "the Far East clause."[13]

Prior Consultation

The provision for prior consultation as contained in the exchange of notes which accompanied the security treaty was declared by the Japanese Government to have the same force in international law as the treaty itself. The language follows:

> Major changes in the deployment into Japan of United States armed forces, major changes in their equipment, and the use of facilities

and areas in Japan as bases for military combat operations to be undertaken from Japan other than those conducted under Article V of the said Treaty, shall be the subject of prior consultation with the Government of Japan.

Although Japan accepted the presence of foreign military forces and bases on her soil, the right of prior consultation was regarded as a protection of sovereignty. As a matter of fact, by this provision Japan was given a veto power over the actions of the United States specified in the exchange of notes. This was confirmed by the Eisenhower-Kishi joint communique issued simultaneously with the signing of the treaty on January 19, 1960, which stated that in cases of prior consultation, "the United States Government has no intention of acting in a manner contrary to the wishes of the Japanese Government." The objects of prior consultation, principally the introduction of nuclear weapons and the movement of troops into combat, were to Japan matters of extreme political sensitivity fully appreciated by the United States. No attempt was ever made to seek Japanese consent through prior consultation; and since the bases on Okinawa were free from all restrictions, the military disadvantages suffered were not of major consequence.

The Japanese Government has developed its own definitions of "major changes." In the deployment of forces, a major change requiring prior consultation is the movement of one Army division, one Navy task force, or one Air Force division, which in the case of fighter-bombers is 75 planes. Major changes in equipment include the introduction of nuclear weapons, intermediate and long-range missiles, and the construction of missile sites (launchers).[14] During discussions in the Japanese Diet, Government representatives were frequently asked whether there was a written agreement between the United States and Japan on the definition of "major changes in equipment." The reply was that an understanding existed but not in written form.[15] As to the deployment of units into combat, Undersecretary U. Alexis Johnson told a questioner during hearings of a subcommittee of the Senate Foreign Relations Committee, chaired by Senator Stuart Symington, in January 1970, that there was no rule of thumb to determine what would constitute a "major change" but referred to various statements and interpretations made by the Japanese.[16]

Port calls, including those by nuclear-powered vessels, did not require prior consultation. The Japanese Government maintained this position consistently during the succession of visits to the naval ports of Sasebo and Yokosuka of American nuclear-powered submarines, and in the face of protests and demonstrations by opposition elements. The visit of the nuclear-powered aircraft carrier *Enterprise* in 1968 brought the most violent reactions to any ship visit which had occurred and revived in the Diet the discussion of prior consultation. The Government declared that the *Enterprise* was not a part of the United States forces stationed in Japan, was not equipped with nuclear weapons, and was not engaging in combat action with Japan as its base.[17]

The very size of the *Enterprise* aroused suspicions; opponents of the Government found it unbelievable that the carrier did not have nuclear weapons on board. To the Socialist contention that everybody knew the *Enterprise* was nuclear-equipped, Government spokesmen countered by citing the opinion of military experts that nuclear weapons were not being carried and by stating that the Government believed this to be the truth. When pressed to offer proof, Foreign Minister Miki explained that no one could board a naval vessel to inspect it and that to protect military secrets, American military personnel could not publicly state whether the ship was carrying nuclear weapons or not.[18]

Nuclear Weapons

Because of the sensitive security question involved, the Japanese Government has had to face continuing pressures and difficulties concerning the presence or absence of nuclear weapons in Japan. The standard prescribed reply by an American official to any question about the location of nuclear weapons has been, "I can neither confirm nor deny. The United States lives up to its treaty obligations." This reply was designed to convey the message that since the United States has not asked for prior consultation with the Japanese Government to make a "major change" in military equipment, which is understood to mean nuclear weapons, the United States is observing the commitment *not* to make such a change, in other words, *not* to introduce nuclear weapons into Japan.

The Japanese have recognized that in the end the effectiveness of the security treaty must depend upon the existence of mutual trust between the two nations, partners in the treaty. After being persistently badgered by Socialist Dietmen about the likelihood of the *Enterprise's* carrying nuclear weapons, Prime Minister Sato replied:

> It is a question of whether America will violate the security treaty or not. America has repeatedly said that it has no intention whatsoever of taking an action which would violate the treaty, and it has declared several times that it will absolutely not take action which runs counter to the will of the Japanese Government. The relations between the two nations are such that if one side cannot trust the statements of the other party to the treaty, the treaty itself cannot be upheld.[19]

Combat Operations

If Japan is attacked, the treaty calls for resistance, not consultation. Prior consultation is required, however, when American troops go directly from their military bases in Japan to a combat area and engage in warfare. Clearly the supply of food and materials to combat zones from Japan can be done without consultation. Japanese Government officials have stressed that the important point is not the going into a combat area but rather the use of a Japanese base to launch a combat operation and the actual engagement in combat when the troops arrive at their destination.

The capture of the *Pueblo* and the shooting down of the EC-121 intelligence plane by the North Koreans in 1969 brought the subject of prior consultation into sharp focus as a live issue between Japan and the United States. Prime Minister Sato clarified in the Diet that if American fighter planes were sent from Japan to escort reconnaissance aircraft, "this is for the purpose of preventing the occurence of unlawful acts against reconnaissance aircraft—and this is important, so please listen closely—it would not be an object of prior consultation because the dispatch itself would not be a combat action." Undersecretary Johnson explained to the Symington subcommittee that the United States could send planes to defend an EC-121 without consulting Japan but to take reprisal action *after* an attack, such as that on the *Pueblo* or the EC-121, would require prior consultation.[20]

In the case of naval vessels and aircraft, if they receive orders while in Japan to engage in combat operations, then prior consultation is required. If a vessel departs from a Japanese port and is then ordered to engage in combat, prior consultation would not be necessary.[21]

It has been assumed that American aircraft can take off from American bases in Japan, proceed to Okinawa, and then promptly take off on combat missions. As Undersecretary Johnson stated in the Senate Foreign Relations subcommittee hearings: ". . . Japan has never raised any questions concerning American aircraft stationed in or passing through Japan being transferred or moved to bases outside Japan from which to engage in combat. Japan has also never raised any question concerning naval vessels en route to or from combat operations calling at our naval bases in Japan."[22]

A New Concept of "Prior Consultation"

The agreement signed in November 1969 by Prime Minister Sato and President Nixon changed the concept of prior consultation. No longer must it be assumed that Japan's response will be a veto. As we shall discuss in more detail in later chapters, Japan by this agreement accepted a greater responsibility to cooperate with the United States in security matters, and the answer in future cases of prior consultation may as well be "yes" as "no."

The Sato-Nixon communique contained the strongest statements yet made of the importance to Japan of "peace and security in the Far East." The phrase "Far East" appears twelve times in connection with "situation," "defense," or "security." The Prime Minister is now on record as stating for his Government that, "the security of Japan could not be adequately maintained without international peace and security in the Far East."[23]

The Military Bases

The American military bases in Japan and the forces which occupy them are the physical manifestation of the United States-Japan security treaty. The bases exist because of the treaty, but the treaty does not exist because of the bases. Every base could be closed and the treaty remain in force. As provided in the treaty, Japan has granted to the United States use of facilities and areas by American land, air, and naval forces "for the purpose of contributing to the security of Japan and the maintenance of international peace and security in the Far East."

89

It is the second purpose mentioned above which justifies retaining the bases today. For some time, those familiar with the American military posture in Japan have known that it was designed not for the defense of Japan but for other areas of the Far East. Undersecretary of State Johnson made this clear in the Symington subcommittee hearings, the text of which was released publicly only in August 1970: "The primary responsibility now for the defense of Japan, direct conventional defense of Japan, is entirely Japanese. We have no forces, either ground or air, in Japan that are directly related to direct conventional defense of Japan."[24] The publication of the Johnson testimony produced a flurry in Japan. Although the phrase "autonomous defense" (*jishu boei*) has become popular in Japanese political discussion, particularly journalism, and although Prime Minister Sato told the National Press Club in Washington in November 1969 that "Japan's self-defense capabilities are already filling an important role in securing the primary defense of Japan," it was nevertheless a shock to many Japanese to learn from an American official that American bases and forces in Japan had *no* direct relation to the defense of their homeland.

The American military bases in both Japan and Okinawa exist primarily to protect Korea and Taiwan, serve other commitments in East Asia, and maintain a military presence which will give confidence to other non-Communist nations in the area. The ports of Yokosuka and Sasebo are important for the operations in East Asian waters of the Seventh Fleet, which forms an essential element of the American deterrent. While the bases may not directly relate to the defense of Japan, the functions they perform contribute to Japan's ultimate security. Whether or not bases are maintained in Japan, the United States has a responsibility for the security of Japan so long as the security treaty remains in effect.

The Extent of the "Presence"

The American military presence in Japan consisted in 1970 of approximately 40,000 service personnel and 50,000 dependents. These figures contrasted with the 260,000 members of the armed forces stationed in Japan in 1952. According to Defense Department information supplied in January 1970, "approximately $490 million is expended annually for support of U.S. facilities in Japan including military pay." The extimate by the Commander-in-Chief, Pacific (CINPAC) of the foreign exchange cost of the United States military presence in Japan, or the net adverse balance of payments, was $573.1 million for 1970.[25]

The installations varied from the important and busy airfields handling the largest and fastest jets, with the resulting noise, pollution, and threat of accidents, to training grounds, housing areas, warehouses, hospitals, service clubs, golf courses (eight with a total area of 693 acres), schools, printing plants, and the well-known Sanno Hotel for officers, in the heart of Tokyo. Total military facilities, which numbered 3,800 in 1952 and covered an area of 270,000 acres, were reduced by the end of 1970 to 123 with an acreage of about 75,000. Further substantial reductions were planned in 1971. Largest areas were used for training and manoeuvres, usually for only temporary periods. Air bases occupied second place, followed by communications facilities. The major bases included the naval installations at Yokosuka and Sasebo, the two major operating Air Force bases at Yokota and Misawa, the Marines' naval station at Iwakuni, and the Army's two main installations, Camp Zama and the Sagami Depot.

Yokosuka, in the Tokyo-Yokohama area, offered to the Seventh Fleet unusually good ship-repair facilities, including six drydocks. Sasebo, on the southwestern island of Kyushu, maintained facilities for servicing fleet units. One drydock could accommodate the largest aircraft carriers of the *Enterprise* class. Misawa, the air base in northern Honshu, is only 250 miles from the Soviet Kuriles and 450 miles from Vladivostok. Located in a fairly remote area, it has been singularly free from "base problems." Community relations between base personnel and Japanese residents in the vicinity have generally been excellent. Yokota, in the Tokyo metropolitan area, has brought complaints from citizens because of noise and the danger of accidents.

Unfortunately, immediately after the surrender, the Occupation forces settled themselves conspicuously and, for them, conveniently, in the Kanto plain area around the cities of Tokyo and Yokohama. The population pressures developing in the intervening twenty-five years created the expected problems arising from spacious foreign-occupied areas in the midst of burgeoning urban growth extending from what soon became the largest city in the world. In 1970, 70 percent of the total area occupied by American military facilities and 77 percent of the total American military personnel assigned to Japan could be found in this Kanto plain area (Table 4-1). A member of the staff of the Senate Committee on Foreign Relations put it vividly:

> What this would mean in American terms would be that there would be three foreign military air bases, one major foreign naval base, a dozen or more minor facilities, four golf courses reserved for the use of the pleasure of foreign military personnel, and an exclusive downtown hotel, all in something similar to the New York metropolitan area. I equate it with New York, not just because of the similarity in population size but also because, as New York could be said to be the hub of our commercial activity, the United States being the greatest economic power in the world, Tokyo is even more so the hub of the second greatest commercial power in the free world, with all that this means for congestion of commercial aircraft and ground transportation.[26]

Japanese Attitudes Towards the Bases

No people enjoy having foreign troops on their home soil. The Japanese are no exception. They feel little threat from the Chinese or Russians and whether they regard American bases in their country as for their own protection or for the defense of the Far East, few share positively the Sato Government's convictions of responsibility in area security and most shun involvement in international conflict of any kind. Knowing these attitudes, one is surprised at the actual tolerance recently shown by most Japanese toward the American military presence. The Left continues to turn out demonstrators to wave banners denouncing American bases and the security treaty, but much of the militancy has been lost. A few years ago any visit of a nuclear-powered submarine produced hundreds of protesters and major rallies in Yokosuka or Sasebo, whichever was the port of call. In October 1970 the nuclear-powered *Plunger* called at Yokosuka, paying the fortieth visit of such a vessel to a Japanese port, and the only notice was an obscure, miniscule newspaper item.

Events can of course set off publicity, and in turn publicity will build events. In 1968 a series of events called the attention of the Japanese public to the "base nuisance" (*kichi kogai*), which was played up enthusiastically and endlessly by Japan's aggressive and imaginative mass media. The year began with the January visit of

Table 4-1

United States Military Installations in Japan as of September 1, 1970

Major facilities

Air bases	6	
Training areas.	2	
Administration	4	
Warehouse/storage	1	(Sagami)
Miscellaneous.	1	(North Pier,
Total	14	Yokohama)

Minor facilities

Air bases	1
Communications sites	37
Ammunition storage and handling	10
Administration	8
POL storage	9
Housing areas	12
Warehouse/storage	7
Firing ranges, training areas	6
Miscellaneous.	19
Total	109
Grand Total	123

Acreage of Installations

Service	Number of Installations	Acreage
Army	32	7,103.00
Navy	38	47,238.73
Air Force	48	18,503.06
Multi-Service	5	2,319.48
Totals	123	75,164.27

Source: American Embassy, Tokyo.

This includes the Fuji training area with an acreage of 22,230.24.

Note: In addition to the 123 facilities included in the above tables, there are two Loran Sites furnished partially by the Japanese Government, with an area of 1,260.28 acres. United States Forces also utilize 15,683.63 acres of "restricted water surface area" for ports, depots, and storage.

the nuclear-powered aircraft carrier *Enterprise*; this provoked demonstrations of unprecedented size and a remarkable cooperation among the opposition parties. In May, monitoring instruments showed abnormal readings in the waters at Sasebo where a nuclear-powered submarine was moored. Thorough investigations revealed not only that the submarine had nothing to do with the suspect readings but that in fact the readings had been in error and no radioactivity had been present. Nevertheless the press and all opposition elements played successfully and sensationally on the special nuclear fears of the Japanese. Then a furor erupted over Oji Hospital, established by the U.S. Army in Tokyo, with charges that sick Vietnam War veterans with communicable diseases were endangering the health of citizens living in the crowded urban area where the hospital was unfortunately located. The story made the front pages of the dailies, then the weeklies, and finally ran its course. The charges were denied, but later the hospital was moved from the unlucky mid-Tokyo site.

In June an American phantom jet from adjacent Itazuke air base crashed on the campus of Kyushu University. In the charged atmosphere of student activism, this was a made-to-order incident. The Itazuke base was close to the University campus and actually part of the Fukuoka municipal airport. It was a constant annoyance to the University, city, and civilian airport officials and the object of repeated protests and demonstrations. Deactivated in 1965, the base was reopened after the *Pueblo* incident and again swarmed with jet fighters. Its proximity to the Korean peninsula enhanced its security value.

The Kyushu University students, insisting on preserving the wreckage as a "monument to American imperialism," physically resisted all attempts by Japanese authorities to remove the crashed plane or to repair the building. Not until sixteen months later, in October 1969, were the American authorities able to clear the site.

In the summer of 1968, a popular Japanese weekly magazine devoted a full issue to "The Security Treaty Damage Which Worries Japan." The subject was American military bases, and the titles of the six articles in the magazine indicated the nature of the worries: (1) noise, (2) plane crashes, (3) electrical interference, (4) radioactivity, (5) morals and crime, and (6) transport of munitions. [27] These are the complaints and fears one might expect from residents of areas contiguous to foreign military bases.

Perhaps the surprising thing is that the complaints caused no more trouble than they did.

Fortunately in 1969 and 1970, no major incidents occurred and the base problem seemed to recede in the consciousness of the Japanese public. Attention to foreign affairs was focused on the reversion of Okinawa and the extension of the security treaty. Public opinion polls in 1969 indicated a relative passivity toward American bases. To one in June which asked whether American bases were necessary for Japan, 50 percent replied "no," but a surprising 30 percent said "yes" and the remaining 20 percent had no opinion. [28] In September the same question elicited a closer vote of 45 percent "unnecessary" against 41 percent "necessary." [29]

Even the problems resulting from the concentration of bases in the Tokyo-Yokohama area were less acute than would be imagined. Once noise-suppressers had been installed at Yokota airbase, the Oji Hospital had been closed, and some arrangements made with local inhabitants whose television reception was hampered by a communications facility, no serious problems arose—at least for the moment! In testimony before the sub-committee of the Senate Foreign Relations Committee in January 1970, Scott George, who had been the officer in charge of politico-military relations in the Embassy in Tokyo was able to say:

> But my main point is there has been less "get out of all the bases around Tokyo" than I would have thought likely to exist. Looking at it as an American, I would have thought there would have been more dissatisfaction than I have ever noticed in the two and a half years I have been there. And I see no likelihood that we will be asked, for example, to get out of Yokota Airbase. I do not see that is in the cards for the next few years in the slightest degree. [30]

The Future of the Bases

Policy in both Japan and the United States suggests a continued reduction in military bases and forces in Japan. On this issue the objectives of both countries coincide. The United States seeks to decrease defense expenditures and, in harmony with the Nixon Doctrine, to reduce the American presence in East Asia. The Japanese Government would like to see fewer American bases in Japan and more military facilities utilized by its own Self-Defense

Forces or at least jointly with the Americans. The rapidity of the change will be affected not only by policy in both countries but by the problems of negotiating satisfactory arrangements for the disposition of the bases. Legal and financial problems arise for the Japanese if they are to assume responsibilities in the operation of these military facilities.

Unquestionably both the Japanese and American Governments contemplate an American military presence in Japan for a considerable period of time. The Director General of Defense, Nakasone Yasuhiro, during a visit to Washington in September 1970, told the National Press Club that he considered "the existence of American military bases in Japan necessary, in the future as in the past . . . ." He went on to say that some of the bases could be disposed of, used jointly, or turned over to the Self-Defense Forces. During Senate committee hearings previously referred to, Undersecretary of State Johnson was pressed to justify the presence of American forces in Japan and to say when they might be withdrawn. He refused to speculate on when this might happen, although he emphasized the hope of continued reductions in forces, adding in a prepared statement, "we will probably need to continue to provide the nuclear deterrent for the indefinite future."[31]

Various proposals have been made for the transfer and joint use of the bases; for example, the Defense White Paper suggested that five categories be set up: (1) exclusive American jurisdiction, (2) American administration with use by the SDF permitted, (3) SDF administration with American use permitted, (4) generally exclusive use by the SDF, and (5) installations returned to civilian use.[32] Conversations between Japanese and American authorities have been proceeding, looking toward arrangements along these lines.

The most important step taken up to then to achieve a changed base structure in Japan was announced by the United States and Japanese Governments on December 21, 1970. In a joint statement issued following a meeting of the Security Consultative Committee in Tokyo, the two Governments outlined certain planned "realignments and consolidations" of American forces and bases in Japan, to take place not later than June 30, 1971. According to this communique, the "U.S. side" explained that the contemplated plans were consonant with the Nixon Doctrine, were designed to streamline operational capabilities and enable maximum use of existing resources, and would not significantly affect the capability of the United States to meet its security commitments to Japan and elsewhere in the Far East. According to the announcement, most of the American forces affected were to be relocated "in Japan or within the Far East."

Briefly, the actions decided upon reduce American military personnel in Japan by 12,000, civilian employees by 360, and require the dismissal of 10,000 Japanese base workers. All American F-4 fighter aircraft at Misawa Air Base are being moved to the United States and to South Korea; those at Yokota, to Okinawa. American activities at Itazuke Air Base in Kyushu and Atsugi Naval Air Station in the Kanto Plains area are to be drastically reduced as are operations at Yokosuka Naval Base. The pattern at most of the bases will be "joint-use" with the SDF.

Japanese comment on the announced American force reductions speculated that the situation described as "stationing of U.S. forces only in case of emergency" was rapidly approaching. As a result, some uniformed members of the Self-Defense Forces were said to favor heavier increases in Japan's armaments to cope with expanded defense responsibilities. Other Japanese felt that present defenses were adequate to meet any presently conceivable threat and that the American nuclear deterrent was still dependable.

The Problem of 1970

Nineteen-seventy, the year in which either party to the treaty could give notice of its termination, was to become the "year of decision" for Japan. During the second half of the 'sixties, the "problem of 1970," which combined the future of the security treaty and the reversion of Okinawa, became Japan's most discussed foreign policy issue. Every Japanese wanted the return of Okinawa to the homeland, and the movement for reversion generated more emotion than did the treaty. Indeed, the convergence of these two issues—Okinawa and the Treaty—in a real sense produced the "problem of 1970." The "problem" provided a much-needed catalyst for the shaky and diverse forces of the Left. When the Okinawa issue was "defused" by the Washington agreements of November 1969, the treaty issue alone lacked the popular appeal to inspire a united and powerful struggle. When the magic date in 1970 came, as we shall see later, the promised crisis did not materialize (see chapter 15).

The attitudes and votes of most Japanese reflected none of the crisis atmosphere which the Left was trying to build up. Just as in 1960 the LDP had claimed the election victory as a *post facto* endorsement of the security treaty, so in 1969 Prime Minister Sato hailed his Party's success in the December election as a mandate for continuing the treaty in effect. Whether Sato's claim was justified or not is difficult to say. Japanese voters, as those in many other countries, do not pick their candidates primarily for the stands they take on foreign affairs. Domestic issues are far closer to the voter's heart, and the activities of parties and candidates on the local level are more powerful determinants of the voter's choices than any issues, foreign or domestic.

In September 1969, when public arguments over the security treaty and Sato's pending visit to Washington were at their height, pollsters for the *Asahi* newspaper asked respondents to name the subject then being most discussed among family and friends. The replies put student unrest as the subject of greatest interest, personal problems next, and prices and taxes third. A mere 6 percent reflected concern over the security treaty and Okinawa.[33]

While the Japanese were never enthusiastic over the security treaty, only a modest minority favored its outright abrogation. According to public opinion polls, popular support for the security treaty was 53 percent in December 1967 and had declined to 40 percent in December 1969. Those who wanted to scrap the treaty have been more constant, varying between 12 percent and 15 percent. The alternative of a medium position between continuation and termination, such as "gradual dissolution," found substantial acceptance. In a survey of September 1969 only 24 percent favored continuation, while 31 percent approved temporary continuation "moving toward" abrogation in the future. The percentage of those replying "no opinion" has been surprisingly large in the more recent polls. In early December 1969, less than a month before the Lower House elections, 38 percent of those asked for an opinion on the treaty replied "don't know." Another survey carried out between May 7 and 9, 1970, approximately six weeks before nationwide anti-treaty demonstrations were scheduled to be held, produced a 32 percent "no opinion" response. In this same poll, 24 percent supported continuation of the treaty, 16 percent chose "revision but with a lessened military coloring," and 12 percent were in outright opposition.[34]

Political Party Positions on the Treaty

Liberal Democratic Party

Japan's political parties have taken a variety of positions on the security treaty. Even within the LDP, opinion was divided for some time on whether renewal should be determined for a specific term of years or whether continuation should be automatic and indefinite. The party officially adopted the latter position October 14, 1969 and at the same time declared that the treaty would be needed for a "considerably long period of time." The Sato-Nixon communiqué of November 21 "affirmed the intention of the two Governments to maintain the treaty on the basis of mutual trust and common evaluation of the international situation."

The Socialist Party

The Japan Socialist Party (JSP), in pursuing its traditional policy of "unarmed neutrality," called for complete abrogation of the treaty in 1970, the disbanding of the Self-Defense Forces, and diplomatic efforts to establish a non-aggression pact with Communist China, the Soviet Union, and the United States. The party demanded the unconditional return of Okinawa to Japan, including the total withdrawal of American forces and abandonment of military bases. The failure of the JSP both at the polls and in the so-called "struggle of 1970" against the treaty left it with little but vague plans and brave words for the future about continuing to battle the treaty system and to achieve the termination of the security pact within the decade of the 1970's.

The Democratic Socialist Party

The Democratic Socialist Party (DSP) advocated revision of the security treaty to eliminate the stationing of American forces in Japan. The party rejected both the "unarmed neutrality" policy of the JSP and outright abrogation of the treaty. Instead it proposed

99

that the United States should supplement Japan's Self-Defense Forces with the deterrent power of the Seventh Fleet and nuclear weapons to be used from sources *outside* Japan. (At least one DSP leader, Sone Eki, stated his willingness to accept continued American use of the naval bases at Yokosuka and Sasebo and of non-nuclear bases in Okinawa.) The DSP also objected to American forces' being stationed in Japan for the purpose of defending the "Far East." A DSP spokesman complained that no other treaty in the world "permits foreign troops to be stationed in a country for the security of areas outside the territorial jurisdiction of that area."[35]

The DSP's position that American deterrent power should only supplement Japan's own military forces later became widely accepted within the Government and LDP, as we shall note later on.

The *Komei* Party

The *Komeito* (Clean Government Party) would like to see the security treaty dissolved by stages during the 1970's. The party does not oppose defense forces for Japan. "Gradual dissolution," as defined by the party, called for a series of steps to be taken during the 1970's, including closing out U.S. bases, opposing further defense build-up, terminating military agreements, and finally abrogating the security treaty. No specific timetable has been set, although presumably Japan would enter a period of "complete neutrality" by the end of the decade.

The *Komeito's* principal target has been the removal of American bases from Japan, by which process the treaty would be "skeletonized" or "scrapped *de facto*." Once this happened, the Self-Defense Forces would be converted into a National Guard, the United Nations would be urged to establish an Asian Headquarters in Japan, and when the U.N. collective security system became fully developed, the National Guard would join the United Nations Police Force. Japan would then enjoy complete neutrality under the United Nations, the ideal already expressed in Article 10 of the security treaty.[36]

The Communist Party

The Japanese Communist Party (JCP) fought the 1960 security

treaty as it fought the peace treaty and the original security pact. It called for a decision in 1970 to terminate the treaty and tried to stay in the vanguard of the "1970 struggles."

Astutely and unlike the Socialists, the Communist Party never championed unarmed neutrality but contended that even in a future Japanese socialist state, the danger of American imperialist aggression would require some "socialist" military forces for national defense.

When the LDP announced that the treaty would be continued for a "considerably long period of time," *Akahata* (Red Flag), the Communist party organ, called this policy an "impermissible outrage" committed by a party unable to win even a majority vote in the last two national elections. *Akahata* interpreted continuation of the treaty as meaning rearmament and the revival of militarism through a conspiracy of American and Japanese reactionary forces. The party contemptuously spurned the JSP's unarmed neutrality and the revisions and gradual dissolution propagated by the "middle-of-the-road" parties (DSP and *Komeito*). The latter were characterized as "turning their backs on the great majority of people who desire dissolution of the Japan-U.S. military alliance."[37]

The JCP repeatedly called for a "united front of all democratic forces." As the Central Committee proclaimed, this should be formed along the lines of the prewar anti-fascist united fronts, to block the United States-Japan military alliance and the revival of Japanese militarism.[38] As we shall see, the "united front" never got beyond the tenuous, temporary "one day joint struggles" which left the JCP, the JSP, and other forces of the Left as deeply divided as ever.

The Future of the Security Treaty

The policy of the Japanese Government to maintain the security treaty with the United States has been expressed consistently and repeatedly and made a matter of record in the 1969 Sato-Nixon communique. The time of the treaty's duration has been left indefinite. The Liberal Democratic Party, in announcing its policy of "automatic continuation," spoke of extension beyond June 1970 for a "considerable period of time." Japanese Government officials described the life of the treaty as "semi-permanent." The White Paper on Defense stated that, "since we do not have nuclear weapons and offensive weapons, the United States-Japan security treaty system will be necessary for Japan's security so long as there is no major change in the international situation."[39]

The Director General of the Defense Agency, Nakasone Yasuhiro, has suggested that the treaty should be reviewed in 1975. He has explained that change in Japan, in the United States, and in the international situation will by 1975 require a flexible response and adjustment by Japan and the United States in their security relationship. He has insisted that this relationship should remain a fundamental policy of Japan.

The United States is also committed to continuing the treaty in force. President Nixon and Prime Minister Sato together "affirmed the intention of the two governments firmly to maintain the Treaty."

Looking forward into the decade of the 1970's, one may reasonably contemplate certain changes coming about in the Japanese-American treaty system, if not in the text of the treaty itself. As the capability of the Self-Defense Forces grows, as Japanese confidence in their own defense potential builds up, and as American forces and installations diminish, a new situation will eventuate. Japan will be far less conscious of a dependence on the military of a foreign country because the symbols of that dependence will be inconspicuous. Bases will be in the hands of the Self-Defense Forces or used jointly when required, and American forces can return in strength if needed. Such a situation is called "emergency use" (*yuji shiyo*) and, interestingly, would be similar to the policy which the Democratic Socialist Party has advocated for a number of years.

But before speculating futher on the future, we should examine the development and status of Japan's Self-Defense Forces.

Notes

1. Mainichi Shimbun, *Nihon no Heiwa to Anzen, Anpo to Jieitai* (Japan's Peace and Security, The Security Treaty and the Self-Defense Forces), (Tokyo: Mainichi, 1969), p. 50.

2. *New York Times*, September 1, 1955; Hirasawa Kazushige, *Japan Times*, August 17, 1957, quoted in George R. Packard, III, *Protest in Tokyo, The Security Crisis of 1960* (Princeton: Princeton University Press, 1966), p. 56.

3. U.S., Department of State, *Bulletin*, Vol. XXXVII, No. 941, July 8, 1957, pp. 51-53.

4. U.S., Department of State, *Bulletin*, Vol. XXXIX, No. 1006, October 6, 1958, pp. 532-33.

5. Young C. Kim, *Major Issues in Japan's Security Policy Debate* (McLean, Va.: Research Analysis Corporation, June, 1969), p. 16.

6. Boei-cho (Defense Agency), *Nihon no Boei* (Japan's Defense), Tokyo, October 1970, pp. 52-53. This document is popularly known as the "Defense White Paper."

7. Asahi Shimbun Anzen Hosho Mondai Chosakai (Asahi Security Problems Research Institute), *Nichi-Bei Anpo Joyaku no Shoten* (Focal Points in The Japanese-American Security Treaty), (Tokyo: Asahi, 1967), p. 177.

8. *Ibid.,* pp. 177-78.

9. *Ibid.,* p. 180.

10. *Ibid.,* p. 182.

11. *Ibid.,* p. 185.

12. Nishi Haruko, "Nichi-Bei Anzen Hosho Joyaku ni tsuite" (Regarding the Japanese-American Security Treaty), November 8, 1962, in Nihon Kokusai Mondai Kenkyujo and Kajima Kenkyujo (Japan International Problems Research Institute and Kajima Research Institute), *Nihon no Anzen Hosho* (Japan's Security), (Tokyo: Kajima Institute, 1964), p. 227.

13. *Yomiuri*, Tokyo, August 7, 1969. The second point of dissatisfaction after "Far East clause" was "base problems" with 23.1 percent followed by "opposition to the security treaty system" with 14 percent, and the "nuclear ban is ambiguous" with 11.7 percent.

14. Kim, *op. cit.,* pp. 25 and 29.

15. *Ibid.,* p. 30.

16. U.S., Congress, Senate, Committee on Foreign Relations, *United States Security Agreements and Commitments Abroad, Japan and Okinawa: Hearings before the Subcommittee on United States Security Agreements and Commitments Abroad*, 91st Cong., 2nd sess., Part 5, January 26, 27, 28, and 29, 1970, pp. 1189-90.

17. Kim, *op. cit.,* p. 32.

18. *Yomiuri*, February 7, 1968.

19. *Ibid.*

20. Senate For. Rel. Subcom., *op. cit.,* p. 1157.

21. Kim, *op. cit.,* pp. 25-26.

22. Senate For. Rel. Subcom., *op. cit.,* p. 1155.

23. *New York Times*, November 22, 1969.

24. Senate For. Rel. Subcom., *op. cit.*, p. 1167.

25. *Ibid.*, pp. 1231 and 1479.

26. *Ibid.*, p. 1232.

27. *Asahi Janaru*, July 7, 1968.

28. *Yomiuri*, August 7, 1969.

29. *Asahi*, October 1, 1969.

30. Senate For. Rel. Subcom., *op. cit.*, p. 1251.

31. *Ibid.*, p. 1288.

32. "Defense White Paper," *op. cit.*, p. 77.

33. *Asahi*, October 1, 1969. The poll was taken September 2 and 3, 1969. As expected, the percentage concerned over Okinawa and the security treaty was 22 percent in Okinawa itself as contrasted to only 6 percent in Japan proper.

34. Sources for the public opinion polls quoted are as follows: *Kyodo News Service*, January 1, 1968; *Yomiuri*, August 7, 1969; *Asahi*, October 1, 1969; *Yomiuri*, December 17, 1969; *Yomiuri*, May 31, 1970.

35. Sone Eki, Chairman, Foreign Affairs Commission and Ad Hoc Commission on Security, Japan Democratic Socialist Party, "For a National Consensus on the Japan-U.S. Mutual Security Treaty" (translation), in *Domei* (DSP organ), May 1968.

36. *Komeito* press releases, "Toward the Realization of World Peace Through the Middle-of-the-Road Principle," "Main Program and Action Policy Adopted at the Seventh Party Convention," January 22, 1969.

37. *Akahata* (Red Flag), "We Call for All People's Struggle Aimed at Abrogation of Security Treaty and at Independent, Peaceful, Neutral Japan: the LDP decision on 'Long-range Extension' of Security Treaty." Statement of Japanese Communist Party Central Committee Presidium, October 14, 1969.

38. *Ibid.*

39. "Defense White Paper," *op. cit.*, p. 39.

5 Growing Pains of the Self-Defense Forces

Chrysanthemum or Sword

"Prewar Japan banished the chrysanthemum from our national life, but postwar Japan has outlawed the sword and by so doing has broken the totality of Japanese culture." Mishima Yukio, Japan's popular contemporary novelist, thus characterized the state of Japanese society today. He viewed with dismay an infatuation among youth over the soft pleasures of life which led the present age to be called "*Showa Genroku,*" a linking of the present reigning Emperor's *Showa* era with the gay, late-17th century *Genroku* period, which saw a brilliant flowering of popular art and theatre. He described present-day Japanese literature as a "paradise of insomniacs, neurotics, impotents, ugly masses of fat, cancer and stomach disease patients, sentimentalists and semi-lunatics." He added, "Those who can fight are few."[1]

Mishima deplored the lack of ideology and knowledge of history among modern Japanese youth. He talked with students who said that, if Japan were invaded, they would bare their chests to the enemy and die rather than resist. He was also concerned over the lack of morale and purpose within the Self-Defense Forces.

Mishima not only wrote about his beliefs but also acted on them. He first joined briefly a unit of the SDF for the experience and then organized a "private army" of some 100 youths whom he trained and exhorted, with the blessing and cooperation of the Self-Defense Forces. Though labeled "right-wing" and representative of a tiny element of Japanese thought, Mishima symbolized a revival of pride in Emperor and country as a reaction to the defeatism of the earlier postwar period and the anarchism of present-day student militants.[2] Mishima carried his glorification of the sword to spectacular consummation when he committed *harakiri* in the Tokyo headquarters building of the Ground Forces Eastern Command on November 25, 1970 after haranguing members of the SDF who gathered in the court-yard below the balcony on which he spoke, and who greeted his appeals with laughter and amused disbelief. Later, the impression of Mishima's deed deepened, not only among the young men of the Self-Defense Forces, but among the youth of Japan. Its effect was not an incitement to revolution nor did it portend a revival of militarism. The act did, however, encourage and stimulate right-wing elements and inspire among some young Japanese sober thoughts about the spirit and purposes of the Japanese nation.

The SDF became twenty years old in 1970, dating its birth from the compliance with General MacArthur's directive of July 8, 1950 in which he proposed to Prime Minister Yoshida the establishment of a National Police Reserve. In twenty years the armed forces grew from a unit of 75,000 "policemen" who braved insults to wear their uniforms in public to the combined ground, air, and sea contingents of 287,000 uniformed and civilian personnel, who by 1970 were at last publicly accepted as respected members of society.

When the Self-Defense Forces celebrated their nineteenth anniversary in 1969, the Prime Minister assured the assembled troops, "The Self-Defense Forces . . . have finally been able to win the confidence and support of the Japanese people."[3] The then Director General of the Japan Defense Agency, in an interview on the same occasion, explained the kind of pep talk he habitually gave the troops:

> I tell them: "You must not forget that, in the background of this wonderful prosperity and precious peace now being enjoyed by Japan, there exists our country's defense set-up, which is based on the principle of gradually increasing its defense power, in keeping with our national ability and national situation, while firmly maintaining the U.S.-Japan security treaty. Consequently, I want you, the members of the SDF, to carry out your tasks with the awareness and pride that you, too, are fulfilling a big role in the prosperity and peace of our country."[4]

Such awareness and pride have not always been easy for the

military that was not a military. In the early days of their existence, the new forces were the "outcasts of society." It was still the period of stunned reaction to defeat. The national flag could not be flown, the national anthem could not be sung. The Emperor was no longer "sacred and inviolable." Until the war's end the sovereignty of the state had resided in his person and he had been the locus of the national polity and culture and the object of all loyalty and devotion. But under the Occupation he had become merely the "symbol of the State" and had publicly divested himself of his "divinity" to become a mere person, respected but not worshiped. The vocabulary of the prewar and wartime years, inculcated in schools, literature, songs, plays, newspapers, and radio was expunged. The word "patriotism" was taboo.

In this atmosphere, it was natural that the postwar armed forces were timid and faltering as they took each cautious, careful step toward building what they could not call a "military." The camouflage went to ludicrous lengths. The terms "Army, "Navy" or "Air Force" were never used; all the traditional military ranks and titles were replaced with contrived, artificial terms. Even weapons were renamed; a tank was a "special vehicle." One was reminded of the Japanese wartime regulations which banned all English baseball terminology and introduced complicated Japanese-Chinese compound words which nobody ever really learned and which were happily and quickly forgotten the moment peace came.

General Sugita Ichiji, who was "Chief, Ground Staff, Ground Self-Defense Forces," recalls that he and his colleagues were startled and delighted when American military officers whom they met addressed them immediately as "General," "Colonel," and the other appropriate ranks. The contradiction was soon apparent that, "to foreigners we were 'military,' to Japanese we were 'non-military.' "[5] This contradiction has not yet been resolved. Prime Minister Sato, pushed hard by the opposition, stated in a House of Councillors debate as recently as March 31, 1967, that "Now and in the future we will *not* call the SDF military (*guntai*)."[6]

Quietly, former professional Army and Navy officers, some of them released from prison after sentences as war criminals, found their way into positions of leadership in the Self-Defense Forces. Other officers came with police backgrounds. Training and recruitment proceeded. By 1952, the Diet had approved increasing the strength of the National Safety Force to 117,000, and by 1954 total personnel of the Self-Defense Forces was 152,000.[7]

The year 1954 marked a turning point in the development of Japan's defense. The Mutual Defense Assistance Agreement was signed with the United States, and the laws establishing the Japan Defense Agency and the Self-Defense Forces were passed. The new legal status and the close interaction and cooperation with the American forces gave new life and incentives to the organization.

However, the SDF suffered, and still suffers, from its origins. Created suddenly out of the Korean crisis by mandate of a foreign occupying power, the Forces missed the proud traditions which glorify the history of most armies. Although the Occupation had instilled in the popular mind ideas of the democratic way of life and the sovereignty of the people, Japan's defense organization came into being without benefit of any initiative, discussion, or referendum by any Japanese popular body. Small wonder that those who wore the uniform were dubbed "American mercenaries" and the SDF a "child of the Americans."

The Challenged Legitimacy

The challenge to their constitutionality and therefore their legitimacy has been a far more serious trauma for the Self-Defense Forces than any rankling over their foreign origin. In spite of Ashida's amendment to Article 9, which, in his mind at the time, made defense compatible with the Constitution, the language left many doubts; and the interpretation of Article 9 has been among the thorniest of Japan's post-Occupation questions.

Arguments have continued over the years both inside and outside the Diet on how much Article 9 restricts the Self-Defense Forces. Constitutional experts, while far from agreed on an interpretation of Article 9 and its legal effect, in general find the difficulties in the preamble and the second paragraph.

The preamble expresses the ideal which General MacArthur so often proclaimed: "We, the Japanese people, desire peace for all time and are deeply conscious of the high ideals controlling human relationship, and we have determined to preserve our security and existence, trusting in the justice and faith of the peace-loving peoples of the world." The latter phrase accords no place to a military force formed for the purpose of preserving the security of the nation.

The first paragraph of Article 9 renounces war as a sovereign right and the threat or use of force as a means of settling international disputes. This article has been interpreted as referring to "aggressive war" and therefore not a prohibition or restriction of the right of self-defense. The second paragraph, however, categorically states that "land, sea, and air forces, as well as other war potential, will never be maintained." As we have seen, Ashida's amendment inserted the phrase "in order to accomplish the aim of the preceding paragraph," which in his mind clearly tied the two paragraphs together and preserved the right of self-defense. However, those who favor revision would like to eliminate the second paragraph in order to remove any doubts about the legitimacy of the SDF, which are likely to remain so long as this article, which in clear language prohibits any armed forces, is retained in the Constitution.

The Opposition Parties and the Constitutionality of the SDF

Both the Socialist and Communist parties have from the beginning declared the Self-Defense Forces unconstitutional. The Socialist point of view is that both the preamble and Article 9 make it clear that "military forces" (*guntai*) are completely outlawed. Otherwise, say the Socialists, there would be provisions for declarations of war, peace treaties, military courts, or some kind of military authority. While admitting that an inherent right of self-defense may exist, the Socialists claim that Article 9 denies to the nation any military force or war potential to be used for purposes of defense. The JSP position is that one cannot limit "war potential" by saying it will not be used for aggressive purposes. "What nation in the world," they ask, "would ever say, 'our country has an armed force for aggression'?" One is reminded that Prime Minister Yoshida, at the time of enactment of the Constitution, before the period when he had to justify defense forces before the nation, commented that every war is fought for "self-defense."[8]

The Socialists, who are the only political party in Japan to advocate unarmed neutrality, admit that if they came to power they would, after dissolving the Self-Defense Forces, establish a "National Construction Corps" and a "Peoples Police Corps." The latter's duties so far have not been defined by the Socialists; they say such a corps would in no way be a military force, as is the present SDF, and that its duties would be rigidly restricted to internal order. [9]

JSP spokesmen have denied that they would ever revise Article 9. They have speculated, however, that, if the party came into power, they might revise the Constitution to make it more suitable to a socialist state. In fact, in 1963 public interest was aroused by the publication of a presumably Socialist-approved draft constitution. Party leaders hastened to play down this document, since to the public it contradicted the JSP's vigorous defense of the present "peace Constitution."

The Japanese Communist Party attacks the SDF as a military force subservient to American Far Eastern strategy and created in violation of the Constitution. The Communists, although rejecting unarmed neutrality, say they would establish a "democratic, neutralist, independent" state liberated from the American security treaty and fighting imperialism. Such a nation would contribute to the peace of Asia and the world by rejecting all military alliances and striving to dissolve all military blocs regardless of the countries which form them. Collective security in its true meaning could then come into existence. Even then, however, armed force might be needed. *Red Flag* stated the party position June 11, 1968 as follows:

> As a future problem, we have to consider that developments both within and without the country may produce a situation in which, in order to defend the independence and sovereignty of the country, some defense measures of a military nature may be required. Over the future, to declare the rigid principle of "unarmed neutrality" is not the right way to defend successfully Japan's sovereignty and independence in every situation. However, this is a problem which the Japanese people themselves, facing a new domestic and international situation in the future, and considering the application of the Constitution, must decide on the basis of the will of all the people. [10]

The Communists have also stated that while they uphold Article 9 they do not regard the Constitution as immutable, and that, in an "independent democratic Japan," revisions might be envisaged which would meet the needs and desires of the people at that time.

The *Komeito* (Clean Government Party) is less positive on the constitutional question than either the JSP or JCP; Secretary General Yano Junya has put it this way: "Our doubts about the

110

constitutionality of the Self-Defense Forces are extremely strong."[11] Yano has enumerated several of the doubts, including the statement of purpose in the law establishing the SDF, the equipment being acquired, such as Phantom jets, and the fact that the SDF is a military force without independence in view of its expected joint action with the United States under the security treaty.

In a conversation with the author, Secretary General Yano emphasized the difference between *Komeito* defense policies and those of the JSP and JCP. He explained that *Komeito* has no desire for immediate abrogation of the security treaty nor for disbandment of the SDF. The strength of the latter is too great, however, and should be reduced. The *Komeito*-proposed "National Guard" would never grow large enough to menace another country; however, the Socialist policy of "unarmed neutrality" is completely unacceptable. Japan needs defense and must provide it herself.[12]

The Democratic Socialist Party rejects the argument that the Self-Defense Forces are unconstitutional and opposes revision of Article 9. The party, in propagating its idea of a "security treaty without stationing of troops," describes its concept as "defensive defense" or "self-reliant defense" based on the Constitution. Like the *Komeito,* the DSP sees a global collective security system under the United Nations as the ideal. Pending this happy juncture, however, the DSP proposes not neutrality, armed or unarmed, but cooperation with the United States (without stationing of American forces in Japan) to supplement Japan's own defense forces. As for the SDF, the party believes the present level of strength to be sufficient; any marked increases in defense potential would be not only unnecessary, but adventurous.[13]

The Courts and the Constitution

Opponents of the SDF have vainly tried to get Japanese courts to rule on its constitutionality. The issue arose first in the Sunakawa case, already mentioned. The decision of the Supreme Court handed down December 16, 1959, determined that Article 9 did not deny to Japan the inherent sovereign right of self-defense, and that the stationing of forces under the security treaty was not unconstitutional since foreign troops were not "war potential" according to Article 9. The Court did not pass on the constitutionality of the Self-Defense Forces and also refused to render an opinion on whether Article 9 prohibits the maintenance of war potential for self-defense.[14]

A second case which attracted wide attention in Japan and which seemed to bear directly on the constitutionality of the SDF arose from the Eniwa incident. Two brothers, farmers in Hokkaido, became irritated by the noise of firing on a Defense Forces training area which they claimed was reducing the milk production and birth rate of their cows. In retaliation they cut communication lines near the firing range, one in five places, another in two. They were charged by the local court for violating Article 121 of the SDF Law, which provides penalties of imprisonment up to five years for destruction or damaging of weapons, ammunition, aircraft, and other defense materials for defense use.

Left-wing and pacifist elements immediately saw an opportunity to challenge the constitutionality of the SDF. Some 300 lawyers were mobilized to support a defense case which would argue that the entire law establishing the SDF and the SDF itself were violations of the Preamble, Article 9, and other provisions of the Constitution and were against the concept of peace.

On March 29, 1967, the Sapporo District Court decided that the defendants were guilty of the crime charged but that cutting communication wires did not fit the definition of "other materials for defense use" in the sense intended by Article 121 of the SDF law; consequently, the law did not apply in the case, and the Court therefore refrained from passing on its constitutionality or that of the Self-Defense Forces.[15]

The failure of the Courts so far to decide whether the Self-Defense Forces exist in violation of the Constitution has kept alive the arguments of the opposition parties. After the judgment was handed down in the Eniwa case, Socialist members of the Diet pressed the Government on this question. On March 31, 1967, just two days after the Sapporo court had announced its decision, Prime Minister Sato presented the Government's "unified opinion," obtained after full consultation among responsible officials and consideration by the Cabinet. The gist of the official statement was that, in interpreting the Constitution, the Government had consistently held the opinion that the Self-Defense

112

Forces Law and the Self-Defense Forces, organized and maintained under the law, were not unconstitutional.[16]

When the White Paper on Defense was published in October 1970, the Director General of Defense, Nakasone Yasuhiro, asserted his "firm belief" that the Self-Defense Forces were constitutional, adding that the public expected the Supreme Court to pass a clear judgment on the constitutionality and limitations of the SDF.[17]

Certainly, until Japan's Supreme Court makes a final decision, the cloud of constitutional doubt will not disappear. As one Defense Agency official remarked ruefully, "Is there another nation in the world whose own armed forces are called illegal?"

Constitutional Revision

Revision of the Constitution became an issue principally because of Article 9 and during the 1950's was hotly debated. Prime Minister Hatoyama and other leading politicians openly espoused the cause of revision, which was made a plank in the platforms of both the Liberal and Democratic parties. When the two parties merged in 1955 to form the Liberal Democratic Party, the plank remained and the present LDP is still on record as favoring constitutional reform.

The policy of the LDP toward the Constitution was determined by a special study group. The rationale follows. Because the present Constitution was enacted under a foreign Occupation and in the period of confusion immediately following defeat, it is natural that after independence, the nation's basic charter should be restudied and revised in a manner befitting a democratic nation, appropriate to national sentiment, and in accord with developments which have occurred in the world. The party position is that revision of the Constitution is a political question of the highest order and that therefore the party should exert every effort to achieve the understanding and cooperation of the entire nation in prudently planning the method, timing, and content of the revision.[18]

Although constitutional revision is party policy, the issue has been seldom mentioned and LDP leaders have expressed no recent intention to try to put it into effect. The obvious practical reason has been that the government party did not command the necessary two-thirds majority in the two houses of the Diet nor could it expect, in the prevailing mood of public opinion, to obtain the required majority popular vote in a national referendum.

In a discussion of this question in early 1969 the then Secretary General of the party, Tanaka Kakuei, recalled that constitutional revision was a live issue in the early 1950's when the party in power commanded nearly three-fourths of the votes in the Diet. Even then, however, it was impossible to win enough support to pass a revision bill. Tanaka admitted that no constitution was a true one unless enacted in a period of complete freedom. There were, furthermore, parts of the Constitution other than Article 9 that should, in his view, be revised, notably the provision for the election of Supreme Court judges, which did not fit national custom. While opinion within the party was divided, he admitted, revision of the Constitution was not a current political question and there was strong sentiment in the country for keeping Article 9.[19] A poll published May 31, 1970 bore him out: only 16 percent of the respondents favored revising Article 9, while 50 percent opposed it.[20]

Successive Japanese governments have chosen the way of constitutional interpretation to permit the steady growth of a defense establishment already preparing its fourth build-up plan. Opposition parties have fought every step of the way. During the last few years the records of Diet debates have bulged from the hours upon hours of clashing exchanges on the "security problem." Again and again questions have been hurled and answers returned: ""Why defense? Defense against whom? How much defense is 'autonomous defense'? Will our own defense involve us in war?" Incidents and "revelations"—involving American nuclear-powered submarines, B-52's taking off from Okinawa, the *Enterprise*, the *Pueblo*, E-112 "spy planes," radioactive water, "secret plans" for Japanese-American military cooperation—all of these provided grist for the opposition and triggered volleys of oratory from Socialist and Communist members of the Diet. While the LDP government with its comfortable majority did not need to bend its policies to meet the verbiage of the opposition, nevertheless, the voice of public opinion being louder in Japan than in most democracies, the Japanese leadership was never insensitive to the effect on the public of its decisions and actions.

Occasionally someone in the LDP bursts the bonds of discretion and calls for an honest Army and Navy. In early 1968, Japanese fishing boats were experiencing more than the usual troubles of harrassment, surveillance, and conflicts of claims in the Japan Sea. On February 6, the Minister of Forestry and Agriculture, Kuraishi Tadao, spoke bluntly in a heated and unthinking moment to some correspondents about "our foolish Constitution" which gives no independence to Japan. He was variously quoted as saying "Japan is like a kept woman . . ." "It's not good, unless we have warships and guns . . ." "By the Constitution we must depend on the faith of others . . . this is 'salvation by faith.'" [21]

Publication of these colorful views in the alert Japanese press produced immediate and violent reactions. The Socialist, Democratic Socialist, and *Komei* parties at once demanded an explanation from the Government and the resignation of the Minister. The Communist Party joined the others in censuring the Sato Cabinet for its "rightist inclination" and denial of the pacifist Constitution and called for Kuraishi's ouster. To back up their demands, the opposition parties refused to participate further in any Diet activities and Japan's Parliament ground to a halt.

Kuraishi apologized but explained he had said nothing that had not been LDP policy since the party's foundation, namely, that the Constitution, enacted under foreign military occupation, should be revised. The Prime Minister and the Secretary General of the Party rose to meet the crisis; they defended the statement as containing nothing new and deplored the obstruction to democratic processes committed by the opposition. However, facing the annual budget and other essential legislation, the LDP could not tolerate indefinite paralysis of the Diet. Party leaders were unable to effect a compromise and on February 23, after 17 days of forced recess, Kuraishi resigned his Cabinet post. In so doing, however, he not only did not retract his views, but pointed out that constitutional revision was still a plank in the LDP party platform and that even the Socialists, who had blocked all Diet proceedings presumably to defend the present Constitution, had themselves promised revision once they came to power. [22] As Diet business resumed, Prime Minister Sato dedicated himself anew to the "cause of peace and preservation of the present Constitution." (In his Cabinet reshuffle of January 1970, following the December elections for the House of Representatives, Prime Minister Sato again appointed Kuraishi as Minister of Agriculture and Forestry.)

A second statement which provoked widespread comment and

criticism in Japan was made by Sakurada Takeshi, director general of the very influential Japan Federation of Employers Association, in a speech to his federation (*Nikkeiren*) on October 16, 1969. He was direct: "People of good sense think the Constitution ought to be revised."[23]

Commentators retorted that very few, if any, Japanese wanted revision of Article 9 and that the "peace Constitution had been fixed among the people."[24] Sakurada, however, in explaining his position, cited the ambiguity of Article 9 and particularly its failure to mention the Self-Defense Forces. He said this doubt of constitutionality affects the recruitment of new members and the martial spirit and morale of the Forces. He also noted that taxpayers, who must support increasing defense expenditures, will question an organization whose legal status remains ambiguous. Finally, Sakurada complained that Article 9 prevents participation in United Nations police forces, which should be a natural obligation for Japan as a member of the United Nations.[25]

Former Prime Minister Kishi, attending a Japanese-Korean conference in Seoul in April, 1970, told the press that the Self-Defense Forces must be recognized officially and that to accomplish this, the preamble and Article 9 of the Constitution should be revised. Kishi said he thought members of the LDP basically approved constitutional revision. However, his brother, Sato Eisaku, while he has been Prime Minister, has been consistent and categorical. He told the House of Representatives January 31, 1968, "I have no intention of revising the Constitution . . . especially the pacifism of Article 9. . . . This is the blood and flesh of the Japanese people now. I will carry through this pacifism."[26]

The Public Image of the SDF

Because of the constitutional and psychological handicaps under which the Self-Defense Forces have had to grow, they have paid very special attention to the cultivation of a favorable public image. In the beginning, a young SDF recruit found his social environment to be a painful one. Defense Academy students were pelted with stones in the streets, and when they attended movie theatres, people rose from their seats and walked away. A young writer charged in a newspaper, "Defense Academy students are a disgrace to our generation." Graduates of the Defense Academy were refused admission to graduate schools in Japanese universities. [27] This latter handicap is still suffered by members of the SDF, who find that their applications to take entrance examinations and enroll in universities are frequently rejected. The Director General of Defense took special notice of this discriminatory treatment in his statement which accompanied the publication of the Defense White Paper on October 20, 1970. [28]

To overcome these prejudices and correct these attitudes, those responsible for the administration of the SDF devised policies to improve public relations, particularly to encourage cooperation with local communities and hopefully develop their support, which could prove inportant in an emergency.

Few details were overlooked in the SDF public relations campaign. Members were cautioned to be modest, gentle, sincere in all their relations with the public. They were told to be "salesmen of the beloved Self-Defense Forces." They were commanded to be clean and neat, and not to throw away empty cans on private property. Young enlisted men were given furloughs and encouraged to travel to their homes and to talk about the SDF and, if possible, recruit new members. All the paraphernalia of public relations were employed, magazines, newspapers, pamphlets, films, slides, and the organization of sports and defense shows. [29]

Article 83 of the Self-Defense Forces Law provides that prefectural governors or other designated officials may request from the Director General of the JDA the dispatch of SDF units to assist in relief activities in case of natural calamities and other disasters. In the early years of the SDF, this provision opened the greatest opportunities for public relations. During the numerous earthquakes, floods, typhoons, and fires which habitually afflict Japan, the SDF responded promptly and effectively. Soon its reputation as an organization ready to bring benefits to the people grew, and the taint of the haughty and domineering military of prewar days began to fade. In fact, in the minds of many Japanese, the SDF became not a force created to defend the country but an organization devoted to relief and welfare.

The Self-Defense Forces have carried out a variety of types of disaster relief. Among these have been: (1) flood relief; (2) fire-fighting; (3) the emergency opening up of roads and waterways; (4) search and rescue of disaster victims; (5) emergency medical care help in the prevention of infectious diseases and in protection from harmful insects; (6) assistance in communications; (7) emergency transportation of medical cases, disaster victims, and relief goods; (8) assistance in setting up emergency kitchens and water supply services; (9) grants or interest-free loans of relief goods; and (10) other urgently needed assistance which the SDF is able to provide.[30]

According to the White Paper on Defense, from 1951 to 1969 the Self-Defense Forces responded to 6,600 calls for relief assistance, using a total of more than three million personnel. In 1969, SDF units were dispatched on disaster-relief missions 590 times, calling for the services of 56,000 members of the Forces.[31]

In addition to disaster relief, SDF units have participated in civil engineering activities and given help to farmers. Engineering projects include road construction, bridge building, playground leveling, and snow clearance. In 1966 more than 58,000 members of the SDF assisted in farming. SDF personnel also engaged in engineering works costing more than five and a quarter million dollars. Indeed, in certain units of the SDF there were complaints that as much as 30 percent of the time set aside for training was being spent on welfare projects.[32] Up to 1969, some 5,000 engineering projects were carried out by the SDF, utilizing about 37 million man-days. In 1969, 290 projects were handled involving about 2.9 million man-days.[33]

Other activities of the Self-Defense Forces have included participation in athletic contests (the Olympic Games 1964, the Annual National Athletic Meet, the Winter Olympics for 1972), in educational training programs (such as courses for civilian pilots), and in the scientific surveys being conducted in the Antarctic.

These image-improving efforts have been successful. No longer are SDF men in uniform insulted in the streets. Although the lengthening term of peace and prosperity has brought the "my-home-ism" which was the despair of Mishima, some pride in country has been revived and respect for men whose mission is to defend the country has risen. Polls show that support for the SDF rose from 58 percent in 1956 to 65 percent in 1959 and to 75 percent in 1969. In fact, some recent opinion surveys have shown as high as 85 percent favorable attitudes. Although the strongest advocates of the SDF in 1969 were those over 50 years old (85 percent), support from youths in their 20's was remarkably high, at 66 percent.[34]

At the same time, recognition of the real mission of the SDF has been growing. Until a few years ago, the percentage of those who saw the principal purpose of the armed forces as coming to the aid of sufferers in time of disaster was always the highest. This has now changed. In 1969 those who replied that the first duty of the SDF was to ensure the security of the nation were 50 percent, or double the number who thought this in 1967 (24 percent). In 1967 those who placed first importance on disaster relief were 33 percent, in 1969, only 13 percent. [35]

In 1970, the year of its twentieth birthday, the SDF could be said to be coming of age, having earned a respectable place in Japanese life. There is, however, no powerful public sentiment for a rapid growth in the strength of the armed services. In fact, as repeatedly tested in recent times, the general attitude of the Japanese people toward their defense establishment is to approve the SDF *but* "at its present level."

Notes

1. Mishima Yukio, "Bunka Boei Ron" (In Defense of Culture), *Chuo Koron*, July 1968, p. 102.

2. Interview with Mishima Yukio, July 19, 1968; *New York Times*, November 9, 1969.

3. *Asagumo* (organ of the Japanese Self-Defense Forces), November 6, 1969.

4. *Ibid.*

5. Sugita Ichiji, *Wasurerarete Iru Anzen Hosho* (The Security Which Can Be Forgotten), (Tokyo: Jiji Press, 1967), p. 40.

6. Asahi, *Nihon no Anzen Hosho* (Japan's Security), Vol. 8, *Nihon no Jieiryoku* (Japan's Self-Defense Power), (Tokyo: Asahi, 1967), p. 152.

7. *Ibid.*, p. 96.

8. *Ibid.*, p. 169.

9. Mainichi, *Shakai-to Seiken-ka no Anzen Hosho* (Security under a Socialist Party Government), (Tokyo: Mainichi, 1969), pp. 110-14. Statements on JSP policy are attributed to Ishibashi Masashi, chairman, Committee on International Affairs.

10. Mainichi, *Kyosan-to Seiken-ka no Anzen Hosho* (Security under a Communist Party Government), (Tokyo: Mainichi, 1969), p. 242. The text of the article is from *Akahata* (Red Flag) of June 11, 1968.

11. Mainichi, *Komei-to Seiken-ka no Anzen Hosho* (Security under a Komei Party Government), (Tokyo: Mainichi, 1969), p. 168.

12. Interview with Yano Junya, Secretary General, *Komeito*, Tokyo, August 18, 1969.

13. Mainichi, *Minsha-to Seiken-ka no Anzen Hosho* (Security under a Democratic Socialist Party Government), (Tokyo: Mainichi, 1969), pp. 85-86; Sone Eki, "For a National Consensus on the Japan-United States Mutual Security Treaty," in *Domei* (organ of the DSP), May 1968. Translation published in pamphlet form by the DSP.

14. Supreme Court of Japan, *Judgment upon Case of the So-called "Sunakawa Case"* (Tokyo: General Secretariat of the Supreme Court, 1960), pp. 62-63. Published in English translation.

15. For the full text of the decision see *Jurisuto*, No. 370, Tokyo, May 15, 1967, pp. 53-55.

16. *Boei Nenkan 1968* (Defense Yearbook), (Tokyo: Boei Nenkan Kanko Kai, 1968), p. 162.

17. "On the Occasion of Publication of 'Japan's Defense.'" Statement by Nakasone Yasuhiro, State Minister and Director General of the Japan Defense Agency, October 20, 1970.

18. Jiyu Minishu-to (Liberal Democratic Party), *"Kuraishi Hatsugen" no Shin-i* (True Meaning of "Kuraishi Statement"), pamphlet, February 1968, p. 12.

19. Mainichi, *Jimin-to Seiken no Anzen Hosho* (Security under a Liberal Democratic Party Government), (Tokyo: Mainichi, 1969), pp. 172-75.

20. *Yomiuri*, May 31, 1970.

21. *Mainichi* (evening), February 7, 1968.

22. LDP, "True Meaning of 'Kuraishi Statement,'" *op. cit.*, pp. 12 and 15.

23. *Yomiuri,* October 18, 1969.

24. *Ibid.*

25. *Nikkeiren Times* (organ of the Federation of Employers' Associations), October 30, 1969.

26. *Yomiuri*, February 1, 1968.

27. *Asahi*, December 4, 1967.

28. "On the Occasion of Publication of 'Japan's Defense,'" *op. cit.*

29. *Asahi*, December 11, 1967.

30. Boei-cho (Defense Agency), *Nihon no Boei* (Japan's Defense), Tokyo, October 1970, p. 62. Known as and referred to as the "Defense White Paper."

120

31. *Ibid.*, p. 62.

32. *Asahi*, December 11, 1967.

33. "Defense White Paper," *op. cit.*, p. 60.

34. *Asahi, Japan's Self-Defense Power, op. cit.*, p. 208; *Seisaku Geppo* (organ of the Liberal Democratic Party), April 1970.

35. *Seisaku Geppo, op. cit.*

6 The Military That Is Not A Military

The Mission of the SDF

What is this military that is not a military? Its purposes and functions are defined by the laws which established the Defense Agency and the Self-Defense Forces in 1954 and in the "Basic National Defense Policy" adopted by the National Defense Council in May 1957.[1]

According to the laws, the mission of the SDF is to defend the nation against direct and indirect aggression in order to preserve peace and independence, maintain national security and, if necessary, take charge of keeping the public order. The Basic Policy adds certain principles: support of the United Nations, promotion of the national welfare and enhancement of the spirit of patriotism, gradual development of effective defense power within the bounds of national capabilities and to the extent necessary for self-defense, and recourse to the joint security system with the United States to cope with aggression and pending effective functioning of the United Nations in preventing and removing aggression.

Thus, the Japanese armed forces are to be defensive, limited, and dependent on cooperation with the United States but must blunt aggression when it comes and, in case of necessity, come to the aid of the police in keeping public order. Until recently the SDF was thought of as supplementing the military power of the United States, whose commitments, specified in a series of treaties, are to preserve peace and security in the Far East, including Japan. However, as the defense forces increased in size and potential, the Prime Minister and other prominent members of the governing political party have more and more cited the need for the Japanese to be able to defend their country with their own hands, backed by the ultimate nuclear guarantee of the United States.

The White Paper on Defense, published on October 20, 1970, explained the security relationship between Japan and the United States as a collective security system. Emphasizing that Japan "has set up the basic policy of coping primarily with aggression by its own power," the White Paper went on to point out that "just as many other nations are adopting systems of collective security, so Japan is coping with and deterring aggression from the outside through a security system with the United States with which Japan shares political, economic, and other interests in common." To refute the critics who argue that this relationship is incompatible with independence, the White Paper affirms that a collective security system is "joint defense," is not contradictory to autonomous defense, and that, in fact, autonomous defense need not necessarily be "single-handed" defense.

Civilian Control

Perhaps the most important single characteristic which distinguishes the present-day Self-Defense Forces from their progenitors, the Japanese Imperial Army and Navy, is the principle of civilian control. During the course of discussions on the Constitution, the Far Eastern Commission on September 25, 1946 reaffirmed a previous decision that "all Cabinet Ministers should be civilians." [2] Told of this decision, Prime Minister Yoshida called it redundant since Japan, under Article 9, would have no armed forces. Nevertheless, because of FEC insistence, MacArthur's Headquarters persuaded the Japanese Government to accept the amendment. Unfortunately, there was no word for "civilian" in the Japanese language, and a new word had to be coined from two Chinese characters (*bunmin*). The draft Constitution was then amended to read: "The Prime Minister and other Ministers of State must be civilians." [3]

The principle of civilian control, patterned after the American system, is firmly established in the Self-Defense Forces. The Prime Minister, instead of the Emperor as in prewar days, is commander-in-chief of the armed forces. Subject to his command and supervision, the Director General of the Japan Defense Agency has immediate authority over the SDF. He is a politician and of course a civilian. By law, his authority over the units and organizations of the SDF is channeled through the uniformed chiefs of staff of the Ground, Air, and Maritime Self-Defense Forces respectively. The post of Director General of the JDA has been passed frequently from one LDP politician to another, resulting in such short terms that an incumbent scarcely has time to master his responsibilities. In the first twenty years of its existence the JDA had twenty-five Directors General! Although the office is equivalent in rank to "Minister of State," the *Agency* has never formally been elevated to a *Ministry*. This would require Diet action, and the SDF has not yet attained the solid status which would encourage a Prime Minister to push through this seemingly small legislative change, which, in Japanese, would make a *cho* (agency) a *sho* (ministry).

Uniformed members of the forces have chafed at the extent of their subordination to civilian control. The bureaucracy of the Defense Agency is largely civilian; no uniformed men occupy posts above that of section chief, and only civilian officials testify in Diet deliberations on defense policy matters. A former professional military officer told the author that the Prime Minister seldom consults and hardly knows personally his own chiefs of staff.

Understandably the older officers with war experience are particularly irked by the extent of civilian domination. One of these is quoted as saying of the civilians: "They are petty functionaries who know nothing. They trample down the SDF by 'stamp' administration. At first they treated uniformed men as 'war criminals.'"[4]

It is worth noting that the most dramatic lesson in civilian control was dealt by the United States to postwar Japan unwittingly when President Truman suddenly dismissed General MacArthur. For a military man who had become the supreme authority of the Japanese nation to be summarily deposed from power by a civilian head of government was a new and profoundly impressive experience for the Japanese.

In late 1969, officers who had received education in the prewar military schools made up slightly more than 10 percent of the total officer complement of the three services, Ground, Maritime, and Air. In 1967, graduates of the postwar Defense Academy barely exceeded those who had attended the old military schools (12.4

percent as against 12.2 percent). [5] The gap is naturally widening, and by 1969 the percentage of Defense Academy graduates had risen to 14.5 percent as against 10.3 percent for alumni of the prewar military schools. Table 6-1 presents the comparison.

Table 6-1

SDF Officers Who Attended Prewar Military Schools
Compared with Graduates of Postwar Defense Academy

	Total number of SDF officers as of:		Prewar military schools (Number and percent)		Postwar Defense Academy (Number and percent)	
	Oct. 31, 1967	Oct. 31, 1969	1967	1969	1967	1969
GSDF	19,171	19,377	1,863 (9.7)	1,625 (8.4)	2,222 (11.6)	2,677 (13.8)
MSDF	6,385	6,667	944 (14.8)	861 (12.9)	836 (13.1)	984 (14.7)
ASDF	6,956	7,086	1,030 (14.8)	928 (13.1)	974 (14.0)	1,165 (16.4)
Total	32,512	33,120	3,837 (12.2)	3,414 (10.3)	4,032 (12.4)	4,826 (14.5)

Sources: *Mainichi,* March 12, 1968; Japan Defense Agency.

Retirement is steadily reducing the ranks of the prewar soldiers, sailors, and airmen, although the top officer grades will probably be filled by men with wartime experience for some years to come. Assuming that officers 45 years of age and over had either some education in prewar military schools or some wartime experience, even though brief—they would have been 16 when Pearl Harbor was attacked—these officers could still be serving in the SDF by 1975, and some, even beyond that year. For example, a colonel who was 46 in 1970 could be promoted to general and continue on active duty until the retirement age of 58, or until 1982. The youngest officers with the rank of general in 1969 were three, aged 52, who could continue in the service until 1975. Eight generals were due to retire in 1974. Disregarding possible promotions, 362 full colonels who in 1969 were 45, 46, and 47 would still be on active duty in 1975. Because of their retirement age of 53, they would be leaving the service in 1975, 1976, and 1977, respectively. Promotions would of course prolong their careers.

The influence which these officers with prewar experience may exert on the men of the SDF is difficult to assess. They are few and their numbers are steadily dwindling so their influence must be judged in perspective. Without doubt many of them deplore the general weakness of patriotic sentiments and the indifference to spiritual and national values which have been characteristics of postwar Japanese youth. It would be suprising if these officers did not try to inculcate in young recruits a sense of mission and loyalty to the country. It would also be surprising if some of the vocabulary and attitudes of the prewar period did not creep into the form and substance of their teaching. In fact, some observers have confirmed that this is true in certain units.

For example, the sea forces seem particularly proud of the traditions of the Imperial Navy, and officers with wartime experience attempt to pass on some understanding of Japanese Navy "spirit." All graduates of the Defense Academy and of civilian universities who expect to become officers spend a year as midshipmen at *Etajima*, an island in the Inland Sea which was the site of the prewar Naval Academy. Here in the same buildings used before 1945, officer candidates receive instruction in the spirit and traditions of the old Imperial Navy. Students at *Etajima* have criticized their seniors for putting too much emphasis on the spirit of the old Navy, which they admit is part of their new way of life but only a part.

The Maritime Self-Defense Forces have also revived their prewar march (the Ground Forces have not) and again display the prewar rising sun ensign on their ships.

In spite of the revival of certain forms and practices of the former military, civilian control seems to be so firmly established that there would appear little danger now of a resurgence of the power and prestige of Japan's prewar military establishment. The Director General of Defense in the strongest terms stressed the importance of civilian control at the time the Defense White Paper was published. Nakasone said that the success or failure of civilian control was the key to whether Japan's "defense policy for peace" would succeed or fail. Blaming the disaster of World War II on the lack of civilian control over the military, he urged that efforts be made to strengthen civilian control still further in the future, centering on the Diet, the "supreme organ of state power."

The Restricted Self-Defense Forces

Constitutionally and legally, the Self-Defense Forces are inhibited in their actions as probably no other armed force in the world, although interpretation and rationalization have limited the effect of the inhibitions.

1. *War potential* is prohibited by the Constitution. Arguments have raged over its definition, how war potential can be distinguished from "defense potential" and at what point the latter becomes the former. As we have noted, the Supreme Court in the Sunadawa case carefully refrained from deciding whether war potential could be maintained "even for self-defense." In 1952 Prime Minister Yoshida said that Article 9 applied to war potential used as a means to settle international disputes but did not prohibit military power for self-defense. He insisted, "We will not *rearm*. To rearm we must ask the consent of the people and revise the Constitution." [6] Friends of Yoshida have said that in his later years he regretted having declared so many times that Japan should not rearm.

2. The Government has interpreted the prohibition of war potential to mean outlawing *offensive warfare* and *offensive weapons*. The Defense White Paper stated that Japan "cannot possess weapons which will pose a threat of aggression to other nations, such as long-range bombers like B-52's, offensive aircraft carriers and ICBM's, for example." [7]

The opposition has forced the Government repeatedly to justify weapons and actions as "defensive" and therefore permissible. The "Honest John" and "Nike-Hercules" missiles can be fitted with nuclear warheads, but officially these have been classified as defensive on the assumption that they will never be converted to nuclear weapons. The Government as early as 1959 asserted that even an attack on enemy bases was allowable if it was the *only* way of defense.

The Japanese Government decided on November 1, 1968 to equip the Air Defense Forces with the McDonnell-Douglas F-4E Phantom Jet. During Diet discussions previous to the decision, the opposition vehemently objected to acquiring an "offensive weapon" in violation of Article 9. Masuda Kaneshichi, Director General of the Defense Agency at the time, replied that the Constitution would be violated only if the planes were *used* for bombing purposes, and he assured the Diet that they would not be equipped for such use. Masuda confirmed the view originally adopted by the Hatoyama Cabinet:

128

Speaking from legal principles, enemy bases can be attacked if our country should be attacked, for example, by guided missiles, and if it is clear that there is no other available means of defense. Hatoyama's reply that it is not the purport of the Constitution to sit idly by and wait for self-destruction by a one-sided attack on our country is the same as my view. [8]

In 1957 Prime Minister Kishi stated that *defensive* nuclear weapons would not be unconstitutional. This has continued to be the official Japanese Government position; legally only amendment of the Atomic Energy Law would be required should Japan decide to build nuclear weapons. The Defense White Paper reiterated and amplified the position:

If small-sized nuclear weapons are within the minimum measure of power required for self-defense, and if they are not such as to pose a threat of aggression to other nations, in principle their possession can be said to be legally possible; however, regardless of the constitutional possibility, the Government's policy is not to have nuclear weapons. [9]

The confirmation in the White Paper of the constitutionality of small "defensive" nuclear weapons was attacked by the Japanese press. One editorial called the statement a "vague" explanation; another commented that the reference to defensive nuclear weapons was "apt to invite unnecessary misunderstanding." [10]

3. The SDF cannot be sent out of the country. Regardless of how Article 9 may be interpreted with respect to the inherent right of self-defense and the maintenance of war potential, the view remains undisputed that the despatch of armed forces abroad is unconstitutional. When the Self-Defense Forces were established in 1954, the upper house adopted a resolution to confirm that the Japanese Government would not despatch troops overseas. This prohibition clearly affects Japan's ability to fulfill the obligations of collective security undertaken in signing the Treaty of Peace and the United Nations Charter. For this reason Japanese ability to assume military responsibilities as a participant in a multilateral security arrangement is open to question.

Whether Japan might join in a United Nations peacekeeping operation has been a subject of keen interest and discussion for a number of years. Support of the United Nations is a fundamental principle of both Japanese foreign policy and the Basic National

Defense Policy. The eventual assumption by the United Nations of responsibility for international peace and security is an ideal expressed in the peace treaty, the security treaty, and the policies of several of the political parties, as we have seen. The difficulty has been to reconcile the constitutional prohibition on sending forces overseas with an active contribution to a peacekeeping unit.

In the past the opposition has been so alert to any conceivable constitutional transgression and so sensitive to expected public reaction that many Japanese have been gloomy about the possibility of ever cooperating with the United Nations. One recalls the ludicrous incident when Mr. Kotani Hidejiro, a civilian instructor at the National Defense College, visited Vietnam and in an indiscreet moment accepted from an accommodating G.I. pilot a ride as a passenger on a fighter-bomber mission. Unfortunately an enterprising Air Force photographer saw a good shot and photographed Kotani, helmeted and seated in the U.S. military aircraft. When the photo hit the front pages of Tokyo's dailies, the ensuing uproar left no alternative for Mr. Kotani but to resign his position at the Defense College. As a "military force" sent overseas he had violated Article 9!

Participation in a peacekeeping arrangement has been seriously considered should this be agreed upon when hostilities cease in Vietnam. Japanese recognize that foreign opinion would not understand refusal by the economically most powerful nation in Asia to join a United Nations force for such a task. Sato's promise in the Washington communique of November 21, 1969 that "Japan was exploring what role she could play in bringing about stability in the Indochina area" was a welcome surprise. He was more explicit in his National Press Club speech, asserting that, if asked, Japan was prepared to participate in "any international peacekeeping machinery which may be set up after the cessation of hostilities." Although the manner of participation remains unspecified, Article 9 apparently will in the future not be allowed to block this kind of peaceful international cooperation.

4. As has been noted, the SDF may assume police duties in time of emergency. Law provides that the Prime Minister may order the Self-Defense Forces into action in case maintenance of peace and order by the civil police becomes impossible. Such action has so far not been necessary, and this provision of the law would certainly be invoked only as a last resort. At the time of the treaty

demonstrations in the spring of 1960, some LDP leaders called for the SDF but the head of the Defense Agency stood firm and use of the forces was averted.

The Government was for some time concerned over the "treaty struggles" threatened for June 1970. Both the police and the SDF planned to be continuously ready to meet emergencies, and the SDF undertook special "public security" exercises. Fortunately the "treaty struggles" of 1970 were no challenge, even for the police. With their training, experience, and improved capabilities and techniques, forged in the fire of previous student riots, they were confident that they could handle whatever turbulence the decade of the 'seventies might bring. Resort to the SDF would signify a total breakdown in public order which no Japanese would like to contemplate.

Men

The Self-Defense Forces now total some 286,000 personnel in authorized strength. Table 6-2 shows the division among Ground, Air, and Maritime forces.

Table 6-2

Authorized SDF Personnel, Fiscal Year 1969

	Uniformed	Civilian
Ground Self-Defense Forces	179,000	12,879
Air Self-Defense Forces	41,183	5,021
Maritime Self-Defense Forces	37,813	4,759
Japan Defense Agency organs and other personnel	78	6,186
Totals	258,074	28,845
		258,074
Grand Total		286,919

Source: *Nihon no Anzen Hosho, 1970 e no Tenbo* (Japan's Security, Outlook for 1970), 1969 edition, Tokyo, August 10, 1969, p. 363. Japanese fiscal year 1969 is April 1969 to March 31, 1970.

Authorized strength for the Ground Forces was increased by Diet action in 1969 from 173,000 to 179,000. Overall actual strength has been almost 10 percent lower, and shortages increased in 1969 and 1970. Actual strength, which in 1968 was 93.8 percent of that authorized, went down to 91.3 percent in 1969 and to 89.7 percent in 1970. Some individual units suffer vacancies up to 20 percent. Air and sea services are more attractive; their actual strength has approached 100 percent but fell off in 1969 and 1970. As in all countries, the infantry is least popular; on the other hand, would-be pilots and sailors find better opportunities for excellent technical training which will qualify them for good jobs in industry after a few years in the SDF.

Tables 6-3 and 6-4 show the authorized and actual strength of the three services from their organization in 1954 through 1970. As can be seen, after the first two years, the Forces were kept fairly near their authorized personnel levels. In the years from 1959 through 1964, recruitment for the Ground Forces became more difficult because of Japan's rapid economic growth, the resulting high demand for labor, and the shortage of young men of recruitment age reflecting the low birth rate during the war. Losses by retirement reportedly went up during this period. After 1964, the eligible age group bulged (the "baby boom"), recruiting methods were improved, and competition from private industry slackened temporarily. Furthermore, regulations were instituted which set minimum terms of service (two or three years) and thus slowed the turnover.

New recruits, who grew up in the atmosphere of the "peace Constitution" and were educated in the Occupation-created system which banned all patriotic indoctrination, felt little respect for the prewar armed forces or their traditions. Discipline was much less rigid, and an informality prevailed which would have been unheard of in the Imperial Army. A journalist, describing his observations of SDF barracks life, noted the privileges enjoyed by the young soldiers and their attitudes. They met their seniors "like friends," they could whistle on duty, they were allowed their own small television sets, their "my-cars," and they could even receive telephone calls from girl friends. The journalist noted that the barracks had none of the "stiffness, gloominess, and cunning eyes" which characterized the living quarters of the old prewar soldiers. Officers in the old Army slapped soldiers on the slightest provocation; slapping is now a punishable offense. New men were said occasionally to become so familiar with their superiors that they called their squad leaders "uncle." Some rookies, rebelling at discipline, were said to have simply shed their uniforms and walked away![11]

The Self-Defense Forces recruit annually about 30,000 people between the ages of 18 and 24 to serve for two- or three-year terms. Recruitment is a necessary and active function; to carry it on, the Defense Agency has established offices in some forty-nine cities in all of the prefectures of Japan. Recruiters, who call themselves "salesmen" and who realize the tough competition they face from the attractive offers of private industry, try to make a career in the armed forces appear as attractive as possible.

Table 6-3

Authorized and Actual Personnel In Self-Defense Forces, 1954-1970

| | Ground SDF | | | Maritime SDF | | | Air SDF | | |
	Auth.	Actual	%	Auth.	Actual	%	Auth.	Actual	%
1954	130,000	99,424	76.4	15,808	9,696	61.3	6,287	2,057	32.7
1955	150,000	132,985	88.6	19,391	16,232	83.7	10,346	7,617	73.6
1956	160,000	149,283	93.3	22,716	20,505	90.3	14,434	11,862	82.1
1957	160,000	152,438	95.3	24,146	23,099	95.7	19,925	16,317	81.9
1958	170,000	160,707	94.5	25,441	24,829	97.5	26,625	22,267	83.6
1959	170,000	158,063	93.0	27,667	26,147	94.5	33,225	30,429	91.6
1960	170,000	147,131	86.5	27,667	27,100	98.0	33,324	31,727	95.5
1961	171,500	142,320	83.0	32,097	31,497	98.1	38,337	35,123	91.6
1962	171,500	145,494	84.8	33,291	32,798	98.5	39,057	37,282	95.1
1963	171,500	143,140	83.5	33,291	32,101	96.4	39,057	37,588	96.2
1964	171,500	145,340	84.7	34,963	32,937	94.2	39,552	37,913	95.9
1965	171,500	151,699	88.5	34,963	34,732	99.3	39,553	38,942	98.5
1966	171,500	153,431	89.5	34,963	34,257	98.0	39,553	38,877	98.3
1967	173,000	156,025	90.2	36,591	35,716	97.6	40,703	39,619	97.3
1968	173,000	158,708	91.7	36,591	36,201	98.9	40,703	39,948	98.1
1969	179,000	158,529	88.6	37,813	36,651	96.9	41,183	40,306	97.9
1970*	179,000	155,686	87.0	37,813	35,988	95.2	41,183	39,653	96.3

* Through August 1970.

Table 6-4

Authorized and Actual Personnel
In Self-Defense Forces, 1954-1970

Totals for SDF

	Authorized	Actual	Percent
1954	152,095	111,177	73.0
1955	179,737	156,834	87.2
1956	197,182	181,681	92.2
1957	204,105	191,854	94.0
1958	222,102	207,803	93.5
1959	230,935	214,682	93.0
1960	230,934	206,001	89.2
1961	242,009	209,015	86.4
1962	243,923	215,649	88.4
1963	243,923	212,904	87.3
1964	246,094	216,268	87.9
1965	246,094	225,450	91.6
1966	246,094	226,280	92.1
1967	250,372	231,436	92.4
1968	250,372	234,935	93.8
1969	258,074	235,564	91.3
1970	258,074	231,405	89.7

Sources: *Boei Nenkan* (Defense Yearbook), editions from 1954 to 1970; *Nihon no Anzen Hosho, 1970 e no Tenbo* (Japan's Security, Outlook for 1970), Tokyo. 1969, pp. 356-57. 1969 and 1970 statistics from Japan Defense Agency.

The speech of one recruiting officer to a class of high school students has been reported as follows:

You don't need to think about difficult things like defense when you join the SDF. Sometimes we have praiseworthy applicants who say, "I am ready to give my life for my country." (laughter). They are really admirable. (laughter). Yes, indeed. (laughter). Since we're not going to take you to Vietnam, you can join the SDF with a light heart. If you want to learn driving or electrical engineering, think of the SDF as an ordinary place of employment. Compare our treatment with private companies.[12]

Radical students have tried to obstruct recruiting on campus, and there have been many high schools where a uniformed SDF officer would not dare to go. Other schools prohibited posters in the schools or even outside the school gates.

The problem of recruitment will become more acute in the future. In 1970 the Forces as a whole were more than 10 percent under strength, and applications for admission in 1969 were one third of the number in 1960. The number of 18-year-olds in 1967 was 1,231,200, reflecting the postwar "baby boom," but by 1975 this age group is estimated to decline to a little over 750,000. This shortage in the eligible age groups combined with the trend toward prolongation of school years into higher education and the accelerating competition of booming industries for high school as well as college graduates, means a much smaller source of supply for the SDF in those years. Conscription is agreed to be politically out of the question.

Anticipating increased difficulties in recruiting, the Defense Forces are trying to make the services more attractive. They are improving food, living conditions, speed of promotions, and offering allowances for leave at home for those stationed in Hokkaido and outlying islands. Probably the greatest inducements are the vocational training received during service and the help in finding employment when mustered out. Efforts are being made to improve the organization and staffing.

In 1954 a Defense Officers Reserve Corps was set up for the purpose of supplementing the regular forces in times of emergency. Many volunteers for the Reserve are former members of the SDF who are glad to report for an annual five-day period of training and to be on call in case of emergency. The authorized strength of the Reserve Corps was increased by 3,000 in July 1969 from a previous figure of 30,000. Actual numbers by September 1969 were reported to be 30,687.[13]

To augment the regular SDF, Funada Naka, former Speaker of the House of Representatives, proposed in the summer of 1969 the formation of a "local defense corps" to be composed of a million volunteers who would receive training and weapons and be subject to call in emergencies. The plan made headlines, but few expected its realization. Funada intended to float a trial balloon and to call attention to manpower needs for defense. The idea was referred to the LDP Security Committee for consideration and study, and nothing further was heard of the plan.

Another proposal suggested in 1969 was to increase the SDF Reserve to 100,000 by adding 70,000 men from those who had retired from the SDF, who then numbered 400,000 and of whom 70,000 had already formed a "Veterans Association."

The problem of "men" is not only one of numbers, but of training. The complex machinery of modern warfare requires technical skills never demanded of prewar armies and navies. To train men to operate the ships, planes, tanks and weapons systems of the electronic age takes time, patience, and brains. Japan's SDF has, according to reports of JDA officials, suffered serious shortages of qualified personnel in areas where training and experience are essential.

The competition by Japanese industry for skilled labor coming out of service in the SDF is now intense. In *Asagumo* (Morning Cloud), the daily newspaper edited and published for members of the Self-Defense Forces, most of the advertisements, often as many as thirty or more and equivalent to three full pages, solicit applications for jobs in private industry. Most of Japan's largest and best-known manufacturing and industrial concerns are represented. The military establishment is an important institution for the flow of skilled manpower to be hungrily devoured by the industrial machine which takes Japan's economy to ever greater heights.

Money

For the future of Japan's defense, money and materials are less critical than men. Quality improvement gets priority attention, but expansion is the accepted way of the future. Japan still spends less than one percent of GNP on defense (see Tables 6-5 and 6-6). The military budget more than tripled between 1962 and 1971 (from $606 million to $1,938 million), but the GNP continues to rise so rapidly that percentages lose their meaning (Table 6-7). Yet relative to other industrial nations, Japan's defense insurance is not expensive. Her 0.8 percent of GNP in 1969 contrasted with almost 8.6 percent for the United States, 8.5 percent for the Soviet Union, 9.0 percent for Communist China, 3.5 percent for West

Germany and 5.1 percent for Great Britain[14] (see Table 6-8). In 1967 the total defense budget was less than 70 percent of the annual amount paid out by Japanese private companies to their more senior employees as the notorious expense accounts which support the bars, night clubs, and geisha restaurants of Tokyo and Osaka.[15]

Table 6-5

Japan's Defense Expenditures Compared with
Budget, National Income, GNP (FY 1970)

Percentage of total budget 7.16
Percentage of national income 0.99
Percentage of GNP 0.79

Source: *Boei-cho* (Defense Agency), "Outline of Budget Request for FY 1971," August 1970, p. 1.

Table 6-6

Defense Expenditures Compared with
Other Budget Expenditures (FY 1969)

Defense .... 7.7 percent of total budget
Social security .... 14.1 percent of total budget
Education, promotion of science ... 12.0 percent of total budget
Public works .... 17.8 percent of total budget

Source: Anzen Hosho Chosa-kai, *Nihon no Anzen Hosho - 1970 e no Tenbo, 1969* (Japan's Security, Outlook on 1970), (Tokyo, 1969), p. 359.

Government party members and industrialists want to step up the increase of military outlays. The Federation of Employers Associations has set a goal of 1½ percent of GNP by the next fiscal year, but this seems unlikely to be achieved so soon. To double the defense budget by 1975 to three billion dollars would put Japan seventh in the world after the five nuclear powers and West Germany (in 1970 Japan was twelfth). If increases continue only at the present rate, the total would be $6 billion by 1980, more than Communist China or France, both nuclear powers, spent in 1970.

Table 6-7

Japan's Defense Expenditures, 1962-1971

Year	Defense Expenditures	Percentage of GNP	Percentage of national income	Percentage of budget
1962	606.3	1.01	1.24	8.34
1963	687.5	1.00	1.24	8.10
1964	780.0	0.98	1.24	8.41
1965	848.3	0.97	1.22	8.16
1966	958.6	0.94	1.18	7.71
1967	1,075.0	0.90	1.12	7.44
1968	1,171.6	0.80	1.05	7.13
1969	1,374.7	0.84	1.06	7.14
1970	1,581.0	0.79	0.99	7.16
1971 (est.)	1,863.6	0.80		7.13

Sources: *Boei Nenkan* (Defense Yearbook), 1969, p. 307; 1970, p. 351; *Boei-cho* (Defense Agency), Outline of Cabinet Approved JFY 1971 Budget Request, January 1971.

If 2 percent of GNP were achieved, as some wish, Japan could rank as high as third, after the U.S. and the U.S.S.R. Needless to say, if Japan should add nuclear weapons to the arsenal, the rise in costs would be much steeper and faster.

SDF, "Child of the Americans"

In the beginning, the SDF was in fact the "child of the United States," not only in historical origin but through the technical, organizational, and financial assistance received from the United States throughout its formative years. Even the uniforms were conspicuously American in style and only very recently have the Japanese decided to change the designs.

The Mutual Defense Assistance Agreement signed in March 1954 established the Military Assistance and Advisory Group (MAAG), which has phased out as military assistance ended. Total American military aid to Japan, from 1951 through September

1968, amounted to $1,600 million.[16] The MAAG did much more than dispense equipment. Its officers engaged in training SDF personnel in the use of weapons and materiel, and their responsibilities for observation and coordination led to relationships throughout the Defense Forces at many levels.

Table 6-8

Comparative Defense Expenditures, 1969 and 1970
(in millions of U.S. dollars)

Country	Amount		Amount per capita (in dollars)	Percentage of GNP
	1969	1970	1969	1969
U.S.A.	79,774	74,400	393	8.6
U.S.S.R.	39,333	39,778	164	8.5
Comm. China*	4,800	4,880	6.4	9.0
France	6,184	5,874	123	4.4
West Germany	5,246	6,111	90	3.5
Great Britain	5,554	5,712	100	5.1
Japan	1,344	1,582	13	0.84

Source: The Institute for Strategic Studies, London, *The Strategic Balance 1970-1971, pp. 110-11.*

*Figures for Communist China are estimates. *The Strategic Balance 1970-1971*, p. 57.

An exchange of notes signed simultaneously with the revised security treaty in 1960 provided for the establishment of a joint Japanese-American Security Consultative Committee. The co-chairmen were the Japanese Minister for Foreign Affairs and the American Ambassador to Japan, assisted by the Director General of the Defense Agency and the Commander-in-Chief, Pacific (CINCPAC), who acted as the Ambassador's principal adviser on military matters. His alternate was the Commander, United States Forces, Japan (USFJ).

The Consultative Committee met infrequently in the early 1960's; but as defense became a matter of increasing interest and debate in Japan, sessions were held more often, at one period at intervals of approximately six months. For a time the meetings were routine, with formal, stilted speeches on both sides. The Committee attracted extraordinary attention from the ubiquitous and hyperactive Japanese press, and at the end of each session a press conference was held by the Foreign Minister and the Ambassador. But in addition to these formal briefings, leaks often occurred of items not reported publicly, leading the Americans to conclude that confidential discussions were impossible. One admiral, Commander-in-Chief, Pacific, remarked that he would include nothing in his report which he would hesitate to publish in full in *Time Magazine.*

Such restraint obviously limited the value of the meetings, which became rather formal exchanges of "sanitized" summaries of the current situation in the Pacific area. Invariably the Americans would manage to include a dig at the Japanese on the small size of their defense budget. On one occasion Foreign Minister Ohira got his word in first; he said, with a twinkle in his eye, "Please don't remind us again that we spend less than 1 percent of our GNP on national defense!"

Depending to some extent on the Director General of Defense at the time (as ambitious politicians, they were inclined to be garrulous), the Committee nevertheless served a useful purpose. In time, officials on both sides became better acquainted, the exchange of information became more substantive, and the opportunity for discussions among responsible officials representing both foreign policy and military points of view benefited all concerned. The wide publicity given to each meeting was also salutary; it contributed to the "defense consciousness" which the Japanese Government was deliberately and consistently trying to cultivate.

A second formal mechanism for coordination between the United States and Japan was the Joint Committee, set up by the Administrative Agreement, signed in 1960 simultaneously with the security treaty. Membership included officials of the Foreign Office, the Japan Defense Agency, the American Embassy in Tokyo, and Headquarters, USFJ. This was the working group, meeting frequently and handling the myriad of day-to-day problems arising from the presence of American troops in Japan and out of the Japanese-American security arrangement. Military-base problems have been a continuing concern of this Committee, involving complaints, incidents, coordination with the SDF, and the greater problems of joint use, transfer, and closing of bases.

United States Forces, Japan (USFJ) is a command without troops, a Headquarters without combat responsibilities. The Commander, USFJ, has been an Air Force lieutenant general who also commands the Fifth Air Force. He does not control the Army and Navy contingents, each of which has its command with direct responsibility to chiefs in Hawaii. The Seventh Fleet is technically based at sea but uses the port installations in Yokosoka and Sasebo, and its principal officers and their families usually live in areas near these port cities. The Commander, USFJ, reports to Commander-in-Chief, Pacific (CINCPAC), Hawaii, but in Japan, he coordinates American military activities and maintains close relations with the Japan Defense Agency and with the American Ambassador; he is a member of the "Country Team" over which the Ambassador presides. When an Air Force jet accidentally crashes into a village, it is the Commander, USFJ, who flies immediately by helicopter to offer a "solatium" to relatives of the victims. If he is a golfer, he plays with the uniformed ranking officers of the JDA. Should B-52's bomb Vietnam from Okinawa, a "Pueblo" be seized, or an E-121 "spy plane" be shot down, the Commander, USFJ and the Ambassador would consult immediately on measures to be taken or recommendations to be made.

The formal channels of communication and consultation between the Japanese and Americans on defense matters are established: Embassy (the defense attaches and one section devoted exclusively to politico-military matters), USFJ, the Joint Committee, and the Consultative Committee. Besides these, however, the continuing informal relationships over the years between American and Japanese military personnel have fashioned perhaps more significant if less tangible ties.

Training and travel in the United States, association with Americans, adoption of American weapons, systems, habits, and nomenclature, have all left an imprint on the Japanese military which will survive for a long time.

Equipment bequeathed to the SDF when American combat troops were withdrawn in 1957 became obsolete and was rapidly being replaced with improved models made in Japan. An example was the M-1 rifle, which was never suitable for Japanese use and which has given way to a much more efficient Japanese model. Operations manuals originally translated directly and literally from English were thoroughly revised as a new Japanese military vocabulary evolved and Japanese concepts developed. Further changes continue to take place, but it will be difficult for the Japanese military to escape totally from this very deep and pervasive American influence.

Of the three services, the Air Self-Defense Force has kept the closest continuing relations with their American counterparts. This is natural in view of the functions performed. When an unidentified object appears on the radar screen, it is of interest to both Japanese and Americans. One commentator, describing the close cooperation of the Japanese and American air forces, called them "literally inseparable."[17]

Sometimes resentment over too active a military role by the United States comes to the surface. When a Japan Air Lines passenger plane was highjacked by the radical "Red Army" Japanese students, a JAL official immediately telephoned, not the Air Self-Defense Forces, but a unit of the U.S. Air Force. Chagrin was expressed in the news media at this bypassing of Japan's own defense forces and the automatic and seemingly subservient turning to the Americans for help in an emergency.

In a panel discussion of Japan's defense problems, a military specialist remarked that the SDF was a "mini-size" American force, in weapons, organization, and command. He recalled that in 1965 when an unknown plane crossed the 38th parallel in Korea, the Air Self-Defense Force planes scrambled, not on the order of their own commander, but at the command of the American Fifth Air Force. During the discussion, the Director General of the JDA commented that if the SDF took over from the United States all military responsibilities in Japan, quite apart from the question of nuclear weapons, four or five times the present defense budget would be required.[18]

Intelligence is an area of some uneasiness between the two governments. While Japan has assumed in the mutual assistance agreement with the United States and in the law establishing the Self-Defense Forces, an obligation to protect classified information, penalties are light and protection incomplete. This situation does not satisfy the American military and consequently limits disclosure of information and cooperation in certain areas.

142

The problem of defense secrets is so politically sensitive that any attempt to enact a stiffer law would meet with violent protests and disruptive tactics in the Diet by the opposition parties. No Government has thus far sought to risk this political confrontation. The Socialists a few years ago revealed in the Diet what was purported to be secret joint plans made by the Japanese and Americans for war contingencies, particularly in case of aggression in Korea. A so-called "Three Arrows" plan, which the Government admitted did exist, was distorted and dramatized far beyond its actual significance, but the incident served to highlight the problem of the discussion and exchange of classified information.

The respective defense responsibilities of the United States and Japan have been described as the spear and the shield. Japan's constitutional limitations have prevented its role from being more than defensive; it has furnished the shield, hopefully to ward off enemies who might come to attack the home islands. For retaliation, for the spear, Japan has had to look to the Americans. And it is natural that, observing events in Southeast Asia and the turmoil within the United States, doubts should occur in Japanese minds. "Is the spear reliable? How long can we depend on it? How rapidly will it come to our help in a sudden moment of crisis? What more should we do ourselves?" These are the questions which inspire the sentiments in favor of the autonomous defense (*jishu boei*) which has become a slogan in Japan today.

Effectiveness

How effective are the Self-Defense Forces, now and for the future, the military which has no chance to fight and which must have no enemies, real or hypothetical? (The Prime Minister has denied repeatedly in the Diet that Japan has any "hypothetical enemies.")

To summarize roughly, the SDF have a thousand aircraft, two hundred naval vessels, and more than seven hundred tanks (Table 6-9). They have missiles and launchers and will continue to concentrate on air and submarine defenses. By 1977 their Air Self-Defense Forces will include 104 Phantom jet fighters, the F-43J, to be produced in Japan under licensing arrangements involving the Mitsubishi Company and McDonnell-Douglas Aircraft Company. If the recommendations of the Fourth Defense Build-up Plan are

Table 6-9

Equipment of Self-Defense Forces as of January, 1970

Ground Self-Defense Forces		
Tanks	660	
Self-propelled artillery	460	
Cannons	4,560	
Armored personnel carriers	570	
Model 30 rocket launchers	25	
Missile launchers		
Surface to surface	55	
Surface to air	50	
Aircraft		
Fixed wing	140	
Rotary wing	210	
Maritime Self-Defense Forces		
Escort ships	40	
Submarines	10	
Minesweepers	40	
Patrol ships	50	
Landing craft	50	
Auxiliary vessels	20	
Total vessels		210
Total tonnage		133,000
Anti-submarine aircraft		
Fixed wing	120	
Rotary wing	35	
Trainer, transport, liaison	100	
Total		255
Air Self-Defense Forces		
Fighters	480	
Reconnaissance aircraft	20	
Search and rescue aircraft	40	
Transport	50	
Trainers	330	
Helicopters	30	
Total		950
Missile "Nike Ajax" Launchers	75	

Source: Japan Defense Agency, *Defense of Japan, 1970*, p. 20.

approved, the 104 Phantom jets would be increased to 158. Japan's objective is to reduce foreign licensing and imports and to build up an armaments industry which will make Japan largely independent in defense production.

Some JDA officials have remarked that the popular use of the term "domestic production" (*kokusan*) is misleading, since it suggests that Japan is already producing substantial quantities of required defense equipment. The figure of "60 percent *kokusan*" has been widely published in the Japanese press. Most of this "domestic production" is actually "domestic assembly," with most vital parts being either imported or produced under license from a foreign company. The phrase "60 percent *kokusan*" can therefore mean that expenditures for 60 percent of acquired defense equipment are paid out in yen, thus saving foreign exchange; but the know-how is still imported from abroad, with most of the *kokusan* constituting merely assembly, like "putting together a model airplane," as one JDA official remarked.[19]

Weaknesses have left the Self-Defense Forces far from constituting yet the ideal of "autonomous defense." It has been popularly understood that the SDF could defend Japan for thirty days, until American help arrived. A prominent JDA official doubted this; he estimated that ammunition supplies belonging to the SDF amounted to only 50 to 70 percent of the requirements for thirty days.[20] He pointed out that gaps in air defense existed: low-flying planes and missiles could enter Japan undetected. Some equipment, such as armored vehicles, was said to be of questionable quality, and ships and other material obtained from the United States had become obsolete. A shortage of trained personnel was perhaps the factor most seriously affecting the readiness of the SDF to meet serious emergencies.

The Fourth Defense Build-up Plan

The outline of Japan's Fourth Defense Build-up Plan, to run from 1971 to 1976, was published by the Defense Agency on October 21, 1970. The total budget projected for the five-year period, which must be approved by the Cabinet and voted by the Diet, was 5.8 trillion yen or approximately $16.1 billion. This sum, which included personnel pay increases, was more than twice the total amount spent on the Third Build-up Plan (1967-1971), but, as Defense Director General Nakasone pointed out, annual appropriations under the Plan would reach only about 0.9 percent of GNP and still be less than the defense expenditures of other major powers. For example, Germany and France each spent approximately six billion dollars on defense in 1970, and the percentages of GNP were considerably larger than Japan's, 3.5 and 4.4 percent respectively. The announcement of the funds required for the five-year Plan drew some immediate critical comment in Japan, certain editorials expressing uneasiness that such huge sums were needed and that Japan should indeed become the "seventh military power in the world." One newspaper, the *Nihon Keizai,* found some inconsistency between the size of the projected defense budget and the Prime Minister's statement to the United Nations that Japan would become economically strong but would never become a big military power.[21]

In presenting the Plan, the Defense Agency discounted the likelihood of a total war but stressed the dangers of limited conflict and indirect aggression. Referring to the situation in Asia, the JDA statement mentioned the complicated relationships among the United States, Soviet Union, and Communist China and specifically cited as factors affecting the situation the development of China's nuclear capacity, the change in the Asian policy of the United States, and the expansion of the Soviet Navy. For Japan it was necessary to preserve strictly "defensive defense power" effective enough to cope with direct or indirect aggression through "maintaining supremacy in the air and command of the sea, in areas surrounding Japan, at an early stage. We will look to the U.S. forces in areas beyond our defense power and rely on the American nuclear deterrent power against a nuclear threat."[22]

The emphasis in the Fourth Build-up Plan will be on the modernization of equipment in the Ground Self-Defense Forces and on the improvement of air and sea defense. No additional personnel will be added to the land forces, but the Maritime Self-Defense Forces will be increased by 5,000 and the Air Self-Defense Forces by 3,000. For the ground troops, additional tanks (making a total of 1,000), helicopters, armored cars, and various types of guns are to be provided. The sea forces, which must assume new responsibilities in 1972 after the reversion of Okinawa, are to receive a total of 80 additional ships, including destroyers capable of carrying helicopters, and torpedo boats. The total tonnage of naval vessels, including those under construction, is planned at

245,000 with 200 ships. The Air Defense Forces will receive 54 additional F-4EJ Phantom jet fighters to bring the total of these planes up to 158. Ground-to-air missile installations will be assigned to Okinawa and the Inland Sea. Replacements are to be made for obsolete fighters, reconnaissance, and transport planes. By the time of completion of the Build-up Plan, the number of aircraft will reach 17 squadrons totalling 900 planes.

Research and development, named as a "pillar" of future defense policy, will receive priority attention. Japan has lagged behind other industrial nations in spending for military research and development and during the Third Build-up Plan allotted only 2.1 percent of total defense expenditures for this purpose, contrasting with the 4 percent spent by West Germany and 10 percent by the United States. An allocation of 3.3 percent has been made in the new plan, which will stress electronic intelligence, communications, aircraft (a new transport plane), a reconnaissance combat vehicle, and missiles.

The words "effective" and "adequate" are meaningless unless one can answer the questions: "effective for what?" and "adequate for what?" Given the limitations of the concept, function, and purpose of Japan's defense forces, the expanded plan for the use of men and armor would seem to be a reasonable one. Director General Nakasone, known for his colorful speech, has said the SDF must combine the qualities of the rabbit and the porcupine: the long ears to know what is going on and the quills to prick the intruder. Rather than opt for some grander, swashbuckling role, Japan may well find this the more satisfying posture in the 1970's.

Military-Industrial Complex

Public statements on defense by industrial leaders during 1969 focused attention on the growing defense industry and led some Japanese to speculate on whether a "military-industrial complex" (the phrase was imported from the United States) was emerging in their own country. The two most powerful organizations in Japan's world of business and industry, the Japan Federation of Employers (*Nikkeiren*) and the Federation of Economic Organizations (*Keidanren*) expressed their support of "defense commensurate with Japan's national power." The *Nikkeiren* set 1.5 percent of GNP as a goal for defense expenditures; and the *Keidanren* passed a resolution, described in the press as "a bugle call to battle," which appealed for the achievement of "autonomous defense."

Since Japan's industrial leaders welcome the expansion of a defense industry as in their interest, and because the close relationship between business and government is historical and traditional in Japan, the development of a "military-industrial complex" is not surprising. It is more important to examine its dimensions, power, and prospects.

As we have seen, Japan's total expenditures for defense purposes are still less than 1 percent of GNP and only half of Government appropriations for social welfare and services. Domestic procurement for defense amounted to $750 million dollars in 1969, only 0.46 percent of total production of mining and manufactured products.[23] Japan's large industrial firms now involved in producing arms and equipment for defense urge in their own business interest the expansion of military potential. For this purpose the *Keidanren* formed a defense production committee and became more active in the promotion of "defense consciousness" and propagation of the principle that "industrial power is defense power."

The industrialists are pushing in two directions, first, for the development of indigenous production (*kokusan*) of defense equipment, which implies lessened dependence on foreign imports and foreign technology, and second, for the creation of an arms-export industry. It is recognized that neither is a goal to be achieved overnight. As one industrialist commented, "autonomous defense really means research and development." Obviously R and D comes before production, and production comes before exports. Some Japanese say that the Phantom jet must be the last plane to be licensed, that its successor must be home-created and home-built. The weak points in the defense industry have been research and development and systems engineering. Japan has not enjoyed the benefits of mass production and of the interaction of large-scale military and civilian efforts, including a major space program, which have greatly assisted industry in the United States. Japanese industrialists have noted that one of the greatest benefits of a defense industry is the technological spill-over for civilian production.

Among producers of defense equipment, Mitsubishi Heavy Industries and Mitsubishi Electric Manufacturing Company have emerged as leaders. Together they concluded with the Defense Agency in fiscal year 1969 thirty-six percent of all defense procurement contracts. This prominence makes the Mitsubishi group vulnerable to labelling as participants in a Japanese military-industrial complex.

The Defense Agency, to avoid the growth of monopolies in defense production, has attempted to encourage competition among private companies. This was one of the policies relating to defense production announced in July 1970. Others were to rely on and encourage the technological and production capacities of private industries in defense production and to bar foreign capital from all enterprises related to defense.

Since procurement called for by the Fourth Build-up Plan is expected to amount to about half of the total cost, or nearly seven billion dollars, the prospects for defense production for the future look favorable, and Japan's leading industrialists are prepared to take advantage of the opportunities. No military-industrial complex worthy of the name exists now, while defense production is 0.4 percent of the industrial production, but it can appear in the future.

Arsenal for Asia

A second area of interest for the industrialists is the possibility of making Japan the "arsenal for Asia." This has been more a political than an economic question. Up to now Japanese exports of munitions and military equipment have been controlled not by law but by principles adopted and enforced by the Ministry of International Trade and Industry (MITI). These principles prohibit the export of arms and ammunition to: (1) Communist bloc nations, (2) countries which are belligerents, and (3) countries subject to a United Nations export boycott (such as South Africa). Total exports of military equipment from 1965 through the first half of 1970 amounted only to slightly more than two million dollars. Recipient nations included Thailand, United States, Republic of Korea, Taiwan, United Kingdom, France, Australia, Peru, Philippine Islands, and Canada. Exports consisted entirely of small arms, rifles, pistols, and ammunition, mostly for police use.[24] Japanese firms have also exported "samples" to various countries, and both Argentina and Peru are said to have inquired from the Kawasaki Heavy Industries Company about the purchase of submarines. Other countries have shown interest in importing munitions plants.[25]

Some businessmen see a promising future for arms exports to Asia after the war in Indochina ends and Government restrictions are removed. They recognize, however, that if exports grew to any considerable degree, the political repercussions could be damaging, not only within Japan but in the recipient countries as well, contributing to the image of a "militaristic Japan" already present in the minds of some Southeast Asians with long memories. A recent public opinion poll in Japan asked the question: "Do you approve of military cooperation with the nations of Asia?" Seventy-four percent replied "no;" only 6 percent said "yes."[26]

The community of interests and easy collaboration between the Defense Agency and private industry are maintained and strengthened not only by the production contracts between them but by the numerous personnel who go from one to the other. The SDF furnishes a continuous flow of technicians to the companies, but more important, ranking officers of the SDF find on retirement lucrative executive positions in industries manufacturing defense equipment. In 1967, twenty-five leading firms who had contracts with the JDA were employing sixty-three former officers of the Self-Defense Forces. From 1960 to 1967, 306 retired officers found employment in private industry.[27] SDF officers are prevented by law from accepting for a period of two years after retirement positions as "officers or any other similar positions" which may be closely connected with duties they have held during the five years prior to their separation from the SDF. However, the positions of adviser, part-time employee, or section chief are not regarded as coming within the intent of the law.

With prospects good for continued economic growth and sharp increases in the defense budget, industry's interest in the future of defense production is understandable. It may be some time, however, before the military element in Japan's total industrial production reaches an impressive figure. Some Japanese have remarked that it takes ten or twenty years to build a defense industry. Others have said that Japan has ten or perhaps even twenty years to enjoy security under the American nuclear umbrella. At the end of that time, they say, the nation should be able to take care of itself.

What does seem certain is that for the foreseeable future, probably during the decade of the 1970's, Japan's defense will be limited and controlled. Nakasone Yasuhiro, Director General of the JDA, has stressed five basic principles he believes should be followed in building Japan's security: (1) protection of the Constitution, (2) harmonization of defense with diplomacy, (3) firm maintenance of civilian control, (4) strict observance of the three non-nuclear principles (not to make, possess, or bring in nuclear weapons), and (5) dependence on the United States-Japan security treaty system to supplement the national defense effort.

After 1972, Japan must take on the responsibility for the defense of Okinawa. This requires plans and budget. In fact, the unravelling by 1972 of the tangled threads which have entwined Americans, Okinawans, and Japanese for these twenty-five postwar years during the American administration of the Ryukyu Islands will demand the application of patience, understanding, ingenuity, and the most diligent effort.

Notes

1. Defense Agency Establishment Law, Law No. 164, June 9, 1954; Self-Defense Forces Law, Law No. 165, June 9, 1954; Text of Fundamental Policy for National Defense is found in *Boei Nenkan 1969* (Defense Yearbook), (Tokyo: 1969), p. 172.

2. U.S. Department of State, *The Far Eastern Commission, A Study in International Cooperation: 1945 to 1952* (Washington, D.C.: U.S. Government Printing Office, 1953), p. 57.

3. Constitution of Japan, Article 66. This episode regarding the question of "civilian ministers" is described in Theodore McNelly, "The Renunciation of War in the Japanese Constitution," *Political Science Quarterly,* Vol. LXXVIII, No. 3 (September 1962), pp. 372-74.

4. *Asahi,* December 5, 1967.

5. *Asahi,* December 3, 1967; March 12, 1968.

6. "Kokkai Rongi no Naka no Jieitai" (The Self-Defense Forces in Diet Discussions), *Keizai Orai* (Tokyo: June 1967), p. 119.

7. Boei-cho (Defense Agency), *Nihon no Boei* (Japan's Defense), October 1970, p. 47. Popularly called and hereafter referred to as the "Defense White Paper."

8. *Mainichi,* October 10, 1968. Testimony of JDA Director General Masuda testifying before the House of Councillors Cabinet Committee.

9. "Defense White Paper," *op. cit.,* p. 48.

10. *Sankei*, October 21, 1970; *Tokyo Shimbun*, October 20, 1970.

11. *Asahi*, December 2, 1967.

12. *Asahi*, March 7, 1967.

13. *Boei Nenkan 1970* (Defense Yearbook), (Tokyo: March 20, 1970), p. 206.

14. The Institute for Strategic Studies, *The Military Balance 1970-1971* (London: Inst. for Strategic Studies, 1970), pp. 110-11.

15. *Asahi*, December 13, 1967.

16. Anzen Hosho Chosakai, *Nihon no Anzen Hosho, 1970 e no Tenbo* (Japan's Security, Outlook on 1970), 1969 edition (Tokyo: August 10, 1969), p. 354.

17. *Asahi*, February 19, 1967.

18. "Japan's Defense: Symposium," *Chuo Koron*, Tokyo, June 1968.

19. Kaihara Osamu, Chief of Secretariat, National Defense Council, Japan Defense Agency, "Boei Sangyo ni tsuite no watakushi no iken" (My Opinion about Defense Industry) in *Kokubo* (National Defense), August 1969.

20. Kaihara Osamu, quoted in *Sankei Shimbun*, October 27, 1969.

21. *Nihon Keizai*, October 23, 1970.

22. "Gist of Draft Fourth Defense Build-up Plan," *Nihon Keizai*, October 22, 1970.

23. *Nihon Keizai*, October 23, 1970.

24. *Asahi*, August 21, 1969; Japan Defense Agency.

25. *Asahi*, August 21, 1969, *op. cit.*

26. *Kyodo* News Service Survey, January 1, 1968.

27. *Hoseki* magazine, July 1967.

7

The Problem
of Okinawa

The Islands and the People

On May 29, 1853, Commodore Matthew Calbraith Perry's squadron, en route to Japan, "found itself quietly anchored in the harbor of Napha, the principal port of the great Lew Chew Island, and the first point where the expedition touched on Japanese territory, if Lew Chew (or, as the natives call it, Doo Choo) be indeed a dependency of Japan." [1]

These islands, for there were many of them besides "the great Lew Chew," were said by a 1933 guide book to Japan to "form stepping stones, as it were, from Kyushu to Formosa." [2] They were called *"Liu-ch'iu"* by the Chinese, a word pronounced "Ryukyu" by the Japanese and spelled variously by Westerners, as "Lew Chew" or Loo-choo." There is no general agreement on the total number of islands and islets in the Ryukyu chain. The Facts Book published by the United States Civil Administration specifies seventy-three, and a recent report on Economic Development in the Ryukyus includes a list and map identifying seventy-two islands, twenty-five of which are uninhabited. [3] Although, strictly speaking, "Okinawa" is the name only of the principal island, it is used by the Japanese as synonymous with *Ryukyus* and to designate the island group which forms "Okinawa Prefecture."

The people of the Ryukyu Islands have been destined in history to be unsure of their identity and their loyalties. Similar in racial origin to the Japanese, they differ nevertheless in certain physical characteristics and a language, culture, and traditions which have naturally grown out of their experiences as an island people. Over the centuries Chinese and Japanese influences penetrated the islands; and although their own government, institutions, and royal line evolved, for many years tribute was paid to both China and Japan. From 1609 the lords of Satsuma, in Japan's southern-

153

most island of Kyushu, established hegemony over the islands, although tribute missions continued to travel to China until 1875.

Perry's judgment at the time of his visit was fairly accurate:

> It is a question yet discussed to what power Lew Chew belongs. By some it is said to be a dependency of the Prince of Satsuma, of Japan; others suppose it to belong to China. The probabilities, however, are all on the side of the dependence, more or less absolute, of Lew Chew on Japan, and probably, also, of some qualified subordination to China, as they undoubtedly send tribute to that country. [4]

The Japanese moved to consolidate their control. In 1872 the Tokyo Government announced that Sho Tai, who had been Ryukyu King, was appointed the King of the Ryukyu Han. *Han* was the designation for a dependent feudal territory. In 1879 the King was forced to abdicate, and the Ryukyus were incorporated into Japan as a prefecture. China's claim to sovereignty continued, however, until Japan's victory in the Sino-Japanese war in 1895 and was again revived during and after World War II. In 1942 Chinese officials announced their determination to recover the Ryukyus; in 1948, before the Japanese peace treaty was signed, Chang Hsinhai, a former Chinese diplomat and author of *Chiang Kai-shek: Asia's Man of Destiny,* wrote in *Foreign Affairs* that "China is asking for the control of the Liuchiu Islands for historic reasons." [5] Later, however, the Chinese raised no objection to the provision for a United Nations trusteeship stipulated by Article 3 of the Japanese peace treaty, and they have not made formal representations to protest reversion to Japan.

Japanese Prewar Rule

Japanese control and influence have been long and continuous, and it is natural that Okinawans consider themselves Japanese and look upon Japan as their homeland. Yet, as has been indicated, their historical experiences have been different from those of their compatriots in the main islands of Japan. Certainly in the prewar period there was a barrier between Okinawans and Japanese.

Okinawa has always been a poor prefecture. In the years 1934-36, Okinawa's per capita annual income was 86 yen or $25, less than half that of Japan in the same years. A comparison of the value of production of different commodities shows that, although per capita agricultural production in the Ryukyus approached the Japanese average in 1937, it was only 82 percent of that of Kagoshima, one of the poorest but largely agriculture prefectures. In per capita value of manufacturing production, Okinawa was 5 percent of that of Japan, 45 percent of Kagoshima. Compared to Kagoshima, Ryukyuan production of silk was 23 percent, lumber 7 percent, and sea products 5 percent.[6] It has been estimated that the 1934-36 per capita average income of 86 yen would have had an equivalent pruchasing power of $119 in 1953, which was close to the actual per capita income that year of $122.[7] By 1969 this figure had risen to $653, which, due to the extraordinarily rapid growth of the Japanese economy, was still approximately one half of the Japanese average, as it had been in 1934-36.

Not only was Okinawa poor, a "sweet potatoes and barefoot" economy, as Okinawans themselves wryly termed it, but the people of the islands were strange to the Japanese, with peculiar dress, names, language, and customs.

The first Okinawan newspaper was founded in 1894, the *Ryukyu Shimpo*. Its editorial policy emphasized two objectives: first, to report the currents of world events and encourage the development of Okinawa, and second, to get rid of the provincial "island mentality" and promote national assimilation. In explaining the importance of the latter, the newspaper noted that Okinawa's historical subordination to both China and Japan had resulted in an abnormal development characterized by mixing of customs and traditions drawn from both countries. This confusion had created a serious obstacle to national assimilation. The editorial concluded that a single-minded policy must be developed to integrate Okinawa fully and completely into the Japanese homeland. Okinawans were exhorted to become exactly like the people of other prefectures of Japan, morally, materially, and regardless of the consequences.[8]

It should be recalled that the Japanese during this period were keenly sensitive to any and all feelings of regional consciousness. The leaders of the new central Government had been faced with rebellions in Kyushu which threatened the survival of the regime, and they were in no mood to brook opposition from the Okinawans. It was natural, therefore, that measures of control intended to obliterate old separatist loyalties and establish allegiance to the central regime were repressive and persistent.

However valiantly the Okinawans struggled to become

"Japanese," they did not succed in eliminating discrimination against them. Japanese continued to regard them as socially separated country cousins; and, unfortunately, Government service in the remote Ryukyus did not always attract the most sensitive and discerning Japanese officials, for whom all principal positions of authority were reserved.

Incidents occurred. In a fair at Osaka in 1904, a building called the "Hall of Races" displayed two Okinawan women who were pointed to by guides with derogatory gestures as if they were "animals in a cage." Loud protests published in Okinawa were echoed in Japan, and the exhibit was finally cancelled.[9]

The Japanese Government showed little zeal in promoting higher education. Okinawa was the only prefecture without a high school in the prewar period. No university existed; the University of the Ryukyus was established only in 1950 by the American administration. The only Okinawan children who could look forward to the opportunity of a university education were those few whose families were wealthy enough to send them to Japan.[10]

As war in China expanded in the 1930's, Japan's leaders felt a greater necessity to control culture and education, not only in the colonies of Korea and Formosa, but in Okinawa as well. The Okinawans began to feel that, although they were nominally Japanese and citizens of a prefecture, they were treated as inhabitants of a colonial possession. Education was increasingly directed toward nationalist aims, in particular, toward "Japanization" or "*kominka*," literally "changing into people of the Emperor," the same system of indoctrination being applied in Taiwan.

In 1940, the laudable attempts of a few Japanese interested in Okinawan history and culture to encourage the people of the islands to preserve and pursue their native language and arts aroused a storm of controversy. After visits by folk art experts from Tokyo had awakened local interest in the study of indigenous culture, the prefectural government reacted sharply and adversely: such activities were manifestations of "irresponsible exoticism" and were contrary to the spirit of *kominka*. At one point the governor proclaimed that "every vestige of Okinawa's provincial individuality must be erased."[11]

While the most vigorous efforts were made in Okinawa by the Japanese administration to inculcate the principles of "spiritual mobilization" and a fighting spirit among the people, complete success was never achieved. In 1935 the commander of the Okinawa Garrison Forces publicly denounced the spirit and conduct of the men of military age. In fact, few were ever drafted for combat duty; 10,000 served in a military labor corps, and only 5,500 local troops were in the islands when the war ended. Japanese stationed in the islands thought the local people were uncouth and difficult to understand.[12]

As George H. Kerr points out in his book, *Okinawa, The History of an Island People*, "No prefecture contributed so little to the preparation for war and its prosecution through the years, but none suffered as much in widespread misery, in loss of human lives and property, and in ultimate subservience to military occupation."[13] Sacrifices were indeed great. Between 110,000 and 115,000 civilians died during the battle of Okinawa. Ninety thousand Japanese soldiers were killed; Americans suffered 12,000 dead and 37,000 wounded.

The Advent of the Americans

The Ryukyu Islanders, torn through the centuries between China and Japan, yet clinging to fragments of their own island culture even as they inevitably began to acquire a Japanese mold, were destined involuntarily to know yet another country and another culture. The islands might have come under American influence or "surveillance" by the United States in 1853. Commodore Perry in correspondence with the Secretary of the Navy remarked that it was self-evident that events would "ere long make it necessary for the United States to extend its territorial jurisdiction beyond the limits of the western continent." He said he assumed the responsibility of urging "the expediency of establishing a foothold in this quarter of the globe as a measure of positive necessity to the sustainment of our maritime rights in the east." Specifically Perry proposed that, if the Japanese Government refused to negotiate a treaty or assign a port of resort for American merchant and whaling ships, he would take "under surveillance of the American flag . . . this island of Great Lew-Chew. . . ." The President promptly rejected Perry's proposal as "embarassing" and American association with the Ryukyus was postponed for almost a hundred years.[14]

But destiny had determined that Americans and Okinawans were again to meet and for an extended time, and so the third foreign influence came in to complicate the ordinarily quiet lives of the islanders.

Revived American interest in Pacific bases was inspired by Japanese rule over the mandated Pacific islands which had been entrusted to them by the League of Nations after World War I. The Navy was determined that never again would a foreign power, especially Japan, gain control over strategically located islands and fortify them as Japan had done illegally, thus threatening American security interests in the Pacific Ocean area.

In a Memorandum to the Secretary of State in January 1945, Henry Stimson, then Secretary of War, wrote that the United States must have the necessary bases for the "defense of the security of the Pacific for the future world." He added: "To serve such a purpose they must belong to the United States with absolute power to rule and fortify them." [15] Stimson was undoubtedly thinking of the Pacific mandated islands more than of the Ryukyus, but after only a few years of occupation, bases on Okinawa were judged necessary to American security. General MacArthur so stated as early as 1947. [16]

Those Americans serving on Okinawa as military government officers as the smoke of battle cleared were not sure of the future of the Ryukyus. The first landings had taken place on the offshore Kerama islands on March 26, 1945, and the battle for the main island of Okinawa opened on April 1. By June 21 hostilities had ceased, and on July 31 General Joseph W. Stilwell became the first Military Governor. On the day the Emperor announced Japan's surrender, August 15, Military Government set up an Advisory Council consisting of fifteen prominent Okinawans. These were able men, most of them school teachers or doctors, the professions open to Okinawans. No member was a government official, since these had all been Japanese and had quickly disappeared. Two members of the Council later became chief executives of the islands.

The confusion in the early Occupation period can be imagined. The agencies of government had vanished, communities were broken up, the population had scattered. On the American side, G.I.'s eagerly awaited transportation home, and the rapidity of transfers—50 percent of the officers were immediately sent to Japan—destroyed all continuity of operations. The people once recovered from the initial shock and fright, gingerly left their places of refuge and came hesitatingly to welcome the American troops. Gradually, as it was to be later in Japan, they saw the conquerors as their salvation. As an officer in military government at the time described it: "Americans were grounded angels in khaki, sword in one hand, perhaps, but the scales of justice in the other."[17]

At the moment neither Okinawans nor Americans thought about the future status of the Ryukyu Islands. Survival and recovery demanded total energy. In 1946 an officer in military government could say that the Okinawans had come to regard themselves as permanent American charges; he felt they were happy with the American administration and, if they had a free choice *at that time*, would vote for American retention of the Ryukyus. In fact, Okinawans had begun to assume that the United States would keep the island chain. For them American generosity outbalanced their suffering, and they could imagine no other source of help. Japan was shattered and China, Russia, Europe, and the United Nations out of the question as alternatives. Moreover, the presence of the United States stimulated the beginning of a psychological transformation of the people; now they felt primarily Okinawan and only secondarily Japanese. In Japan's defeat their identity as Okinawans suddenly acquired a dignity they had not experienced before, and a new pride in their own home islands was born.

In spite of these attitudes, some senior military government officers concluded as early as 1946 that the United States should not annex the Ryukyu Islands, that "Americanization" at best would never be completely successful and that, as the Occupation continued, inevitable irritations and grievances would accumulate. Okinawans had already been pulled to and fro between two cultures; to try to force them into still another direction would be neither in their interest nor in that of the United States. The Okinawans, they argued, were Japanese, and the only satisfactory permanent future for the Ryukyus lay in their return to Japan.[18]

In 1946, at least for those on the spot, there was little thought of Okinawa as a great military base for the future. In the euphoria of peace and hope for harmony with the Russians, military units were disbanded, men were sent home, installations dismantled, and equipment left to rust. From the view point of one military government officer on Okinawa, a garrison of a thousand men, stationed not on Okinawa itself but on the tiny adjoining islet of Ie-jima, would for the future prove adequate for America's security needs! [19]

Outposts for Defense

The Cold War revamped America's global interests and drastically changed the strategic outlook from Washington. Just as Japan's role was viewed in a new light, so the sleepy outposts in the islands of the August moon suddenly became a focal point of strategic concern. On March 1, 1949, General MacArthur described the Pacific as an Anglo-Saxon lake and drew the American defense line through the Ryukyu archipelago, "which includes its main bastion, Okinawa." In the same year the Army Chief of Staff, General Joseph Lawton Collins, announced during a visit to Tokyo that the United States would keep Okinawa "indefinitely." In the summer of 1949, construction started on base installations in Okinawa, to cost $50 million. On January 12, 1950, Secretary of State Acheson repeated the delineation of MacArthur's defense line and specified: "We hold important defense positions in the Ryukyu Islands, and these we will continue to hold."

Only to be resolved was the form in which the United States would retain the islands. Annexation, a form of territorial aggrandizement, could not be considered. The United Nations Charter had provided for a system of trust territories, and in 1947 a general trusteeship agreement was signed. It was logical, therefore, that the United States should propose inclusion of the Ryukyu and Bonin Islands in the United Nations trusteeship system.

The future of Okinawa was determined in what became Article 3 of the treaty of peace with Japan, which provided that Japan would concur in any proposal of the United States to the United Nations to place certain islands, including the Ryukyus and the Bonins, under its trusteeship system, with the United States as the sole administering authority. A proviso was added that "pending the making of such a proposal and affirmative action thereon, the United States will have the right to exercise all and any powers of administration, legislation and jurisdiction over the territory and inhabitants of these islands, including their territorial waters." Whether so intended at the time or not, this sentence became the basis for the succeeding twenty years of American

160

control over the Ryukyu Islands. The treaty was ratified April 28, 1952. The date later came to be observed annually as "Okinawa Day" in Japan and the Ryukyus with demonstrations against continued American administration and in favor of reversion to Japan.

At the San Francisco conference, John Foster Dulles referred to the divergent proposals of the Allied Powers for disposition of the Ryukyu Islands, including the assumption of sovereignty over them by the United States and their complete restoration to Japan. He then stated: "In the face of this division of Allied opinion, the United States felt that the best formula would be to permit Japan to retain residual sovereignty, while making it possible for these islands to be brought into the United Nations Trusteeship system with the United States as administering authority." [20]

Consequently, although rule by the United States was to be absolute and indefinite, it was not to be permanent; and the Ryukyus were promised to Japan once a need for the bases had ceased to exist.

It was expected that the Ryukyu Islands would be placed under a strategic trusteeship, with the United States as the sole administering authority. This would impose Security Council jurisdiction and inevitable Big Power veto. In such a situation the persistent obstructionism of the Soviet Union was not difficult to foresee, and it is understandable that no move was ever made by the American Government to carry out the intent of Article 3 of the San Francisco treaty by proposing to make the Ryukyus a strategic trust territory under the United Nations.

The Movement for Return to Japan

The movement for reversion of the Ryukyu Islands to Japan, which dates its formal beginning to the formation by a group of Okinawans in 1951 of an Association for the Promotion of Reversion, steadily gained support through the years. As the Occupation continued, disillusionment with American control nourished a nostalgia for Japan. In the years between 1946 and 1949, Okinawa was for Americans the "forgotten island," the "rock" where Army misfits were sent, where the zeal of the early military government officers had evaporated, and where local corruption and crime were rampant. [21]

Above all, the United States had no determined policy for the future of the islands. Even after the peace treaty had been signed and Dulles had declared "residual sovereignty" for Japan, a general from Washington visiting Okinawa told the press that the Ryukyus might "attain independence or revert to Japan in the future." [22] At the same time American authorities were suspicious of and irritated by the growing agitation for return to Japan. In October 1951, the American commanding general and deputy governor wrote to the Okinawan chief executive that "continued movements for reversion would hamper the work of the American Government and breach the close cooperation of the Ryukyuan people and the American authorities." [23]

Okinawans themselves were not unanimous in their views of the future. Some wanted independence, and others favored international trusteeship under the administration of the United States. Many could not believe the United States would ever leave the islands. A commentator writing in an Okinawan newspaper in 1952 predicted that "barring some fundamental change in the world situation, the United States would never leave Okinawa." [24] Some Okinawans continued to hold this view. The permanency of American installations and the comfortable, settled attitudes of the American military led to the conclusion that Americans intended to stay in Okinawa forever.

In February 1951, the four political parties of the day held different positions on the future of the Ryukyus: two favored reversion to Japan, one supported trusteeship under United States administration, and the fourth proposed a kind of independence. Even in 1951, however, public opinion polls showed large majorities favoring return to Japan. A collection of signatures on a petition asking for reversion and said to represent 72 percent of the eligible voters was sent in August by the Okinawa provincial assembly to Prime Minister Yoshida, Ambassador Dulles, and Secretary of State Acheson.

In succeeding years, as the reversion movement grew, the bases became more important to the United States. The Korean war dramatically demonstrated their usefulness. As army visual-aids so vividly portrayed, Okinawa was the "keystone of the Pacific," the crucial center in the off-shore island chain. Naha is only 400 miles from Communist Chinese territory, 410 miles from Taiwan, 480 miles from the American naval base in Sasebo, Japan, 830 miles from Seoul, and 970 miles from Tokyo. Bases in Okinawa were regarded as essential to American commitments to Japan, to South

Korea, to the Philippines, and to Southeast Asia through SEATO. They constituted a major forward springboard of the nuclear deterrent to Communist power in Asia.

As the conflict in Vietnam developed, military activities in Okinawa rose proportionately; facilities and manpower kept pace with the expansion of the war. American independent control of the Ryukyus guaranteed unmitigated freedom to use the bases, a privilege highly prized and rarely enjoyed elsewhere in the world. The situation contrasted vividly with that in the main islands of Japan where the obligation of "prior consultation" prevented the introduction and storage of nuclear weapons and the free movement of combat troops.

The retention of Okinawa by the United States has invariably been justified in terms of military imperatives, yet it has always been recognized that retention and effective use of the bases depended not only on international legalities, but also on the tolerance of the local population. Thus a practical policy aim on the islands has been, in the words of a Headquarters briefing paper, the "reasonable acquiescence of the people." To achieve this result two salient policies were pursued: first, to increase gradually the autonomy of the Government of the Ryukyu Islands (GRI) and, second, to improve the education, welfare, and livelihood of the people. The hope was that a successful pursuit of these policies would blunt the agitation for reversion.

Yet, while the economy rose sharply and steadily and the standard of living reached unprecedented heights, not only did sentiment in favor of reversion not dwindle, but reversion became a doctrine which no one could oppose and an issue which all political parties could exploit. Differences between government and opposition were reduced to questions of timing. The Okinawan Liberal Democratic Party (OLDP), like the LDP in Japan, conceded the security role of the bases and expressed willingness to accept a delayed reversion. Leftist parties demanded immediate and total reversion, including American withdrawal from the bases. Intermediate positions emerged with the passage of time.

Separation of Bases from Administration

As early as a year after the peace treaty went into effect, it was suggested that the United States should retain the military bases

163

but return the administration of the islands to Japan. Joseph W. Ballantine, a former Foreign Service Officer and Japan specialist, recommended this solution in an article in *Foreign Affairs* in July 1953. He described the arrangement as one whereby "Japan would grant military bases in the islands to the United States and the United States would restore the islands to Japanese rule." He pointed out that Japan would welcome such a proposal, the Okinawans would gain economically from a continued American presence, and the moral stand of the United States would be improved in Asia. Sixteen years before the promise to return Okinawa was finally made, Ballantine wrote: "The return of the islands to Japan would be hailed by the Ryukyuans and the Japanese as giving heed to their aspirations. It would tend to cement their friendship with us, to instill confidence, and to dispose the Japanese Government to wholehearted cooperation in the defense of the free world in East Asia." [25]

The American military has generally opposed such a divorce of the bases from the administration of the islands. In January 1954, Major General David A. D. Ogden, deputy governor of the Ryukyus, argued that "the peculiar nature of the military defenses in the Ryukyus makes control of civil administration inseparable from the military for security reasons." [26] A briefing paper prepared by the United States Civil Administration for the Ryukyus (USCAR) in 1966 presented the official line, describing the unique value of the Okinawa bases, which would be destroyed by giving up the administrative rights over the islands:

> . . . Okinawa is useful primarily because of the freedom of the United States to make military decisions. If Okinawa were to resume its former position as a prefecture of Japan, the area would come under the provisions of the security treaty between the United States and Japan. . . . The value of our bases here would be vastly diminished if we had to consult with any nation on the decisions that had to be made. [27] *

---

* It is interesting to compare these statements with one made by the High Commissioner of the Ryukyu Islands, Lt. Gen. James B. Lampert, on January 28, 1970: "Reversion itself will not basically alter the strategic importance of our Okinawan bases which are a tremendously valuable investment of the United States. Our Okinawan bases will continue to be a key element in the deterrence of aggression." *United States Security Agreements and Commitments Abroad*, Hearings before the Subcommittee on United States Security Agreements and Commitments Abroad of the Committee on Foreign Relations, U.S. Senate, 91st Congress, 2nd Session, January 26, 27, 28, and 29, 1970, p. 1490.

A milestone in the history of American administration of Okinawa was President Kennedy's statement of March 19, 1962, which was based on the recommendations of an Interdepartmental Task Force appointed to investigate conditions, policies, and programs in the islands. The President reiterated the importance of the bases in maintaining American deterrent power and in assuring our allies of our willingness and ability to come to their aid in case of need. But the statement also included the most direct recognition yet made of Japanese sovereignty and of American intention to return the islands: "I recognize the Ryukyus to be part of the Japanese homeland and look forward to the day when the security interests of the free world will permit their restoration to full Japanese sovereignty." The President went on to say that in the meantime a "spirit of forbearance and mutual understanding" was required and that the specific actions he was recommending were intended to "discharge more effectively American responsibilities toward the people of the islands and to minimize the stresses that will accompany the anticipated eventual restoration of the Ryukyu Islands to Japanese administration." President Kennedy's principal recommendations embraced additional economic assistance, increased autonomy for the Ryukyu Government, and reduced controls over the freedoms of individual citizens.[28]

The Japanese Role

The Kennedy statement opened more fully a door to the participation by the Japanese Government in Okinawan affairs. At the time of the statement, suspicion and wariness of Japan colored the attitudes of many American military men who dealt with Okinawan affairs in the Pentagon and in the Islands. These men were convinced that Japan was intent upon undermining the authority of the United States in the Islands by extending its influence in devious and inauspicious ways. "Salami tactics" described the charge most often aimed by the military against the Japanese. The fear was that by gaining access here, sending a representative there, winning participation in one program, breaking down travel regulations, establishing advisers in Okinawan governmental departments, and through a multitude of other small actions, the Japanese would be able to subvert the constituted authority and control of the United States in the Ryukyus.

Japanese aid programs were suspect for these reasons. At one point, because of the strong influence emanating from the Pentagon and American military authorities in Okinawa, American officials were actually discouraging the Japanese Government from raising its level of aid to the Ryukyus. The theory was that if Japan gave more than the United States, American prestige and influence would drop and the Japanese would reap the benefit. This would be one more slice of the salami. However, keeping Japanese aid down and American aid up soon became impossible in the face of refusals by the American Congress to raise the Price Act ceilings, which set the aid funds for Okinawa. Finally, and fortunately, attitudes changed, and suddenly American officials could welcome a Japanese figure which began to mount precipitously. American appropriations for economic assistance were locked at $17.5 million by the failure of the most strenuous efforts to break through the Price Act ceiling.

By 1964 the United States was ready to cooperate formally with the Japanese on aid programs, and a joint consultative committee was established. Terms of reference were drawn up very carefully, however, to ensure that the committee could do no more than coordinate aid for economic development and for the welfare of the people. The American representative was scrupulous in rejecting any agenda item which, regardless of how pertinent it was to conditions in Okinawa, did not directly relate to economic or technical assistance. There were still American fears that the Japanese might try to insinuate their influence beyond the strict terms of reference and erode the American authority to rule the Islands.

Autonomy

As promised by President Kennedy in his statement of March 1962, genuine efforts were made to delegate increasing powers to the Government of the Ryukyu Islands (GRI) and to reduce controls, encourage greater responsibility for the Legislature, and improve cooperation with the Japanese Government. Members of the military continued to resist what they believed to be derogation of the ultimate authority of the United States. On March 5, 1963, High Commissioner Caraway spoke out on the "myth of autonomy." He asserted that the time was not yet ripe to transfer authority to the GRI, which was not yet ready to assume such responsibilities, and that "autonomy at the present time is a myth." He went on to criticize severely the low efficiency of the executive, legislative, and judicial branches of the Ryukyuan Government. The pro-government party leaders were ready to absorb the criticism, but opposition party spokesmen denounced the speech as revealing the colonial status of Okinawa and the new American policy as in fact designed to deceive the people. The press quoted Japanese Government sources which termed the High Commissioner's expression of distrust improper and injurious to Japanese-American relations. [29]

After 1964 the autonomy of the Government of the Ryukyu Islands was rapidly enlarged. Succeeding High Commissioners eliminated ordinances and controls to the point that by 1969 direct American rule was minimal. Of course, the power of veto vested in the High Commissioner and the ultimate power of *de facto* sovereignty remained in American hands, not to be relinquished until reversion.

Choosing the Chief Executive

The evolution in the procedures for choosing the Chief Executive illustrates the devolution of American authority. Until 1962 the Chief Executive was directly appointed by the High Commissioner; from 1962, in accordance with the Kennedy statement, the Chief Executive was nominated by the Legislature and appointed by the High Commissioner; in 1965, the system was again changed to permit *election* by the Legislature. Not until February 1968 did the American administration agree to the direct, popular election of the Chief Executive, an objective of many years of political agitation in the Islands.

The democratization of procedures for selecting the Chief Executive, from appointment to popular election, presented the United States Government with difficult dilemmas. Obviously, the security of the bases was always a primary consideration, and the election of a leftist Chief Executive, which would mean strengthened opposition to American policies and actions, was a prospect no American official viewed with pleasure. Particularly frightening was the possibility that disturbances might be fanned to levels of violence where local police could or would not act firmly and that then, unavoidably, American bayonets would be pointed at Okinawan citizens.

When the free election of the Chief Executive was permitted and set for November 1968, the race was expected to be close. Yara Chobyo, a popular school teacher, veteran in the reversion movement, and president of the Okinawa Teachers Association, was endorsed by all opposition parties. The government party, the Okinawan Liberal Democratic Party (OLDP), had managed to keep a majority in the Legislature and campaigned with extraordinary vigor, with massive support from the LDP in Japan. However, Yara won the election. After taking office, to the gratification of American authorities in Okinawa, Yara did not prove to be a fire-eating militant; in fact, he displayed impressive moderation and understanding of the problems facing Okinawa in its transition toward reversion. Moreover, his leftist affiliation proved useful in one sense: he could influence the elements who elected him in a way no OLDP Chief Executive could ever have done.

Sato's Visits to Washington and Okinawa

In 1965, Prime Minister Sato visited Washington in January and Okinawa in August. Both visits significantly spurred the movement toward reversion. In the joint communique signed by President Johnson and Prime Minister Sato, both recognized the importance of American military installations in the Ryukyu and Bonin Islands for the security of the Far East. The President, "appreciating" the desire of the Japanese Government and people for the restoration of the administration of the Islands to Japan, went on record that "he looks forward to the day when the security interest of the Free World in the Far East will permit the realization of that desire." Johnson and Sato also agreed to broaden the scope of the consultative committee matters related to the well-being of the Okinawans.

Sato's visit to the Ryukyus, extensively reported in the Japanese press, provided a slogan which became the battle cry of the reversionist movement in both Japan and in Okinawa. At his airport press conference in Naha, the Prime Minister, after expressing respect and gratitude to his "nine hundred thousand compatriots" for all they had endured, stated that *the postwar period would not be over for Japan until Okinawa had been returned to the homeland.* Although marred by demonstrations by opposition groups who sought immediate and total American withdrawal, the visit gave a dramatic impetus to the agitation for reversion, especially in Japan. From that time on, the movement was in high gear, and hardly a day passed without reference to Okinawa in Japan's all-pervasive mass media.

Both Tokyo and Washington realized that timetables had to be advanced. American officials began to consider seriously what the Army and Defense Departments had consistently called impossible, namely, separation of the administration from the bases. No one could think of giving up the Okinawa bases while the Vietnam War went on. But it was also evident that a hostile Japanese Government could make bases in either the Ryukyus or Japan quite useless. A relationship of mutual trust and cooperation with Japan was fundamental to the American position in the Pacific.

Sato-Johnson Communiqué, 1967

Consequently, by 1967 the idea had become generally accepted within the United States Government that a rapid resolution of the "Okinawa problem" was required and that the only possible way was agreement to return the administrative rights to Japan while continuing to operate the bases. Thus, when President Johnson met Prime Minister Sato again in November, the joint communique issued after the conferences included a promise to keep "under joint and continuous review the status of the Ryukyu Islands, guided by the aim of returning administrative rights over these Islands to Japan. . . ." In the same communique the Prime Minister emphasized that agreement on a date for this return should be reached "within a few years," a phrase which in its Japanese version was interpreted to mean "two or three years." The schedule was met when two years later Prime Minister Sato returned to Washington and agreed with President Nixon on November 22, 1969, that the return of the administrative rights over the Ryukyu Islands should take place in 1972.

Notes

1. Francis L. Hawks, *Narrative of the Expedition of an American Squadron to the China Seas and Japan. Performed in the Years 1852, 1853, and 1854* (2 vols.,

169

Washington, D.C.: published by order by the Congress of the United States, 1856), I, p. 151.

2. *An Official Guide to Japan* (Tokyo: The Japanese Government Railways, 1933), p. 449.

3. United States Civil Administration of the Ryukyu Islands (USCAR), *Facts Book*, FY 1967, p. 51; Daniel, Mann, Johnson, and Mendenhall and Japan Economic and Engineering Consultants Ltd., *Economic Development Study Ryukyu Islands*, March 1968, pp. xvii and xix: Map 1; p. 16, Table 5. Hereafter referred to as DMJM Report.

4. Hawks, *op. cit.*, p. 151.

5. Chang Hsin-hai, "The Treaty with Japan, A Chinese View," *Foreign Affairs*, April 1948, p. 509.

6. DMJM Report, *op. cit.*, p. 64.

7. *Ibid.*, p. 61.

8. Ota Masahide, *Minikui Nihonjin* (The Ugly Japanese), (Tokyo: Simul Press, 1969), p. 23.

9. *Ibid.*, p. 24.

10. *Ibid.*, p. 8.

11. *Ibid.*, p. 29.

12. George H. Kerr, *Okinawa, The History of an Island People* (Tokyo, Rutland, Vt.: Charles E. Tuttle Co., 1958), pp. 462-64.

13. *Ibid.*, p. 463.

14. U.S., Senate, *Correspondence Relative to the Naval Expedition to Japan, 1853-1854*, U.S. Senate Documents, 33rd Congress, 2nd session (1854-1855), vol. 6, Ex. Doc. no. 34, Serial 751, quoted in Kerr, *op. cit.*, p. 327.

15. Henry L. Stimson and McGeorge Bundy, *On Active Service in Peace and War* (New York: Harper and Brothers, 1947), p. 600.

16. Frederick S. Dunn, *Peacemaking and the Settlement with Japan* (Princeton: Princeton University Press, 1963), p. 55.

17. James T. Watkins IV, *Government, I* (undated, unpublished manuscript), p. 47.

18. James T. Watkins IV, *Okinawa USA?* (undated, unpublished manuscript).

19. *Ibid.*

20. *Japanese Peace Conference, San Francisco, California, September 1951*, "Statement by John Foster Dulles, on behalf of the Delegation of the United States of America as co-sponsor of the Draft Treaty of Peace with Japan," Second Plenary, Sept. 5, 1951 (Press Release PR ∕9, Sept. 5, 1951), p. 5.

21. Higa Mikio, *Politics and Parties in Post-war Okinawa* (Vancouver: University of British Columbia, 1963), p. 8.

22. Research and Evaluation Division, Public Affairs Department, USCAR, *A Chronological Report on Public Election of Chief Executive and Reversion (as reported by the Ryukyuan press) for the period September 1950—September 1965,* p. 7. Hereafter referred to as *Chronological Report.*

23. *Ibid.,* p. 8.

24. Nakasone Genwa, "Okinawa kara Ryukyu e, Nihon Fukki Ron to Sekinin" (From Okinawa to the Ryukyus, the Argument for Reversion to Japan and Responsibility), *Okinawa Times,* July 24, 1952.

25. Joseph W. Ballantine, "The Future of the Ryukyus," *Foreign Affairs,* Vol. 31, No. 4 (July 1953), p. 674.

26. *Chronological Report, op. cit.,* p. 21.

27. Public Affairs Department, USCAR, *The Ryukyu Islands under United States Administration,* January 1966, pp. 10-11.

28. USCAR, *Facts Book, op. cit.,* pp. 2-13.

29. *Chronological Report, op. cit.,* p. 80.

8

Back to Japan: Okinawa, 1970 to 1972

Hondo-nami, Kaku-nuki

The Nixon-Sato agreement of November 1969 calling for the "reversion" of the Ryukyu Islands to Japan in 1972 marked a high point in post-Occupation Japanese-American relations. The agreement not only blunted the sting of the outstanding territorial issue dividing the two countries, but it also represented in Japanese eyes, a formal American recognition of Japan's sovereignty and independent power.

While the sting was thus blunted, however, it was not removed completely. Reversion was expressed in the agreement as the return by the United States to Japan of the administrative rights over the Islands. There remained the question of continued American use of the bases.

In Japanese contemplations of post-reversion use of the bases by the United States, two questions became central: whether the security treaty would be applied and whether nuclear weapons would be permitted. While the Left in both Japan and Okinawa continued to demand total reversion, including removal of all military bases, most Japanese realized that this solution was impractical and indeed undesirable for the security of Japan. They believed, however, that if the bases were to remain, they should be subject to the restrictions of the security treaty with a ban on nuclear weapons. In other words, there should be no difference in the status of bases in Okinawa and in Japan. The watch-word became *hondo-nami, kaku-nuki* (homeland level, without nuclear weapons).

The Okinawans complained that not only had they suffered enormous losses of lives and property through invasion and battle, which the Japanese had escaped by their surrender, but also they

173

alone had been subjected to twenty-five years of continuing foreign rule. They believed that the Americans' unrestricted use of the bases in Okinawa had involved them—without their consent—in America's war in Vietnam. American B-52's could take off from Okinawan bases, but not from Japanese bases, to bomb targets in Vietnam; and nuclear weapons banned from Japan, could be freely moved and stored in Okinawa.

Opinion solidified in both Japan and Okinawa that failure to apply the security treaty to the Okinawan part of the homeland after reversion would be intolerable. Even the Sato Government, while fully supporting the continued maintenance of effective American military bases for the defense of the Far East, could not oppose *hondo-nami, kaku-nuki* and survive politically. Although for a period Sato avoided taking a categorical position on the nuclear question, explaining that he must keep a "clean slate" before the negotiations, he gradually shifted to a bolder stand, presumably sensing that the American Government would in the end not insist on complete and unrestricted freedom to use the bases after reversion.

During 1968 and 1969 the tempo of discussion of the reversion issue accelerated in Japan and Okinawa, and meetings between Japanese and American Government officials became more frequent. In November 1968, as we have noted, the worst fears of USCAR were confirmed when the first direct election for Chief Executive was won by the candidate proposing complete and immediate reversion and supported by the combined opposition forces. Yara's victory proved again, if further proof were needed, the strength of reversionist sentiment in Okinawa and the urgency of a Japanese-American agreement which would defuse the issue. As 1970 drew nearer, the conclusion was inevitable that, politically, reversion was potentially a more explosive issue than was the security treaty and that, unless an Okinawan solution could be achieved before 1970, the Japanese Government would face serious troubles during that year, with the opposition forces making the most of a campaign combining Okinawan reversion and treaty termination.

The meetings between the Prime Minister and the President in November 1969 were well timed, and the success of their agreement was quickly tested in the December elections for the House of Representatives. The Liberal Democrats won the largest number of seats (302 out of 486) held by any party since the war.

In Tokyo the Sato-Nixon communiqué of November 21, 1969 was termed as significant for Japan as the Potsdam Declaration or the Japanese peace treaty. The provisions relative to the return to Japan of the administration of the Ryukyu Islands received the greatest public attention.

Two points of view had to be reconciled. The Japanese required the controls over nuclear weapons and the use of bases in Okinawa provided by the security treaty, and the American needed assurances that the bases would in fact be usable and effective. The agreement was drawn up to meet these demands. After its publication, newspaper headlines in Japan could proclaim *"hondo-nami, kaku-nuki,"* and the United States could point with satisfaction to the numerous references to Japanese recognition of the security value of the bases.

Early in the communiqué the Prime Minister "stressed that it was important for the peace and security of the Far East that the United States should be in a position to carry out fully its obligations." He further stated that "the presence of United States forces in the Far East constituted a mainstay for the stability of the area." Later, both the President and the Prime Minister recognized the "vital role played by United States forces in Okinawa in the present situation in the Far East," but agreed that the "mutual security interests of the United States and Japan could be accomodated within arrangements for the return of the administrative rights over Okinawa to Japan." They again emphasized security by stating that consultations between the two Governments would be carried out in order to accomplish early reversion "without detriment to the security of the Far East." [1]

The key to the use of the bases was the "prior consultation" system. After agreeing that the security treaty and its *related arrangements* (the exchanges of notes describing prior consultation) would apply to Okinawa without modification, Sato affirmed the recognition of the Japanese Government that "the security of Japan could not be adequately maintained without international peace and security in the Far East and, therefore, the security of the countries in the Far East was a matter of serious concern for Japan." In the light of such recognition, the return of the administrative rights in the manner prescribed "should not hinder the effective discharge of the international obligations assumed by the United States for the defense of countries in the Far East including Japan."

This language and the additional recognition by Japan, in another part of the communique, that the "security of the Republic of Korea was essential to Japan's own security" and that "the maintenance of peace and security in the Taiwan area was also a most important factor for the security of Japan," made it clear that the United States would not expect a "no" answer in case prior consultation became necessary in the future.

The question of the introduction and stationing of nuclear weapons in Okinawa was handled by indirection: "The Prime Minister described in detail the particular sentiment of the Japanese people against nuclear weapons and the policy of the Japanese Government reflecting such sentiment. The President expressed his deep understanding and assured the Prime Minister that, without prejudice to the position of the United States Government with respect to the prior consultation system under the Treaty of Mutual Cooperation and Security, the reversion of Okinawa would be carried out in a manner consistent with the policy of the Japanese Government as described by the Prime Minister."[2] Sato's critics at once charged that while nuclear weapons might be removed from Okinawa at the time of reversion, Japan thenceforward would have to agree to bring them back whenever the United States so desired.

In his speech to the Washington National Press Club, Sato underscored the point that prior consultation would, after reversion, apply equally to bases in both Japan and the Ryukyus. Speaking of the Japanese bases, he said, ". . . and it would be in accord with our national interest for us to determine our response to prior consultation regarding the use of these facilities and areas in the light of the need to maintain the security of the Far East, including Japan." He went on to say that an armed attack against South Korea would seriously affect the security of Japan and that, in such a case, if the United States wished to use Japanese bases for combat operations to meet the attack, the Japanese Government would decide its position in prior consultation "positively and promptly." He implied that an attack on the Taiwan area would evoke a similar response.

The value of the Okinawan bases rose with the expansion of war in Indochina, and it is not surprising that American military authorities resisted the restrictions on their freedom of action which reversion would bring. It was therefore inevitable that the Sato-Nixon communique should contain a proviso that if peace had not been achieved by 1972, the Japanese and American Governments would then consult, "so that reversion would be accomplished without affecting the United States efforts to assure the South Vietnamese people the opportunity to determine their own political future without outside interference."

Reactions to the Sato-Nixon Agreements

The Japanese press in general welcomed the Sato-Nixon communique, hailing the Prime Minister's diplomatic success in obtaining agreement to the reversion of Okinawa in 1972. Predictably, the opposition was critical.

The Liberal Democratic Party called the Washington meetings a triumph and emphasized that Japan's three objectives had been achieved: (1) reversion in 1972, (2) no nuclear weapons, and (3) bases on the "homeland level." Opposition critics found the wording of the communique deliberately vague, giving rise to contradictory interpretations in Japan and the United States. While the Japanese Government contended that Okinawa would be "nuclear free," the Americans could feel confident that Japan would agree to the reentry of nuclear weapons if the United States invoked prior consultation to meet an emergency. Japan's repeated declarations regarding security were interpreted by opposition elements as proof that Japan would become involved in future Asian wars. The specific references to South Korea, the Taiwan area, and Vietnam strengthened this view.

Several points arose out of Okinawan reversion which were basic to Japan's security policy in the 1970's: (1) the introduction of nuclear weapons; (2) Japan's obligations to the Republic of Korea and the Republic of China on Taiwan; (3) the influence of the Vietnam War on reversion; and (4) the status of the security treaty after reversion, which we have already discussed and to which we shall again refer in later chapters.

Socialists, particularly, hit out at the "policy" on nuclear weapons, which the United States "understood," but which could so easily change in the future. In reply both the Prime Minister and the Foreign Minister repeatedly insisted that the "three non-nuclear principles" (no possession, production, or introduction of nuclear weapons) would be continued and categorically denied that the Government would agree to bringing in nuclear weapons even in time of emergency. When pressed to confirm that the Government would say "no" to an American proposal to introduce nuclear weapons, Foreign Minister Aichi asserted emphatically, "Yes, I mean that." [3]

Aichi was circumspect, however, in discussing the permanency of the present nuclear policy. He limited himself to saying that *the present Cabinet* has no intention of giving up the three non-nuclear principles and quoted a Sato statement that Japan would disapprove bringing in nuclear weapons "as long as an LDP Cabinet is in office." He explained that the fate of the non-nuclear principles after the resignation of the present Cabinet depended on Japan's attitude toward the security treaty. [4]

In spite of these strong statements, the Government's position, as expressed in the communique, certainly suggested a cooperative attitude in an emergency situation, and the communique was so interpreted in Washington. Not without some reason, Ishibashi Masashi, a prominent Socialist member of the House of Representatives and director of the party's International Bureau, took the position that it was illogical for Japan, as an ally of the United States, to refuse cooperation when asked for it through prior consultation.* He commented that it was absurd for officials of the Government to say Japan would never approve the introduction of nuclear weapons and at the same time claim protection under the American "nuclear umbrella." [5]

Korea, Taiwan, and Vietnam

The relating of Japan's security to that of South Korea and Taiwan was a special target of attack. This unprecedented affirmation of a security link with neighboring countries raised the specter of Japan's involvement in war, not only for Socialists and Com-

---

*A representative of the Communist party, speaking in a round table conference of political party leaders, noted that Sato in his Washington statement had promised that Japan would take a "positive" attitude toward prior consultation. He remarked that the English word "positive" had been used to translate the Japanese word *mae-muki* or "forward-looking." "Positive," he said, was much stronger than "forward-looking," being in fact equivalent to "affirmative." *Yomiuri*, Dec. 6, 1969.

munists but even for such middle-of-the-roaders as the Democratic Socialists. Critics professed alarm over inclusion of the "Taiwan area" in the sphere of Japanese security interest, particularly in the face of hostile reactions in Peking. The Foreign Minister defended Japan's concern over tension in the Korean peninsula but went to some pains to differentiate this situation from the less dangerous one in the Taiwan area. He stressed that the milder reference to a security interest in the Taiwan area reflected the strong desire of both Japan and the United States not to antagonize mainland China.

Some opponents of the Government predicted that the agreement to consult if war in Indochina still continued in 1972 could delay reversion indefinitely. Japanese Government spokesmen promptly denied this, and Aichi explained that the United States could hardly assure Japan that the war would indeed be over by 1972. Agreement to consult did not mean postponing return of the islands. "Reversion in 1972," Aichi said, "is an absolute prerequisite."[6]

The American Government undoubtedly expects that Japan's defenses will have strengthened, base transfers will have taken place, and Japanese readiness to cooperate in security measures will have further developed. It would, however, be totally unrealistic to believe that any Japanese Government, unless faced with an unprecedented change in the international situation, could accept any interruption in the determined schedule of reversion.

The use of Okinawan bases by B-52 strategic bombers for missions over Vietnam has been a continuing source of irritation. One recalls the public outcry, the protests, and the official unhappiness in both Japan and Okinawa in late July of 1965 when B-52's, which had moved temporarily from Guam to Okinawa to escape a typhoon, then promptly took off on a bombing mission over Vietnam. Opposition parties in Japan made vigorous representations to the Japanese Government and the American Embassy in Tokyo. Even the Foreign Office, while admitting that operations out of Okinawan bases were completely within American rights and not subject to prior consultation, expressed anxiety because of the raids and their effect on the "people's feelings" (kokumin kanjo).

In early 1968, B-52 bombers were stationed provisionally at Kadena Air Base in Okinawa. Badgered in the Diet by opposition protests, particularly by those who foresaw continued bombing of

Vietnam from Okinawa after 1972, Foreign Minister Aichi tried to quell the clamor by insisting that "regardless of the situation in Vietnam in and after 1972," it would be up to the Japanese Government to prevent the strategic bombers from operating from Okinawa. [7] Fortunately, on September 24, 1970 the American Embassy in Tokyo officially notified the Japanese Foreign Office that the B-52's would be removed from Okinawa in the near future, although they would be returned should the need arise. This decision was welcomed in Japan and Okinawa although, as to be expected, the Left objected to the escape clause, which meant the planes might in emergencies fly again from Okinawan bases.

Opponents of the Japanese Government fear the possible "yes" answer which, they charge, would "Okinawa-ize" Japan (Japanese bases would be like Okinawan bases before reversion) and destroy Sato's non-nuclear principles. But as Kosaka Zentaro, former Foreign Minister and prominent member of the LDP, has aptly remarked, the three nuclear principles are valueless unless considered as inseparable from the nuclear guarantee of the security treaty. [8] In turn, the mutual objectives of peace and security expressed in the treaty and the Sato-Nixon agreements are valid only if prior consultation produces mutual agreement and not a veto.

The Defense of Okinawa

The Prime Minister and the President agreed in Washington that, following reversion, Japan would gradually assume responsibility for the immediate defense of Okinawa. At the same time the United States would, under the security treaty, retain bases in Okinawa "as required in the mutual security of both nations" (Japan and the United States). In other words, the Self-Defense Forces would take over the local defense of the islands while American forces and facilities would be utilized for the maintenance of security in the Far East.

General James B. Lampert, High Commissioner of the Ryukyu Islands, testifying before the Symington subcommittee on security agreements and commitments abroad, gave his concept of the post-reversion Japanese role in the defense of Okinawa:

> The United States shifted defense responsibility to Japan gradually over a course of a number of years and we foresee the same general approach to defense arrangements for Okinawa. This would entail shifting responsibility for air defense, coastal surveillance, sea lane security and internal security to Japanese forces, as is presently the case in Japan. [9]

General Lampert went on to say that the levels and timetable for the introduction of the SDF into the Ryukyus would be the subject of further discussions between the Governments of Japan and the United States.

One official of the Japanese Defense Agency spoke cynically about the assignment of the SDF to "take over the defense of Okinawa," bluntly calling it "meaningless." In his opinion, as expressed to the author, so long as American bases remain in the Ryukyus, any SDF presence would be more symbolic than real. Potential enemies threatening the security of Okinawa would never be deterred by a token Japanese military contingent. The only real guarantee of the defense of the islands would be the American forces stationed on their own bases. The Director General of Defense has estimated that it will require the implementation of both the Fourth and the Fifth Defense Build-up Plans (through 1981) before Japan has "adequate" defenses for her territory, including the Ryukyus.

However realistically one may evaluate the measure of Japanese defense potential to be built up in the Ryukyus, the assignment has added a new incentive for the expansion of Japan's military forces. The extension of Japanese waters to within sight of Taiwan will spur the development of the Maritime Self-Defense Forces. Without violating constitutional limitations, Japanese patrol ships will find large, new acreages of water where they may exert their responsibilities.

The Japan Defense Agency on October 7, 1970 announced the outlines of a first deployment of forces to Okinawa, to be completed within six months after reversion. The published plan called for the assignment of 3,200 men to make up the combined complements from the Ground, Maritime, and Air Forces. These would include: (1) GSDF: a guard unit formed from infantry and engineering troops numbering 1,100 and an aviation unit of four helicopters and one liaison plane; tasks: local defense, public

181

security, response to emergency needs for disaster relief; (2) MSDF: two minesweepers, one landing ship, two landing craft; six P2J anti-submarine patrol planes; total personnel, 700; tasks: submarine warning, security of transportation of necessary materials in times of emergency; (3) ASDF: F104J jet fighters, three F104DJ trainers, and six T33 jet trainers, two MU2 search and rescue planes, and two rescue helicopters, deployed at Naha airport; personnel, about 700. The Defense Agency announced that since the Third Defense Build-up Plan contained no appropriations for stationing SDF units in Okinawa, supplemental funds amounting to approximately $14.4 million would be requested in order to begin preliminary deployment in 1971.[10]

It was understood that Japanese operation of air warning systems, radar networks, and air-to-ground missile systems would be worked out with the American forces and that sea defense responsibilities would be closely coordinated with those of the Seventh Fleet.

The Defense Agency expected that after the deployment following reversion, the SDF contingents in Okinawa would be later augmented, probably to twice the original strength. This would occur during the course of the Fourth Defense Build-up Plan; it was expected, for example, that the F104J jet fighters would be replaced by the newer Phantom jets and that additional ships, radar sites, and anti-aircraft missile installations would be provided.

Effect of SDF Entry into Okinawa

The effect of the entry of the Self-Defense Forces into Okinawa on the military personnel and the base facilities maintained by the United States can only be surmised. In harmony with the trend of Asian policy under the Nixon Doctrine, a phasing down of bases and people appears inevitable. These changes will produce frictions and irritations; base problems will not disappear but will only alter in character. Lay-offs at Okinawa bases have already resulted in strikes, demonstrations, and protests. The United States in 1970 employed about 50,000 Okinawan workers, about 11.7 percent of the total labor force of 428,000.[12] (About half of the 50,000 are United States Government employees; the remainder are employed by American contractors and by American personnel.)

After reversion had been removed as an issue, leftist parties and organizations in the Ryukyus channeled their agitation toward three objectives: (1) removal of all American bases and personnel, (2) cessation of the dismissal of Okinawan base workers, and (3) prevention of the Japanese Self-Defense Forces from taking over the defense of the islands.

The inconsistency of the first and second demands seemed clear to everyone but the agitators themselves. The *Japan Times* of Tokyo in an editorial of October 4, 1970 entitled "Madness in Okinawa" put it bluntly:

> It is not difficult to figure out just what it is that the leftist elements in Okinawa really want. But, then one wonders whether they are in their right mind. The Okinawa leftists and radicals, for instance, have shown themselves capable of screaming for the United States forces to go home and for the American bases to be pulled out while protesting the reduction in the employment of the islanders as a result of the announced cutbacks of the U.S. bases. [13]

General Lampert described a telegram he had received from one of the small labor unions which said, "Put the displaced, the discharged workers back on the payroll and all Americans leave Okinawa." [14] In trying to escape the charge of inconsistency, labor and leftist organizations have been emphasizing their opposition to "rationalization," which they define as the use of fewer workers while maintaining and even strengthening base operations.

The coolness of many Okinawans to the return of Japanese troops to their soil could have been foreseen. They know the modern Self-Defense Forces are not the Imperial Army and Navy of old, but the image in their minds is not a particularly happy one. Besides, the Japanese soldiers and sailors will never be the spenders that the American G.I.'s are, and the merchants who have profited handsomely from the American military presence can look forward to no comparable experiences when their own Japanese defenders come to the islands.

But the leftist elements who resist the coming of the SDF do it on very different grounds. They say that the expansion of the Japanese military forces into the Ryukyus and their plan to replace the Americans or use the bases jointly with them are signs of the "revival of Japanese militarism," which Chou En-lai has described so ominously from Peking. The *Japan Times* gives them short shrift:

... if the presence of the Japanese SDF is going to be a source of irritation and trouble with the Okinawan people, it might have been much better for Japan to have left the situation as it was. ... Sharing in the defense of the Okinawa Islands is, indeed, a responsibility which Japan has shouldered in reaching an agreement with the United States on their reversion. We hope the people there will understand this. ... Those concerned have enough on their hands without the professional agitators trying to interfere with their madness." [15]

As time goes on, pressure will grow, not only from leftist opposition elements but from broader segments of Japanese and Okinawan political life, for continued reductions in the American bases in Okinawa. The Okinawa Problems Study Committee, a group of journalists, professors, and professional men, organized several years ago to promote the return of Okinawan administration to Japan, was reorganized as the "Security Treaty Problems Study Committee" and made its new goal the speedy reduction of American military bases and personnel in Okinawa. In a report submitted after a visit to the Ryukyus, the Committee found that, while there were no signs that the United States intended to augment its strength in Okinawa, neither were there indications of intentions rapidly to reduce the bases. The Committee recognized that a too rapid curtailment and merger of facilities in the Ryukyus would adversely affect the economy, so dependent on American expenditures. Consequently, the Committee recommended expediting negotiations for the partial evacuation of occupied land and the transfer or abandonment of bases. Priorities listed were: (1) over-populated areas not used for direct military purposes, such as oil depots and facilities in Naha city and residential areas for American families; (2) areas needed to serve the Okinawan economy and public welfare, such as Naha airport and Naha port; and (3) facilities needed by the Self-Defense Forces. [16]

The points made by the Committee suggest the kind of pressure which the United States may expect to receive from Japanese official and private sources before and immediately after the date of reversion. Defense Director General Nakasone and other Japanese visitors to Okinawa in late 1970 were profoundly impressed by the size of the American establishment in the Ryukyus. In 1970 it numbered 53,000 military personnel with 30,000 dependents and occupied 75,000 acres—about 26 percent of the land on the main island of Okinawa and 22 percent of the land in the Okinawa group, consisting of the main island and surrounding smaller islands. [17] While it will obviously be in the interest of the United States to reduce personnel and facilities in Okinawa as well as in Japan, the problem will be to synchronize American objectives and desires with those of Japan and hopefully to agree on a calendar of reduction in which the speed and numbers will be successfully coordinated.

Transition

Administration

American and Japanese negotiators face in the period between 1970 and 1972 the task, so long declared "impossible," of working out for the Ryukyus detailed arrangements for the separation of civil administration from military bases. Problems range from traffic to money to property to communications to the minute details of the daily lives of a million people. Should one now drive on the left instead of the right? How can a dollar economy be changed to a yen economy? On what terms will Japan take over the facilities and assets of the United States? Who will have jurisdiction over roads, power, telegraph, and telephones? Where does civilian control end and base control begin? How does one draw the lines of authority when military installations are so intermingled with the private institutions and facilities used by the islanders? These are only a few of the questions to be answered.

To prepare for the transition to Japanese rule, an Advisory Committee representing Japan, the Ryukyus, and the United States, was formed in early 1968 with the task of advancing the "identification" (*ittaika*) of the Okinawans with Japan. Specifically the Committee was to recommend changes which would bring the institutions and procedures established by the American administration into harmony with comparable systems in effect in Japan. Affected were laws, education, taxation, insurance, health services, welfare programs, and other matters concerned with the daily life of the Okinawan people. In 1969 the Advisory Committee was replaced by a Preparatory Commission with more direct responsibility to prepare for the transfer of administrative rights, including the necessary assistance to the Government of the Ryukyu Islands (GRI). [18]

Although no rigid timetable was set, the Japanese hoped that the reversion agreement could be signed by Japan and the United

States and ratified by the Diet and the Senate in 1971, with the actual transfer of administration to occur in early 1972.

Among the problems to be resolved were: (1) a Status of Forces Agreement regulating the American military forces and facilities to be retained in Okinawa after reversion; (2) the conversion of currency from dollars to yen; (3) the transfer of authority over transportation and communications systems, including airways, airports, telephone, telegraph, radio, television, and other facilities; (4) the disposition of American assets in the islands.

The total value of American investments was estimated at three quarters of a billion dollars; these included off-post military roads, some administrative structures, some civil-use navigational and communications aids, and properties of the Ryukyu Domestic Water Corporation (RDWC), Ryukyu Electric Power Corporation (REPC), and the Ryukyu Development Loan Corporation (RDLC). Over the years the United States has built schools, hospitals, and other facilities for the Okinawan people; titles to these properties were given to the GRI or to the municipalities at the time of completion.

The reversion agreement was drafted in the form of a treaty and signed June 17, 1971, simultaneously in Tokyo and Washington. As expected, it provided for the application to Okinawa of the U.S.-Japan security treaty and its related arrangements and for retention by the United States of bases in the islands. Japan was to pay compensation for American assets in the amount of $320 million.

Of particular interest to Americans will be the treatment of foreign private investments and business after reversion. Authorized American private investments in Okinawa in 1970 amounted to $271.9 million. The actual investment was less than the amounts authorized, since several investors, including the Aluminum Company of America (ALCOA) and the oil companies, had either not commenced or completed their construction by the end of 1970. The actual American investments therefore totaled only $102 million at that time.

American businessmen are understandably concerned about their treatment after reversion. The United States succeeded in including in the joint communique a reference to the financial and economic problems arising from American business interests in Okinawa and a promise of detailed and prompt discussions relative to their solution.[19] Worries of the American businessmen are concerned with the application of tax laws, licensing regulations, work permit practices, the protection of real estate leases, imposition of restrictive duties and quotas, and possible currency restrictions.

Economy

The economy of the Ryukyus has advanced rapidly in the postwar period, spurred largely by the expenditures of American military forces. In prewar years, Okinawans' per capita annual income was well below that of all prefectures in the main Japanese islands. In 1965, at $344, it exceeded that of at least three Japanese prefectures, Kagoshima, Miyazaki, and Tottori, and was more than twice that of Taiwan and the Phillippine Islands. By 1969 per capita income had almost doubled, to $653. Gross national product more than quadrupled between 1959 and 1969, from $177 million to $727 million.

During the ten years from 1958 through 1968, the annual growth rate for Okinawa in real terms averaged over 12 percent, one of the highest in the world. On a per capita basis, the rate of growth was about 10 percent, which is near Japan's 10.3 percent during the same ten-year period.[20]

The total United States input into the Ryukyus, including the expenditures of government agencies and personnel, aid programs, private investments, and exports from Okinawa to the United States, amounted in 1967 to $257 million, almost 50 percent of the GNP at that time. Since 1967 a slackening in construction and other outlays for military purposes has brought down the percentage of GNP originating from strictly base costs. Still, total American expenditures were $258.6 million in 1968 and rose to $271.2 million in 1969, representing about 37 percent of the GNP.[21]

American economic assistance to the Ryukyus originates from two sources, appropriations of the United States Congress, now limited by the Price Act to $17.5 million, and the USCAR General Fund. For FY 1969 the former amounted to $15.6 million and, as stated, $17.5 million for FY 1970. The General Fund embraces income from the sale of petroleum products, earnings from the three public corporations (loans, power, and water), plus interest and dividends. This fund totalled $16.6 million in 1969 and was projected at $17.1 million for FY 1970.[22]

Japanese Government aid increased rapidly during the last few

187

years, more than doubling between 1968 and 1970. The total planned for FY 1970 was over $63 million; $97 million was forecast for FY 1971.[23] Statistics for Japanese and American aid appear in Table 8-1.

After reversion Okinawa will receive direct government subsidies, just as any prefecture. It has been estimated that if Okinawa had enjoyed this status in 1968, the central government subsidies would have been about 50 percent above the official economic aid which Tokyo gave to the GRI in that year. A Tax Study Commission has concluded that when the Japanese tax system is put into effect in Okinawa, most taxes will rise but income taxes alone will decrease. In any case, Okinawa can expect payments from the national treasury well in excess of the amounts required to be paid as national taxes, although in terms of the total Japanese budget the additional obligations for Okinawa will probably not be great.

Most calculations for future economic development of the Ryukyus are based on the assumption that American military bases will be retained for the foreseeable future. If so, continued growth is a reasonable expectation. However, barring a fresh Asian crisis, the implications of the Nixon Doctrine as well as political forces active in Japan suggest a steady and continuing retrenchment in American military facilities and personnel. The future economic viability of the Ryukyus thus becomes a question of urgency, primarily for Japan, but also for the United States. Economic and political stability are interrelated, and they can determine the use and effectiveness of bases which the United States will retain.

Numerous studies of the Okinawan economy have been made, and numerous recommendations formulated. One of the most recent and thorough reports was done jointly in 1968 by two economic and engineering consulting firms, one American and one Japanese. The report pinpointed the most crucial element in economic development as a sharp increase in the exports of goods and services. It estimated that to maintain an annual increase in per capita real income of 7 or 8 percent, exports would have to reach $406 million by 1977.[24] Since in each of the two years 1968 and 1969, Okinawan exports were only about $89 million (Table 8-1), they would have to more than quadruple in eight years to meet this goal. Although imports decreased by a million dollars from 1968 to 1969, they were almost four times greater than exports: $378.1 million.[25] This gap will not be easily closed. More than half

188

Table 8-1

Okinawa Statistics

1. Gross National Product (in millions of dollars)

1955 -	$ 131.3	1966 -	$ 436.9
1960 -	199.0	1967 -	521.7
1965 -	373.0	1968 -	641.9
	1969 - $ 727.1		

2. Per capita national income

1955 -	$ 149	1966 -	$ 424
1960 -	202	1967 -	497
1965 -	366	1968 -	578
	1969 - $ 653		

3. Per capita natl. income compared to Taiwan, Philippines, Japan

	Ryukyus	Taiwan	P.I.	Japan
1965	$402	$223	$161	$861
1968	578	237		

4. Foreign Trade (in millions of dollars)

FY	Exports	Imports
1967	81.2	347.3
1968	89.4	379.2
1969	89.8	378.1

5. U.S. Government aid (appropriated) (in thousands of dollars)

1964 -	$ 7,859	1967 -	$ 11,994
1965 -	11,993	1968 -	11,974
1966 -	11,997	1969 -	18,910
	1970 - $ 17,500		

6. Japanese Government aid (in thousands of dollars)

1964 -	$ 5,208	1967 -	$ 25,800
1965 -	7,964	1968 -	28,758
1966 -	16,114	1969 -	42,714
	1970 - $ 63,192		

Sources: USCAR, *Facts Book, FY 1967;* USCAR, *Report for Period 1 July 1968 to 30 June 1969;* DMJM, Japan Economic and Engineering Consultants, *Economic Development Study Ryukyu Islands,* March, 1968.

of Okinawa's exports are sugar products, subsidized by the Japanese Government. Only a sudden and dramatic upsurge in exports—which did not appear on the horizon as 1970 ended—could bring the needed boost to the islands' economy.

The report recommended, in addition, an active search for foreign investment, the encouragement of new industries, and revolutionary improvements in agricultural productivity. Sectors which promised most increases in export earnings were identified as manufacturing, tourism, and the livestock industry. [26] The question as to how much would be done to achieve these needed results remained unanswered as reversion approached.

Oil and Okinawa

The position of American oil companies in post-reversion Okinawa has been one of the most lively and controversial of the issues facing the United States and Japan in preparing for the transfer of administration in 1972. The American oil companies began to file applications for foreign investment licenses as early as 1967. In February of 1969 a ten-year contract was entered into with ESSO Standard which included the supply of fuel oil to the Ryukyu Electric Power Corporation and the construction by April 1972 of a refinery in Okinawa with a daily production capacity of 80,000 barrels which could supply oil products called for in the contract. In addition to ESSO, the Gulf Oil and Caltex Companies were granted licenses by the Government of the Ryukyu Islands and planned to build refineries in Okinawa.

After the date of reversion had been set for 1972 by President Nixon and Prime Minister Sato, officials of the Japanese Ministry of International Trade and Industry (MITI) began to express apprehension over an American oil "rush-in" in Okinawa. The basic policy of MITI was that (1) no new foreign capital in the oil industry would be permitted and (2) in no case would a joint venture including more than 50 percent foreign capital be approved.

The American oil companies, recognizing the difficulties they would face once the Ryukyus came under Japanese control, have shown a readiness to work out joint arrangements with Japanese companies which would save their investments. Caltex and the Toyo Oil Refining Company are reported to have reached an agreement; and should other arrangements be successfully completed, the refineries originally planned by the three American companies will be built, but in partnership with Japanese oil concerns.

The Senkaku Islands

For some time rumors circulated that rich oil resources lay beneath the East China Sea, especially in the vicinity of the Senkaku Islands, part of the Ryukyu chain. In 1968 an oceanographic research vessel, operating under the joint auspices of the United States Naval Oceanographic Office and a committee formed by the United Nations Economic Commission for Asia and the Far East (ECAFE), carried out investigations near the Senkakus; and in 1969 a Japanese survey mission reported to Prime Minister Sato the results of soundings made in the same area.

Survey reports indicated that the region was underlain by a series of ridges which trapped sediments from the drainage of the Yellow and Yangtse rivers in China. The report made to the Prime Minister by the Japanese team was apparently optimistic, stating that the area north of the Senkaku Islands could be an important source of oil for Japan, that it was "extremely promising." [27] Published comments in news dispatches were more enthusiastic: ". . . the region may prove to be one of the world's major off-shore oil fields" . . . "oil deposits which could radically tilt the balance of power in Asia" . . . "unless the oceanographers have made the error of the century, a vast new source of oil will be trapped." [28]

The Senkakus, eight tiny, uninhabited bits of land with a total area of 4.2 square miles, are found in the East China Sea 118 miles northeast of Taiwan and about the same distance north of Ishigaki Island, in the Yaeyama group of the Ryukyus, of which they have been considered a part. Ignored for centuries, their history has suddenly become important. The Japanese Government maintains that the Senkaku group is unmistakeably a part of the Ryukyus, claiming they appear as such on a map published in 1881, two years after Japan annexed the Ryukyu Islands. However, other later maps, some as recent as 1924, have been cited as failing to make any mention of the Senkakus as part of the Ryukyus.

The Republic of China on Taiwan has shown interest in possible oil deposits on the continental shelf near the Senkakus. Chinese scholars are reported to have found mention of the islands in books as early as 1534, when the Kings of the Ryukyus were paying tribute to the Ming Emperors. The ROC Government did not officially claim sovereignty over them, although a Nationalist Chinese flag was raised on the islands in mid-September 1970 and very promptly and hastily removed by Okinawan authorities. According to published reports, the Taiwan Government gave contracts to several American oil companies, including the Pacific Gulf Company, a subsidiary of the American Gulf Oil Corporation, for oil exploration rights in the waters over the continental shelf in the East China Sea, which would include the Senkaku Islands. [29]

The Japanese Government took the position that the question of the legal possession of the Senkaku Islands, now under American administration and to revert to Japan in 1972, was separate from that of the continental shelf, which is subject to international discussion. The Government was prepared to discuss the rights over the continental shelf with both the Republic of China and the Republic of Korea, also interested. The United States Department of State affirmed on September 10, 1970 that the Senkaku Islands were part of the Ryukyus, administered by the United States under authority of the peace treaty with Japan, that Japan enjoyed residual sovereignty over the Ryukyus and was due to assume the administrative rights over them in 1972. A Department spokesman asserted that conflicting claims over the sovereignty of the Senkaku Islands would be a matter for resolution by the parties concerned. The Japanese were disappointed by this latter phraseology, which left the question of final ownership of the islands still undecided. [30]

The international complications surrounding the future of the Senkaku Islands in the center of a possible oil-rich area can be surmised. The Governments of Japan and of the Republics of China and Korea, all of which have claims over the continental shelf, have shown readiness to work out joint understandings. Communist China broke its silence on this subject in early December 1970 with a strong assertion of sovereignty over the islands, as part of Taiwan and therefore part of mainland China. The Peking press agency, *Hsinhua*, accused the Japanese, South Koreans, and Nationalist Chinese of plotting aggression with the support of American imperialism and said their plan of joint development meant to "surrender their sovereignty and let Japanese militarism plunder and occupy the islands and resources as well."[31]

As 1972 approaches with Japanese administration of the Ryukyus becoming a fact in that year, the dispute over the Senkaku Islands and the nearby continental shelf has ominous potentialities. Involving both mainland China and Taiwan, as well as South Korea, Japan, and the United States (our bases will still be in Okinawa), Senkaku could become a crisis of the 1970's.

The Japanese Future of Okinawa

Once return to the homeland had been decided, the thoughts of many Okinawans turned to the future and the great changes which their new status under Japanese rule would bring. Memories of suffered slights revived. Older citizens recalled the discriminations of prewar days. Younger Okinawans thought of snubs received as students in Japan, where they were made to feel, if unsuccessful in hiding their origin, that being Okinawan was different from being Japanese.

Okinawan employees of the United States Government worried about job security, and Okinawan businessmen whose trade has depended on American customers saw reversion as a threat to their livelihood. In the summer of 1969, a group of Okinawan businessmen tried to put a full-page advertisement in the three leading Tokyo dailies pleading for "postponement of reversion until 1980." No newspaper would accept the advertisement.

Conservative Okinawans were dissatisfied with the "progressive" government symbolized by the elected Chief Executive; they worried over its policies and actions as well as over the leftist influence which they feared would more freely enter from Japan once the administrative control of the United States was removed.

Fears of increasing leftist influence in Okinawa may not be unjustified. The strong showing made by the Socialist and Communist-oriented parties in the first elections held in postwar Okinawa for Diet seats on November 15, 1970, in which these parties elected three out of five candidates of the lower house and one out of two for the upper house, suggests a possible trend. The firm position which Yara Chobyo has achieved as Chief Executive and the growing uneasiness over future Japanese policies in the islands (dispatch of the Self-Defense Forces, lack of concern for Okinawan interests, and the return to treatment as a mere "prefecture") coupled with the economic uncertainties ahead could well substantially encourage and benefit the future successes of the parties of the Left.

Some Okinawans are indeed pessimistic about how vigorously Japan will work for the interests of the people of the Ryukyus once reversion is a fact. They fear the Japanese Government will lose interest and that private Japanese industry will find little incentive to develop the islands. They are well aware of Okinawa's handicaps: lack of a good water supply, low productivity of labor, and costs higher than Japan for both water and electric power. Okinawan average industrial wages may be lower than in Japan ($98 per month as compared to $125) but they are higher than in Taiwan, and a Japanese industrialist calculating his profits may well without compunction skip Okinawa and build his factory in Taiwan.

The key to Okinawa's economic future is industry. Much will depend on whether Japanese companies decide to establish factories in Okinawa, thus creating the needed employment opportunities and export industries. Both the Japanese Government and private industry have sponsored research groups to investigate the opportunities and possibilities for the economic development of Okinawa. Some conclusions are more hopeful than had been expected. For example, land reclamation can provide good industrial sites, and the labor supply is plentiful; export industries for South Asia would be nearer their markets.

Some Okinawans have great hope for tourism, which at present brings in $30 million a year. The Ryukyus can indeed boast of tropical island scenery, stretches of smooth, white beaches, and a warm, alluring climate, marred only by typhoons at certain times of the year. As tourist travel in the Pacific area grows, especially from Japan, Okinawa could win a greater share. The President of the Tourism Development Corporation in Naha believes that, with Japanese and American help, tourist revenues could be increased to $100 million by 1973. This is an optimistic prediction. Tourists demand more than sun, sea, and sand, and before Okinawa can be transformed into another Hawaii, hotels, swimming pools, roads, airports, and golf courses must be added to the gifts of nature.

The Japanese Government has announced plans to promote the

establishment of industries in Okinawa, and the Ministry of International Trade and Industry has published a draft law which would accord certain benefits and exemptions designed to encourage Japanese industries going into the islands, help the local economy, and benefit the small and medium-sized industries existing in the Ryukyus. Although in mid-1969 Japanese investments approved by the GRI amounted to only $8.8 million, additional applications were submitted subsequently, the most important being from the Japan Light Metal Company, Ltd., consisting of five aluminum companies. Furthermore, during 1970 many Japanese nationals acquired interests in Okinawan firms; these ranged from 20 percent to 50 percent of the capital of the concern. In other cases, Japanese became directors and managers in ostensibly Ryukyuan companies. This type of penetration exceeded the other formal so-called "foreign" investments by Japanese.

If American investors should find the Okinawan market a contracting one and Japanese regulations too onerous, if Japanese industrialists fail to enter the islands to build power plants, factories, and ports, if tourism does not flourish, then Okinawa must again depend on its sugarcane and pineapple and must again export its people. Okinawans look apprehensively at the example of Amami-Oshima, north of the present Ryukyus, which the United States returned to Japan in 1953 and which in ten years lost 80,000 of their 250,000 people and lapsed into a sleepy, forgotten backwater.

In any case, it seems inevitable that a substantial migration of labor to the main Japanese islands from the Ryukyus will take place. Already, with reversion in sight, the recruiters for private companies have been competing frantically with each other for employees to relieve the acute labor shortage in Japan. Newpapers described a "mad rush" to sign up middle school and high school students ahead of graduation. The Labor Department of the Ryukyu Government, which limited visits of recruiters to the months of June through September, stated that during this period in 1970, from 1400 to 1500 companies sent representatives to hire young men. The numbers of youths leaving the Ryukyus to take jobs in Japan Proper increased markedly in recent years, from 4,747 in 1968 to 8,272 in 1969 to nearly 10,000 (9,927) in the nine months through September 1970. [32] Many observers believe this stream will continue to grow, as young Okinawans ponder their own job prospects and the uncertain economic future of their islands. At the same time, one hears of disillusioned young workers who found, as did their compatriots before the war, that discrimination against them had not disappeared and who, after a try in Japan, decided to return to their native Okinawan homeland.

Perhaps Japan will not allow Okinawa to become a forgotten backwater. In spite of its return as a prefecture, Okinawa can never be a Kagoshima or a Miyazaki. Japan lived only seven years under American occupation; by 1972 the Okinawans will have known twenty-seven years of all-embracing, ever-present American administration. As an Okinawan professor remarked to the author, "We cannot go back to being the bottom prefecture. Twenty-five years of American influence have changed us. We can never be the same again." For better or for worse, the Okinawans have been treated as the inhabitants of a foreign country. They have spent American dollar bills. They have travelled to their own motherland as foreigners, with passports and permits. Their ships have flown a special "Okinawan" flag. In spite of General Caraway's "myth" of autonomy, the GRI enjoyed much autonomy. Its Chief Executive was treated as a head of State. The unique traditions, history, and culture of Okinawa were revived and respected under American rule as they never were under the Japanese. In spite of his conviction and feeling that he is Japanese, the Okinawan is also conscious of his own separate identity, which is something not to hide or suppress but to cherish with pride.

The Okinawan consciousness will become stronger as the islanders contemplate the return to Japan which they have wished for so long. As Nishime Jinji said in his victory statement after election as an Okinawan Liberal Democrat to the Japanese Diet in November 1970: "Okinawa representatives in the Japanese Parliament should stand together whatever their party affiliations and make sure that there would be no betrayal of the islanders' interests once the Ryukyu chain has again come under Japanese rule." [33]

Notes

1. For the text of the communique, see *New York Times*, November 22, 1969, p. 14.

2. *Ibid.*

3. *Yomiuri,* December 5, 1969.

4. *Ibid.*

5. *Yomiuri,* December 8, 1969.

6. *Yomiuri,* December 7, 1969.

7. *Ibid.*

8. *Yomiuri,* December 10, 1969.

9. U.S., Congress, Senate, Committee on Foreign Relations, *United States Security Agreements and Commitments Abroad, Japan and Okinawa,* Hearings before the Subcommittee on United States Security Agreements and Commitments Abroad, 91st Cong., 2nd session. Part 5, January 26, 27, 28, and 29, 1970, p. 1294. Hereafter referred to as For. Rel. Subcommittee Hearings.

10. *Asahi,* October 8, 1970.

11. *Ibid.*

12. Source: United States Civil Administration of the Ryukyu Islands (USCAR).

13. *The Japan Times,* October 6, 1970.

14. For. Rel. Subcommittee Hearings, *op. cit.,* p. 1303.

15. *The Japan Times,* October 6, 1970.

16. The Security Treaty Problems Study Committee, "Suggestion on the Negotiation of Reversion based on the Investigation in Okinawa," October 17, 1970.

17. For. Rel. Subcommittee Hearings, *op. cit.,* pp. 1296-97.

18. Joint communique, para. 10, *New York Times,* November 22, 1969.

19. *Ibid.,* para. 9.

20. Sources for statistics and estimates, unless otherwise identified, are State Department and USCAR.

21. USCAR, *Report for Period 1 July 1968 to 30 June 1969,* Vol. XVII, pp. 45 and 313. Hereafter referred to as USCAR, *Report 1968-1969.*

22. *Ibid.,* pp. 49-50.

23. *Ibid.,* p. 51.

24. Daniel, Mann, Johnson, and Mendenhall and Japan Economic and Engineering Consultants, Ltd., *Economic Development Study Ryukyu Islands,* A Study con-

ducted for the Joint USCAR / GRI Committee on Economic Development, March 1968, p. 234. (Hereafter referred to as DMJM Report).

25. USCAR, *Report 1968-1969, op. cit., pp. 73-76.*

26. DMJM Report, *op. cit.,* pp. 233-35.

27. *Nihon Keizai,* August 8, 1970.

28. "Oil Resources in Senkaku Are Promising," AP despatch datelined Tokyo in *Daily Star,* Beirut, Lebanon, August 29, 1969; "Oceanographers Discover Huge Oil Deposits in Yellow Sea," despatch datelined Hongkong, in *Daily Star*, Beirut, November 5, 1969.

29. *Nihon Keizai,* August 8, 1970; *Japan Times*, October 22, 1970.

30. *Mainichi*, September 18, 1970.

31. Tillman Durdin, "Peking Claim Disputed Oil-Rich Isles," *New York Times,* December 6, 1970.

32. *Asahi,* October 5, 1970.

33. *New York Times*, November 17, 1970.

Part 3

Relations in East Asia

9 The Communist Neighbors: China

Japan and East and Southeast Asia

"East Asia," in which Japan is destined to play an increasingly important role, embraces those countries that form an arc around the western edge of the Pacific Ocean, on the rim of the mainland and on the adjacent islands. The arc begins in Alaska, follows the coast of Asian Russia, including the Kamchatka Peninsula and the island of Sakhalin. Southward, the countries are mainland China, North and South Korea, and the islands of Japan, the Ryukyus, and Taiwan. Southeast Asia consists of the Philippine Islands, the mainland nations of North and South Vietnam, Cambodia, Laos, Thailand, Singapore, and Malaysia, and the great Indonesian archipelago.

Both superpowers, the United States and the Soviet Union, are very much involved in this East and Southeast Asian region. In the words of a contemporary Japanese writer, the Asian problem is "structurally interwoven in the central power balance of the world."

Australia and New Zealand are not included in this group of countries, because their identity and interests thus far have set them apart from the Asian nations in the area. This is not to suggest that Australia and New Zealand do not figure prominently in the region. Australia's trade with Japan is substantial, and Canberra's likely assumption of increasing defense responsibilities, especially to supplement decreased British forces in Singapore, will become a prominent factor in the politics of the area. Australia and New Zealand, as developed countries, form part of the so-called Pacific Basin Community, and their economic interests are common with those of the other advanced nations of the Pacific region who naturally fall into this grouping: Japan, Canada, and the United States.

Burma is usually included in Southeast Asia, but its presence has hardly been felt politically. From the vantage point of Japan, Burma is somewhat remote, and its closed society has prohibited an active foreign policy for participation in regional arrangements and activities. In trade as well, Japan's relations with Burma are miniscule in comparison with those of other nations of the area.

Even more remote are India and Pakistan. The relations of these countries with Japan are important in their own right, but they do not bear directly on the political, military, and economic problems of East Asia.

Japan's trade and investments are now global. A principal thrust of Japanese foreign policy is to seek sources of essential raw materials wherever they may be found and to diversify markets for exports. Japan is, therefore, not economically dependent upon East Asia—this notwithstanding the fact that a substantial percentage of her foreign trade is carried on with the countries of the region. According to estimates, by 1980 half of the trade of the Southeast Asian nations will be carried on with Japan.

While Japan's economic interests are world wide, they focus politically on East and Southeast Asia. As a leading world power, Japan will not remain content with a purely economic role, and it is natural that Japanese leaders should also contemplate the extension of political influence. Yet, political strategy must cater to security interests, and for Japan security is a function of relations with the two Communist powers, mainland China and the Soviet Union, and secondarily, with its near neighbors, Korea and Taiwan.

The "China Problem"

A well known Japanese writer on international affairs, Royama Michio, has labeled the "problem of China" a "political obsession of the Japanese."[1]   The obsession issues from a sense of guilt over Japanese aggression committed in war, the desire to restore full relations with mainland China while continuing to recognize and support Taiwan, and the frustrations resulting from the contradictions in these latter policies. Japanese apprehensions over the military stance of Communist China and the lack of popular enthusiasm among Japanese for Chinese are counterpointed by the legacy of historical and cultural ties with China, the natural

204

Japanese desire for trade in an enormous market, and the urge to be on good terms with the next-door neighbor of long standing.

The first postwar event that spotlighted relations between Japan and Communist China was the "treaty of friendship, alliance and mutual assistance between the People's Republic of China and the Union of Soviet Socialist Republics," signed on February 14, 1950. The principal object of the treaty, as set forth in Article I, was to prevent "the resumption of aggression and violation of peace on the part of Japan or any other state that may collaborate with Japan directly or indirectly in acts of aggression." The treaty provided that if either party were attacked by Japan, the other would immediately give "military and other assistance by all means at its disposal."[2]

The treaty was signed at a time when Japan was completely disarmed and still under allied occupation. Under the circumstances, the Soviet Union and Communist China could scarcely have felt seriously threatened by Japanese aggression. The true target of the treaty obviously was not Japan but the United States, then ensconced militarily in Japan and the Ryukyu Islands.

In actuality, Japan's postwar "China problem" dates from the San Francisco peace conference of September 1951. Since neither Communist China nor Nationalist China was at the conference or signed the peace treaty, the Government of Japan was to be free to formulate its own China policy after regaining sovereignty under the treaty. Indeed, as early as June of 1951, John Foster Dulles and Herbert Morrison, then Foreign Secretary of Great Britain, had agreed that "Japan's future attitude toward China must necessarily be for determination by Japan itself in the exercise of the sovereignty and independent status contemplated by the Treaty."[3] Consequently, Foreign Minister Yoshida expected that his Government would have ample time to consider the matter and that the choice would be neither hurried nor forced. However, he did not reckon with sentiment in the United States, particularly as reflected in the Congress.

The Communists had conquered China less than two years before, and the anger and frustration among Americans were still fresh and deep. In the Senate, which would have to ratify the peace treaty, opinion was swinging to the notion that Japan should recognize the government on Taiwan. Fifty-six senators, a majority, wrote to President Truman threatening to withhold ratification if this choice were not made: "Prior to the submission of the Japanese Treaty to the Senate, we desire to make it clear that we would consider the recognition of Communist China by Japan or the negotiating of a bilateral treaty with the Communist Chinese regime to be adverse to the best interests of the people of both Japan and the United States."[4]

To make sure that the point would register with the Japanese, Dulles traveled to Tokyo with two members of the Senate Foreign Relations Committee, and their conversations left no doubt about the American position. The Japanese Government saw quickly that a peace treaty and an end to the Occupation depended upon Japanese recognition of Nationalist China. On December 24 Yoshida wrote Dulles that Japan wanted peace and trade with mainland China but that he would negotiate a treaty with the government on Taiwan, applicable however only to territories then or thereafter controlled by the National Government of the Republic of China. Subsequently, in accordance with Yoshida's letter, the Japanese Government negotiated and signed a treaty of peace with Nationalist China.

Although Chiang Kai-shek's efforts to be recognized as the government of all of China were resisted and Yoshida's restrictive language was inserted in the treaty, Japan became bound diplomatically and politically to the Republic of China on Taiwan. Yoshida's references to mainland China did, however, define the ultimate aims of Japanese policy, upheld consistently by every succeeding Government: "The Japanese Government desires ultimately to have a full measure of political peace and commerical intercourse with China, which is Japan's close neighbor."[5]

Japan pursued her China policy as a delicate and hazardous balancing act, trying to develop trade and travel with the mainland and at the same time keeping reasonably stable diplomatic relations with the Nationalists in order to take full advantage of economic opportunities on Taiwan. The course has not been smooth: Peking suddenly stopped trade in 1958, and Taipei almost broke relations in 1963. Japan proclaimed a policy of "separation of politics and economics," which, although repeatedly and vehemently rejected by Communist China, has in fact worked. Despite sporadic invective, disruption, and retaliation, Japanese trade with both Taiwan and the mainland has continued, Japan has probably enjoyed more contacts with the Chinese mainland than any other non-Communist nation, and policy toward the Chiang Kai-shek Government has been consistent and unchanged.

Economic Relations

China and Japan are the two great East Asian powers, but the disparity between them is enormous. China has seven and a half times as many people as does Japan but a GNP only two-fifths as large. [6] Japan's economy is so far ahead of China's that there seems little chance of closing the gap in the foreseeable future. All statistics for China are guesses, but expert observers conclude that in 1970 the national economy might have just inched ahead of the 1966 level after the disruption of the Cultural Revolution. Annual per capita income in China was estimated at about $100, whereas Japan's is $1500. Japanese economic growth was projected at 12.4 percent for the period 1970-1975, but a rapid growth rate in China seemed doubtful. [7]

Foreign trade has never loomed large in China's economy, notwithstanding the fact that it has been crucial in obtaining materials for Chinese industrialization and during famine periods, desperately needed food supplies. Exports and imports together have constituted roughly 3 to 5 percent of the Chinese GNP, although totals have risen in recent years. According to Japanese estimates, Chinese trade reached a peak of $4.3 billion in 1966, then declined in the next two years, rising to $3.8 million in 1969—not yet up to the 1966 figure but a 7 percent increase over 1968. [8] China's total foreign trade in 1969 was less than Japan's exports to the United States alone during that year.

The direction of Chinese trade shifted away from the Communist countries in the 1960's, due in large part to the Sino-Soviet conflict. China's principal trading partners became, first, Japan, then Hong Kong, Australia, Canada, and Germany.

Trade

Trade between Japan and Communist China was under way even before the Communists had proclaimed themselves masters of China on October 1, 1949. In August of that year a Chinese mission had traveled to Japan to buy railway equipment. In early 1950 the Japanese House of Councillors passed a resolution urging trade with the mainland. Trade totalled $59 million in 1950, but was cut back sharply by the Korean war, which stimulated stiffer Occupation controls and allied restrictions on exports of strategic commodities. Not until 1954 did Japanese-Chinese trade climb back to approximately $60 million (See Table 9-1).

In the period between 1955 and mid-1958, Japanese trade with the PRC improved markedly. In October of 1954 Moscow and Peking jointly declared their readiness to open normal relations with Japan. Hatoyama Ichiro, who succeeded Yoshida as Prime Minister at the end of 1954, announced a policy of normalizing relations with the two Communist neighbors, which he set about to accomplish as quickly as possible. In 1955 the first official Chinese trade mission visited Japan and Japanese trading companies began doing business with the Chinese; the first China Fair was held in Tokyo and Osaka in 1955, and a Japan Fair took place in China the next year. Trade suddenly jumped beyond the $100 million figure to a peak of over $150 million in 1956.

The accession of 1957 of Kishi Nobusuke as Prime Minister changed the nature of relations with the mainland. Kishi, who had served in Tojo's war cabinet, was trying to establish himself as pro-American and pro-Asian. Pursuing his "Asian" policy, he visited Taiwan in the course of a tour of Southeast Asia, but he also attempted to improve relations with the PRC. Later, to placate Taiwan while arranging a trading agreement with Peking, Kishi sent a friendly personal message to Chiang Kai-shek. This provoked Peking to turn its propaganda barrage against Kishi and accuse him of disrupting China-Japan trade.

The climax came in early May of 1958, when a Japanese youth tore down a Communist Chinese flag from an exhibit of Chinese goods being held in Nagasaki. This was pretext enough. Japanese companies were notified by Peking that all commercial transactions between the two countries were suspended. The real Chinese motivations were undoubtedly irritation at Kishi for his attitude toward Taiwan, hopes that Kishi's position could be undermined (elections were due), and the desire to influence Japanese businessmen against the Kishi government. If these were the expectations, the move backfired. Japanese saw it as intervention in their internal affairs, and Kishi's Liberal Democratic

Table 9-1

Japan's Trade with Communist China (in thousands of U.S. dollars)

	Exports to China	Imports from China	Total Trade
1950	19,632	39,328	58,960
1951	5,828	21,606	27,434
1952	599	14,903	15,502
1953	4,539	29,700	34,239
1954	19,097	40,770	59,867
1955	28,947	80,778	109,725
1956	67,339	83,647	150,986
1957	60,485	80,483	140,968
1958	50,600	54,427	105,027
1959	3,648	18,917	22,565
1960	2,726	20,729	23,455
1961	16,639	30,895	47,534
1962	38,460	46,020	84,480
1963	62,969	74,567	137,536
1964	152,739	157,750	310,489
1965	245,036	224,705	469,741
1966	315,150	306,237	621,387
1967	288,294	269,439	557,733
1968	325,439	224,185	549,624
1969	391,100	234,500	625,600
1970	571,708	253,769	825,577

Sources: A. M. Halpern, ed., *Policies Toward China: Views from Six Continents* (New York, Toronto, London: McGraw-Hill Book Company, 1965), p. 138; Tsusho Sangyo-sho (Ministry of International Trade and Industry), *Tsusho Hakusho* (Foreign Trade White Paper) *Kakuron* (detailed), 1968 (Tokyo: MITI, July 10, 1968), p. 616; *Ibid.,* 1970 (Tokyo: MITI, July 10, 1970), p. 659. Totals for 1970 are Japanese Government preliminary figures.

Party won the election handsomely. Japanese exports to China plummeted from $50 million in 1958 to less than $4 million in 1959 and to a new low of less than $3 million in 1960.

In 1960 Peking signaled a willingness to resume trading

relations. Prime Minister Chou En-lai proposed trade by direct agreements, private contracts, and special arrangements. This procedure has continued; it provides for trade through certain designated Japanese "friendly firms" and by "Memorandum Agreement." The first of the memorandum agreements was signed in Peking in 1962 by Liao Cheng-chih, President of the China-Japan Friendship Association, and by Takasaki Tatsunosuke, a former Minister of Internation Trade and Industry and a venerable member of the LDP. Trade under this agreement, which was to last for five years, was known as L-T (Liao-Takasaki) Memorandum Trade. After 1967 the "L-T" designation was dropped because of Takasaki's death.

"Friendly firms" were Japanese companies designated either by Peking or on the recommendation of leftist parties and groups in Japan. "Friendly firm" trade has always exceeded that under the L-T agreement, with the proportion growing in recent years. For example, in 1964 "friendly firms" carried on 58.6 percent of the trade; in 1967 this percentage had risen to 72 percent, and in 1969 to as much as 90 percent. [9] The explanation was the growing Chinese hostility to the Sato government and the increasing difficulties of negotiating the annual trade agreements.

In 1960 Chou En-lai announced the three political principles controlling trade with Japan which have been repeated in succeeding years: (1) the Japanese Government must not be hostile to China, since the Chinese Government is not hostile to Japan; (2) the Japanese Government must not support the "two Chinas plot"; and (3) the Japanese Government must not obstruct the normalization of Sino-Japanese relations. On the Japanese side, succeeding governments have consistently supported the principle of "separation of politics and economics"; hence, all negotiations carried on with Peking are, for Japan, private, and no members of the executive departments of government participate in them. (Usually the delegation consists of LDP Diet members of the pro-Peking faction).

PRC officials reject the Japanese thesis and repeat frequently that politics and economics cannot be separated. This difference of approach, however, has not hindered the negotiation of successive agreements. The Japanese negotiators are prepared to tolerate extensive political harangues from the Chinese at each meeting, and the discussions and communiques have become more political in content with each successive occasion. In fact, of course, the Japanese Government very closely monitors the negotiations, and trade with mainland China is conducted as a matter of official policy.

Events more political than economic have continued to plague Sino-Japanese trade. One occurred in 1963, when the Kurashiki Rayon Company sold a $20-million vinylon plant to China on a five year deferred payment plan. The President of the company, Ohara Soichiro, euphemistically justified the sale as putting clothes on the backs of poor Chinese and thus atoning in a small way for the atrocities Japanese soldiers had committed in China during the war. Unfortunately the plant sale coincided with the widely publicized repatriation by the Japanese Government of a Chinese citizen who had defected from the Communists and then changed his mind. Incensed by both these events, the Taipei Government threatened to break relations and, indeed, recalled from Tokyo its Ambassador and most of his senior staff. To reassure Chiang Kai-shek, former Prime Minister Yoshida hurriedly visited Taiwan and wrote another "Yoshida letter," which promised that trade with Communist China would not be financed by the Government's Export-Import Bank. Yoshida held no official position, and his letter was no more than a personal communication; but such was his prestige that the letter continued to be honored and no EX-IM credits were extended to China. The "Yoshida letter" provoked anger in Peking.

Yet trade continued to grow, rising to $621 million in 1966. In addition to trade, travel and two-way exchanges in other fields surpassed those of any other non-Communist nation. Nine Japanese journalists stationed in Peking (the same number of Communist Chinese journalists were allowed in Tokyo) reported exhaustively to their Tokyo papers and, although constrained in their movements in China and in their access to Chinese, provided some of the most useful information to be filtered out of China. Numerous Japanese business, cultural, and educational missions visited the mainland and published extensive accounts of their observations upon their return to Japan. Nearly 4,000 Japanese visited China in each of the years 1965 and 1966. In the same two years about 875 Chinese came to Japan. [10]

All this was changed by the confusion of the Cultural Revolution and disruption of the Red Guards after 1966. Trade and travel dwindled, and tensions rose.

In 1967 Premier Sato visited Taipei and Saigon, and Chiang Kai-shek's son Chiang Ching-kuo visited Tokyo. Sato traveled to Washington and signed a joint communique with President Johnson that recognized the "threat of China." The Chinese retaliated: the expiring trade agreement was renewed for only one year; many of the Japanese correspondents and businessmen in China were either expelled or jailed, usually on charges of espionage; Sato's visit to Taiwan was denounced as a provocation against China's more than 700 million people and as a "criminal act" aimed at wrecking Sino-Japanese relations.

Despite the fury in Peking, however, trade continued. After a dip in 1967 and 1968, the figure for 1969 jumped to $625 million, and the total two-way exchange in 1970 was estimated at the all-time high of $800 million.

In 1969 exports to Communist China amounted to $390.8 million, against $234.5 million in imports. The most important exports were iron and steel ($163 million), chemical fertilizers ($80 million), machinery ($44 million) and textiles ($17 million). Leading imports were food products, largely fish, vegetables and fruits ($53 million), soya beans ($42 million), textiles ($26 million), raw silk ($20 million), clothing ($10 million), and coal ($4 million). [11]

The agreed-upon amount of Memorandum Trade for 1970 was $70 million, a $3 million increase over 1968, which included $49 million in exports and $21 million in imports. The principal exports were to be fertilizers and steel; the imports, soya beans, salt, and miscellaneous beans and peas. [12]

Politics

As the value of Memorandum Trade declined in relative terms until in 1970 it was less than 10 percent of Sino-Japanese exports and imports, the annual negotiations became a political forum rather than a session of economic bargaining. In 1970 political talks droned on for forty days, the negotiators wrapped up the trade agreement in one morning!

The Chinese have exploited the negotiations as a forum to propagandize the Japanese about the iniquities of their government and its policies, preaching that politics cannot be separated from economics. The Japanese have so far been willing to tolerate the yearly torrents of abuse in order to keep open this one channel of communication with officials of the PRC.

212

Over the years, as hostility to the Sato government grew, the political tirades became more shrill and strident. The Japanese negotiators, invariably members of the anti-Sato wing of the LDP, were patient and forbearing, too much so by some standards, and seemed to have few qualms about signing communiques not only sharply critical of their own party and government but contradicting party policy.

The 1968 communique referred to the promotion by American imperialists and Japanese authorities of policies hostile to China and the inseparability of politics from economics in Sino-Japanese relations. With regard to the former, the Japanese "showed deep understanding"; as for the latter, they "agreed to it."

In 1969 more protracted sessions, devoted largely to political issues, produced a communique laced with even harsher language than was used in 1968. The Chinese affirmed that the Peoples Republic of China was the only legitimate government of China, including Taiwan; that the peace treaty Japan had signed with Nationalist China was illegal; and that the United States-Japan security treaty was an "aggressive military alliance." The Japanese negotiators supinely "agreed to" or "appreciated" these statements. Trying to calm the resulting furor in LDP and Government circles in Japan, Foreign Minister Aichi blandly assured everybody that the Government had no formal connection with Memorandum Trade and sternly disavowed the political views expressed in the communique.

The Japanese participants described the Chinese attitude in the 1969 meetings as extremely hard. Chou En-lai spoke with unusual sternness. He told the LDP Diet members who were conducting the talks that not only was the Sato government following American imperialism but that it showed less understanding of China than did the United States! Asked when Japan and China might expect to establish diplomatic relations, Chou answered by referring to two of the Japanese delegates: "When Mr. Utsunomiya is as old as Mr. Matsumura is now." Utsunomiya was 62, Matsumura 86.[13]

During the latter part of 1969, comment from Peking increasingly raised the specter of a remilitarized, aggressive Japan. A main article in the September *Peking Review*, entitled "Japanese Reactionaries' Pipe Dream," described Japan's defense build-up as a frantic and futile adventure designed to realize a fond dream of Asian hegemony. The author saw reversion as the "fraud of Okinawa," set up to disguise new military expansion, and Japan's economic advance in Southeast Asia as "outright colonial gang-sterism" masquerading under the signboards of aid and cooperation. The article spoke of frenzied war preparations catering to Nixon's Asia policy and Sato's "subservience to United States imperialism, collaboration with Soviet revisionism, and opposition to China, Communism and revolution." [14]

Publication of the Sato-Nixon communique in November 1969 produced shock waves in Peking. The very shrillness of the commentaries which poured out of the Chinese information media in subsequent weeks and months suggested that a sensitive nerve had been touched and that behind the violent verbiage some genuine fears had been aroused.

The focus was on the revival of Japanese militarism, alleged by the Chinese to be revealed by the reference in the communique to security, particularly to the tying together of Japan's security with that of South Korea and the "Taiwan area." The Peking *Peoples Daily* attacked the Sato-Nixon agreements as a "criminal plot of the United States and Japanese reactionaries," and Chou En-lai cited the communique as proof of Sato's ambition to revive Japanese militarism and build another "Greater East Asia Co-Prosperity Sphere." [15] Japan, according to Peking, was being groomed to become the "gendarme of Asia" to suppress liberation movements and preserve U.S.-led imperialism, and Japanese forces were to be equipped with offensive arms including nuclear weapons. [16]

The barrage of propaganda denouncing the Japanese Government for ambitions to dominate Asia and to rearm continued in 1970 unabated. In March the *Peking Review* described Japan's ambitions in Asia:

Harping on the "theory of Japan as a master race" a shopworn tune often played by the old-line militarists, the Japanese reactionaries nowadays fly the tattered banner of "aid" and "trade" and strut about in South Korea, Indonesia, Thailand, Malaya and other countries. There they carry out economic infiltration, stop at nothing in extending their influence and voraciously plunder the natural resources of the Asian countries and make the people there sweat for them. [17]

In early April Chou En-lai visited Pyongyang, North Korea. As we shall discuss in a later chapter, speeches, articles, and the com-munique issued after meetings with Premier Kim Il-song of the

Democratic Peoples Republic of Korea, all stressed the theme of "revival of Japanese militarism."

The Japanese recognized that, in the atmosphere which had developed in Peking, negotiations for the renewal of Memorandum Trade would be thornier than ever. Matsumoto Shunichi, a distinguished former diplomat and member of the Diet, returned from Peking in early April to express the extreme opinion that "China's hatred has now shifted from the United States to Japan." He dated this attitude toward Japan from the November agreements signed in Washington. [18]

Representatives of associations of Japanese "friendly firms" paid a "good-will visit" to Peking in April and held discussions with the China Council for the Promotion of International Trade. Their communique issued on April 14 condemned the Washington agreements, noting "unanimously" that the Sato-Nixon statement revealed the "Japanese reactionaries' wild ambition to annex Taiwan, swallow up Korea and lay their fingers on the region of Indochina." Japanese militarism was declared to be not a distant threat but a reality. Since the "friendly firms" are fully sympathetic with Communist China, there was no hesitation on the part of the Japanese representatives to sign the statement. [19]

The negotiations for Memorandum Trade began March 10 and ended with the joint communique issued April 19. On the same day, Chou En-lai announced his "four principles" for the conduct of foreign trade. The gist of these was that China would not trade with firms which (1) carry on trade with South Korea and Taiwan, (2) invest in South Korea and Taiwan, (3) export weapons for American use in Vietnam, Laos, and Cambodia, and (4) are affiliated as joint ventures or subsidiaries of American firms in Japan. [20] The Chinese made it clear that existing contracts with companies which violated these principles would be canceled. Some Japanese firms immediately announced their intention to abide by Chou's principles; others refused. Announcements also appeared of new Japanese companies—obviously dummies—which would be formed especially for trade with Communist China. This transparent circumvention of Chou's four principles would probably be winked at by Peking authorities if the trade concerned were judged to be in China's interest. The April 19 communique recorded some differences between the opinions expressed by the Chinese and the Japanese parties to the agreement. However, the Japanese delegation agreed with the

Chinese that the Sato-Nixon communique should be condemned, that the PRC is the only government representing the Chinese people, and that the "plot to create 'two Chinas'" should be opposed in all its forms. To the charge that Japanese militarism was "already a grave fact," the Japanese admitted a danger of turning Japan into an American military base like Okinawa and did not deny the threat of a revival of Japanese militarism, which they were determined to try to "renounce and smash." While the Chinese called the reversion of Okinawa an "out-and-out" fraud, the Japanese conceded that provisions for the islands' return were "deceptive."

Peking's sharp sensitivity to Japan's dealing with Taiwan showed through in the joint agreement's unusual stress on Japan's public recognition of the relation of her own security to that of the Taiwan area. The linking by Nixon and Sato of Japan with Taiwan, South Korea, and Indochina in a security context was clearly infuriating to the Chinese. They put this language in the Memorandum Trade communique:

> The purpose of the U.S. and Japanese reactionaries in stepping up military collusion is obvious, that is, to perpetuate the forcible occupation of China's sacred territory of Taiwan Province and prevent the Chinese people from liberating Taiwan; to pertetuate the forcible occupation of South Korea, obstruct the reunification of Korea and even invade anew the Korean Democratic People's Republic; and keep Vietnam divided forever, prevent the Vietnamese people from liberating the south, defending the north and reunifying the country, and to this end, go to the length of expanding the war of aggression against Indochina. [21]

In Japan, reaction was prompt. The Government, on April 21, rejected the charge of revived militarism as showing no understanding of Japan's peaceful policies since the war. The Government defended Japan's interest in the security of nearby Taiwan and Korea as natural, and called the Chinese interpretation of Okinawan reversion a distortion of the genuine Japanese desire for the return of the islands in a "nuclear-free, homeland-level" state and of the true intentions of the United States in responding to this desire.

An LDP caucus with a majority of members favorable to Sato in attendance and from which Furui Yoshimi, the chief negotiator in the Peking talks, walked out, approved a much stronger statement.

It termed the accusations that militarism had been revived "a slander against the Japanese people, filled with maliciousness" and arousing suspicion that China intended to obstruct Japan's friendly relations with other Asian nations. The statement strongly defended the security treaty with the United States and the Sato-Nixon communique and denounced the declaration issued after the trade talks for its intention to alienate the Japanese people from their Government "which is the government the Japanese people chose themselves." The LDP statement continued: "We also find it extremely regrettable that the Communist Chinese side does not understand the self-evident principle that this kind of criticism and slander against the government of another nation is an insult to the people of that country." [22]

The Japanese delegation was assailed in the Japanese press for having accepted so many of the Chinese charges and for failing to explain the true situation in Japan, especially to refute the groundless charges of a revival of militarism. Sharp arguments arose in LDP circles, many questioning the passive attitude of their party colleagues in the face of such violent attacks on their Government and Prime Minister. Still, most responsible LDP leaders believed that as long as the trade talks offered the only channel for any contact with government officials in Peking, it was worth preserving, even though, as one party official said, the "pipe line" had become a slender thread.

Furui, a veteran of many conferences in China, and a pro-Peking LDP "dove," tried to explain the differences in attitudes between the Japanese and Chinese and urged his LDP friends to appraise them calmly. The theme of militarism in Japan was universal in China, being written about daily in the public press and repeated on every level and by every method of communication. The Japanese should not be disturbed, he said, After all, the Chinese don't want militarism to revive in Japan and, he added, "neither do we."

Security

Communist China is a military power with three million men under arms and a nuclear capability expected to produce an intercontinental ballistic missile by the middle of the 1970's. The annual defense budget has been estimated at nearly $5 billion, which is less than one eighth of Soviet military expenditures ($42 billion) but still almost five times Japan's military spending in 1969. To continue the comparison with the Soviet Union, Communist China is superior in manpower but the Russians are far ahead by every other standard of military strength, notably in artillery, air power, and nuclear forces. The concentrations of forces in the Sino-Soviet border areas were estimated in 1969 as 814,000 Chinese as against 658,000 Russians. [23]

The conflict between the U.S.S.R. and Communist China had by 1970 pitted the two Communist giants openly against each other for ten years. The rift grew out of a combination of factors, a natural historical antipathy between the Russian and Chinese peoples, long standing boundary disputes, and differences over Communist ideology.

The confrontation became intense in March 1969, when fighting broke out on an island in the Ussuri River, which forms the border in an area near the trans-Siberian railway, roughly 150 miles south of Khabarovsk. So far as is known, the Chinese attacked first; the Russians retaliated in strength on March 14 and on the following day seized the island. Other incidents followed at widely separated points; as far west as the Sinkiang-Kazakh border, near the Amur River, and again near the Sinkiang frontier. In all, some sixteen clashes took place from March to August.

Soviet propaganda escalated with the tension, and in the fall of 1969 threats emanated from Moscow that a preemptive strike against Chinese nuclear installations was a possibility. Throughout the period China protested but maintained a generally defensive attitude. The theme, repeated frequently and attributed to Mao Tse-tung himself, was "We will not attack unless we are attacked; if we are attacked, we will certainly counter-attack." [24]

During 1970, tension between the two Communist powers moderated. The talk of a Soviet preemptive strike died down. Border negotiations begun in Peking in October 1969 continued; some troop withdrawals from the border were made. Ambassadors were exchanged and a trade agreement signed in November 1970. The Peking government sent a message of congratulation to the Soviet Union on November 7, the anniversary of the Russian Revolution, expressing admiration for the "courageous and inexorable struggle of the Soviet people for a victorious revolution." The message also referred to the "deep desires" of the two countries to solve unsettled problems and make relations "friendly and good neighborly." A thaw had set in, but the basic conflict was not yet resolved and the Chinese had not yet removed the Soviet "socialist imperialists" from their list of enemies. Furthermore, intelligence sources were reporting the deployment along the Soviet border by Communist China of small numbers of nuclear-type missiles with ranges of 1,500 to 2,000 miles. Some observers believed that because of the priority given to the Russian threat, Chinese emphasis would be on medium, intermediate-range missiles rather than on intercontinental missiles which could reach targets 6,000 miles away, in the United States. [25]

How China looks at Japan

China fears first the Soviet Union. While the United States remains a primary "enemy," the Peking leadership can scarcely believe seriously in an American military threat. Japan, however, is an uncertainty for the future. Japan is near, is economically powerful and technologically advanced, and is acquiring a respectable military capability. While they are proclaiming the revival of Japanese militarism by Sato, the "imperialist stooge," the Communist Chinese may genuinely envision a Japan again rampant, a future nuclear power challenging them for hegemony in East Asia.

A Chinese nightmare must be an anti-Chinese Communist front in which Japan, the United States, and Soviet Russia would join. The Chinese fear collaboration between the American "imperialists" and the Soviet "revisionists" as they view with alarm any signs of closer relations between Japan and the Soviet Union. The Peking news service has colorfully put it, "The Soviet revisionist renegade clique . . . is stepping up its collusion with Japanese militarism in political, economic, military, and other fields, thus giving immense encouragement to Japanese militarism to carry out frenzied expansion and aggression abroad." [26] Keeping the Chinese trade channel open to Japan, apart from its economic value, also serves to keep a balance against the cooperation which can develop between Moscow and Tokyo.

After Sato announced in Washington how important South Korea and Taiwan were to Japan not only were the cries in Peking loud and long, but the Chinese hastened to mend fences with the estranged Communist regime in North Korea. Hence, when Chou En-lai visited Pyongyang in early April, the communique he signed with Kim Il-song featured Japanese militarism as a chief villain and prime menace to the peace-loving revolutionary peoples of the world.

The Chinese Communists warned that an "anti-revolutionary front," formed by Japan, South Korea, Taiwan, and the United States, was hatching a plot against the "revolutionary forces" of Asia, operating in three sectors, Korea, Formosa, and Indochina. Efforts to assemble these "revolutionary forces" culminated in rallies held in Peking and Pyongyang on June 25, the anniversary of the beginning of the Korean War and just two days after the Japanese-American security treaty became open to notice of cancellation. The Asian revolutionary front consisted of North Korea, North Vietnam, Prince Sihanouk's government in exile, and Communist representatives from Laos and South Vietnam.

Peking's nerves respond quickly whenever Japan strengthens relations with the governments of either the Republic of Korea or Nationalist China. Particularly irritating are the regular meetings held between South Korean and Japanese officials to discuss economic and other problems. The formation in Japan of the Committee to Promote Cooperation between Japan and the Republic of China (Taiwan) drew special fire. Chou En-lai in a revealing interview with Matsumura Kenzo, distinguished Japanese politician, old friend of China, and veteran of many meetings in Peking, enumerated the causes of China's ire. He singled out Japan's relations with Korea and Taiwan, accusing Sato of planning to send Japanese troops to take the place of Americans being withdrawn from South Korea. He showed alarm at the growth of Japan's defense expenditures, at the extension of Japan's defense line to Korea and Taiwan, and at the importance Japan attached to the Malacca straits as a "life-line." He specifically charged Japan with the intention of intervening in Indochina and contended that Sato followed a policy of overseas expansion and dreamed of the reestablishment of the co-prosperity sphere. [27]

China not only fears Japan as a rival in East Asia but fears it even more seriously as an armed, and potentially nuclear-armed, adversary. The Chinese appreciate Japan's superior technology and its rapid development of nuclear energy, including nuclear power plants and a nuclear-powered merchant ship, and may calculate that weapons production is logically the next step. The Japanese proved they could launch missiles into space by orbiting a 50-pound satellite on February 11, 1970, two months before China's first space shot. The Chinese Communist press ignored the Japanese achievement but revealed uneasiness by accusing Japan of hoping to "equip the Japanese 'Self-Defense Forces' with nuclear missiles so as to unleash wars of aggression." A few days later, the Chinese charged that "the Japanese have intensified their plunder of uranium resources in Africa, Southeast Asia and other parts of the world under the pretext of the 'peaceful use' of atomic energy." [28]

The significance of Chinese nuclear weapons so far is more political and psychological than military, although Peking must hope that China's nuclear power is enough to deter a Russian preemptive strike. Weapons and ballistic missiles are badges of power which Chinese leaders hope to use to win influence in East Asia. Leaving aside the Soviet Union, Peking may see in the future a possible confrontation with the combined military power of the United States and Japan. The Nixon Doctrine seems to have impressed the Chinese less with its promise of American disengagement from East Asia than with a heightened American dependence on nuclear weapons. Thus, for the Chinese the nuclear equation takes on greater importance, both with respect to the United States and with respect to Japan. A nuclear-armed Japan becomes at once a competitor with China in nuclear power and a competitor for the leadership of Asia.

For China this contingency would mean new confrontation, which would affect the balance of power in Asia. The result would likely be heightened Chinese-Japanese tension, with the Chinese nuclear threat becoming a serious danger to the Japanese instead of the present hardly believed possibility. Furthermore, the revulsion throughout Asia against a Japan which had blatantly thrown off what would be seen as only a mask of a "no war" constitutional policy would make China acceptable in contrast. The integration of economic and military power with a nuclear dimension would deeply alienate Asians from a Japan whose history of cruelty and oppression would be quickly and vividly recalled.

China might use nuclear blackmail against Japan if Japan had already started on the road to becoming a nuclear power. In such circumstances, the temptation might be strong. Otherwise, given China's recent cautious, careful stance, this course seems unlikely. The crucial point would be the credibility of an American response in defense of Japan. The nuclear umbrella is useful only so long as it is believed in. Action and policies of the United States could erode the confidence of the Japanese in it and the belief of the Chinese that it would work.

How Japan Looks at China

Japanese attitudes toward China and the Chinese are complex and contradictory. They have vacillated from feelings of inferiority to superiority and again to inferiority. They include a sense of common race, common culture, and common writing. They arise out of an amalgam of Japanese national experience; from victory in the war of 1895 to the long, frustrating war of attrition in the 1930's, including the occupation of large areas of China; guilt over atrocities committed by the Japanese soldiery; and ignominious withdrawal from the continent after defeat in 1945. Feelings of admiration and affinity are mixed with guilt and condescension. Most Japanese believe that normal relations should be established with the mainland as soon as possible—but without, of course, abandoning Taiwan. At the same time, they are wary of China's nuclear power, although they feel no threat from it now. Traditionally, the Japanese have never particularly liked the Chinese as people. Surveys of popular attitudes toward various nationalities usually show the Chinese to be the third most disliked, Koreans and Russians being first and second, respectively. [29] But these personal feelings probably have relatively little influence on attitudes toward China as a nation or toward Japanese national policies toward China.

The Japanese Government seeks to open new doors to China and encourages the annual trade talks in spite of the humiliating communiques which members of the LDP so blandly sign. Eyes are constantly on Washington with genuine envy that, while Japan is far ahead of the PRC in trade and travel, American and Chinese Communist ambassadors have been able from time to time to talk at Warsaw. The Japanese Foreign Office has repeatedly tried to arrange similar channels, without success. Although the idea of being a "bridge" between Americans and Chinese titillates the imagination of some Japanese, many ruefully admit that

Washington may break through first to Peking. They fervently hope the Americans will keep them posted in advance. A joke widely publicized in Japan had it that while serving in Washington, Ambassador Asakai had a recurring nightmare that Secretary of State Dean Rusk telephoned him at two o'clock in the morning to remark dryly, "Oh, by the way, we have just recognized Communist China." In retrospect the Japanese Ambassador's nightmare seemed prophetic when, on July 15, 1971, Secretary of State William P. Rogers telephoned Japanese Ambassador Ushiba Nobuhiko to inform him that within thirty minutes President Nixon would announce his acceptance of Mao Tse-tung's invitation to visit Peking.

Japan's China policy, like America's, has been locked to Taiwan. Japan's economic, political, and security interests in Taiwan (the latter now officially recognized by the Sato-Nixon agreements) are impossible to abandon. In spite of popular pressure to the contrary, the Government, at least through 1970, had shown no inclination to recognize the People's Republic in place of the Republic of China or to vote to seat the PRC in the United Nations if the resolution also called for the expulsion of Taiwan. The Sato government was content to continue the tightrope walk, risking bombast in Peking and grumbles in Taipei, profiting economically, and trusting that in due course changes in personnel and policies in the two capitals would permit more stable relationships to become possible.

Japanese political perties are divided on the China issue. The LDP has pro-mainland and pro-Taiwan factions. The opposition parties favor relations with the Communists but only the Socialist Party actively supports the Mao regime. The JCP broke with Peking in 1967, after splitting with Moscow in 1964, and is now one of the "four enemies" of the Chinese, the others being "American imperialists, Soviet revisionists and Sato reactionaries."

When the Chinese in 1964 detonated their first nuclear weapon, the Japanese reacted with almost unruffled calm. After all, they had for a long time lived next door to Soviet nuclear power and the explosion of a small Chinese "device" scarcely heightened a threat already there. More recently, as the Chinese have added hydrogen bombs and ballistic missiles to their arsenal, the thoughts of the Japanese have sobered, although a sense of threat has not developed.

In the future, as Japan's own defense and foreign policies

evolve, a Chinese threat may appear more real. Japan's stake in the security and stability of the countries of East Asia will rise as her political and economic involvement deepens. Especially if the Sino-Soviet conflict continues, China will seek to rally the "revolutionary forces" and steal their leadership from the Kremlin. This activity and the prime interest of both China and Japan in Korea and Taiwan point to possible collisions for the future.

In the 1970's Japanese governments will probably judge that the Chinese threat can be contained by a continuation of present policy, a combination of Japanese defense strength plus the American nuclear deterrent. So long as the modest posture in Peking continues, this would seem to be sufficient. Moreover, the Japanese aim would be to achieve through diplomacy an accomodation with Communist China which would assure continuing and increasing trade, progress toward normalized relations, and a relaxation of tensions. Whether this objective can be accomplished in the face of many conflicting interests and obligations is probably the most important question facing the leaders of the Japanese nation.

Notes

1. Michio Royama, "The Asian Balance of Power: A Japanese View," *Adelphi Papers,* No. 42, November 1967, The Institute for Strategic Studies, London, 1967, p. 6.

2. The text of the treaty appears in Theodore McNelly, ed., *Sources in Modern East Asian History and Politics* (New York: Appleton-Century-Crofts, 1967), pp. 297-300.

3. Dean Acheson, *Present At the Creation, My Years in the State Department* (New York: W.W. Norton and Company, 1969), p. 603.

4. Acheson, p. 603.

5. See Acheson, NOTES, p. 759 for complete text of Yoshida's letter to Dulles.

6. Estimates of China's population (750 million) and GNP ($80 billion) are from *The Military Balance, 1970-1971*, The Institute for Strategic Studies, London, 1970, p. 57.

7. On Communist China's growth rate after 1969, see Robert Michael Field "Industrial Production in Communist China: 1957-1968, *The China Quarterly,* London, April-June 1970, No. 42, p. 54: ". . . The rate of growth after 1969, therefore, will certainly be lower than that of the First Five Year Plan or the period of recovery from 1962 to 1966 until fewer resources are diverted to military programmes or until the economy is able to generate a large volume of funds for investment."

8. Chinese foreign trade figures are from JETRO (Japan External Trade Organization) reported in *Nihon Keizai*, "Chinese Foreign Trade Increases by 7 percent as compared with last year." Tokyo, August 6, 1970.

9. George P. Jan, "Japan's Trade with Communist China," *Asian Survey*, December 1969, p. 916.

10. Eto Shinkichi and Nagai Yonosuke, *Nihon no Shorai* (The Future of Japan). Vol. 3, *Sekai no Naka no Nihon, Anzen Hosho no Koso* (Japan in the World, Concept of Security), (Tokyo: Ushio Publishing Company, June 23, 1969), p. 83.

11. Tsusho Sangyo Sho (Ministry of International Trade and Industry-MITI), *Tsusho Hakusho Kakuron, 1970* (White Paper on Foreign Trade, Detailed), (Tokyo, Tsusho Sangyo Chosa-kai, July 10, 1970), pp. 661-63.

12. "Japan-China Memorandum Trade to Show Big Excess of Exports This Year," *Nihon Keizai*, Tokyo, April 25, 1970.

13. "Premier Chou Discusses Japan-China Relations," *Asahi* Tokyo, April 9, 1969.

14. Hung Chih, "Japanese Reactionaries' Pipe Dreams," *Peking Review* (Peking, September 19, 1969), pp. 26-27.

15. "Gulf likely to develop between Japan and China" *Tokyo Shimbun*, Dec. 1, 1969 (Kyodo News Service, Peking, November 30, 1969).

16. Peking, New China News Agency (NCNA), November 23,24, 28, 1969.

17. "Aggressive Designs of the Japanese Reactionaries Will End in Bubbles," by the Fighters' Commentaries Group of the Dagger Company of a unit under the P.L.A. Wuhan Command, *Peking Review* (Peking, March 20, 1970), p. 25.

18. "Difficult to Break Deadlock with China Under Present Situation; Interview with Matsumoto Shunichi," *Mainichi*, Tokyo, April 9, 1970.

19. See Peking, NCNA, April 15, 1970, for full text of communique after meeting with "friendly firms."

20. "Memo on Chou En-lai's Statements at Talks with Matsumura," *Mainichi*, Tokyo, April 24, 1970.

21. See Peking, NCNA, April 19, 1970, for full text of China-Japan Memorandum Trade communique.

22. "Full Text of Draft LDP Statement in rebuttal of Japan-China Communique," *Mainichi*, Tokyo, April 27, 1970.

23. The Institute for Strategic Studies, *Strategic Survey 1969* (London, 1970), p. 71.

24. Joint editorial in *Jen-min Jih-pao* and *Hung Ch'i*, Peking, NCNA, International Service, July 31, 1969.

25. *New York Times*, November 23, 1970.

26. Peking, NCNA, April 13, 1970.

27. "Memo of Cho En-lai's Statements at Talks with Matsumura," *op. cit.*

28. Peking, NCNA, February 17, 1970; Peking, NCNA, February 21, 1970.

29. In one 1969 poll, 43 percent "disliked" the Soviet Union; 33 percent "disliked" China (*Yomiuri*, August 7, 1969). Another poll in 1969 asked "With which country should Japan develop most friendly relations in the future?" The replies were: Korea, 1 percent; Soviet Union, 2 percent; Communist China, 10 percent. The United States received the largest vote, 40 percent. (*Asahi,* October 1, 1969).

10 The Communist Neighbors: The Soviet Union

Japan and Russia: War to War (1904-1945)

In decision and actions, the Russian approach to Japan has been more traditionalist than revolutionary, more pragmatic than ideological. In 1904 Lenin exulted over the Czarist Russian defeat at Port Arthur, but in 1945 Stalin called it a "black spot on our country." In 1920 Lenin was prepared to hand over extensive economic and even military concessions in Kamchatka to the United States, believing Russia would thus be protected from Japan. In 1941 Stalin was delighted to sign a neutrality pact with Japan, and in 1945 he was even more eager to break it and attack Japan for revenge and territorial gains. And today, while the Soviets encourage what leftist elements they can and denounce the Sato Government for leading Japan toward war and militarism through the security treaty with the United States, they pursue trade and economic cooperation with far greater ardor than they propagate idology and revolution.

The Kamchatka episode was an example of the desperate need of the new Soviet state in 1920 for economic help from abroad. More significantly, the episode reflected Lenin's desire to pit American power against Japan. The concession contemplated by Lenin was to a syndicate headed by an American named Washington Vanderlip and was for the exploitation of oil, coal, and fisheries resources in Kamchatka. The same syndicate was apparently also dickering for concessions in Siberia. What is surprising in Lenin's proposal, as shown in the Soviet documents, was his apparent willingness to permit the Americans to build a military and a naval base near the source of oil.

At the time, troops of the nations who had intervened to oppose the Bolshevik Revolution, including those of Japan, were still in Russia. Lenin discussed the Kamchatka concession at a party meeting and was asked what would happen if Japan took Kamchatka and refused to hand it over to the United States. Lenin replied that Japan was then in fact occupying Kamchatka but that if the concession were granted, the Japanese, for fear of the United States, would not refuse to yield the territory. Lenin was also asked what Russia would do if, as he was predicting in 1920, war broke out between Japan and the United States. Lenin answered that if this happened, the Soviet Government would of course become an ally of the United States against Japan. He explained that it was quite permissible to form an alliance with one inperialist nation against another in order to preserve the socialist republic.

Lenin defended the Kamchatka concession, assuring his critics that "when life is hungry," choices are limited, that the Soviet system would survive unharmed, and that in any case the capitalists were blind pawns caught in their own burgeoning crises. [1]   Lenin clearly believed that the most important task was to bring in the Americans, representatives of a far-away "imperialist" power, to counteract the nearer and more dangerous Japanese. Maxim Litvinov recalled this policy in 1933, when he stated that the United States had helped protect Russian territory against Japan through its intervention in the Far East.

As for Vanderlip, who was not the important financier Lenin thought him to be, he failed to arouse enthusiasm or funds in New York and Washington and "the concession faded into thin air." [2]

Similar security motives impelled Stalin in the 1940's. In the spring of 1941, a neutrality pact with Japan had advantages for the Soviet Union; it represented an insurance policy against a Japanese attack, and thus against a two-front war, and encouraged Japan's southward—instead of northward—expansion. At the same time, Japan saw the pact as a useful complement to the Axis entente with Germany and Italy and as protection for Japan's northern flank. The Japanese also believed that signing the treaty might exert some influence on Chiang Kai-shek to come to terms with Japan in settling the "China Incident," as the Japanese called their war on China's mainland. The Army Chief of Staff made a point, at the Imperial Conference, to approve the Axis pact (September 19, 1940): "Improvement of relations with the Soviet

Union is extremely important both for the settlement of the China Incident and for future defense policies." He urged the Government to "redouble its efforts in this area." [3]   The Soviet Government did little to settle the "China Incident;" on the contrary, the Stalin regime aided the Nationalist Chinese Government and continued to recognize it until October 2, 1949, the day after the Peoples Republic of China was formally inaugurated in Peking.

Those who lived in Tokyo in March and April 1941 recall the daily exuberant press accounts of Foreign Minister Matsuoka's triumphant progress to the Axis capitals, Berlin and Rome, and thence to Moscow, to add, as Herbert Feis has said, the missing number to the "grand combination which would hold the United States in check." [4]   The Japanese correspondents, as enterprising, energetic, and omnipresent then as today, reported each minute detail of the diplomatic whirlwind trip of this—so rare for a Japanese—flamboyant character.

The climax came in Moscow after the signing of the neutrality treaty on April 13. After a Kremlin reception and much conviviality (Stalin had delayed the trans-Siberian express so the party could be held) Stalin, in an unprecedented gesture, went to the Kazan railway station and there on the platform embraced Matsuoka warmly and, in a glow of good feeling, uttered the famous words, "We understand each other. We are Asiatics." [5]

Within the year, Russia attacked Germany and Japan attacked the United States. As the war wore on and victory in Europe was in sight, the Allied Powers calculated what it would take to defeat Japan. Although by late 1944, Japan was in a desperate state, deprived of most of its shipping, air force, and island outposts, military estimates as late as February 1945 concluded that fighting for eighteen months after V-E Day, including invasion of the Japanese islands with enormous casualties, would be required to bring Japan to surrender. To reduce these casualties, use of the atomic bomb and the entry of the Soviet Union into the Pacific war were both believed essential.

On October 30, 1943, Stalin told Secretary of State Cordell Hull at a dinner in the Kremlin that the Soviet Union would join in the war against Japan as soon as Germany was defeated. To underscore his promise, Stalin showed an after-dinner film depicting Red partisans fighting treacherous Japanese interventionists in Siberia during the revolutionary period. [6]

The Yalta agreement, signed February 11, 1945, formalized Stalin's commitment and specified that the Soviet Union would enter the war against Japan "two or three months" after Germany's surrender. In return, Russia would receive the Kurile Islands, the southern part of Sakhalin, and certain other rights in the Far East, such as a dominant position in Manchuria, the safeguarding of "preeminent interests" in the port of Dairen, and the restoration of Port Arthur as a naval base of the U.S.S.R. In insisting on these concessions, Stalin was obviously mindful of the neutrality pact with Japan and of the fact that the Russian people harbored no special hatred for the Japanese and would not welcome war on another front. He told Roosevelt during the Yalta meetings that if his conditions were not met, he would find it difficult to explain to his nation why Russia was going to war against Japan. The Russian people "understood clearly the war against Germany which had threatened the very existence of the Soviet Union, but they would not understand why Russia would enter a war against a country with which they had no great trouble." However, Stalin suggested, if the political terms were met the Russian people would understand that a national interest was involved. President Roosevelt replied that he foresaw no difficulty in the transfer to Russia of the Kurile Islands and half of Sakhalin. [7]

The Northern Territories

The territorial question, born in Yalta, is the most difficult issue between Japan and the Soviet Union and has been the obstacle to the signing of a peace treaty between the two nations. Japan has never questioned the right of the Soviet Union to retain southern Sakhalin and the northern Kuriles, but it claims three islands and one small island group forming that part of the Kurile chain nearest to Japan's Hokkaido. These are Kunashiri and Etorofu, known as the southern Kuriles, with areas of 579 and 1,212 square miles, respectively, and Shikotan and the Habomai Islands, with a combined area of 138 square miles, which had been administered by Japan as part of Hokkaido before World War II. The Yalta agreement stated merely that "the Kurile Islands should be handed over to the Soviet Union." Charles Bohlen, who was present at the Yalta conference, pointed to this later "as a case where lack of precision was so important to future events." [8]

A State Department document dated December 28, 1944, distinguished clearly among three groups of the Kuriles: southern, central, and northern. According to the study, the southern group, extending north of Hokkaido and including the island of Etorofu, contained "90 percent of the total population of the Kuriles and has been admittedly Japanese since about 1800." The study affirmed that Japan had a strong claim on this island group on grounds of nationality, self-determination, geographic propinquity, economic need, and historical possession, and it recommended that the southern Kuriles be retained by Japan. Ironically, according to the official record in *Foreign Relations of the United States*, this document was not included in the Yalta Briefing Book, nor was it apparently ever brought to the attention of President Roosevelt or Secretary of State Stettinius.[9]

The Japanese claim dates to a treaty signed with Russia in 1855 which gave the islands from Uruppu north to Russia and those from Etorofu south to Japan. In 1875 Japan gave up Sakhalin in exchange for *all* of the Kuriles, and then in 1905 it regained southern Sakhalin by the Portsmouth Treaty. The Japanese have contended since 1955 that the southern Kuriles—Kunashiri and Etorofu—are distinct from the rest of the Kurile chain, did not rightfully belong to Russia, and are legally Japanese.[10]

Japan renounced all rights to the Kuriles in the San Francisco peace treaty. Again, however, the wording was "the Kurile Islands" without definition. Prime Minister Yoshida denied at the conference that Japan had taken the Kuriles and South Sakhalin by aggression and insisted that Russia in the past had never disputed Japanese ownership of the southern Kuriles; he also charged that the Soviets were occupying without authority islands which were part of Hokkaido (Shikotan and the Habomais). Ambassador Dulles told the conference that the United States believed the Habomai Islands not be a part of the Kuriles, but he omitted mention of Kunashiri or Etorofu.

Japanese-Soviet Negotiations

The Soviet Union refused to sign the Japanese peace treaty and for five years kept Japan out of the United Nations by its veto power. Finally, in 1955, Japanese and Soviet diplomats met in London to begin negotiations which, after long delays and interruptions, resulted in the resumption of diplomatic relations but in no agreement on territories, and consequently no treaty of peace. The Joint Declaration, signed on October 19, 1956, provided that the Soviet Union would transfer to Japan the Habomai Islands and the island of Shikotan only after a peace treaty had been concluded.[11]

The Japanese Government has weakened its case by not being consistent in its claim to Kunashiri and Etorofu. At San Francisco, although both Yoshida and Dulles singled out Shikotan and the Habomais as not being part of the Kuriles and therefore rightfully Japanese, neither mentioned the two larger islands, Kunashiri and Etorofu. The Japanese in 1951 considered the "Kurile Islands," as specified in the peace treaty, to include both the northern and southern groups and therefore limited their claim to the Habomais and Shikotan. Yoshida confirmed this position to the Diet as did the Foreign Office Director of the Treaties Bureau. The latter stated on October 19, 1951, that the Kuriles embraced both northern and southern islands. He added that historically the situation of the two groups had differed, one from the other, a fact which the Government would continue to recognize.[12]

The official change in position came during negotiations with the Soviet Union in London in 1955. Apparently Japan had originally been prepared to accept the return of only the Habomais and Shikotan. However, when the Russians were about to agree, the Japanese suddenly shifted ground and raised their demand to include the southern Kuriles. Angered at this unexpected reversal, the Soviets broke off the talks. They were not resumed until the following year, when they again foundered on the territorial issue.[13]

Since 1955 the Japanese Government has consistently demanded the return of the southern Kuriles (Etorofu and Kunashiri), arguing that they have been historically separate from the rest of the island chain and have been traditionally and legally Japanese. Neither government nor party officials have mentioned the shift in position which occurred in 1955.

In obvious attempts to curry public favor, both the Socialist and Communist parties have argued for return of the islands, but in terms different from both the official Japanese and Soviet positions. The JSP and the JCP published their policies in detailed statements in 1969, the JCP in March, the JSP in December. The JSP dated its position from a Central Executive Committee decision of October 1961. Both parties contended that *all* of the Kuriles are historically and legally Japanese, that the Yalta agreement was not binding on Japan, and that the renunciation of rights over the islands in the San Francisco peace treaty was a serious error, or "crime," as the Socialists called it. Both parties propose that the Government should negotiate a peace treaty with the Soviet Union to obtain reversion of the Habomais and Shikotan in accordance with the Joint Declaration of 1956. Subsequently, after Japan has broken the security treaty with the United States—which they assume the Soviets would require—the Government should again approach the U.S.S.R. to ask for the return not only of the southern Kuriles but of the entire island chain.[14] It is noteworthy that the JSP and JCP would go further than the LDP or the Japanese Government has ever suggested.

The Secretary General of the Japan Socialist Party and other colleagues, during a visit to Moscow in late 1970, raised the territorial issue; the discussion, they reported on their return to Tokyo, was useless; they were talking in "parallel lines."[15]

The United States has supported Japan's claim to the islands. In September 1956, a month before the Soviet-Japanese Declaration, the State Department affirmed that the two islands of Etorofu and Kunashiri, as well as the Habomais and Shikotan, were part of Japanese territory and should be recognized as subject to Japanese sovereignty. During the same period Secretary Dulles excited the Japanese by a statement to the press which sounded like a threat to keep the Ryukyus and Bonins if Japan gave up the northern islands to Russia. State Department spokesmen hastened to assure the Japanese that while American military forces might stay in Okinawa for a long indefinite time, the United States had no intention whatsoever of annexing any Japanese territory.[16]

The Soviet View of the Northern Territories Question

The position of the Soviet Union is that "there is no territorial problem" with Japan. Soviet spokesmen deny that any "negotiations" or even "talks" have taken place with Japanese officials on this subject. In fact, for the Russians it is a "non-issue."

There are several elements in the Soviet position. The first is the historical claim. This includes the Cairo Declaration, the Yalta Agreement, the Potsdam Proclamation and the San Francisco peace treaty, all of which the Russians cite to prove that the Kuriles were ceded to them. They declare the 1855 and 1875 treaties, quoted by the Japanese, to be irrelevant and bring forth their own chapters in history to prove Japan's old sins: the inequities of the Portsmouth Treaty and Japan's illegal occupation of Soviet Far Eastern territory in the 1920's. The Soviets refuse to recognize any difference in status between the northern and southern Kuriles.

Second, the Soviet Union opposes changes in any frontiers existing since World War II. The Japanese are called "revanchist" for their attempts to revise the results of the war. After the signature of the treaty between the U.S.S.R. and the Federal Republic of Germany on August 12, 1970, the Soviet attitude toward Japanese territorial claims hardened. This treaty pledged the two parties to "respect without restriction the territorial integrity of all states in Europe within their present frontiers." [17] The Kremlin wanted to hold up this treaty as a precedent for freezing boundaries with Japan. As one commentator in the Moscow *New Times* wrote on November 20, 1970:

> The positive tendency . . . in the signing of a USSR-FRG treaty is clearly not to the taste of certain Japanese circles. These circles are dissatisfied with the fact that the treaty has confirmed the stability of postwar frontiers developed in Europe and has thus restressed the irreversibility of historical processes. . . . The Japanese ruling circles clearly have misgivings lest the principles on which it is founded knock the ground away from under Japan's territorial claims against its neighbors. [18]

The Soviet Union is reluctant to return territory to Japan in the face of the principles incorporated in the treaty with West Germany and the troublesome border problems with Communist China. It is not surprising that the Russians cling to the "irreversibility of historical processes." Soviet experts in the Japanese Foreign Office have long thought that this Russian position was the most serious obstacle to their demands for the northern islands.

Third, the Soviets have regarded the United States-Japan security treaty as the principal impediment to a peace treaty with Japan. In 1960, after the signature of the revised treaty, the Soviet Government made it clear that it would not make formal peace with Japan so long as foreign troops were stationed there. [19] Little reference has been made to this position in recent years, but it was recalled by a Radio Moscow commentator in November 1970. He repeated that the "new situation" created by Japan's signing the military pact in 1960 made it impossible for the Soviet Government to fulfill its promise to transfer the Habomais and Shikotan to Japan. [20] This restatement of the 1960 position suggested a stubborn Soviet attitude and offered little hope to the Japanese for the recovery of even the smallest islands—the Habomais and Shikotan.

Finally, while the islands are of no great economic value, the Soviets may regard them as of some importance to their security. This would mean primarily the effect of the islands on free access through the Sea of Okhotsk to the Pacific Ocean.

Stalin described the strategic interest to Ambassador Harriman in December 1944:

> He [Stalin] went into the next room and brought out a map. He said that the Kurile Islands and the lower Sakhalin should be returned to Russia. He explained that the Japanese now controlled the approaches to Vladivostok, that he considered that the Russians were entitled to protection for their communications to this important port and that "all outlets to the Pacific were now held or blocked by the enemy." [21]

The Japanese lay no claim to the northern Kuriles, and the Habomais, Shikotan and Kunashiri are close to Hokkaido and would seem of limited importance in affecting Soviet freedom of movement into and out of the Sea of Okhotsk. The question of strategic value might arise for Etorofu, which is the largest island and is a little farther out in the Kurile chain. The Soviet Navy would no doubt be loath to give up either Kunashiri or Etorofu, which sit like clumsy aircraft carriers across the southern stretch of sea marked by the Kurile chain. Moreover, the traditional Russian distrust of Japan, renewed and reenforced by uneasiness over a revival of militarism, probably magnifies in the Russian mind whatever strategic worth these bits of territory may seem to possess.

Against the advice of the Foreign Office—which saw nothing to be gained except the antagonism of the Russians—Prime Minister Sato appealed for the return of the northern territories in his speech to the Twenty-fifth Anniversary Session of the United Nations General Assembly on October 21, 1970. Very shortly thereafter, the Soviet media opened a barrage of attacks on Japan, accusing Sato of wishing to change the map of the world drawn after World War II, and raising the specter of a dangerous, revived militarism in Japan. The unprecedented vehemence of the comment in newspapers and radio was in sharp contrast to the friendly tone which had generally characterized Soviet references to Japan during 1969. An American journalist writing in the *New York Times* in late November 1970 noted that "hardly a day passes without such strident attacks as a long article in *Pravda* yesterday warning of a growth of 'revanchism' in Japan and reasserting Moscow's refusal to part with the islands." He remarked on the sharp contrast with the attitude in the summer of 1969, when a Soviet publication had commented that "an absolutely new favorable atmosphere has appeared in relations between the Soviet Union and Japan, distinct from that twenty or even ten years ago."[22]

There were several probable reasons for the campaign. One was the treaty with West Germany; another was the improvement of relations with Communist China. The Russians may have temporarily put less importance on wooing Japan away from China, thinking that a too friendly stance toward Japan might toughen the Chinese position in border negotiations. The Soviet Government also probably welcomed an opportunity again to highlight the Japanese-American security treaty as a block to a formal Russo-Japanese peace, hoping to erode the Japanese-American relationship and Japanese faith in the United States.

A few examples of Soviet propaganda directed to Japan during late October and November 1970 suggest the character of the continuing stream of invective.

Izvestia, October 29: . . . Sato's speech sounded like a call for a revision of the results of World War II. And this is revanchism. . . . the Soviet Union and the Soviet people cannot ignore statements and utterances involving the question of the inviolability of Soviet territory and calling for a revision of the results of World War II.

Radio Moscow, October 30: Undoubtedly, U.S. imperialism and the militarism being revived in Japan are threatening the Asian peoples' security.

Radio Moscow, November 6: As is well known, the revanchist program of the Nazi regime of Germany started with making territorial demands against countries adjacent to Germany. . . . The Japanese revanchists seem to have decided to take a similar path.

Radio Moscow, November 12: Japan's territorial claim has begun to take on a more dangerous nature. The fact that Japanese militarism is being stepped up can be proved by the recent Japanese white paper on national defense and Japan's fourth defense buildup plan . . . these documents provide theoretical grounds for the possibility of arming the Japanese Self-Defense Forces with nuclear missiles.

Izvestia, November 13: . . . the revanchist campaign launched in Japan is aimed not only against the Soviet Union but also against all the Asian countries which suffered from Japanese aggression in 1941-1945, and which some people in Japan are eyeing greedily in our time too.

Pravda, November 21: A journalist . . . compared the "White Paper" on defense . . . with "an axe in a peaceful wrapping.". . . Those circles who even today dream of Japan at the head of the "Great East Asia Co-prosperity Sphere" . . . and who even today would not be averse to flexing the muscles of the second industrial power of the capitalist world, did not disappear with the defeat of Japan in World War II.

Pravda could not resist attacking obliquely the Japanese Socialist and Communist parties for their failure to support the Soviet position on the northern islands: "Unfortunately, the members of certain opposition parties, who have been unable to discern which circles' interests their actions are serving, have appeared in the company of those who are whipping up the territorial hysteria."[23]

Japanese public attention has turned from south to north, from Okinawa to the Kuriles. But reversion in the north will never pack the punch of reversion for Okinawa. A million Japanese live in Okinawa, none in the Kuriles. Even the displaced fishermen, after twenty-five years, think more of their catch than of going back to former homes.

At some point in the future, changed circumstances, such as a different Japanese-American relationship, could motivate the Soviet leaders to return the Habomais and Shikotan and sign a peace treaty with Japan. Any willingness to return the larger islands, Kunashiri and Etorofu, seems quite unlikely in the foreseeable future. However, in spite of their propaganda, the Russians will probably not let the territorial impasse affect their interest in Japan's economic cooperation, both in trade and in the development of the resources of Siberia and Sakhalin.

The Economic Interest

Fish and Troubled Waters

On Japan's northernmost island, Hokkaido, one can stand at Nossapu point at the end of Nemuro peninsula, a stick of land jutting into the Sea of Okhotsk, and watch Russian soldiers on patrol on an island less than three miles away. The local inhabitants of Nemuro are fishermen and collectors of tangle, a special kind of seaweed found in these waters and highly prized by the Japanese. A visiting Japanese journalist found in 1963 that the fishermen were eking out a marginal existence, a family of seven or eight living on an income of $638 a year. The Soviets prohibited tangle-collecting in the vicinity of their islands and were constantly seizing Nemuro fishermen, sometimes keeping them in detention for several years. Now the situation has changed. In 1963, a "private" tangle agreement was signed in Moscow providing that specified numbers of Japanese boats would be permitted to operate in the waters near the Soviet-held islands. In 1969, 300 boats were in service and the annual family income of the fishermen had risen to an average of over $4,500. [24]

Nemuro's citizens have not, however, been relieved of all harassment from the Russians. Seizures of boats and men have become less frequent but have not ceased. Japanese fishermen are still detained in the Soviet Union. The people have other complaints. The Soviets often use the area for military manoeuvres and test firings, which disturb the fishing grounds. The closeness of Soviet and Japanese territories makes it inevitable that fishermen of both countries ply the same waters, and clashes result.

Hokkaido fishermen have two principal aspirations: safe fishing and return of the islands. The prewar Japanese population of the Kuriles numbered some 16,500. After the war the Soviets moved out all who were left and later repatriated them to Hokkaido. Most settled in the Numuro area and formed the nucleus of the reversionist movement. However, after 25 years, time has taken its toll; some survivors have prospered and are satisfied with their present life. Others, younger and without adult experience in the lost territories, care little about returning to islands they hardly knew. As time passes, Nemuro families became more interested in the state of the fishing grounds, the size of the catch, and the safety

238

of their men and their boats than in agitating for reversion. Their watch word is "Fish before Territory." [25]

Fishing has long been important in Soviet-Japanese relations. The perennial embroilment of Russians and Japanese in the northern fishing areas near Soviet territory are described in statistics: 1,312 Japanese fishing boats seized between 1945 and 1969, of which 809 were returned and twenty-one were sunk; 11,974 Japanese fishermen captured, of whom 10,974 were returned and thirty-two were killed. [26]

Fisheries were finally responsible for normalizing Japanese-Soviet relations in 1956. After negotiations in London were broken off in March, Moscow suddenly announced restrictions on Japanese fishing in the northern Pacific and the Bering Sea. Pressure from the powerful Japanese fishing industry mounted immediately; in response, the Minister for Agriculture and Forestry was sent to Moscow for an emergency conference to negotiate a temporary fisheries agreement. The Russians would sign the pact only on condition that negotiations to restore diplomatic relations be resumed at once. The Japanese Government, subjected to intensive lobbying by the fishing companies, pursued the talks and reached agreement in October.

Trade

When the Soviet Union restored diplomatic relations with Japan in 1956, trade was not the first priority, as it has been with Communist China. However, in recent years, Japanese-Soviet trade has climbed steadily, and from 1967 through 1969 it surpassed Soviet trade with China (Table 10-1).

Japan has imported raw materials from the Soviet Union—timber, chrome, pig iron, coal, asbestos, crude oil, and raw cotton—and has exported machinery, steel, textiles, and manufactured goods. Imports exceeded exports each year through 1969. At trade talks held in Tokyo in January 1970, the volume of trade for the ensuing year was set at $720 million, with exports of $370 million and imports of $350 million. Japan would thus for the first time attain an export surplus. [27] In March the president of the Japanese Chamber of Commerce and Industry predicted that two-way trade with the Soviet Union would soon reach the billion-dollar mark. [28]

Table 10-1

Japan's Trade with the Soviet Union and Communist China (in thousands of dollars)

	Exports to USSR	Exports to China	Imports from USSR	Imports from China	Total trade with USSR	Total trade with China
1965	168,358	245,036	240,198	224,705	408,556	469,741
1966	214,024	315,150	300,361	306,237	514,385	621,387
1967	157,688	288,294	453,918	269,439	611,606	557,733
1968	179,018	325,439	463,512	224,185	642,530	549,624
1969	268,247	390,803	461,563	234,540	729,810	625,343

Source: Tsusho Sangyo-sho, *Tsusho Hakusho* (Ministry of International Trade and Industry, White Paper on Trade and Commerce), 1968, 1969, and 1970, hereinafter called MITI, *White Paper*.

Cooperation in Economic Development

Soviet interest in economic cooperation with Japan, particularly in Siberia and Sakhalin, has been keen. In March of 1966, the first meeting of the Joint Soviet-Japanese Economic Committee was held; succeeding meetings took place in July 1967, January 1969, and February 1970. The first project to be agreed upon (July 1968) was for the development of Siberian timber resources. Japan was to supply machinery, equipment, and consumers' goods to the Soviet Union and in return was to receive timber of comparable value over a five-year period.

The Japanese reciprocated interest in cooperative projects in the underdeveloped areas of eastern Soviet Russia but have been sensitive to the obstacles involved. The Ministry of International Trade and Industry (MITI) pointed these out in an official publication. [29] One problem was the size of investment required for each project. In the case of mining development, for example, huge investments would be needed to build railroads, housing, and roads and to establish administrative organs, waterworks, and facilities for the distribution of the necessary consumers' goods. A second problem was a shortage of reliable labor; population density in Siberia is two persons per square kilometer. A third obstacle was the problem of access. Although mineral resources were enormous, no organized system of distribution existed, and the requirement of shipment for long distances overland and to foreign countries loomed as an extremely costly one.

The Japanese have been disappointed by the lack of concrete Soviet proposals that would specify the content, scale, timing, and amount of investment required for each project. Moreover, the Japanese deemed unacceptable Soviet terms entailed in some of

240

the projects, which called for a barter of Japanese machinery and technology for raw materials such as ore or natural gas.

The Joint Committee met for the fourth time in Moscow, from February 10 to 17, 1970. Nagano Shigeo, President of the Japan Chamber of Commerce and Industry and chairman of the fifty-man Japanese delegation, appeared encouraged, commenting that understanding had improved and concrete discussions had replaced exchanges of polite formalities. The Japanese mission reported that the Russians showed greater friendliness than previously and were obviously eager for economic cooperation with Japan. The Japanese attributed this change of Soviet attitude to the stagnation of the Soviet economy, Russia's keen need for technical assistance, and the influence of the Sino-Soviet conflict. Although an economic mission, the Japanese group insisted on raising the issue of the northern territories. Prime Minister Kosygin gave a totally negative response, commenting any change in borders would be taken advantage of by "a third country," by which the Japanese were sure he meant Communist China.

Three principal items were on the agenda: (1) production and transportation to Japan of natural gas; (2) construction of the port of Vrangel, near Nakhoda in Siberia, and (3) imports of timber.[30]

The piping of natural gas for use in Japan had been talked about for several years. The Japanese were most interested in a proposal to build a pipeline from Okha, in northern Sakhalin, to Hokkaido, a distance of about 925 miles. The gas, annual supplies of which had been estimated at 2.4 billion cubic meters, would be consumed by industries in Hokkaido. However, at the February meetings the Soviet representatives presented a new plan: construction of a pipeline of larger size from the remote Yakutia region of Siberia, not far from Yakutsk, to the port of Magadan on the Sea of Okhotsk, a distance of about 746 miles. This pipeline would permit shipment of the gas in liquefied form by tanker to Hokkaido or would connect up with the pipeline to be built from the northern part of Sakhalin and would furnish Japan ten billion cubic meters of gas per year. The Japanese were less than enthusiastic over this latest proposal, which would be expensive, require much greater capital, involve construction of a pipeline in difficult, uninhabited, and rough terrain, and would supply much more gas than Hokkaido industries could consume. No decision was reached. The Japanese delegation agreed to study the proposal.

Questioned in Moscow by a Japanese correspondent, the deputy leader of the Soviet delegation said that his Government considered agreement to develop the port of Vrangel the most significant result of the meeting. The Japanese delegates also stressed the importance of the new port, when completed, in affording opportunities for exporting Japanese technology and machinery to the Soviet Union, and greatly facilitating transportation in the Northeast Asia region.[31] Final agreement on the port project was reached in June 1970.

The Joint Committee agreed, at the February meeting, on the import of Siberian timber into Japan. This supplemented the 1968 arrangement and provided for Japan to supply technical assistance and machinery in return for timber shipments of equivalent value. Timber was the single largest export item from the Soviet Union to Japan in 1969: $170.2 million. Among the numerous development projects proposed for Soviet-Japanese cooperation, the two timber agreements have been the only ones actually to be put into effect. The cooperative development of Vrangel port will be the third.

For eight years Soviet-Japanese cooperation in the economic development of Siberia has been discussed. Soviet representatives have dangled before the eyes of the Japanese prospects of the unlimited, unexploited riches of Siberia. The possibilities for cooperative effort have included the construction of a 3,000-mile pipeline to bring oil to the Soviet Far East and thence to Japan, the joint working of the Udokan copper mine in the Chita region north of Lake Baikal, said to be the world's largest undeveloped copper mine, with deposits of more than a billion tons of ore, and other projects to tap resources of iron, coal, and electric power. That relatively little has been accomplished was due to factors which we have mentioned. Negotiations have been particularly difficult on the subjects of price, terms, capital investment, and credits. The Soviets have expected large infusions of Japanese capital and long term credits at favorable interest rates, which the Japanese have not been able or willing to offer. Although the successive meetings between Japanese and Russians have removed some of the distrust which existed, and economic cooperation between the two countries has been discussed on a businesslike basis, the atmosphere for easy agreement has not prevailed. Soviet rigidity on the northern territories inescapably affects the attitudes of Japanese negotiators, who will have to see very clear and unmistakeable advantages for Japan in any bargain they make. They will scrupulously compare what they can get from the Russians with what is possible elsewhere, and to win their assent the Russian offer will have to bring an added and exceptional lure.

A recent writer on Soviet-Japanese economic cooperation aptly summarized the attitudes of the two partners:

> The record of these Soviet-Japanese negotiations shows that the Japanese are in no hurry to rush into any Siberian project however otherwise attractive, unless the terms are acceptable, while for their part the Soviets, with their inflated credit and price demands, seem to have greatly over estimated Japanese eagerness to get a footing in Siberia, irrespective of costs.[32]

Security and Strategy

Japanese wariness *vis-a-vis* the Soviet Union is reinforced by the stark facts of georaphy and power. One need not be privy to the secrets of the Self-Defense Forces to surmise that much Japanese military planning is directed northward.

The island of Hokkaido is nearly surrounded by Russian territory to the north, east, and west. The consciousness of the power and proximity of the Soviet Union is ever present in the minds of the people of Hokkaido. Many of them recall their luck in escaping Soviet occupation at the end of the war. The United States firmly refused the demand of the Soviet Government in August 1945 to station troops in Hokkaido and to make it a Soviet zone of occupation. Three of the twelve infantry divisions and the one mechanized division in the Ground Self-Defense Forces are stationed in Hokkaido. Together these form nearly a third of the effective manpower of the GSDF and half of its firepower. In addition, sizeable air and sea forces are poised in the northern area, which embraces the island of Hokkaido and Aomori, the northernmost prefecture on the main island of Honshu. Hokkaido is suitable for military training and hardening of troops, because of extensive, uninhabited space, rough terrain, and a severe, cold climate.

Eight American military installations have been located in Hokkaido and seven in Aomori, several of them jointly used with the Japanese Self-Defense Forces. Camp Chitose on Hokkaido hosts the mechanized division of the GSDF and units of the Japanese air forces. Wakkanai, on the very northernmost tip of Hokkaido and facing Soviet Sakhalin across only thirty-six miles of water, is the site of important communications facilities, part of which are used jointly by Japanese and American forces. The most important air base in northern Japan is Misawa, on the east coast of Aomori prefecture, which has been the headquarters of American tactical air units and support groups. The Northern Command of the Air Self-Defense Forces jointly used part of these facilities. Japanese-American military cooperation has been particularly noteworthy in this northern area. [33]

While the Russians on the spot eye the Japanese and their American friends across the thin strips of water and play hide-and-seek in the cloudy air space which separates them, their masters in Moscow obviously are thinking about bigger stakes. For some time the Soviet Union has sought to expand and strengthen its prestige and authority in the Asian and Pacific area. Political, economic, and military means have been harnessed to this endeavor. The most powerful goad has been the conflict with China and the competition with Peking for power and influence in Asia.

Clearly Soviet moves to bolster defenses in the Far East have been primarily addressed to China. Soviet troops stationed along the Sino-Soviet border and in Mongolia were increased from 21 divisions in July 1969 to 28 divisions by the end of the year and to 30 divisions in 1970. Troop strengths in the border areas in the 1969 numbered 834,000 Chinese compared with 658,000 Russians. However, manpower is the only Chinese advantage. According to the London Institute for Strategic Studies, the Soviet forces enjoy an overwhelming military superiority by every other measure. They are particularly strong in artillery and air power. The Soviet nuclear capability is preponderant, including as it does tactical missiles and medium range ballistic missiles; the latter are probably already deployed within reach of Chinese targets. [34]

During the past few years the Soviet Union has taken giant strides to expand its sea power. The Soviet Pacific fleet is estimated at about one-third of the total Soviet navy, commanding some 750 vessels, including 105 submarines, about ten of which are estimated to be nuclear powered. Fifty missile-carrying submarines are divided between the Arctic and Far East fleets. In additions to its warships, the Pacific fleet operates 150 helicopters and up to 400 other shore-based naval aircraft. [35]

The Commander in Chief of the Soviet Navy, Admiral Sergei Gorshkov, expressed the spirit of Soviet ambitions for sea power: "Our fleet can not only break the attack of an aggressor but also inflict annihilating blows in distant oceans and deep in enemy territory . . . the flag of the Soviet Navy proudly flies over the oceans of the world. Sooner or later, the United States will have to understand that it no longer has mastery of the seas."[36]

To solidify its claim to global power. and to gain inroads of political and economic influence in Asia at the expense of Peking, the Soviet Union has actively wooed Asian countries on the periphery of China. Moscow's successful mediation of the India-Pakistan dispute over Kashmir, resulting in the declaration at Tashkent in 1966, has bought friendly relations with both of these countries. Especially in India, where the Chinese threat continues to cast its shadow, the Russians are looked upon as useful friends in times of crisis, and the Soviet navy is welcomed to the waters of the Indian Ocean.

Soviet Policy Toward Southeast Asia

The Soviets have also extended their influence in Southeast Asia against the background of an ostensibly weakening American position and the possibility of a British pull-out. As one journalist described it, Moscow's is "trying to play both sides of the street in Asia."[37] The Russians have invested heavily in North Vietnam and in national liberation movements but at the same time would like to cultivate useful relationships with the non-Communist nations of Southeast Asia, especially to keep ahead of the Chinese. They have established diplomatic relations with Singapore and Malaysia, opened trade with the Philippines, tried to better their relations with Australia, and made tentative approaches to the Asian Development Bank. There have even been unofficial exchanges of visits between Taiwan and the Soviet Union.

Leonid I. Brezhnev, Secretary General of the Soviet Communist Party, caught the attention of Southeast Asians by proposing at a conference of Communist parties in Moscow in June 1969 the formation of a collective security system for Asia. The project appeared to be directed against China and the United States, and especially at the security agreements in effect between the United States and various Asian countries. Brezhnev was accused of

245

trying to perpetrate a Russian version of "Dulles pact diplomacy."

Radio Moscow declared that the collective security pact was intended to bring about the neighborly and friendly cooperation of all Asian countries, including China, that its aim was to eliminate the settlement of disputes by military means and establish a system which would protect the countries of Asia from intervention and aggression from outside. Another aim of the pact was to be the removal of all foreign military bases from Asia and the establishment of a "peace zone." Subsequently, Moscow's *Izvestia* protested that the security arrangement was directed against no country but would be realized by the collective efforts of and for the benefit of all the countries of Asia. What the Soviet Union was proposing was a structure designed for very broad purposes: political, economic, scientific, and cultural cooperation between the Asian countries.[38]

Peking did not take long to respond and did not accept Moscow's invitation to join. Chou En-lai told a visiting Pakistani delegation in Peking on July 13 that the Soviet proposal was a step further toward socialist imperialism, which aimed to build a strong military alliance against China. Its objective, said Chou, was aggression and expansion against the countries of Asia, with the objective of destroying their sovereignty and independence. Soviet insistence that the pact did not have an anti-Chinese objective and that the Mao government would be welcome to participate was not very convincing.[39] An article by V. Matveyev, a well-known commentator, which appeared in *Izvestia* a little over a week before the Brezhnev speech, could hardly be described as a welcome to China: "Judging by what the Peking press says, Mao and his henchmen entertain quite definite designs on a number of countries in this part of the world. . . . The main thing is that the Maoists are intensively exploiting the numerous Chinese communities in several Asian countries."[40]

Asians were intrigued by but skeptical of the Brezhnev scheme; for several months after its announcement, the Soviet plan was a subject of discussion in the capitals of Southeast Asia. Diplomats attempted to pry from their Soviet colleagues more concrete explanations of the form the collective security arrangement might take, but they were unsuccessful. The Soviets clearly hoped that the American security treaties with Asian nations would be abrogated, but journalists reported hints from Soviet sources that their collective security system might allow for existing bilateral defense treaties. [41] Just how the North Koreans and the South Koreans, the North Vietnamese and the South Vietnamese would all join happily in the Soviet-sponsored club was never explained.

The Brezhnev proposal remained as it had been set forth, with no action taken on it and no action probably expected. A Russian research specialist in international relations, visiting the United States, expressed to the author his "personal opinion" that nothing more would happen to the collective security system for Asia so long as Communist China remained hostile to the Soviet Union. He believed that some day, when the time was ripe, the Asians themselves might take up the proposal as their own and bring the arrangement into being. In the meantime, it has not been forgotten in Moscow. A commentator in *Izvestia*, writing in November 1970 about the struggles of the Southeast Asian countries for their independence and against the "war machine" of the United States, noted that these countries were thinking about how to make the continent of Asia a zone of peace. The commentator insisted that the Soviet-proposed system for Asian collective security had received "ever wider support in Asia," but added, with refreshing candor and monumental understatement, "though its practical implementation will certainly require considerable efforts." [42]

The success of Soviet fence-mending in Asia was enhanced by China's absorption in the Cultural Revolution and resulting temporary retirement from the diplomatic scene. (For a time, all Ambassadors except the one accredited to Cairo were recalled to Peking.) Peking's reentry into international affairs can be said to have been signalled by Chou En-lai's dramatic visit to North Korea in April 1970 and the pronouncements which emerged from his meetings with Kim Il-song. The Soviet leaders were reminded that competing with the Chinese in non-Communist Asian nations was less difficult than the struggle they would face with their Chinese adversary in Communist nations such as North Korea and possibly North Vietnam.

The depth of Soviet rivalry with China for power in Asia has been revealed by the tone of pronouncements coming out of Moscow. On May 18, 1970, *Pravda* accused China of seeking domination "if not of the whole world, then of Asia." In the same month, *New Time*, the Soviet foreign affairs periodical published in Western languages, warned that Peking's leaders are trying to use the national liberation movements of Southeast Asia as tools for "asserting Chinese domination in Asian countries and to condemn them to defeat and destruction." [43]

Soviet Policy Toward Japan

While Soviet strategic planners fix priority attention on the United States and China, they, like their Chinese neighbors, also focus on Japan, third most powerful nation in the world, geographically on their doorstep, and traditionally hostile. Analyzing public opinion in Japan, they may find an impressive degree of dissatisfaction with Government support of American policy in Southeast Asia and may conclude that the political climate has many elements exploitable in Soviet interests. At the same time, they will note that the Liberal Democratic Party is in a stronger position than it has enjoyed in years, that the Left is in disarray, with the Socialists on the verge of break-up and the Japan Communist party following a so-called independent line, shunning Soviet control and influence. Although the Kremlin planners may count on some futher student unrest and foresee the for them favorable prospect of a declining American military presence, they may also decide that growing nationalism and doubled defense budgets, with the American security tie-up continuing for an indefinite number of years, make a future antagonist worthy of close attention.

Recognizing the long-range possibility of conflict, the Soviet planners might project policy toward Japan for the immediate future, at least for the 1970's, along the following lines:

1. Although the continued military buildup in the Soviet Far Eastern region will be directed primarily toward maintaining a strong nuclear capability against American military power in the western Pacific and superior defenses against China, a third target will be Japan. Certainly, while the security treaty is effective and American bases still exist, Soviet reconnaissance and intelligence-gathering aimed at Japan will expand.

2. The Soviet leadership will try to woo Japan away from China, although, as we have seen, circumstances may seem to interrupt the policy from time to time, and we can conceive of a temporary Soviet effort to woo China away from Japan. Soviet policy in general, however, will be directed toward keeping Japan from becoming too closely involved with China, either economically or

politically. Soviet policy makers will no doubt hope that the attractions of economic cooperation in Siberia and trade with the Soviet Union will offset the lure of a rapid expansion of Japanese economic relations with mainland China. While a *friendly* Japan would not necessarily be expected and while Soviet desires to win the Japanese would not be translated into territorial concessions, the Soviets would hope for mutually beneficial relationships. A Soviet "expert on Japanese affairs," who spoke in Tokyo in May 1970, was probably expressing more than a personal opinion when he outlined the basic points in Japanese-Soviet relations. Although his topic was economic interchange, he emphasized political factors. He described Asia as the most dangerous area in the world and cited China and its adventurous policy as one of the causes. He declared that Japan and the Soviet Union, as the two most industrially developed nations in the Far East, must work together and cooperate to ease tensions in Asia.[44]

3. The fear of the "Pandora's Box" of both territorial and strategic considerations will probably dictate Soviet retention of the northern territories, at least for the time being. Should some change occur in the Japanese-American security relationship, including total or near-total American withdrawals or some other circumstance offering patent advantage to the Russians arise, they might find it expedient to sign a peace treaty with Japan and, in accordance with the 1956 declaration, agree to give back Shikotan and the Habomai Islands. There is little likelihood that the southern Kuriles, Kunashiri and Etorofu, would be returned. Whether the Japanese Government would accept a solution which it rejected in 1956 is questionable. It would depend upon a Japanese judgment of the advantages a treaty would bring at the time.

4. The Soviet Union will not abandon attempts to try to influence sympathetic elements within Japan, particularly the Socialist party and Labor organizations. Hope of persuading the Japanese Communist Party to "lean" more in their direction will not die, particularly in view of the vitriolic attacks which the JCP has carried on against what they call the Mao Tse-tung clique. At the same time, the Soviet Union will use "invitation diplomacy" and other methods, as it has in the past, to attempt to influence leading politicians of the Liberal Democratic Party, usually of the middle and conservative factions, and not of the left-wing

members, who are known for their sympathy toward Communist China.

5. In the unlikely case of an open conflict with China, Soviet leaders would put forth extraordinary efforts to assure Japanese neutrality, "friendly neutrality," if possible, and at a minimum, "strict neutrality." The Soviets would wish to use naval power freely, establish a blockade of Communist China, and be able to purchase supplies from both Japan and the United States. Japanese defense specialists have written that the Soviet-American nuclear balance would be an important consideration and that the United States would probably take a position of either strict or at most friendly neutrality toward China. Japan's attitude, they concluded, would follow that of the United States. [45]

6. The Soviet Union will continue efforts to develop economic cooperation with Japan in the exploitation of natural resources in Siberia and Sakhalin. The Japanese response will be dictated by the economic benefits which are judged to result, and these will be weighed against similiar opportunities in Pacific Asia and other parts of the world.

Japanese Governments in the 1970's will probably take a calm and cautious view of Soviet policy. Emphasis will continue to be placed on the defense of Hokkaido and north, and for the long run the Soviet Union will remain marked as Japan's most feared potential enemy. However, in the immediate years ahead, Japan will feel little threat from Russian arms but will endeavor to develop profitable economic relations with the U.S.S.R. while maintaining a continuing record of protest against Soviet retention of the northern territories. The Japanese will try to glean what advantage they can from Sino-Soviet rivalry and will respond to the respective enticements of both China and Russia in the way they judge will, at the time, best further interests of the Japanese nation.

Notes

1. *Novi Dokument V. I. Lenina, O Kontsessiax* (New document of V. I. Lenin, "About Concessions"), December 21, 1920; in *Voprosi Historii CPSU* (Problems of History, Communist Party of the Soviet Union), No. 4, 1963.

2. Antony C. Sutton, *Western Technology and Soviet Economic Development, 1917 to 1930* (Stanford: Hoover Institution, 1968), p. 297.

3. Nobutaka Ike, *Japan's Decision for War, Records of the 1941 Policy Con-*

ferences (Stanford: Stanford University Press, 1967), p. 13.

4. Herbert Feis, *The Road to Pearl Harbor* (Princeton, N.J.: Princeton University Press, 1950), p. 145.

5. I. Deutscher, *Stalin, A Political Biography* (New York, London: Oxford University Press, 1949), p. 452.

6. Cordell Hull, *The Memoirs of Cordell Hull* (New York: The Macmillan Company, 1948), Vol. II, pp. 1309-11.

7. U.S., Department of State, Foreign Relations of the United States, *The Conferences at Malta and Yalta 1945* (Washington, D.C.: U.S. Government Printing Office, 1955), Department of State publication 6199, p. 768.

8. Charles E. Bohlen, *The Transformation of American Foreign Policy* (New York: W.W. Norton and Company, 1969), p. 35.

9. Foreign Relations of the United States, *op. cit.,* Memorandum of the Division of Territorial Studies, Department of State, *Japan: Territorial Problems: The Kurile Islands,* December 18, 1944, pp. 379-83.

10. Japan: Gaimusho, Joho Bunka-kyoku (Foreign Office, Office of Information and Culture), "Warera no Hoppo Ryodo" (Our Northern Territories) in *Sekai no Ugoki* (Trends of the World), No. 216, December 1969.

11. For text of declaration, see Donald C. Hellmann, *Japanese Domestic Politics and Foreign Policy, The Peace Agreement with the Soviet Union* (Berkeley and Los Angeles: University of California Press, 1969), p. 161.

12. Japan: Shugiin (House of Representatives), *Heiwa Joyaku oyobi Nichi-Bei Anzen Hosho Joyaku tokubetsu Iinkai Giroku* (Journal of Proceedings of Special Committee on Peace Treaty and Japan-United States Security Treaty), No. 4, 12th session, October 19, 1951, pp. 18-19.

13. Hellmann, *op. cit.,* p. 59.

14. *Akahata* (JCP organ), March 6, 1969; *Shakaito* (JSP organ), December 1969.

15. *Shakai Shimpo* (organ of the JSP), November 15, 1970.

16. *New York Times,* August 29, 1956; August 30, 1956.

17. Soviet-German Treaty Texts, *Washington Post,* August 13, 1970.

18. V. Pronin, "On A Dangerous Road," *New Times,* November 20, 1970.

19. *Soren Gaiko to Ajia* (Soviet Diplomacy and Asia), (Tokyo: Asahi, June 15, 1967), p. 184; in Asahi book series No. 7, *Nihon no Anzen Hosho* (Japan's Security).

20. Ukraintsev commentary, "The Problem of the Northern Territories: Who Needs It and Why?", Radio Moscow, November 10, 1970.

21. Foreign Relations of the United States, *op. cit.,* Telegram from Ambassador in

251

the Soviet Union (Harriman) to the President, December 15, 1944; p. 378.

22. Bernard Gwertzman, "Soviet Reverses Stance in Japan," *New York Times,* November 29, 1970.

23. A Biryukov, "The Dark Shades of the Past," *Pravda,* November 21, 1970.

24. Natsubori Masamoto, "What Will Become of the Northern Territory?", *Bungei Shunju,* July 1969.

25. *Ibid.*

26. Omori Shigeo, "Japan's Northern Territories," *Japan Quarterly,* January-March, 1970, p. 26.

27. *Japan Times,* February 4, 1970.

28. *Yomiuri,* March 3, 1970; March 4, 1970.

29. Japan: Tsusho Sangyo-sho (Ministry of International Trade and Industry), *Tsusho Hakusho* (White Paper on Trade and Industry), *Soron* (General Survey), 1969, pp. 391-392.

30. *Asahi,* February 16, 1970; *Yomiuri,* February 17, 1970; *Nihon Keizai,* February 16, 1970.

31. *Ibid.*

32. Violet Conolly, "Soviet-Japanese Cooperation in Siberia," *Pacific Community,* October 1970, p. 65.

33. Anzen Hosho Chosakai (Security Research Council, *Nihon no Anzen Hosho, 1970 e no Tembo* (Japan's Security; Outlook on 1970), 1969 edition, August 10, 1969, pp. 116-17.

34. The Institute for Strategic Studies (ISS), *The Military Balance 1969-1970* (London: ISS, 1969), p. 7; *The Military Balance 1970-1971* (London: ISS, 1970), p. 7.; *Strategic Survey 1969* (London: ISS, 1970), p. 71.

35. ISS, *The Military Balance 1970-1971, op. cit.,* p. 9; *Japan's Security, 1969* edition, *op. cit.,* pp. 167-68.

36. Georgetown University, Center for Strategic and International Studies, *Soviet Sea Power* (Washington, D.C.: Georgetown, June 1969), Special Report Series No. 10, p. 54.

37. Bernard Gwertzman, "Soviet and Indochina," *New York Times* (Moscow dateline), June 17, 1970.

38. Japan: Gaimusho, Joho Bunka-kyoku (Bureau of Information and Culture, Foreign Office), "Ajia ni mukau Soren no Shisei" (Position of the Soviet Union toward Asia in *Sekai no Ugoki* (Trends of the World), No. 213, September 1969. Quotations from Radio Moscow and *Izvestia* are from this article.

39. *Ibid.*

40. Quoted in A Diplomatic Correspondent, "Russians Planning to Build Up Security System in Asia," *The Times,* London, June 27, 1969.

41. Richard Halloran, "Soviet May Propose Asian Security Talks," *New York Times*, October 24, 1969.

42. TASS, November 18, 1970.

43. *New York Times,* June 6, 1969.

44. Report of lecture by Dmitri Petrov, "Soviet Economy and Japan," *Mainichi,* May 14, 1970.

45. *Japan's Security*, 1969 edition, *op. cit.*, p. 194.

11 The Former Colonies: Korea and Taiwan

The Heritage of Colonialism

On a hot September day in 1969, the publisher of one of Seoul's important newspapers sat in his cluttered upstairs office. To get there one sidled between the tables of a crowded restaurant on the first floor, with the clatter, talk, laughter, smells, and scraping chairs of a seemingly continuous lunch hour. The office was dark, with stacks of books and papers on chairs, tables, and on the floor. The publisher excused himself for having lunch at his desk; he was munching corn on the cob, almost hidden behind the piles of papers and with eight telephones before him. He looked up and spoke brusquely, "Japan? Japan is *not* solving its problems with Korea!" He called an assistant, who dug into a pile of papers in one corner of the room and finally, after much searching, unearthed a mimeographed text of a speech the publisher had delivered in Japanese not long before at a meeting in Tokyo. The speech had cited fifteen problems in Japanese-Korean relations which the Japanese were not solving. "And the Americans are basically to blame" he blurted between chews of corn, "You divided Korea and left it crippled. Then MacArthur gave Japan a stupid constitution and encouraged socialism, which is now the main influence on youth. Yet the United States kept helping Japan while Japan made profits from the Korean War." His parting shot at the end of the interview was, "Don't believe the Japanese! You can never trust the Japanese!"

In Taipei the clean-cut, handsome, successful young Taiwanese executive, sitting in the office of an important Taiwanese trading company, said that Taiwan was friendliest to Japan of any Asian country. His elementary schooling had been in Japanese; his wife teased him for acting like a Japanese—he was a tyrant at home! "Taiwanese over 35 speak Japanese, were educated in Japanese, and are sympathetic to Japan. The younger generation knows nothing about Japan, but they read what Japan did in China and Southeast Asia; they are anti-Japanese, and they don't like Japan's push in Taiwan now."

These are the reactions of two individuals in Japan's prewar colonies twenty-four years after their liberation from Japanese colonial rule.

By the end of the war in 1945, Japan had ruled Taiwan for 50 years and Korea for 35. Taiwan was a prize won from China after war in 1895; Korea was annexed in 1910, after some years of submission to dominating Japanese influence. Russia had been defeated by 1905; and the Portsmouth treaty, blessed by Theodore Roosevelt's mediation, recognized Japan's "paramount interest" in Korea.

Both the Taiwanese and the Koreans fought Japanese occupation. A short-lived "Republic of Taiwan" was proclaimed at Taipei in May of 1895, and resistance on the island continued for some months. It took seven years to suppress the last guerilla holdouts and establish complete military and police control over the Formosan Chinese inhabitants. (The head-hunting aborigines, who lived usually in remote mountain villages, continued to cause disturbances. Incidents were reported as late as 1934.) In Korea, opposition to the conquerors was far stronger, more stubborn, bitter, widespread and long lasting. During the two years before annexation, the Japanese were literally at war in Korea, with 12,000 people killed in one twelve-month period. [1] The independence movement, although it went underground after annexation, continued as a formidable force with a strong, enduring influence over the Korean people.

The two colonies were important to Japan, first as suppliers of food and needed industrial materials, and second, as bases for the developing policies of military expansion on the Asian continent and toward the South Seas. During the 1930's Korea and Taiwan provided almost two thirds of Japan's food imports, including the rice required to supplement homeland production. Economics were organized to benefit the mother country; rice production in Korea and Formosa was related not to local consumption but to Japanese demands. Domestic per capita consumption in Korea decreased 45 percent in the fifteen years before 1935, although the percentage of the rice crop exported to Japan rose from 14 percent to 48 percent in the same period. One writer put this exploitation of Korea in perspective: "There are few countries in the world, even among the colonies, where such a large portion of the goods is taken out of the country." [2]

Taiwan supplied Japan with rice and sugar, which together made up about three quarters of the island's total exports. Ninety percent of Taiwan's total exports were shipped to Japan. Items exported in smaller quantities included alcohol, bananas, canned pineapple, and camphor. Farmers in Taiwan were better off than those in Korea; their crops were worth more per acre, the soil was richer and because of the climate, they could grow two crops instead of one.

As Japan proceeded to build the Co-prosperity Sphere in East Asia, Korea became the gateway to the puppet state of Manchukuo and to Japanese-dominated North China, while Taiwan was the "aircraft carrier pointing south." In this sense, Korea belonged to the Army, Taiwan to the Navy. As war with China ravenously consumed materials, the resources of the colonies, human and material, were mobilized to service the war machine.

In Korea, given the impetus of espansion on the continent, industrialization progressed rapidly and successfully. Value of industrial production increased fifteen times from 1932 to 1945, and the number of industrial corporations operating in Korea jumped from 484 in 1929 to 1,812 in 1939. The Japanese reaped most of the benefits; in 1938 they owned 90 percent of the paid-up capital of all corporations. The Koreans owned some small businesses, but according to one estimate, their share in industrial capital was no more than 6 percent in 1940. They were able to find some opportunities for employment in large organizations and for technical training. A few became financially well off. [3]

In 1939 the Governor of Taiwan singled out the three most urgent tasks: expansion, industrialization, and Japanization (*kominka*). [4] The achievement of these three goals was seen as essential to the establishment of the New Order in East Asia, in which Taiwan was to play a unique role. It would be the nerve center and take-off point for the advance into South China and the South Seas. Industrialization of the island would permit the quickest and most profitable use of the benefits of the southern conquest: with more electric power, more raw materials from the South could be processed. One hydroelectric power plant, built by American capital, near Sun and Moon Lake was functioning. A plant to produce aluminum from bauxite found in the Netherlands

East Indies was in operation. Other projects were planned. Taiwan's industrial development was to become a model for Japan's spheres of influence in China and Southeast Asia.

The third policy, *kominka,* or Japanization, was a kind of spiritual mobilization directed to the Formosan Chinese. *Kominka* meant literally "changing into imperial subjects" and sought to root out Formosan and Chinese culture, religion, language, and customs, creating in their place a total "Japanese-ness" designed to capture the body and soul of the individual.

In both colonies, Japan tried to destroy the identity of the people as Taiwanese and Koreans and inculcate into them unquestioning loyalty to the Emperor of Japan. Education was directed to these ends. However, except for endowing the generations who grew up during these years with a knowledge of the Japanese language, the efforts were not successful. Koreans, particularly, were bitter, outraged, and determined in their resistance. At the war's end, more than 50 percent of the adult population in Korea could still read the Korean native script. As one observer said, "The Japanese educational system failed completely in its express purpose of making the Koreans loyal Japanese subjects and of obliterating all vestiges of Korean identity." [5] The Taiwanese, more easy-going than the Koreans, gave lip service to Japanese indoctrination but were not deeply influenced. A young Formosan told the writer in 1939 that his contemporaries had little feeling for the teachings of their Japanese "tutors," and he questioned then whether *kominka* could ever be successful.

Japanese colonial rule offered little chance for the inhabitants of the colonies to participate in government. Most important official positions in both Korea and Taiwan were held by Japanese. In Korea, Japanese monopolized more than 80 percent of the highest positions, 60 percent of those of intermediary rank, and 50 percent of the minor jobs in government. Very few Formosan Chinese occupied positions of any importance. At the university at Taipei, only one professor was Taiwanese. Japanese residents made up only 5 percent of the population, but Japanese students greatly outnumbered Taiwanese in all secondary and higher educational institutions except the School of Agriculture. [6] As an indication of the separation of occupations, in both colonies about three fourths of the local population were engaged in agriculture, while 41 percent of the Japanese residents were employed in government service.[7]

Japan's colonial policy was designed to serve Japan's interests, not the welfare of the Koreans and the Taiwanese. As one writer described the policy in Korea, it was "despotic though purposeful."[8] The legacy of colonialism was resentment and bitterness, deeper and more alive among Koreans than among the Formosan Chinese.

However, Japan left behind efficient railway systems, highways, hydroelectric power plants, postal and telecommunications systems, a considerable industrial base in Korea, and the beginnings of industrialization in Taiwan.[9] In spite of the postwar division of Korea, which cut the industrial north from the agricultural south, both the Republic of Korea and the Chinese Nationalist Government benefited from the economic structure which the Japanese had built.

Contrasting Korean and Taiwanese Views of the Japanese

Although the Koreans and the Taiwanese experienced Japanese colonial rule for approximately the same period of history, their attitudes toward Japan and the Japanese have contrasted sharply in the postwar period. Koreans have done everything in their power to erase the imprint of Japanese occupation. Taiwanese, on the other hand, have readily and easily renewed relationships with the Japanese and have seemed to harbor little rancor over the injustices of the colonial period. These differences of attitude are explained by the influences of character, culture, policy, and history.

1. Clearly, the character of the two peoples is different. Koreans are more volatile, combative, and quick-acting than are the more easy-going, relaxed Formosan Chinese. Perhaps the tropical climate of Taiwan and its history of less well organized turbulence have made the Taiwanese more placid and more tolerant than Koreans. Former Prime Minister Kishi once said that the reason Taiwanese like Japan and Koreans do not lies in the "different personality of the Taiwanese: easier for anybody to govern, no long tradition of nationalism, and so much politer than Koreans."[10]

2. Korea has a language and culture uniquely its own and a long

history of independence. The Taiwanese have always lived under outside rule. They were absorbed by Japan before the Chinese nationalist movement got under way and thus missed its direct influence. The few abortive attempts by the students and others to form independence movements, especially during the 1920's, made little headway and attracted little support.

By contrast, the Koreans, proud of their art, language, and thousands of years of history, have traditionally felt culturally superior to the Japanese. Politically unified at the end of the seventh century, Korea remained much the same country in language, culture, and geography until partition in 1945. Before the Japanese occupation, one dynasty ruled continuously for 518 years, from 1392 to 1910. The Korean independence movement was very much alive throughout the Japanese period, both within the country and outside. By the end of the war, rival independence groups were active in Hawaii, Chungking, Yenan, and the Soviet Union. They were united only in their opposition to Japan and their zeal for an independent Korea.

3. Then too, Japanese colonial policy, while it was directed toward the same ends in both Korea and Taiwan, differed in character and implementation in the two colonies. The military kept continuous control in Korea for the entire 35 years of occupation, whereas in Taiwan, for the 17 years after 1919, civilians served as governor general. In 1936 the Navy took over, and admirals held the post of governor general of Taiwan until the war's end. Although military and police controls were tight in Taiwan, as foreigners sojourning there in the 1930's will so well remember, the hand of the Navy was probably never quite so harsh as that of the despotic Army, building its iron empire in Korea.

4. The Japanese traditionally disliked the Koreans and discriminated against them; it is natural that the ill will should have been reciprocated. Although Japanese popular opinion of China and the Chinese was never high, there was no special Japanese feeling of prejudice against Formosan Chinese. Hideyoshi's conquest and devastation of Korea in the 16th century produced a historical memory which can still bring feelings of bitterness to the Koreans and of arrogance to the Japanese. As the only significant foreign minority group in Japan, the 600,000 Korean residents are Japan's "race problem." Keeping to their own schools and ghettos, many of them refusing repatriation and integration, they have endured discrimination for decades. Today

Koreans rate lowest in Japan's popularity polls. In a recent comparison of Japanese feelings toward Americans, Russians, British, French, Germans, Italians, Indians, Thais, Chinese, Indonesians, Filipinos, Koreans, Negroes, and people of mixed blood, Koreans were disliked more than any of the others. Respondents were asked to indicate, with respect to each nationality or category, whether they would approve, disapprove, or be indifferent to becoming friends, travelling together, living as neighbors, entering the same public bath, and marrying a brother, sister, or child. Koreans were highest in "disapprovals" in every category. For example, 62 percent of the respondents disapproved of marriage with a Korean; the next highest disapproval percentages were 61 percent for Negroes and 45 percent for Chinese.[11]

5. The final and perhaps most important reason for differing Korean and Taiwanese perceptions of Japan relates to their contrasting postwar experiences. Japan's defeat in World War II brought independence to Korea but continental Chinese rule to Taiwan. This occupation of Taiwan by the mainlanders determined the present composition of the population. In 1970 there were an estimated 14.4 million inhabitants, of whom about 12 million were native Formosans, 2 million were Nationalist Chinese from the mainland, and some 170,000 were aboriginal tribesmen. The way in which the mainlanders took power in 1947 has never been forgotten: the first eager expectations, the crushing disillusionment, the revolt, the massacre and blood bath, and the ruthless oppression which succeeded these events. Although the Taiwanese have adjusted to life under mainland domination and have shared in the remarkable prosperity of the island, their activities have been carefully controlled and their participation in government, although greater than under Japanese rule, is still minimal. Only one Formosan was admitted to the Central Committee of the ruling party, the Kuomintang, and high positions in Government were held exclusively by mainlanders. In December 1969 Taiwanese candidates campaigned openly for the first time in the first national election held since the Nationalists fled the mainland. Enjoying an unprecedented and remarkable freedom of speech at that time, candidates echoed the "taxation without representation" cry of the American colonists and daringly compared their status to the "slave mentality" of the Rhodesian blacks.[12]

The Koreans have suffered the partition of their country and a bloody civil war and live with continuing tension, crisis, and threat. Still, they have not had to submit to rulers from the outside, as have the Taiwanese. For the Taiwanese, this experience has mellowed their memories of Japanese colonial exploitation; the suppressions of the present are more vivid than the indignities of the past. In September 1969 a leading Taiwanese journalist admitted frankly to the writer that the Taiwanese preferred the Japanese to the mainlanders.

The relationship between the ruling mainlander crust—14 percent of the population—and the 84 percent of the people who are Taiwanese (aborigines 2 percent), affects Taiwanese attitudes toward the Japanese but, more important, suggests who will rule the island in the future. Of the Chinese who escaped from the mainland, 600,000 were soldiers; most of these left wives and families in China and were not permitted to marry in Taiwan, since they had to assume they would be reunited with their families when the Nationalist forces reconquered the homeland. Some did, however, marry Taiwanese, formally or informally, and a few married aborigines. Thus, their progeny lost any "mainland" identity.

Of the elite mainlander leadership class, the children and grandchildren have emigrated and are emigrating in large numbers, most of them to the United States, presumably to obtain an education. However, very few ever return to Taiwan; most marry Americans or Eurpoeans and seek careers abroad. Their Eurasian children would never fit into a Chinese elite society. The implications for the future are unmistakeably a steady drain from the mainlander population, with no compensating infusions of new blood. If these natural processes continue, the result can only be the eventual take-over of the island by the Taiwanese. Such a new kind of leadership could guide Taiwan toward one of several destinies: independence, reabsorption into the mainland, or some other form of relationship with the government on the mainland.

Normalization of Relations Between Japan and South Korea

Japan signed a treaty of peace with the Government of Chiang Kai-shek in 1952, shortly after the Japanese peace treaty had come into effect, but it took thirteen more years before relations could finally be normalized with the Republic of Korea. Japanese and South Korean representatives first met together in 1951, while Japan was still under American occupation. They failed to reach an agreement then and in subsequent repeated attempts. Twenty years after Japan's surrender, these two close neighbors had still been unable to establish normal diplomatic relations with each other.

In the fall of 1964, talks were again resumed. This time President Park took a determined stand to accomplish normalization. However, prospects were still gloomy, especially in Korea. One found deep fears and apprehensions about the Japanese among Government officials in Seoul. Remembering the cruel rule of the prewar period, Koreans saw themselves overwhelmed by the Japanese economic giant, whose weapons might be different now but whose aim would again be domination. The President gave his Foriegn Minister, the young, bright, able and enthusiastic Lee Tong Won, the assignment of normalizing relations with Japan. As the Foreign Minister said at the time, he was young, with many years ahead of him; he would put all of his energies into this task; if he failed, he was willing to be expendable. The opposition forces in Korea were dead set against the treaty; they were determined to block it. Many observers expected the struggle to tear the country apart.

Intensive negotiations continued until all documents were signed on June 22, 1965. The ratification process in both Seoul and Tokyo aroused violent demonstrations and parliamentary turmoil, which caused both Governments to resort to unusual tactics to force the bills through. After a stormy Korean ratification in August, the treaty was submitted to the Japanese Diet in October. The opposition parties used every conceivable device to delay, obstruct, and disrupt, including the *gyuho*, or "cow-walk," a well-known parliamentary tactic in which members stroll to the ballot box in slow motion to delay action in the Diet. The treaty was blitzed through the House of Representatives in fifty seconds in a surprise midnight session;[13] when it was submitted to the Upper House, opposition members boycotted the session. By December 8, 1965, the treaty had been ratified in both countries and was in effect.

Few international agreements have been so complex as the Japan-Republic of Korea treaty. The first and most difficult issue was the "basic relations" agreement. Japan was determined not to foreclose the possibility of carrying on some relations with North Korea, regardless of how informal or tenuous these might be. The ROK was equally determined to be formally recognized as the sole legitimate Government for *all* of Korea. In an exchange of notes accompanying the 1952 treaty with Nationalist China, Japan had succeeded in restricting recognition to territories actually or thereafter to be under the control of the Republic of China. The Koreans flatly rejected any such language. Only after prolonged and bitter controversy were the Korean negotiators persuaded to accept recognition as "the only lawful government in Korea as specified in the resolution 195 (III) of the United Nations General Assembly." Since this resolution identified the "lawful government as the one exerting effective control and jurisdiction of that part of Korea opened to United Nations observation, there was no question but that South Korea was meant. At least this was the Japanese interpretation. Foreign Minister Shiina told the Diet, ". . . as far as this treaty is concerned the problem of North Korea is still in the state of *carte blanche.* The area of the treaty application is limited only to the area where the present jurisdiction of South Korea extends." However, the Koreans could give a different interpretation. Foreign Minister Lee Tong Won declared that "with the conclusion of this treaty the Government of Japan hereafter could not establish any legal relationship with North Korea such as diplomatic relations or an exchange of diplomatic representatives, without abrogating the treaty itself."[14] The phraseology was useful and helped ratification in both countries.

The other most important elements of the treaty were (1) economic issues, (2) fisheries, and (3) treatment of Koreans in Japan. A territorial question plagued the negotiators until a few hours before the treaty was to be signed: sovereignty over Takeshima, a tiny uninhabited rock island which both countries claimed. Finally, the only possible solution was to agree not to agree: the question of Takeshima would be left for diplomatic negotiations. At one point someone facetiously suggested that the Americans would do everybody a great favor by using the island for target practice and nuclear bombing it off the map and off the agenda!

The economic issues boiled down to the amount of aid Japan would give Korea. The Japanese called this "economic cooperation"; the Koreans insisted on "claims" for compensation justly due for the years of insult and injury inflicted on the Korean people. In the end it was left to each side to describe the funds in its own way. Amounts finally agreed upon were $300 million in grants, $200 million in loans, and $300 million in commerical credits, to be paid generally over a ten year period.

The fisheries problem was complex. Korean harassment and seizure of Japanese fishing boats had continued unabated for years; between 1947 and 1965 the South Koreans captured 327 boats and 3,911 crewmen.[15] Japan objected to the "Rhee Line," which limited fishing areas, and protested discriminatory treatment. The Koreans claimed that the Japanese were far advanced in equipment and methods and asked for help to repair their deficiencies. The agreement in effect abolished the Rhee Line, delineated a most complex system of fishing zones and areas, and provided Japanese technical assistance for the Korean fishing industry.

Matters concerning the 600,000 Koreans resident in Japan, although taken up in the treaty, have continued to be bothersome. Of these 600,000, some 200,000 have registered as nationals of South Korea and the remaining 400,000 wish to be considered nationals of the northern Democratic Peoples Republic of Korea (DPRK). The problems of their treatment, registration, education, and repatriation have not yet been satisfactorily settled and are continuing sources of friction between Seoul and Tokyo.

Of the Seoul publisher's fifteen complaints about Japan, noted at the beginning of this chapter, four related to relations with North Korea, three concerned the treatment of Koreans in Japan, and the remainder embraced economic problems: trade imbalance, tariffs, credits, quotas, investments, and taxes. While North Korea has none of the lure or dimension of Communist China, Japan does reserve the right to deal with the North Koreans, informally, unofficially, and in the spirit of the separation of politics and economics. Trade with North Korea is not large; it amounted to $56 million in 1969, more than a 50 percent increase over the 1967 figure but still less than one sixteenth of Japan's trade with South Korea. As an official of the Foreign Office said to the author in Seoul, "The Korean government is not happy with the Japanese 'neutralist' attitude toward the Communist states. Their deportation of Koreans to North Korea (they call it repatriation) and continuing trade with the Communist North make things difficult for us. But we realize that Japan has political problems of its own."[16]

In spite of the publisher's complaints, five years after normalization, relations between Japan and the ROK have gone remarkably well. The principal economic question has been the imbalance in trade, a problem that Japan, with her stupendous growth, is facing with many countries, not least of all the United States. Japan in 1969 sold to South Korea almost six times as much as she bought: $767 million versus $134 million. This has been a continuing difficulty and worried Koreans even before normalization. They have urged the Japanese to buy more Korean products, especially seaweed, and to reduce tarriffs on Korean imports, in particular on manufactured articles processed in Korea and reexported to Japan.

Korean Government officials interviewed in late 1969 were generally optimistic about the progress of economic cooperation with Japan. In addition to the Japanese payments on grants and loans, which were being made on schedule, Japanese technical assistance programs were expanding. About 80 Korean trainees have gone to Japan annually for technical training and several research and technical training projects function in Korea with Japanese cooperation. Japanese officials believed that their technical assistance projects could be carried out more effectively in Korea than in Southeast Asia; the language and the ability of the Koreans were advantages.

The top priority item on the Korean agenda for economic talks held in Tokyo in August 1969 was an integrated steel mill. The Japanese were dubious but concluded that the political importance of the steel mill overshadowed its uncertain economic justification. In the joint conference communique the Japanese "showed deep understanding" of the Korean request and agreed to make a survey and produce a plan.

A prominent Korean, a former minister in the Park government, exuded optimism for the future of the ROK and for relations with Japan. He recalled the doom predicted by the opponents of normalization and how wrong they had been. Now much depended on the North. If the North left the South in peace, the future was very bright indeed. South Korea could compete with Japan. The people are inspired by Japan, but they workharder than the Japanese. This human drive and a still cheap, plentiful labor supply are Korea's advantages. Koreans imitate Japan as Japan imitated the West. They can make radios and gadgets as well as the Japanese, but copies. The conversation ended, as did so many in Seoul, with a plea to the United States, "We are glad to have the Japanese take more responsibility, but the Americans must stay here." [17]

Japan's Relations with the Republic of China

Although Japan and the Republic of China have enjoyed normal diplomatic relations with each other since 1952, the course of these relations has not always been smooth. It has been complicated by Japan's insistence, as we have seen, on trading with Communist China and on encouraging a policy toward Peking of the "forward posture." Taipei has reacted according to its judgment of how far Japan leans to the mainland, in one instance approaching a break in diplomatic relations. Always, however, the Nationalist Government has prized its ties with Japan; in turn, Tokyo has dealt cautiously and carefully with Taipei.

Economically Taiwan is of no small importance to Japan. Two-way trade in 1969 surpassed that with Communist China by more than $161 million ($786.8 million with Taiwan; $625.3 million with mainland China). Trade with both Taiwan and mainland China jumped appreciably in 1970 ($953 million and $825 million), but the balance was still in favor of Taiwan ($127 million). In 1965 the Japanese Government extended credits to the Republic of China amounting to $150 million, utilized mainly for the construction of a dam. In 1970 negotiations were conducted for an additional loan of $300 million, to be used principally to build the port of Taichung and main north-south highways. Japanese private investments in Taiwan by the end of 1968 were $50 million, only a third of the American total but far greater in diversity, representing 264 separate ventures as opposed to 114 for the United States.[18] By 1970 Japanese investments had increased to 307 joint enterprises, valued at $63 million.

Most Japanese joint ventures are with Taiwanese, not mainlanders. Many firms appear to be Taiwanese but in fact are Japanese in financing and control. Business relations between Taiwanese and Japanese appear to be good; the common language, for those Taiwanese over 35, is a great advantage. One prominent Taiwanese industrialist complained of unfair practices by the Japanese, who, he said, were aggressive in their trading methods and not above using "silver bullets" (bribes) to gain their ends. He also objected to the Japanese practice of staffing their companies from Japan instead of hiring local citizens, as the Americans did. Japanese employees, being exempt from conscription, had a great advantage over Taiwanese, whose em-

267

ployment was constantly interrupted for military service.[19]

As can be expected, the Japanese are active in certain key industries, although their interests extend to a great variety of manufacturing enterprises. Out of fourteen electronics companies, two are Japanese and control 60 percent of the electronics business. The only automobile plant in Taiwan manufactures the Japanese Nissan Bluebird; the Government requires 60 percent of the parts to be made in Taiwan. (In Korea a Japanese automobile is made, but with a Korean name, "Shinjin.") As in Korea, numerous factories take advantage of a cheaper labor supply to produce Japanese radios.

The trade balance was more than three to one in favor of Japan in 1969 ($606 million in exports; $180.5 million in imports). This is a smaller gap than the six to one ratio with the ROK, but it is still a problem. Japan exports manufactured goods and machinery to Taiwan and, instead of the sugar and rice of prewar days, imports bananas ($57 million worth in 1969). Taiwan depends on this market. Relations were shaken in 1969 by the great "banana scandal," involving fraudulent diversion of some $2.5 million dollars, with government employees and officials of farmer cooperatives profiting at the expense of farmers. Bananas were sold at inflated prices, but the Taiwanese farmer lost his fair share. Numerous individuals were arrested and tried, and several high ranking officials removed from office. The affair revealed the complex relationships which can develop between Japanese entrepreneurs, affluent Taiwanese businessmen, and vulnerable mainlander bureaucrats.[20]

The Nationalist Chinese Government fears too close association between Taiwanese and Japanese and too much cultural influence from Japan. Japanese films, books, magazines, newspapers, and popular songs are banned. Suspicion attaches to students who go to Japan (as well as to the United States), where Taiwanese independence organizations are active, since many of the students who leave Taiwan are reported to join these movements abroad. In the summer of 1969, the Taipei Ministry of Education announced that for at least the rest of the year no more students would be permitted to study in Japan. Arrests of students and professors returning from abroad have understandably discouraged others from coming home and have added to an already serious brain drain. Even tourist travel is tightly controlled; in early 1970 the Government prohibited visits to Japan's EXPO '70.

Nationalist Chinese officials have been uneasy over both American and Japanese overtures to Communist China. They were dismayed at the resumption of talks between the American and Chinese ambassadors in Warsaw and would be further perturbed should the Japanese Foreign Office succeed in arranging contacts on the ambassadorial level with the Peking government. Taipei will pay the closest attention to the China policies of both Japan and the United States in the light of the changing situation in the United Nations and the recognition by a succession of other countries of the Government in Peking.

Reversion of Okinawa and the Sato-Nixon Agreements

The prospect of the return of the Ryukyu Islands to Japan produced qualms in both Taipei and Seoul.

In the fall of 1969, before the Washington meetings had decided on Okinawa's reversion, a Taiwanese Foreign Office official spoke emotionally to the author. The United States, he felt, was making a grievous mistake in consenting to reversion. Since agreements made at Cairo, Potsdam, and San Francisco affected Okinawa and were multilateral, other countries were now entitled to a voice in the disposition of the Ryukyus. Furthermore, they should be returned to Japan only on condition that the Soviet Union at the same time give back the northern territories. Of course the Soviets would refuse, and as a consequence reversion would be delayed. But that would be a good thing. Once the United States hands over administration of the islands, free use of the American military bases will be lost and a helpless Japan will confront a leftist Okinawa. Speaking Japanese rapidly and with his voice shaking, the official blurted out his feelings about Japan. Americans had been too soft on Japan; we seemed to be giving in so easily on Okinawa; the result could be disastrous for the security of Asia. Japan does not understand China and has no firm foreign policy toward China. Like the publisher in Seoul, he declared with emotion, "We do not trust Japan!"[21]

Koreans also viewed with dismay the prospect of Okinawa's reversion to Japan. A Korean military specialist visiting Japan was quoted as listing the consequences as he saw them for the Republic of Korea: (1) the withdrawal of American troops from the Korean peninsula would become inevitable; (2) observing the withdrawals, Kim Il-song would likely embark upon his adventure of the "second Korean war"; (3) if war did break out again, the strategic value of Japan would be decisive to United Nations forces in the ROK; however, because of the strength of leftist elements in Japan, one could not count on the cooperation which was given in 1950; (4) consequently, if the Okinawan bases are not left unrestricted, as at present (free use, free movement of nuclear weapons), the security of the ROK would be seriously impaired.[22]

Chinese Communist and North Korean Reactions

The recognition by the Japanese and American Governments in the Sato-Nixon communique of November 1969 that the security of the Republic of Korea is "essential" and security in the Taiwan area "a most important factor" for the security of Japan, evoked reactions in Pyongyang and Peking which were shrill, violent and prolonged. The theme, elaborated are repeated in the press of both capitals, was that Japanese militarism had been revived under the direction and patronage of the American imperialists and Japan was setting out to repeat the prewar expansionist policy, menacing the peace of Asia and threatening the establishment of a Japanese-controlled "Greater East Asia Co-prosperity Sphere," but this time with the strong backing of the United States.

The climax in vituperation against Japanese militarism came in April 1970, with the meetings in Pyongyang between Premiers Chou En-lai and Kim Il-song and the negotiations held in Peking later the same month to conclude the Chinese-Japanese Memorandum Trade Agreement. On March 29, before the Chou-Kim conference took place, *Rodong Sinmun* of Pyongyang published a lengthy article entitled "Let Us Oppose the Revival of Japanese Militarism." Later reprinted in English translation in both *The Pyongyang Times*, taking up seven and a half pages, and in *The People's Korea* of Tokyo, the article denounced Japanese imperialsim and aggression from the Meiji period to the present, emphasizing the reappearance of a Japanese threat to Korea, Taiwan, Vietnam, and all of Asia and the close and nefarious collaboration with the imperialistic designs of the United States. The characterization of the Sato-Nixon communique was vivid: "It is a concentric manifestation of piratical ferocity and shamelessness of modern imperialism and adds a new, heinous criminal page to the blood-stained history of two bloodthirsty imperialisms—the U.S. and Japanese."[23]

270

Within the vivid verbosity and among numerous other charges, the *Rodong Sinmun* thesis specifically accused President Johnson and Prime Minister Sato of concluding in January 1965 a secret agreement that Japan, in return for active participation in the Vietnam war, would be allowed to reinvade South Korea and "share the right of domination over it with U.S. imperialism." [24]

Condemnation by the Peking press of the Sato-Nixon agreements and Japanese militarism was no less vitriolic, as we have seen in Chapter 9. The same theme was repeated often: Japan was being turned into a military base for United States imperialism under the deceptive guise of a return of Okinawa and was directing a "spearhead of aggression squarely against China, Korea, Indochina and Asia as a whole." The article in the communique linking Japan's security with that of Korea and Taiwan always drew fire: "Such a few words have completely laid bare the U.S. and Japan's ambitions of aggression against the whole of Asia." [25]

The communique published April 7, after the meetings in Pyongyang between Chou En-lai and Kim Il-song, attacked American imperialism as the principal enemy but found Japanese militarism almost as dangerous, devoting nine paragraphs to its denunciation, the first of which set the tone:

> The two sides vehemently condemn Japanese militarism which, revived again as a dangerous force of aggression in Asia under the active patronage of U.S. imperialism, is embarking on the road of open aggression against the Asian people with a delusion to realize the old broken dream of "Greater East Asia Co-prosperity Sphere" with the backing of U.S. imperialism and in conspiracy and collusion with it. [26]

Chou En-lai's appearance in Pyongyang marked a public reconciliation with Kim Il-song after several years of cool relations between the two regimes. The Communist Party of North Korea had been pursuing an "independent" course similar to that of its sister party in Japan, and during the period of the Cultural Revolution, Kim Il-song had been denounced in the wall newspapers of Communist China. For example, after three days of silence following the *Pueblo* incident, the Peking press found no words of praise for Kim Il-song but only heaped anger on the Soviets for collaborating with the United States. In 1969 some signs of thaw began to appear, and on July 11, for the first time in several years, receptions were held in both Peking and Pyongyang to commemorate the anniversary of the Chinese-North Korean treaty of friendship and cooperation. Chou's April visit seemed to signify a Chinese effort to repair one diplomatic relationship which had been allowed to lapse. Probably the immediate stimulus, besides the ever present motive of competing with Moscow, was the Washington agreements and their specific references to Taiwan and the Korean peninsula.

Chou and Kim attacked Japan for assisting the United States both in provoking a new war in Korea and in "insidiously machinating to include Taiwan, the sacred territory of the Chinese people, in their sphere of influence." In the joint communique, the Chinese expressed support for the efforts of the DPRK to achieve unification of the country "after making the U.S. imperialist aggression army withdraw from South Korea." Korea, in turn, extended "full support to the righteous struggle of the Chinese people to liberate Taiwan from the occupation by U.S. imperialists and achieve territorial integrity."[27]

Security: Japan, South Korea, Taiwan

Responsible leaders in Taiwan and South Korea reacted calmly to Chou's and Kim's cries of alarm at the perils of Japanese militarism. Still, they obviously have not themselves been entirely sure about the kind of role Japan might play in the future. As we have seen, the agreement to transfer Okinawa's administration to Japan created uneasiness in the Republics of both China and Korea. The tying together of Japanese, Korean, and Taiwanese security was designed to reassure the people of both Taiwan and South Korea and indeed they have welcomed this American-Japanese agreement. But they are not quite confident of how much protection it in fact extends to them.

In the eyes of these nations, the key to security in the Pacific lies not with Japan but with the United States. Their attitude toward Japan is ambivalent. They believe that Japan, with its strong economic power, should assume a rightful share of responsibility for security in the region. However, while not swayed by the kind of hysteria emanating from Peking and Pyongyang, they nevertheless harbor their own small fears that Japan might again become fascinated with military power and revert to the swaggering arrogance which older men in their countries still remember. For them, the believable assurances must come from the United States.

In Taipei and Seoul the American hears voiced many times the plea that the United States stay. The Nixon doctrine that Asians should take care of Asian problems has a sensible sound and a natural appeal, but judged against the background of the United States leaving Vietnam and a shaky outlook for Indochina, it generates uneasiness in responsible men who must think about the security of their own countries. In the minds of leaders in Taiwan and South Korea, security has always been irrevocably tied to an American presence. The Americans are wanted not only for the security they are believed to bring but also because of the feeling that it is good to have them around while the Japanese grow so rapidly in power and confidence. Some of those one met in Seoul and Taipei seemed not to understand that the years of American tutelage over Japan were long gone, and they tended to exaggerate the influence which the United States could in the future bring to bear. They did not seem to realize that the nation which expected to become the second most powerful economically in the world and was experiencing a fast developing spirit of nationalism and independence would make its own decisions based on cold calculations of self-judged self-interest; that American leverage had already diminished and would be even less potent in the future.

Published reports that the United States might in 1971 begin to reduce its military forces in South Korea set off the strongest protests in Seoul. President Park Chung Hee immediately declared that keeping American troops at their present strength was essential to face the threat from the North. ROK officials wrung their hands over the uncertainties of the next few years, reminding Americans that this is the year Kim Il-song is most likely to pick to invade again. They asked that American forces stay at least until 1975—an even quarter of a century after the first crossing of the 38th parallel, one recalls—when the ROK would assuredly be strong enough to defend the country with its own forces. As a senior editor of the *New York Times* expressed it on a recent visit to Seoul: "The one country in the world where an American is least likely to be greeted with that bitter slogan 'Yankee Go Home' is the Republic of Korea . . . the South Koreans . . . want the Americans on hand if they have to face another invasion."[28]

Japan sees the gravest and nearest outside danger in the Korean peninsula. Although the Japanese public is still relatively un-concerned about a possible second Korean war, responsible political leaders realize that the danger is real and that, like it or not, Japan is for the first time involved. The Sato-Nixon agreements completely changed Japan's relationship to conflict in Korea. During the war of the early 1950's, Japan was occupied by American troops and, while serving as a base for American military operations and reaping the enormous economic benefits of war expenditures, took no part in and had no responsibility for the hostilities. But should war erupt a second time, Japan's security would be affected and appropriate action would be expected. Probably this would mean an immediate alert of the Self-Defense Forces and an approach by the United States in "prior consultation."

Sato has himself made clear that either a "yes" or "no" answer is possible to requests by prior consultation. However, should the United States suddenly need to use Okinawan and Japanese bases to resist an agression committed against South Korea, it is hard to believe that a Japanese Government would refuse the request. The expected "yes" would mean full cooperation in logistics as well as the free use, without restrictions, of American bases and facilities.

The Self-Defense Forces would act to meet the threat to Japan's security. The sea forces would assist the Seventh Fleet and would doubtless take responsibility for patrolling the Soya, Tsugaru, and Tsushima straits. The air defense forces would work closely with the Fifth Air Force in maintaining the air defense of Japan and Okinawa. American combat aircraft would doubtless assist the ROK air force in defending air space over South Korea. No one would suggest the dispatch of Japanese forces outside of the country, and this could not be expected even in the emergency of war in Korea. At the same time, it is not difficult to imagine that once the SDF became engaged in defensive operations, the difficulties of respecting national boundaries in air space and the fine line between offensive and defensive warfare might well involve Japanese personnel in action the Government might prefer, for political reasons, to avoid.

One can only guess how much public support the Japanese Government would receive should it decide to cooperate with the United States in the case of war on the Korean peninsula. First, many Japanese are generally unsympathetic to Koreans. Second, while Japan enjoys normal relations exclusively with the ROK in the South, there has always been an effort, as we have seen, to keep the door open to eventual relations with the DPR in the North. In a recent public opinion poll, more than 70 percent of the respondents favored improving relations with North Korea, either through establishing diplomatic ties, expanding trade, or gradually settling problems and arranging exchanges of persons.[29] Third, the Japanese public as contrasted to the Government, does not fully support involvement in Korean security. Another poll asked the question: "Should the Japanese Government refuse the direct deployment of American forces from Japanese bases in case the ROK is attacked?" Fifty-four percent replied, "Yes, refuse." Only 16 percent approved American deployment and 13 percent gave the equivocal reply, "It depends on the circumstances."[30]

One Japanese journalist, foreseeing the Government's "yes" in prior consultations at a time of trouble in Korea, concluded that this was the necessary price which Japan had to pay for the return of Okinawa. He emphasized that in such a case the Government would need the full understanding of the Japanese people that the security of the nation was indeed directly related to Korean security and their complete cooperation in carrying out the obligation of the agreement.[31]

The adverse sample of public opinion and popular Japanese attitudes might lead to doubts that a Japanese "yes" would be reliable. No one can foretell the circumstances of the crisis which might arise in the Korean peninsula, the reaction in South Korea, the response of the United States, or the mood in Japan at the time. Let it be said, however, that public opinion polls, while useful in suggesting trends are rarely indicators of policy, especially in Japan. Sato and his party won an impressive election victory after he made the commitments contained in the agreements reached with President Nixon, and his subsequent reelection confirmed his position as leader of the party. For Japan the trend toward assuming greater international responsibility is irreversible. The Government will have the duty, and it will be a serious and continuing one, to explain to the public what this will mean in the future.

Since Japan has also recognized the relation of security in the Taiwan area to the security of Japan, the same obligations apply should trouble occur there. Most Japanese do not now believe that the Peking regime, in spite of constant fulminations and threats to "liberate" Taiwan, is going to initiate military action to recapture the island in the near future. They are confident that in spite of all hazards and pitfalls, they will be able to continue the present, very profitable diplomacy of maintaining a lucrative and solid position in Taiwan while at the same time promoting the trade and other exchanges that are possible with the Government of Communist China. The "China problem" is yet for the future.

Notes

1. John K. Fairbank, Edwin O. Reischauer, Albert M. Craig, *East Asia, The Modern Transformation* (Boston: Houghton Mifflin Company; Tokyo: Charles E. Tuttle Company, 1965), p. 482.

2. Andrew H. Grajdanzev, *Modern Korea* (New York: International Secretariat, Institute of Pacific Relations, 1944), quoted in George M. McCune, *Korea Today* (Cambridge, Mass.: Harvard University Press, 1950), p. 30.

3. Gregory Henderson, *Korea, The Politics of the Vortex* (Cambridge, Mass.: Harvard University Press, 1968), pp. 94-97.

4. U.S., Navy Department, Office of the Chief of Naval Operations, *Civil Affairs Handbook, Taiwan (Formosa)* OPNAV 50 E-12 (Washington, D.C.: June 15, 1944), p. 49.

5. McCune, *op. cit.,* p. 27.

6. *Civil Affairs Handbook, op. cit.*, p. 36.

7. Henderson, *op. cit.*, p. 75. Cites Grajdanzev, *op. cit.*, *Civil Affairs Handbook, op. cit.*, p. 12.

8. Henderson, *op. cit.,* p. 72.

9. Industrial production in Taiwan rose from 37 percent of total production in 1914 to 48 percent in 1937, while agricultural production more than trebled in the same period. See Maurice Meisner, "The Development of Formosan Nationalism," in Mark Mancall, *Formosa Today* (New York: Praeger, 1964), p. 157.

10. Douglas H. Mendel, Jr., "Japanese Policy and Views Toward Formosa," *Journal of Asian Studies,* Vol. XXVIII, No. 3 (May 1969), p. 521.

11. Wagatsuma Hiroshi and Yoneyama Toshinao, *Henken no Kozo* (Structure of Prejudice), (Tokyo: NHK Publishing Company, May 20, 1967), pp. 131-34.

12. Donald Shapiro, "Candidates Speak Minds in Taiwan," *New York Times,* December 14, 1969.

13. Hans H. Baerwald, "The Diet and the Japan-Korea Treaty," *Asian Survey,* Vol. VIII, No. 12 (December 1968), p. 956.

14. Soon Sung Che, "Japan's Two Koreas Policy and the Problem of Korean Unification," *Asian Survey*, Vol. VII, No. 10 (October 1967), pp. 706-07.

15. Doba Hajime, "The Japan Sea," *Chuo Koron*, April 1968.

16. Conversation in Seoul, September 11, 1969.

17. *Ibid.*

18. Republic of China, Foreign Office, *Table of Investments of Overseas Chinese and Foreigners by Years, 1969* (Taipei: 1969). According to the Foreign Office, Japanese investments by the end of August 1969 had increased to 316 with a total value of $65.9 million.

19. Conversation in Taipei, September 12, 1969.

20. Mark Plummer, "Taiwan: Toward a Second Generation of Mainland Rule," *Asian Survey*, Vol X, No. 1 (January 1970), pp. 21-22.

21. Conversation in Taipei, September 13, 1969.

22. Murakami Kaoru, *Nihon Boei no Koso* (The Concept of Japan's Defense), (Tokyo: The Simul Press, June 15, 1970), p. 26.

23. *The Pyongyang Times,* Pyongyang, DPRK, No. 14 (272), April 6, 1970, p. 11 *The People's Korea*, published by *Chosun Shinbosa*, Tokyo, April 8, 1970, p. 4.

24. *The Pyongyang Times, op. cit.,* p. 9.

25. *Hsinhua*, Peking, April 18, 1970, Peking NCNA International Service.

26. *The Pyongyang Times, op cit.,* April 13, 1970, p. 11.

27. *Ibid.,* p. 11.

28. John B. Oakes, editor of the editorial page, "Yankee, Please Stay a Little While," *New York Times*, November 23, 1970.

29. *Yomiuri*, May 31, 1970.

30. *Asahi*, June 23, 1970.

31. Murakami, *op. cit.,* p. 27.

12

Japan and Southeast Asia

Japan's Prewar Position in Southeast Asia

On July 20, 1936, the *Straits Times*, a leading newspaper in Singapore, warned of the dangers of Japanese economic domination: "Within a very few years, the whole of trade and banking of this colony will be dominated by the Japanese if effective preventive measures are not taken promptly." [1]   Thirty-two years and much history later, a Singapore civil servant spoke to the author about the "economic aggression" of the Japanese in his country. They think only of profits, he said, only of pushing the sale of their own products and not of the interests of the developing countries. Another civil servant was more pessimistic; he was convinced Japan would again build armed forces to defend her economic interests in Southeast Asia.

A British businessman with long experience in Asia, both prewar and postwar, and who himself had been a prisoner of the Japanese told the author one evening in Taipei, "The Japanese are winning by economic means the co-prosperity sphere they sought before World War II. And it's a good thing! They have the power, the know-how, and the expertise."

A Japanese journalist, reflecting on Japan's prewar and postwar interests in Asia, commented in 1969, "The only difference between then and now is that the Japanese leaders of that period were thinking of a 'take-over' in terms of military expansion, while today's leaders are thinking of a 'take-over' in economic terms." [2]

Few recall today the meaning and the motives of the old Greater East Asia Co-prosperity Sphere. Certainly no Japanese wishes to revive this tattered and tainted concept. Yet the enormous weight of Japan's present drive in Asia inevitably arouses memories and comparisons, and a mere three decades are not too vast a segment of history to bridge.

279

The ideology of Japan in the 1930's was always difficult for foreigners—and perhaps for many Japanese—to grasp. No one convenient text existed, no *Mein Kampf*, no little red book of Mao. But pronouncements such as the Imperial Rescript on Education and the "Way of the Subject," a handbook published by the Education Ministry in August 1941, bore the authority of holy writ. Every child learned from his primary school text books and throughout his school life of the divine origins of Japan and of the nation's unique position in the world.

The year 1940 was the 2,600th anniversary of the founding, in 660 B.C., of the Japanese Empire by the ascension to the throne of Jimmu Tenno, direct descendant of the Sun Goddess and the first Emperor. Nineteen hundred and forty was to have been the year of years—the Olympic Games, a World's Fair, and commemoration of the nation's beginning. Spreading war cancelled the Games and the Fair—the U.S. State Department had early in 1940 recommended the evacuation from the Far East of all dependents of American citizens—but Jimmu Tenno's anniversary was honored on two days, November 10 and 11. A formal ceremony on the first day was followed by a celebration on the 11th in the spacious plaza facing the Imperial Palace grounds. Fifty thousand people attended, including diplomats and distinguished guests in formal attire, the Japanese ladies in their most prized kimonos. All were given box lunches with bits of fish, beancake, rice, and even a bottle of sake (protection against the cold!), all beautifully wrapped in the artistic Japanese cloth of a thousand uses, the *furoshiki*.

At a hushed moment the red limousine (no one but the Emperor could own a red automobile) appeared at the palace gate, and the Emperor and Empress were driven slowly the short distance to the bunting-draped platform. American Ambassador Joseph C. Grew, then dean of the diplomatic corps, sat on the platform with the Emperor, the Empress, and honored guests and delivered a speech of congratulation. With the conscientious care of a professional diplomat preparing a state paper, Ambassador Grew obtained State Department approval for his brief complimentary remarks, which were neither profound nor pointed, and carried no urges nor warnings. "This anniversary symbolizes and marks the long continuity and tradition for which Japan is deservedly distinguished," intoned Mr. Grew, ". . . may the nation ever increasingly contribute to the general culture and well-being of mankind." The Emperor was seen to nod approval several times during the Ambassador's reading, a gesture thought so politically significant by the French Ambassador that he hastily cabled the fact to his government. [3]

The Imperial Rescript set the tone of the anniversary:

> Ye, Our subjects, should let your minds go back to the great task of the Empire-founding achieved by the Emperor Jimmu, and then think how profound were the Imperial plans and how difficult and deep the Imperial policy. Ye, therefore, should work in harmony and cooperation to enhance the glory of the fundamental character of the Empire, surmount the difficulties confronting the current situation, and make manifest the national dignity, so that all this can answer the Heavenly spirits of Our Ancestor." [4]

The myth of Japan's origins, the constitutional position of the Emperor as "sacred and inviolable," and the continuity of the imperial line "for ages eternal" nurtured the nationalism which the country's early leaders believed necessary to build a powerful state. Looking back on this "ultra-nationalism," a Japanese professor wrote in 1946: "Ultra-nationalism succeeded in spreading a many-layered, though invisible, net over the Japanese people, and even today they have not really freed themselves from its hold." [5] A Japanese was taught to think, not as an individual with freedoms and personal choices, but as a disciplined part of a unique Japanese state and society.

The homogeneity, the inward-looking closeness, of the Japanese, and long isolation, had created curtains between themselves and foreigners. These were partially torn apart by the flood into Japan of knowledge and know-how which characterized the Meiji Restoration in the years after 1868. But the national experience with foreigners was not a happy one. There were the wars with China and Russia, quarrels with the Western Powers over unequal treaties, and later an aggravating dispute with the United States over discriminatory immigration.

The Meiji leaders had placed great store in a strong Army and Navy, and these acquitted themselves well against China and Russia. Modern Japan's first heroes, General Nogi, Admiral Togo, and Field Marshall Oyama, arose out of the war with Russia, which gave the nation great confidence and high morale.

With Western technology and arms, tried and successful, Japan's leaders saw for the future the vision of a great Japanese

Empire. Leaders with the prescience to think ahead might have wondered whether Japan's destiny could be fulfilled without understandings with the two great neighbors, China, the mammoth land power, and the United States, the great ocean power. Japan's tragedy was that she could achieve understanding with neither and that she went to war with both.

The concept of a divine mission, not only in the Japanese Empire, whose growth was inevitably a matter of pride, but in the world, evoked response from an insular people. After 1931 Japanese military power spread from Manchuria into North China and southward. Racial and national pride grew out of the inspiration of grandiose opportunities to save Asia for the Asians. Later it was tempered by the sobering facts of logistics, economics, and the singular lack of Chinese enthusiasm for the "New Order" being bestowed upon them.

The concept of Japan's mission to free Asians from the yoke of Western control and bless them with the unique moral virtues of the Imperial Way was symbolized in the phrases which masked the policies: the New Order in East Asia, the Eight Corners of the Universe under one Roof, and the Greater East Asia Co-prosperity Sphere.

The "Way of the Subject," carefully prepared for the edification and education of the Japanese people, particularly the youth, was announced as a new code of ethics for the nation. It denounced the evils of Western civilization—individualism, liberalism, utilitarianism, and materialism—and proclaimed Japan's destiny to build a universal order based on moral principles. Japan's "victories" were aimed to stir the Asian conscience as Japan proceeded to emancipate and stabilize the East Asian nations. This mission was described in the "Way of the Subject":

> Until the elimination of the evils of European and American influences in East Asia that have led China astray is realized, until Japan's cooperation with New China as one of the links in the chain of the Great East Asia Co-prosperity Sphere yields satisfactory results, and East Asia and the rest of the world are united as one on the basis of moral principles, Japan's indefatigable efforts are sorely needed. [6]

The role of the military in this scheme was central. The "Way of the Subject" made it clear: "Defense is absolutely necessary for national existence. A nation without defense is one that belongs to a visionary world." The "Way" called for a total war structure, without which no victory would be possible. [7]

Other forces impelled Japan toward expansion besides the sacred task of conferring on Asians the blessings of the imperial destiny. First was the determination that the independence from the West and strong military power should be primary national objectives. The Japanese described this policy as their Monroe Doctrine; it meant a free hand in China, Southeast Asia, and in the South Seas, and its logical implication was a clash of interests with the United States and the Soviet Union, not to speak of the colonial powers holding territories within this area. Second and equally important was the economic domination of East and Southeast Asia. This was stated in terms of population pressure and requirements for access to essential raw materials and to markets for Japanese goods.

Ambassador Grew gave the Tokyo Embassy's view of the situation in November 1940:

> The program of the Japanese extremists, who today are definitely in the saddle and are supported by at least a substantial section of the public, is to sweep on through "Greater East Asia including the South Seas," gaining provisional economic and ultimate political control, as fast and as thoroughly as circumstances permit. [8]

As penetration progressed, led by the military, the inevitable obstacles arose. By mid-1941, the cry in Tokyo was to break the so-called tightening encirclement of the "ABCD Powers": America, Britain, Chiang Kai-shek's China, and the Dutch. The Japanese urge for security and equality was fast turning into desperation.

It was November 1941 when the author, then a junior Foreign Service Officer, returned to Washington from the Embassy in Tokyo and called on Dr. Stanley K. Hornbeck, special adviser for the Far East to the Secretary of State and senior officer in the Far Eastern Division of the Department of State. The stiff, bald, forbidding doctor scowled: "What do you people in the Embassy think about war with Japan?" The answer: "Japan wants domination in Asia and hopes to get it without war. But, if this looks impossible, Japan will go to war in desperation." A snort of derision came from the other side of what one remembers in awe as a high, vast mahogany desk: "When did a nation *ever* go to war in desperation?"

On November 27, only a few days after this frigid meeting, Dr.

Hornbeck wrote a long memorandum on the chances of war with Japan that concluded: "Stated briefly, the undersigned does not believe that this country is now on the immediate verge of 'war' in the Pacific." [9] In just ten days Japanese bombs fell on Pearl Harbor.

Japan's Postwar Approach to Asia

It is fair to ask how Japan's view of Asia in 1970 differed from the prospect of 1940. Population pressure had intensified. In 1940, 73 million people lived in the main island; by 1970 there were more than 103 million, equalling the population of the 1940 Japanese Empire, which included Sakhalin, Korea, and Taiwan. Trading patterns changed as much as the population. After 1913 more than half of Japan's foreign trade was with Asia; by 1939 this had increased to two thirds. The American share of Asian trade was 20 percent in 1936, 18 percent in 1939. [10] Today the directions are reversed. Japan's trade with Asia in 1969 was only 22 percent of her trade with the world, whereas the United States, her most important trading partner, accounted for almost 30 percent of all Japanese exports and imports. Second to the United States was Southeast Asia.

Raw materials are just as crucial in the 'seventies as they were in the 'thirties. Japan must buy from abroad oil, coal, iron, phosphate, bauxite, steel scrap, cotton, wool, hides, rubber, and many other materials, all required for the functioning of a modern industrial state. In the 'thirities the Japanese envied the Western colonial powers, whose Asian possessions guaranteed them secure access to the necessities for industrialization. Japan owned Korea and Formosa but nothing in Southeast Asia. A powerful impetus to those who advocated the "southward advance" was the need for raw materials essential to an industrial economy. In the minds of Japan's leaders, the surest and shortest way to this end was the expansion of political and military power.

The Japanese have twice built a successful producing economy, reaping profits from international trade. Before the war the lure of colonies, controls, "stabilizing missions," and the passion of military power halted and destroyed the successful development that was in progress. William Lockwood, in his history of Japan's prewar economic development, refers to the "militaristic leadership not only politically chauvinist but economically quite illiterate" and notes that "at the very crest of their economic expansion, accordingly, the Japanese were coerced and cajoled into withdrawing from the world system and making instead a supreme bid for political hegemony in East Asia." [11]

Following their defeat in World War II, the Japanese, with precise method and intense concentration, constructed the productive capacity which led to their industrial power. Moreover, this time they geared their economy to the world system, which they had failed to do before, and as Peter Drucker has said, for the past twenty years have "systematically projected the trends of the world economy onto their economic policy, both domestic and international." [12]

Although materials and markets are as essential as ever, Japan's economy is far less dependent on international trade than in the 1930's. In 1938, 40 percent of the nation's manufactured goods were exported and foreign trade was 28 percent of GNP. By 1959 only a fourth of manufactured product was sold abroad, and ten years later, in 1969, foreign trade reached only 19 percent of GNP. [13] With exports and imports each accounting for 10 percent or less of GNP, Japan relies less on foreign trade, in monetary terms, than any industrial nation except the United States. [14] However, because of its nature, trade is still the vital lifeline.

Japan has approached Southeast Asia in recent years with care and circumspection, recognizing natural links which had to be repaired but fully aware of the handicaps in returning to the area. Japan had to achieve through normal international trading the economic results which colonies, special interests, and military and political controls had so disastrously made impossible before. The remarkable consequences are well known. Japan is now either the first or second trading partner of every country in Southeast Asia except Cambodia, of which it is third. Through fantastic increases in productivity and changes in Japanese dietary habits, the need to import rice, and therefore the old dependence on Korea and Taiwan for essential food, has disappeared. Understandably, new problems have arisen. Instead of colonies, both her own and those of Western nations, Japan must deal with sensitive, proud, newly independent, emerging countries. These regard the only industrial power in Asia with a mixture of expectations and misgivings.

Reparations

Japan began independent life in 1952 with the obligation to settle accounts with nations still bearing the scars of Japanese military occupation. Scaled down drastically from the vast sums demanded in the days of the Far Eastern Commission, reparations agreements totalling more than a billion dollars were finally signed with four countries; the Philippines, Vietnam, Burma, and Indonesia. Amounts ranged from $39 million for Vietnam to $550 million for the Philippines. Japan also agreed, in lieu of reparations, to give economic assistance to Laos, Cambodia, and Thailand. The former two countries were to receive $6.95 million, and Thailand was given a special yen account equivalent to $26.5 million, due by May 1970.

Reparations debts were paid by mid-1969 except for $225 million owed to the Philippines and about $6 million for Indonesia. The latter was settled in April 1970, and the Philippine debt is to be liquidated by 1976 but may well be paid off before that date. Finally, after the separation of Singapore from Malaysia, both countries demanded payment of "blood debts," compensation for wartime destruction of life and property by the Japanese military. In 1967, agreements with these countries awarded grants and loans amounting to $16 million for Singapore and $8 million for Malaysia.

Thus, the Japanese Government hoped to have written an end to obligations arising out of the war. Most of the payments financed the purchase of Japanese goods and services and were therefore not without benefit to the donor. Sukarno spent reparations for projects more flamboyant than useful, but since his downfall and Japan's present heavy aid commitments to Indonesia, reparations follies have been largely forgotten.

Trade

Although Japanese trade statistics usually lump all countries from South Korea to Pakistan under the rubric "Southeast Asia," geography and Japan's priority interests more accurately fix on ten countries: Indonesia, Thailand, the Philippines, Malaysia, Singapore, Hongkong, and the Indo-Chinese states South Vietnam, Cambodia, Laos, and North Vietnam. Trade with these countries has amounted to about half of the total for Asia, a little more than two fifths of that with the United States, and about 12 percent of Japan's trade with the world (Table 12-1).

Table 12-1

Japan's Trade with Southeast Asia (in millions of U.S. dollars)

	1968			1969		
	Exports	Imports	Total	Exports	Imports	Total
Indonesia	146.6	251.8	398.4	235.8	397.3	633.1 (3)
Thailand	365.4	147.0	512.4	433.8	167.4	601.2 (4)
Philippines	411.1	397.9	809.0	475.6	468.0	943.6 (1)
Malaysia	104.5	343.4	447.9	133.4	406.7	540.1 (5)
Singapore	209.2	61.8	271.0	312.6	66.0	378.6 (6)
Hongkong	467.6	54.0	521.6	614.6	68.1	682.7 (2)
South Vietnam	199.0	2.7	201.7	223.2	3.3	226.5 (7)
Laos	6.5		6.5			
Cambodia	20.3	6.6	26.9	23.5	7.3	30.8 (8)
North Vietnam	2.4	6.1	8.5	7.3	6.0	13.3 (9)
Southeast Asia	1,932.6	1,271.3	3,203.9	2,459.8	1,590.1	4,049.9
U.S.A.	4,086.5	3,527.4	7,613.9	4,957.8	4,089.9	9,047.7
World	12,971.7	12,967.2	25,938.9	15,990.0	15,023.5	31,013.5

Source: Ministry of International Trade and Industry, *White Paper on Foreign Trade 1970.*

By far the largest item of export to all Southeast Asian countries, except Hongkong and Singapore, is machines and machinery. This category includes textile machinery, sewing machines, radios, television sets, and the thousands of trucks, buses, and passenger cars which choke the streets of Southeast Asian cities today. To Hongkong and Singapore, the value of exports of industrial materials, including textiles and non-metallic manufactures such as cement, glass, and miscellaneous products, supersedes machines. The countries with export surpluses *to* Japan furnish indispensable raw materials. Indonesia supplies crude oil, timber, and some natural rubber; Malaysia sells timber, tin, iron ore, and natural rubber.

North Vietnam is the source of high quality Hongay coking coal, much desired by Japanese industry. Japanese trade with North Vietnam, which in 1966 amounted to $15 million, dipped by almost half ($8.5 million) in 1968 but recovered to a total of $13 million in 1969, when Japan for the first time achieved an export surplus, attributed to reconstruction going on in North Vietnam. Almost $5 million on the 1969 trade consisted of imports of coal.[15]

A problem Japan faces with Southeast Asian countries, as with developing nations the world over, is the one of trade imbalances. With all but two of the Southeast Asian countries, Indonesia and Malaysia, Japan had an export surplus in 1969. Markets for Japanese products grow rapidly, but except for the countries with sought-after resources, what to sell Japan becomes more perplexing and irritating as trade figures mount. Japan hopes that these situations can be alleviated through investment and other methods of economic cooperation.

Investment

Japan's direct investments overseas have been small compared with those of other industrial nations: about $2 billion by 1969, as contrasted with $65 billion for the United States and $18 billion for the United Kingdom. Only 18 percent or $355 million of Japan's investment ventures, were with Southeast Asian nations.[16] According to Japanese Foreign Office statistics, investments more than doubled from 1967 to 1969, increasing from $85 million to $200 million. In 1969, 48 percent ($96 million) of direct investments were in Asia; 33 percent, or $67 million, were in Southeast Asia.

Several factors characterize Japanese investments in Southeast Asia. First, they are largely related to Japan's need for raw materials. This is to be expected, since almost 70 percent of Japan's imports from Asia consist of primary products. Of all investments between 1951 and the end of March 1967, 42.8 percent were for projects designed to secure needed materials. The same percentage of investments in Asia was devoted to the development of mining, agricultural, and forestry resources.[17]

Second, the domestic labor shortage has led industrialists to invest in plants overseas for the processing of raw materials. The textile industry took early advantage of available and cheaper labor in Southeast Asia. In 1967 this industry moved into Thailand, the Philippines, and Hongkong, and in the same year 85 percent of Japan's textile imports were made up of semiprocessed goods from Southeast Asian countries. Other industries followed this trend.[18]

A third characteristic of investment in Southeast Asia is its attraction to small and medium-sized industries. As of March 31, 1968, 124 out of 142 investments by enterprises capitalized at less than 100 million yen ($278,000) were in Southeast Asia. A prominent Japanese banker has written that many small industries are turning to overseas investment for better opportunities and a more favorable atmosphere than they find in Japan. They are apprehensive especially over the effect on them of continued liberalization of trade and investment by the Japanese Government and the resulting stiffer competition from foreign products.[19]

Thailand has been especially attractive to Japanese capital. In August 1969, Japanese projects in Thailand were reported to make up 36.7 percent of all foreign investment in the country, ahead of the United States, with only 18.5 percent of the total. Moreover, in 80 percent of these joint enterprises, the Japanese partners held more than 50 percent of the shares. The extent of Japanese investment and the continuing excess of Japanese exports over imports led to criticism by the Thais, including the expression of fears that Japan was on the way to dominating the economy of the country.[20]

An example of the kind of cooperative enterprise appealing to the Japanese was the announcement in September 1970 of an agreement on a copper concession in Sabah, Malaysia. The copper deposit, reputed to be potentially the richest in Southeast Asia, was to be developed by a joint venture between a Japanese concern with a 51 percent interest and the Sabah Government, holding the remaining 49 percent. The initial investment on the Japanese side was reported to be $66.7 million, with much greater sums expected to be required in the future. The project involves the construction of a road to the mountainous area where the copper is located and a port from which the ore will be shipped.[21]

Although Japan's Southeast Asian ventures may not in the future exceed their present modest percentage of the country's worldwide investments, they will no doubt increase rapidly in the number of projects and in total value. In addition to the economic motives mentioned—the requirement for critical raw materials, the pressure of the labor shortage, and the opportunities for small business—Japan has a political interest in contributing to the stability of the Southeast Asian nations. For the long-term future, the Japanese stake in the viability and tranquillity of the nations to the south is the most important interest of all.

Foreign Aid

Economic Assistance

The present program. Japan is very much in the "aid business." Pressure to increase aid programs has grown in the last few years and has come from both the United States and the Organization for Economic Cooperation and Development (OECD), to which Japan belongs. The agency of the OECD directly responsible for economic cooperation is the sixteen nation Development Assistance Committee (DAC). (DAC members: Australia, Austria, Belgium, Canada, Denmark, France, West Germany, Italy, Japan, Netherlands, Norway, Portugal, Sweden, Switzerland, the United Kingdom, and the United States.) In 1968 Japanese economic cooperation for the first time exceeded one billion dollars ($1.049 billion) and Japan moved to fourth place among aid giving countries, after the United States, France, and West Germany. In 1969 Japan's aid figure increased by 20.4 percent, to $1.263 billion, which represented 0.78 percent of GNP, a slight rise over the 0.75 percent for 1968. These percentages of GNP compared with 0.49 percent for the United States, 1.3 percent for West Germany (which had moved to second place in aid) and 1.24 percent for France. [22] In 1970 Japan's aid increased by 44 percent, or $1.8 billion, reaching 0.93 percent of GNP.

Japanese aid has been criticized because so much of it has been "private-based" as contrasted with direct government appropriated funds. For example, in 1968 and 1969 private-based economic assistance, that is, export credits and overseas investments, made up 63 percent and 64 percent, respectively, of Japan's total aid. Official development assistance, including reparations payments, accounted for the remaining 37 percent and 36 percent. As a percentage of GNP, this government component was only 0.26 percent in 1969, compared with 0.69 percent for France, 0.39

percent for West Germany, and 0.33 percent for the United States. (In 1969 DAC created a new reporting formula called "Official Assistance," which added certain categories of aid to "Official Development Assistance." In the case of Japan, this meant the inclusion of export credits extended by the official Export-Import Bank and the Overseas Economic Cooperation Fund, loans in connection with direct investments, and the Central Bank's purchases of securities of international financial institutions. Under this new formula, Japan's "total official flows" in 1969 amounted to .49 percent of GNP.)

The principal interests of DAC have been to increase the total flow of economic assistance and to improve the terms of aid. The second United Nations Conference for Trade and Development (UNCTAD), held in New Delhi in 1968, recommended that the industrialized countries devote 1 percent of their GNP to assistance for the developing nations. The members of DAC associated themselves with this target; those who achieved it in 1969 were Belgium, Denmark, France, West Germany, Italy, and the Netherlands.

Terms should be improved, according to DAC, in three ways: (1) by enlarging the proportion of official development assistance; (2) by softening loan conditions; and (3) by increasing the grant, or "concessional" element, as it is called, in the aid flow. Japan's record on terms of aid is not exemplary. In fact, the prevalent complaint heard in the developing countries of Southeast Asia is that Japanese terms are tough and difficult. The report by former Canadian Prime Minister Lester Pearson, "Partners in Development," recommended a target of 0.7 percent of GNP for *official* development assistance. By 1969 no DAC nation had reached this mark, although France was near with 0.69 percent. Japan, with a percentage of only 0.26 percent, had far to go. Japan was also behind the other DAC nations in financial terms accorded for loans. The DAC country averages for loans were maturity at 27.8 years, an interest rate of 2.7 percent, and a grace period of 6.7 years. Japan's average terms were 19.5 years at 3.7 percent, with 6.1 years of grace. Only France and Austria had harder terms. For the United States, average maturity was 35 years, the interest rate 2.7 percent, and the grace period 8.7 years. West Germany's terms were 26 years at 3.2 percent, with 7.6 years grace. As for the grant element in official development assistance, Japan was behind all other DAC countries, with 42 percent. Grant elements for the

United States, West Germany, and France were 70 percent, 51 percent, and 75 percent, respectively. [23]

Table 12-2

Japanese Economic Cooperation (in millions of U.S. dollars)

1. Categories

	1967	1968	1969
GOVERNMENT			
a. Grants	138.4	117.0	123.4
b. Loans	207.5	190.5	216.2
c. Multilateral Contributions	44.6	48.8	113.9
Totals	390.5	356.3	453.5
PRIVATE			
a. Export credits	322.4	570.5	609.5
b. Investments	84.6	122.6	200.0
Totals	407.0	693.1	809.5
Grand Total	797.5	1,049.8	1,268.1
Annual Growth Rate (Percentage)	27.8	22.7	20.4
Percentage of GNP	0.71	0.74	0.76
Percentage of national income	0.89	0.93	0.96
Percentage of Government Aid to GNP		0.25	0.26

2. Aid Recipients

	1967 Amount	1967 % of total	1968 Amount	1968 % of total	1969 Amount	1969 % of total
Asia	500.3	62.7	559.0	53.3	847.4	67.1
(Southeast Asia)	(215.8)	27.1	(218.8)	20.8	(338.7)	26.8
Near and Middle East	69.3	8.7	89.5	8.5	109.0	8.6
Europe	-4.0	0.5	51.5	4.9	57.5	4.6
Africa	-1.1	0.1	70.6	6.7	56.0	4.4
Latin America	44.9	5.6	102.6	9.7	77.2	6.1
Oceania	-	-	-0.2	*	-0.1	*
Unallocated	188.1	23.6	176.3	16.9	116.1	9.2
Totals	797.5		1,049.3		1,263.1	

*Amounts less than $50,000.
Figures marked (-) indicate amount extended was less than amortization received from same area during year.
Source: Japanese Ministry of Foreign Affairs.

It is natural that geography, as well as economic and political interests, should determine that Japan's largest aid component should go to Asia. The gap between Japan and the developing countries of Asia has steadily widened. Between 1960 and 1968, the growth rate in GNP was less than 5 percent for Southeast Asia and more than 16 percent for Japan, whose GNP in 1960 was $43 billion as contrasted to a $28 billion total for nine countries of Southeast Asia (Burma, Cambodia, Laos, South Vietnam, Indonesia, Malaysia, Philippines, Singapore, and Thailand). By 1968 Japan's GNP had jumped to $142 billion, more than four times the $33 billion total GNP of the nine Southeast Asian countries. As shown in Table 12-2, Japan's economic assistance to Asia in 1969 amounted to 67 percent of her total aid that year, or $847.4 million, which was more than the entire assistance program in 1967. Aid to Southeast Asia (the nine countries listed above) in 1969 was 26.8 percent of the total, or $338.7 million.

The Japanese Position on Foreign Aid

Japan's philosophy of foreign aid has contained little of the missionary zeal which has motivated Americans. Although the Government has fully recognized the obligations of an industiral power of the first rank to extend economic assistance to developing countries, in practice a guiding principle seems to have been, "What is good for Japan is good for Southeast Asia," or, to exaggerate a little but perhaps not too much, "what is good for *Mitsubishi* is good for Southeast Asia." There has been a resistance in the past to softening terms of loan aid. As a Japanese official in Manila put it to the author, "We have a different philosophy of aid giving from yours. We do not believe in give-away programs. The very best terms should be 25 years at 3 percent."

The rationale for Japan's economic cooperation program has been clearly stated by the Ministry of International Trade and Industry (MITI) in its Annual Report on Economic Cooperation. Japan has no "Aid Agency" as such; significantly, the Report is published by MITI, whose well known aim is to promote with unflagging vigor Japanese economic interests abroad, Aid objectives are listed as first to secure access to essential resources; second, to increase exports and strengthen the international base of Japan's economy; and third—to include an idealistic note—to

293

fulfill Japan's obligation as the only advanced nation in Asia. The report does remind its readers that with a national income greater than the combined national incomes of all Asian countries east of Afghanistan except Communist China and with great expectations on the part of these Asian countries, it is Japan's "mission" to meet their expectations and "extend the warm hand of assistance to them." [24]

Japan would like safe and cheap access to natural resources. In Southeast Asia these are conveniently located, but the possessors lack capital and technology to exploit them. It is logical for Japan to furnish money and know-how to these countries and to help them develop their own export industries. In fact, the MITI report calls this indispensable to the future of Japan. Developing countries in 1969 bought 42.6 percent of Japan's exports and sold 41.2 percent of her imports. Southeast Asia is Japan's best market after the United States, and the Japanese believe that increased trade will speed the development of nations which in turn will buy more from Japan. Japanese industrialists look especially to opportunities for the export of plant equipment, which would combine aid in capital and technology. The Report on Economic Cooperation stresses that in the long term such projects will strengthen the international elements of Japan's economy and contribute to the nation's long term expansion. [25]

Technical Assistance

Thus far, technical assistance has been a very minor element in Japan's economic cooperation programs, amounting in 1969 to less than 1.5 percent of total aid funds ($19 million) and to only .44 percent of official development assistance. Many European donor countries give as much as 20 percent of their official aid in technical cooperation.

Japan's modest technical cooperation program began in 1954. During the fifteen years from 1954 to 1969, more than 10,000 trainees studied in Japan (9,000 from Asia, of whom 5,000 were from Southeast Asia) and 1,502 Japanese experts were sent overseas (1,100 to Asia, of whom 600 went to Southeast Asia). Total funds expended from 1953 to 1968 were $48 million ($33 million for Asia, of which $20 million went to Southeast Asia.) [26]

The Japanese face special problems in bringing technical assistance to foreign countries.

First, Japanese technicians in Southeast Asia, although respected for their expertise, risk unfriendly reactions from people whose countries were occupied by Japanese troops in time of war. In some countries, the Japanese still have to work their way back into full acceptance and win the confidence of the local people.

Second, the recruitment of talented, qualified personnel is unusually difficult. Yet the Foreign Ministry estimated that from 300 to 500 aid experts would be needed in the near future. [27] Not only is there a skilled labor shortage in Japan, but the traditions of lifetime employment and the rigidity of the Japanese industrial system mean that few technicians are willing to take up temporary service overseas, at possible sacrifices of salary, promotions, and guaranteed employment upon return home.

Finally, language and cultural differences seriously impede the adjustment of Japanese to a foreign environment. Language is a formidable barrier, and yet the technical expert is valuable only if he can communicate. In Southeast Asia he must know either the language of the country or fluent English or French. Unfortunately, the Japanese are not generally adept at foreign languages. The ablest and best-trained expert often finds that language is his most formidable obstacle. [28]

In spite of these problems, the Japanese recognize how important it is to expand their technical aid programs, including their Youth Volunteer Peace Corps-type projects, so far organized on a small but selective scale. Successful instruction by competent, trained Japanese experts will be the best way to improve the Japanese image in Southeast Asia. Specialists can make major contributions in fields in which the Japanese have shown outstanding competence, such as agriculture, fisheries, industry, mining, and health.

Regional Cooperation

Secretary of State William Rogers was asked in a press interview in January 1970 whether he thought the non-Communist nations of Asia could put together a defense force and if so, whether the Japanese would be a part of it. He replied that this might happen eventually but that it was much too early to think about it now. Regarding the Japanese, he answered: "Probably, but I think that is a long way down the road. I think what is more important are regional organizations that would improve the economic viability of the area, and I think in that connection that Japan might take the lead." [29]

Japanese and Southeast Asian officials agree with Secretary Rogers that Japan should play a leading role in multilateral aid-giving organizations in Asia. Prime Minister Sato has said, "Pacific Asia is indeed the outcome of the spirit of regionalism in Asia . . . the Japanese Government intends, for its part, to play a positive part in the progress and development of this region as a whole." [30] Bunchana Atthakor, Minister of Economic Affairs of Thailand, probably expressed the opinion of many Asian leaders when, in discussing regional cooperation in Asia, he wrote: ". . . Japan has the moral obligation to provide a significant amount of technical and economic assistance to developing Asian countries. . . . Japan's destiny . . . is tied to a large extent to the destiny of the countries in this region." [31]

Beginning with the Colombo Plan, Japan has participated in most of the multilateral groupings organized for economic development in Asia, including the Economic Commission for Asia and the Far East (ECAFE), consortiums for aid to India and Pakistan, the Foreign Exchange Operations Fund (FEOF) for Laos, the Mekong Valley project, and the nine-nation consortium for economic aid to Indonesia. Japan has taken part in numerous specialized regional efforts; those related to education (conferences of Southeast Asian Ministers of Education) and transportation (the project for an Asian Highway) are but two examples. According to the Japanese Foreign Office, the principal channels for regional cooperation in the 1970's, the "decade of development for Southeast Asia," will be the Asian Development Bank, the Ministerial Conference for Economic Development in Southeast Asia, and the Mekong Development Program. As a founding member of the Bank, and with Watanabe Takeshi, a Japanese financial expert, as President, Japan takes a special interest in its activities. The Ministerial Conference, organized at the initiative of Japan in 1966, has met annually and performs valuable functions as a forum for consideration of development problems and for coordination with the Asian Development Bank and other organizations and agencies engaged in development projects in Asia.

Besides the institutions in which governments participate, the Private Investment Company for Asia (PICA) was formed in Tokyo in February 1968 by 112 private companies from 12 countries: Japan, the United States, Canada, the United Kingdom, Australia, West Germany, France, Italy, Switzerland, Sweden, Denmark, and the Netherlands. The chairman was Iwasa Yoshizane, President of the Fuji Bank and Vice President of the Japanese Federation of Economic Organizations. PICA's functions were to seek investments for private enterprise, arrange joint ventures, and make loans. The organization expected to concentrate on manufacturing and processing industries rather than undertake large development projects.

Both Japan and the United States support the principle of regionalism in Asia, and the outlook is for increasing use of multilateral means for assisting developing nations. However, Japan is a world power, with rapidly expanding global interests, whose participation in Asian regionalism must be put in perspective. The Asian segment of Japan's combined trade and aid amounts to less than 5 percent of GNP. Japan's interest and role in East and Southeast Asia will be continuing and of crucial importance; nevertheless, Japan will not again, as in prewar days, create a confining regional focus of primary national interest.

A Thai professor, knowledgeable about the problems of regionalism, has characterized regional institutions and activities in Southeast Asia as "long on communication and consultation, but . . . extremely short on commitment." Admitting that sentiment for regional cooperation was strong in Southeast Asia, he concluded that, in concrete terms, little had been accomplished. [32] The problems of nation-building are enormous; diversity within the region is great; and interests frequently do not coincide. Still, the mere fact that important initiatives have been taken by the Southeast Asians is encouraging. ASEAN (Association of Southeast Asian Nations) is an organization exclusively Southeast Asian in membership and seems to be taken seriously by its members.

The Asian Development Bank is the central institution for development financing. It has been criticized for its conservatism in lending policy, for super-caution in doling out loans and for thinking more about blue-chip investmenst than about loans for urgently needed development. The Japan-sponsored Agricultural Fund has been unfairly called, by the representatives of some countries, a Japanese effort to perpetuate agricultural economies in Southeast Asia and slow down industrialization.

The Japanese Executive Director of the ADB, in a speech

delivered at the East-West Center in Honolulu in 1969, named the three factors indispensable to development: passion, brains, and money. He listed the first, "enthusiasm in the mind and heart of the people," as most important, beyond the function of any international institution or even creation by human efforts; it "just happens," he said. International agencies could help with the second, "brains," by extending technical assistance and with the third, "money," by grants and loans. He knew that no one would ever find the ideal combination of all three ingredients but thought mixtures of varying quantities would make interesting patterns in the development process. [33]

Regionalism has its limitations, and those who expect neat, friendly, cooperative arrangements between countries efficiently working together to solve the development problems of Southeast Asia are expanding their hopes beyond reality. Japan, as the only donor nation in Asia, must necessarily find a place in these organizations; otherwise, they would be meaningless. And for some nations, the dilution of Japanese aid in a multilateral mix would make it more palatable. But Japan's presence in Southeast Asia will be too big to be confined in international organizations; it will continue to burst forth in the energetic push of its great concerns, as in the past, and in the calculated action of the Japanese Government to make bilateral aid more important and more conspicuous.

Popular Attitudes

Foreign aid has never been a popular issue in Japan; in fact, polls show that many Japanese have never heard of the term "economic cooperation," and few have any idea of how much foreign aid their country gives. Certainly, no Japanese politician would ever think of trying to win votes by advocating bigger aid programs. As one observer put it, "No citizen groups wrapped towels round their heads and paraded in Tokyo or picketed the Diet chambers in favor of foreign aid." [34]

If aid has aroused little enthusiasm, neither has it been the target of organized opposition. The Japanese Government has used various official organs, such as the Export-Import Bank and the Overseas Cooperation Fund, for aid purposes. It has never established a single administration, such as the succession of American agencies, from TCA to AID, which have so stirred the fluctuating emotions of congressmen over the years. Largely because so much of Japanese aid has been "private," it never became an issue of controversy in the national Diet.

Public apathy over aid was demonstrated in answers to a 1968 survey which asked the question: "What do you think should be emphasized to make Japan a better nation?" "Aid to developing nations" was at the bottom of the list, receiving only 5 percent support, while expansion of social security, economic growth, and promotion of science, technology, and education drew the priority votes. Next-to-last place was "build-up of defense capacity" (7 percent).[35] As in many such polls, the answers illustrate the preoccupation of ordinary Japanese with domestic problems, their concentration on "my-home-ism," and their relative indifference to the international relations in which their country is engaged.

The future of economic cooperation. Prime Minister Sato confirmed in his speech to the United Nations General Assembly on October 21, 1970, what Japanese officials had already publicly stated: that the Government of Japan intended to reach the target of 1 percent of GNP for aid to the developing nations by 1975.[36] With the GNP in that year projected at $400 billion, Japan's $4 billion would probably surpass American aid. Predictions are that by 1980 this sum would have risen to $5 billion.

Whatever the figures turn out to be, Japanese official policy under LDP governments will be to up the total amount of assistance, to better the terms and character of aid in accord with DAC recommendations, and to give more importance to technical cooperation. The expectations of the world are directed to Japan; her commitments are on the record; and the response of trading partners will be harsh if these expectations and commitments are not fulfilled.

At the Tokyo meeting of the DAC in September 1970, Japan took the gratifying step of accepting the principle of untied aid. Traditionally, Japanese loans were tied to the purchase of Japanese goods and were thus an integral part of Japan's export drive and industrial expansion. Outside pressure has mounted to convince Japan that, as a first rank economic power, she should free loan aid from these restrictions. The director of the Economic Cooperation Bureau in the Foreign Office wrote frankly, "We must untie our aid before the criticisms of the developing countries are concentrated solely on our country."[37]

299

Japanese Government sources affirm an intention to increase *official* development assistance from the present 0.26 percent of GNP to 0.42 percent or .5 percent of GNP by 1975. At the same time, grant aid will be substantially enlarged. Yen credits are also to be extended in greater amounts with, however, less emphasis on Asia in the future. The limitation of absorptive capacity and the lack of projects have led to the conclusion that some spreading of credits to other areas would be useful. At the same time, the Japanese, through technical assistance, will help the Southeast Asian countries acquire the capacity to use loan aid effectively.

However much Japanese economic cooperation is expanded in the developing countries of Africa and Latin America, political and economic considerations will still make Southeast Asia an area of primary attention. In the past, the greatest assistance for this area has gone to Indonesia, the Philippines, Thailand, and Malaysia. This pattern is likely to continue in the future.

Indonesia has been of special interest and will undoubtedly remain so, because of the attractive combination of rich resources and an extensive market—the largest population of any country in Southeast Asia. Japan is a member of the international aid consortium established in 1966 to restore the Indonesian economy after the end of the Sukarno regime. Japan and the United States have each been pledging roughly one third of the funds raised by the consortium. The total amount of consortium aid to be extended to Indonesia in 1971 was determined, at a meeting in December 1970, to be $640 million, an increase over 1970 of $40 million.

Raw materials swing the balance of trade in favor of Indonesia. Japanese imports from Indonesia in 1969 exceeded exports by more than $161 million. An Indonesian professor recently wrote that his country recognizes Japan as "one of the largest potential partners for economic cooperation." He noted three advantages for Japan: (1) the wealth of raw materials which can serve Japanese industry: oil, rubber, timber, tin, copra, and maize; (2) the vast Indonesian market of 120 million people for Japanese products; and (3) benefits from capital investment in Indonesia.[38]

Two professors, one the Indonesian head of the Department of Japanese Studies at the University of Indonesia and the other a Japanese professor of anthropology at Kyushu University, have written an article on Indonesian-Japanese relations. They concluded that "cordial relations between Indonesia and Japan are essential not only to the stability and prosperity of the two countries involved but also to the stability and prosperity of Southeast Asia and the world at large." They find the one problem to be overcome in Indonesian-Japanese relations a psychological one, "evolving around the so-called 'superior attitude' of the Japanese and the inferiority complex of the Indonesians." They advise:

> If good willing Indonesians and Japanese will make a supreme effort to break the psychological barrier that has been causing so many misunderstandings and frictions, so as to induce their peoples to rectify the mental picture they have of each other more in accordance with present-day reality, then, perhaps, we can face the future of Indonesian-Japanese relations with more confidence and optimism than the present seems to warrant. [39]

In addition to Indonesia, Thailand, the Philippines, and other Southeast Asian countries where Japanese aid programs will undoubtedly continue to expand, Indochina will receive greater attention over the next few years. Because of the war, recent assistance to South Vietnam took the form of "humanitarian" goods, such as medical and hospital supplies and equipment. In 1970, however, the Government decided to extend other kinds of aid without waiting for warfare to stop. New projects were to be initiated, based on recommendations of a survey team visiting Saigon in October 1970. A first, preliminary figure of $30 million was published, and $4.5 million was immediately earmarked for the construction of an electric power plant in Saigon. [40]

Ever since President Johnson tried to persuade Asian countries to contribute more substantially to the war in Southeast Asia, to "show more flags" in Vietnam, as he said, the American Government has been irritated that Japan, with growing exports to South Vietnam ($200 million in 1969) and an estimated annual billion dollars received from procurement for the war, did not see fit to give more economic aid to the Saigon Government.

Tokyo expects to contribute substantially to the economic recovery of South Vietnam after hostilities end (it would be a profitable enterprise in the long run) and also hopes to be able, if at all possible, to assist North Vietnam, an action that would be politically popular in Japan. After all, President Johnson once held out the hand of aid to Hanoi. Many Japanese feel that their country's historic experience in Vietnam was less tragic than that in some other Asian countries and that future influence there is not an illusion.

Japan's assistance in Laos and Cambodia has been largely carried on through multilateral organs or through projects arising from the Mekong River scheme. After Prince Sihanouk's departure, $2 million in medical supplies was sent through the Japanese Red Cross to Cambodia, and in November 1970 a second grant of $2 million was publicized. This was to be used for repairing roads and bridges and to buy trucks and ferryboats. When the Cambodian Chief of State, Cheng Heng, visited Tokyo at the end of October, Prime Minister Sato refused him military aid but promised suitable economic assistance. The Japanese press commented critically that trucks given to Cambodia might well be diverted to military use. [41]

Japan's future aid to Southeast Asia will continue to be affected by profits and foreign policy. What Mitsubishi believes may not always coincide with the ideas of the Foreign Office. The Government has in the past been accused of grudgingly pledging small amounts of aid in Indochina "because the Americans wanted it." The Japanese flag has never loomed very large in South Vietnam, except in the "Honda-ization" of Saigon! Future Japanese programs will grow as peace and stability return.

The Southeast Asian View of the Japanese

In Southeast Asia the view of Japanese trade and aid is a contradictory mixture of admiration, expectation, desire, suspicion, irritation, anxiety, and fear. Asians are overwhelmed by the tremendous visible impact of Japan. The evidence of successful Japanese economic advance strikes the visitor to every Southeast Asian capital: the *Toyotas*, *Datsuns*, and Japanese-built taxis making the traffic jams; the textiles, transistor radios, and TV sets crowding the shop windows; and the blazing signs monopolizing the night skies: SONY, NATIONAL, MITSUBISHI, TEIJIN, HITACHI, NISSAN. Asians in business profit from Japanese trade, joint ventures, and the stimulation to local industry, employment, and enterprise. Besides the flood of goods labelled "Made in Japan," an ever enlarging crowd of eager, well-regimented Japanese tourists and indefatigable, persistent businessmen is becoming visible in the cities of Southeast Asia.

Attitudes vary from country to country, but several themes are repeated: (1) Japan will again become a military threat; (2) the Japanese exploit natural resources in their own selfish interest; (3) the Japanese will dominate Southeast Asia economically; (4) Japanese business methods are sharp, harsh, and unfair; (5) Japanese aid is given primarily to benefit Japan; and (6) The Japanese are aloof, clannish, mysterious—and numerous. These elements, forming the image of Japan held by many Southeast Asians, seriously concern Japanese Government officials, especially the ambassadors who represent their country in the capitals of Southeast Asia.

Memories of wartime cruelties condition present attitudes to a small degree, although in Singapore a monument was erected only a few years ago to commemorate those who died victims of Japanese atrocities. Most Southeast Asians begin conversations about the Japanese by assuring the listener that wartime deeds are forgotten, that it is present actions which disturb them. Surprisingly, some take seriously the threat of a revived Japanese militarism. In a discussion with a group of Singapore civil servants, several expected Japan to rearm in order to protect growing economic interests in Southeast Asia. Two Indonesian officials, interviewed separately, expressed worry about future Japanese efforts to dominate Southeast Asia by military power. One quoted a visiting Japanese parlamentarian who had boasted over a drink, in what the Indonesian interpreted as a menacing tone, "We can make nuclear weapons tomorrow!" Likewise, in the Philippines fears of a Japanese military comeback have not disappeared. The Japanese Ambassador to Manila reported publicly to a discussion panel in Tokyo that he had heard such fears expressed. [42] President Marcos was asked during a visit to the United States in 1967 whether he favored rearming Japan; he replied—some afterwards said too hastily—"Yes, but under control." [43]

Much more general, however, are the anxieties over Japanese economic exploitation and domination. In both Indonesia and the Philippines, where the Japanese are busy tapping the resources of oil, timber and rubber, one heard charges that they were denuding the countries of precious raw materials in Japan's selfish interests. A young Indonesian librarian spoke with emotion in her voice: "We do not like the Japanese! They only *take* from our country. They take out our pearls, our fish, our precious resources!" A professor at the University of the Philippines called Japan's aid to agriculture a "policy for Asians," intended to discourage industrialization and keep the developing countries in a retarded agricultural stage.

Japan is accused of economic domination and economic aggression. A Thai government official was alarmed at the growing Japanese control of Thai industry. He said Japanese would outbid competitors by 35 percent to 40 percent to get business; their future domination of the Thai economy would give them political leverage and enable them to apply powerful pressures difficult to resist. Thailand's large negative trade balance has been particularly irritating. The Thais complain, "Why don't the Japanese buy more from us!?" The Japanese reply, "What can we buy? We don't need your rice, and we use just so much tapioca!"

In Singapore, an official warned of Japan's economic aggression: the Japanese thought only of profits, only of the sale of their own products; they did not have the true interests of the developing countries at heart.

Criticism of Japanese business methods came from a variety of sources. An Indonesian member of Parliament commented with exasperation, "With the Japanese, we always get the short end of the stick!" A Djakarta businessman was adamant that he would never deal with the Japanese again; they were untrustworthy, with an eye only for profits, now or later: they might sell cheap now but only to capture a market for the future. A Filipino professor complained that Japanese businesses with local partners insisted on a monopoly of every phase of the business activity, management, advertising, and transportation. They left no authority or discretion in the hands of their local representatives; the minutest detail was dictated from Tokyo. An Indonesian official found the Japanese businessmen "mysterious, always holding back"; he felt they thought only of profits and the aggrandizement of their own nation. Motives of Japanese traders were questioned; they were said to try to exploit, reap maximum immediate advantages, and gain influences, rather than to develop mutually beneficial trading relations.

Japanese business methods were more dispassionately appraised by other observers as simply combinations of the initiative, aggressiveness, persistence, and persuasion which make successful traders. An American in Djakarta remarked that he had told his compatriots doing business in Indonesia that if the Japanese were outselling them it was their own fault; they would have to take a leaf from the Japanese book and go after business with more energy and ingenuity. The Japanese, he noted, were achieving great successes in spite of local resentments against them. [44]

The Japanese "presence" in Southeast Asia now stands out as much as does the American, and "the Ugly Japanese" is crowding out "the Ugly American" as a popular cliche. In every capital one heard the complaint, "The Japanese are taking over the golf courses!" spoken as though the *Kami-kazes* had staged a comeback! Japanese were described as clannish golfers who played in their own foursomes and never joined the people of the country. One heard of rules passed and of unwritten understandings designed to exclude Japanese from the golf clubs. Socially, the Japanese were said to keep to themselves; few learned the language of the country; in living and working, they created a closed Japanese environment and became "inscrutable" to their fellow Asians.

The Thai Minister of Economy let the press know of his irritation at the clannishness of Japanese tourists: "Japanese tourists arrive in Bangkok in their Japan Air Lines plane, get in their Japanese bus, go to their Japanese hotel, eat at their Japanese restaurant, go to a Japanese-owned night club, then get back to their plane and return to Japan. Where is the benefit for Thailand?" [45]

Japanese officials are aware of the problems created for Japan's trade and aid by the resentments and fears, real or imagined, among Southeast Asians. One Japanese ambassador in a Southeast Asian capital admitted that his principal task was to try to improve local attitudes toward his compatriots and establish better relations between the Japanese community and the citizens of the country in which he served. Asked in a press interview about unfavorable feelings toward resident Japanese in the developing countries, Foreign Minister Aichi agreed that this was a difficult problem, particularly at a time when Japan must substantially increase economic cooperation and when greater numbers of Japanese are becoming residents of countries overseas. He felt that the unpopularity of Japanese living abroad results largely from their being "unskilled in the art of social intercourse and their tending to form their own communities, which are a kind of national characteristic of our people." The Foreign Minister thought that such problems arising out of the private and business conduct of Japanese citizens abroad would be very hard for the Government to correct. He could only advocate greater cultural exchange, arrangements for families to accompany businessmen abroad, a restudy of the methods of trade and aid, and an increase in Government as opposed to private-based aid. [46]

While attitudes toward the Japanese in Southeast Asia have so far produced no perceptible effect on the quantity of trade, which continues to grow by ever mounting percentages, or on economic cooperation, which is needed and expected by the developing countries, they create problems for Japan's total relationships in Asia. Unless the Government and the companies represented in Southeast Asia are able to improve the methods of doing business and the skill and sensitivity of personnel in the field, problems for Japan's economic advances in Southeast Asia will increase, and profits and policy will suffer.

The Strategic Importance of Southeast Asia

In an article proposing a revision of Japan's Basic Defense Policy, Kotani Hidejiro, a well-known commentator, argued that the guarantee of peace and independence based on democracy was not enough for present-day Japan, that the economic prosperity of the nation must also be protected. This meant, he said, the freedom to buy required materials from abroad and to sell freely in markets abroad. He concluded that the logical consequence of the necessity for such freedom was a significant broadening of the concept of defense. [47]

For several years Japanese politicians and journalists have speculated about the strategic importance of Southeast Asia to Japan. For a time attention was focussed on the Malacca Straits, especially the narrow, difficult-to-navigate, island-dotted strip of water between Singapore and Sumatra. Much of Japan's Arabian oil is hauled through these straits. Those huge tankers unable to navigate the straits, and therefore forced to go around Sumatra and even Java, add three days to their travel time and more than $100,000 to transportation costs. Some Japanese have worried about how to defend the straits of Malacca! Others, more practical, have considered how to widen and deepen the channel. Surveys have been made, others planned; the channel can be enlarged and obstacles to navigation removed, so that the giant tankers can safely pass through the straits.

A Japanese destroyer squadron of the Maritime Self-Defense

Forces visited Southeast Asian ports in the fall of 1969. This was the first visit of Japanese "warships" since World War II, and officials in Singapore and Djakarta were edgy about the popular reactions. The visit went off without incident. In Singapore the reception was "correct" but not cordial. The visit inevitably suggested to Southeast Asians that Japan might one day return as a military power. An Indonesian editor wrote in October 1970: "Japan's need to protect her investments and economic interests in Southeast Asia could grow correspondingly greater with the increase of her investments. Her growing trade with the Middle East, Africa and Europe makes the Malacca Straits more vital. Japan would need to secure this important trade route." [48]

Japanese specialists have derided as fantasy the proposition that Japan should develop a military capability to defend the Malacca Straits. They point out that another Seventh Fleet would be required and that an undertaking on such a scale is out of the question. The Director General of Defense, Nakasone, stated positively that Japan would assume responsibility for the defense of sea routes in "nearby waters," but that any guarding of sea lanes in the vicinity of the Malacca Straits would be completely outside of Japan's purview and out of the question for the Japanese Maritime Self-Defense Forces. [49]

There can be no doubt that as Japan's stake in trade and investment in Southeast Asia grows, the security and stability of the area will become more important in Japan's national interest. Japan will watch intently the moves of the Soviet Navy in the area and, of course, the degree to which British and Australian forces and, most important, American air and naval forces remain available. The Japanese Government will probably be eager to participate in regional conferences of Asian nations to discuss mutual problems, including security. The Djakarta conference, which met in May 1970, after Cambodia, while it accomplished little, set an example which can be followed in the future. Japan's only weapon will be economic aid—at some future date, military aid, perhaps. But the day Japanese military forces appear again in Southeast Asia—except on training cruises—is probably still a long way down the road.

Notes

1. *Straits Times*, quoted in William Henry Chamberlin, *Japan Over Asia* (Boston: Little, Brown and Co., 1938), p. 189.

2. Goto Motoo, "Japan in Asia," *Japan Quarterly*, Vol. XVI, No. 4 (October-December, 1969), p. 390.

3. Joseph C. Grew, *Ten Years in Japan* (New York: Simon and Schuster, 1944), p. 353. Copy of speech in Grew Papers, Personal Notes, November 1940.

4. Otto D. Tolischus, *Tokyo Record* (New York: Reynal and Hitchcock, 1943), p. 419.

5. Maruyama Masao, *Thought and Behaviour in Modern Japanese Politics* (New York: Oxford University Press, 1969), p. 1.

6. An English translation of *Shimmin no Michi* (Way of the Subject) appears in Tolischus, *op. cit.*, p. 415.

7. *Ibid.*, p. 419.

8. Grew Papers, *op. cit.*, Personal Notes, November 1940, p. 4619.

9. U.S., Department of State, *Foreign Relations of the United States, 1941*, Vol. IV, *The Far East*, Dept. of State publication No. 6325 (Washington: U.S. Government Printing Office, 1956), pp. 672-73.

10. William W. Lockwood, *The Economic Development of Japan* (Princeton: Princeton University Press, 1954), pp. 395-96; Schumpeter-Allen-Gordon-Penrose, *The Industrialization of Japan and Manchoukuo, 1930-1940* (New York: The Macmillan Company, 1940), p. 856. Percentage distribution of Japanese exports and imports by countries of destination 1900-1939, pp. 832-33.

11. Lockwood, *op. cit.*, p. 403.

12. Peter F. Drucker, *The Age of Discontinuity* (New York: Harper & Row, 1969), p. 68.

13. Leon Hollerman, *Japan's Dependence on the World Economy* (Princeton: Princeton University Press, 1967), p. 68. 1969 statistics from : Tsusho Sangyosho (Ministry of Trade and Industry MITI), *Tsusho Hakusho 1970 Kakuron* (White Paper on Foreign Trade Detailed) (Tokyo: MITI, July 10, 1970). Hereafter referred to as: MITI, *White Paper.*

14. Drucker, *op. cit.*, p. 68.

15. MITI, *White Paper 1969 Detailed*, pp. 653-54; MITI, *White Paper 1970 Detailed*, pp. 697-98; *Nihon Keizai*, March 19, 1970.

16. MITI, *Tsusho Hakusho 1970 Soron* (White Paper on Foreign Trade 1970 General), pp. 245-47.

17. Iwasa Yoshizane, "Japan Ventures into Southeast Asia," *Fuji Bank Bulletin*, Tokyo, May 1970, p. 83.

18. *Ibid.*, p. 84.

19. *Ibid.*, p. 85.

20. *Mainichi*, June 17, 1970.

21. *Yomiuri*, English edition, September 23, 1970.

22. Source: Ministry of Foreign Affairs and OECD, DAC "Development Assistance 1969 and Recent Trends," Press/A (70) 41, Paris, July 20, 1970. In latter, see table, p. 22.

23. DAC, "Development Assistance 1969," *op. cit.*, table 10, p. 26.

24. Tsusho Sangyo-sho, Boeki Shinko-kyoku (Ministry of Trade and Industry, Trade Promotion Bureau), *Keizai Kyoryoku no Genjo to Mondai-ten 1969* (Present Status and Problems of Economic Cooperation 1969), (Tokyo: MITI, January 10, 1970), pp. 77-80.

25. *Ibid*, p. 79.

26. Japan: Overseas Technical Cooperation Agency, *Technical Cooperation of the Japanese Government, '69 Report* (Tokyo: December 1969), pp. 119-23; pp. 131-32.

27. *Mainichi*, August 8, 1970.

28. Sawaki Masao, Director of the Office of Economic Cooperation, Ministry of Foreign Affairs, *Kongo no Ajia Enjo Mondai* (The Present and Future Problems of Aid to Asia) (Tokyo: Jiji Hyoron, October 1, 1970), pp. 10-11, p. 29.

29. U.S., Department of State, *Bulletin*, Vol. LXII, No. 1601, March 2, 1970, p. 223.

30. Sato Eisaku, "Pacific Asia" (From an Address to the Fourth Ministerial Conference of ASPAC, Kawana, Japan, June 9, 1969), *Pacific Community*, Vol. 1, No. 1, Tokyo (October 1969), p. 3.

31. Atthakor Bunchana, "Agenda for Southeast Asia," *Pacific Community*, Vol. 1, No. 2, Tokyo (January 1970), p. 187.

32. Somskadi Xuto, "Regional Cooperation in Southeast Asia," *Bulletin of the International House of Japan*, No. 24 (October 1969), p. 42.

33. Fukuda Masaru, Japanese Executive Director, Asian Development Bank, "The Role of Asian Development Bank in Economic Development of Asia," Paper read at Second Pacific Trade and Development Conference, East-West Center, Honolulu, Hawaii, January 8-11, 1969.

34. Lawrence Olson, *Japan in Postwar Asia* (New York: Praeger, 1970), p. 139.

35. Mainichi, January 1, 1969. Answers to question "What do you think should be emphasized to make Japan a better nation?" were as follows, with percentages (maximum of three choices): (1) expansion of social security system, 54; development of economic strength, 50; expansion of science and technology, 43; positive promotion of diplomacy of peace, 37; modernization of politics, 26; promotion of arts and culture, 10; build-up of defense capacity, 7; aid to developing nations, 5; no answer or don't know, 5.

36. "Text of Premier Sato's Address at U.N.", *Japan Times*, October 23, 1970.

37. Sawaki, *op. cit.*, p. 29.

38. Selo Soemardjan, "Stability in Economy Gained," *Japan Times*, August 17, 1969.

39. Dr. Lie Tek-Tjeng and Professor Yoshida Teigo, "Some Remarks on the Problems and Difficulties Besetting Present-Day Indonesian-Japanese Relations," Djakarta, March 13, 1968.

40. *Asahi*, November 6, 1970.

41. *Sankei*, October 29, 1970; *Asahi*, October 26, 1970.

42. *Asahi*, July 2, 1969. Ambassador Yasukawa Takeshi, then accredited to the Philippines, is quoted.

43. Lawrence W. Beer, "Some Dimensions of Japan's Present and Potential Relations with Communist China," *Asian Survey*, Vol. IX, No. 3 (March 1969), p. 173.

44. John K. Emmerson, "Uncertainty in Pacific Asia," *Pacific Community*, Vol. 1, No. 3, Tokyo (April 1970), p. 483.

45. "Thailand Complaints Against Japanese," *Hokubei Mainichi*, San Francisco, March 21, 1970, p. 1.

46. *Sankei*, February 4, 1970.

47. Kotani Hidejiro, "Kokubo no Kihon Hoshin wo Soten-ken Suru" (Overall Assessment of the Basic Policy for National Defense), *Kokubo* (National Defense), Tokyo, September 1970, p. 20.

48. Mochtar Lubis, publisher and editor of Indonesia Raya, Djakarta, "A Bold New Conception for Southeast Asia," *Pacific Community*, Tokyo, October 1970, p. 94.

49. Conversation with Nakasone Yasuhiro, Tokyo, October 26, 1970.

Part 4

Decisions for the 1970's

13 The Nuclear Option: Technology

Japan Comes Late: R and D

A decision by Japan to produce nuclear weapons would be a decision to become a military power, to rearm in the full sense of the word. It would affect all of Japan's international relationships, particularly those in Asia and those with the United States. To understand the nature of this option and the consequences of choice, we should first consider Japan's progress in technology.

The destruction of factories and equipment and the wartime break in normal intercourse with the Western world created a gap which the Japanese hastened to fill as rapidly as their resources and the strictures of the Occupation would permit. Momentum quickened as time went by.

"Coming late," as Japan has done, has not been without advantages. There was the chance to "leap-frog" to the latest techniques. The fires of war swept clean, destroying the superannuated machinery and clearing the way for imports of the latest, most modern equipment from around the world. This is exactly what Japan did. To close the serious technological gap between them and the advanced industrial nations at the end of the war, Japan chose licensing arrangements as the best and fastest way to develop the needed capabilities. They saved the time required for modernization through research and development and avoided possible foreign control over key sectors of Japanese industry. From 1950 through 1963, Japanese companies signed 2,545 technical agreements, 62 percent of them with the United States and 10 percent with West Germany, America's nearest competitor. During the same period, Japanese industry borrowed more than $2 billion from sources in foreign countries.[1]

Although during the fifteen years after 1950 much basic required technology was absorbed by Japanese industry, imports of know-how by no means ceased at the end of that period. On the contrary, in recent years they have increased. The number of class "A" technology agreements (those entered into for periods longer than one year) made by Japan in the four years 1965 through 1968 reached 5,840.[2] Many of the recent contracts are for improvements in techniques already licensed in the past. In 1968, 70 percent of total technological imports were in this category rather than in new technology. The number of arrangements made in 1968 was 1,744, a 66 percent increase over the 638 of 1967. Payments were $313.8 million in 1968, against $238.8 million in 1967. The United States continued to hold first place, with 56.7 percent of the 1968 total; West Germany was second, providing 14.3 percent. Japan is also an exporter of technology; the total in 1968, $33.8 million, was not much over 10 percent of imports but was well ahead of the $26.9 million in exports for 1967. In 1969 Japanese imports of technology amounted to $400 million, of which 60 percent were purchased from the United States; exports were only $47 million.[3]

Japan has also won access to foreign technology through direct investment by foreign companies and joint ventures between Japanese and foreign firms. Japanese industrialists have generally preferred to buy licenses, which leave them independent in ownership and management. At the same time, many foreign companies have lost their enthusiasm for licensing in the face of toughening Japanese competition. They prefer to provide technology through joint ventures or, better still, to establish wholly owned subsidiaries. Permission for the latter has become almost impossible to obtain, the Japanese Government generally holding to the principle of maximum 50 percent foreign equity. In recent years direct investment has become one of the persistent and irritating economic problems between Japan and the United States. While the Japanese Government has promised continuing liberalization of the regulations and practices which have prevented American and other foreign investors from sharing the profits of the Japanese markets, the process has been slow and unsatisfactory, contributing to mounting complaints and exasperation of foreign companies, particularly American firms.

The Japanese have long since shaken off their prewar notoriety as slavish copyists and makers of cheap and shoddy goods. They have proved that they can not only successfully absorb foreign technology but adapt, improve, and innovate. Japanese accomplishments which can accurately be called innovations have been made in a wide variety of fields, including electronics, optics, materials, mechanics, and chemicals. Specialists recognize Japanese excellence in computer technology. The largest computer manufacturer in Japan, Fujitsu, held out against a technology link with the United States and was the first Japanese company to sell computers on the American market.[4]

As we have seen in the case of defense equipment, some machines have been an assembly of components, both foreign and domestic-made, rather than completely original products. For example, the YS-11, the passenger airplane which was so successfully sold abroad, used Rolls Royce engines. The Japanese have said they are determined that the successor to the YS-11 will be "all Japanese." Making a jet engine is high on the list of priorities for the future.

Some observers appraise modestly Japan's capacity for innovation, at least as shown thus far. A British science writer has found Japanese innovative ideas "solid, sensible and not too expensive" with a value that is "immediately meaningful to cautious industrialists." He cited an OECD review of Japan's science policy which criticized research in government laboratories as "low-level and ill-coordinated" and concluded that the allocation of money for research and development was inflexible and should be "more experimental and more venturesome."[5]

Heavy dependence on imports of foreign technology during the last twenty years has unquestionably retarded accomplishments in research and development, for which Japan has only recently begun to allocate funds that would appear adequate for an advanced industrial nation. Expenditures for R and D multiplied more than five times during the decade of the 1960's, from $513 million in 1960 to $2.66 billion in 1969.[6] In terms of GNP, the 1969 figure was about 1.6 percent, roughly the same percentage as that achieved in 1967 when expenditures were only $2.2 billion. Japan lags behind other advanced countries in relative expenditures on research and development. In contrast to Japan's 1.6 of GNP, the Soviet Union spends 3.3 percent, the United States 3 percent, France 2.3 percent, and West Germany 2 percent.[7]

Private companies in Japan bear about three-quarters of the total expenses for research and development, including technology imports, with the Government contributing the remaining one fourth. In the United States the Government pays

315

53 percent of the bill for R and D. Furthermore, of the modest Japanese Government share, only about a quarter is spent for the purposes which require such major appropriations in the United States: defense, space, and atomic energy. From these statistics, one can see that the financial responsibility of the Government for science and technology is limited and that of the industrialists very great indeed. This does not mean that the Government loses control of policy; it means, in fact, that it is the "government-industrial complex" which bears responsibility for the promotion of science and technology, including the determination of national policy.

All forecasts point to sharply increased programs in research and development. Japan will probably surpass Great Britain, Germany, and France to become third among nations of the world, as already achieved in GNP. Japan is giving special attention to research in the fields of nuclear energy, computer technology, space, and oceanography. Expenditures for R and D have been projected, at a five-fold increase by the end of the decade, to be $10 billion per year. This would be equivalent to the rate of increase between 1960 and 1969. One Japanese economist is even more optimistic. He believes that imports of technology will phase out by 1975 and that total spending for research and development in that year will reach $13 billion, or more than four times the estimated 1970 figure of $3 billion.[8] This forecast, especially the proposition that imports of technology would cease by 1975, appears a little too rosy even for the miraculous economy of Japan. The change in policy toward the space program alone, which will be discussed later on, suggests increased imports of technology on a major scale. What seems reasonably certain for the future is that Japanese will spend much more on R and D, will stress independent development, and will check their reliance on imports. At the same time, the Government share in the science and technology budget will become larger.

R and D for Defense

The R and D effort for defense purposes is small, both actually and comparatively, but like the civilian program has grown rapidly in recent years, and sharper increases are planned for the future. It represents less than 2 percent of the defense budget and less than 5 percent of total government appropriations for scientific development. In 1960, funds for defense research were $5.8 million; they rose to $10.5 million in 1965, and exceeded $25 million in 1969. The 2 percent allocation from defense funds contrasts with 10 percent for the United States and United Kingdom; 25 percent for nuclear-equipped France, and 5 percent for West Germany. The 4th Defense Build-up Plan (1971-1976), which will cost an estimated $14.4 billion (excluding basic pay increases), is to include $472 million, 3.3 percent of the total, for research and development. [9] The defense budget for FY1971 contains $62 million for R and D, already 3.2 percent of the total defense expenditures planned for that year. [10]

With small appropriations and a small staff, the Defense Agency has directed its efforts toward basic-weapons research, experimentation, and trial production of new weapons. Subjects of research have been electronic intelligence-gathering equipment, including radar and sonar, new aircraft, and missiles, rockets and torpedoes. Several missiles and rockets, including air-to-air, surface-to-air, and anti-tank, have been developed. Necessarily, the JDA works closely with private industry, but because of the political sensitivities involved, there is little coordination between its rocket program and the civilian space efforts.

Space

For some years Japan's goal has been to become fourth in space. Its first satellite was planned for September 1966, to take its place after the Russian *Sputnik* of 1957, America's first *Explorer* of 1958, and the French satellite of 1965. Success was not to come, however, until February 11, 1970, after four failures but, fortunately, just two months ahead of the Chinese singing satellite and therefore in time to capture the coveted fourth place. The 84-pound satellite was called *Osumi,* after the peninsula from which it was launched, a pointed jut of land which forms the southernmost extension of Japan's main southwestern island, Kyushu.

The national pride stirred by *Osumi's* successful thrust into orbit was diminished somewhat by the later failure, in September, to orbit a scientific satellite weighing 136 pounds, using a four-stage, solid-fuel *Mu* rocket. (Japan's second satellite, *Tansei,* weighing 138.6 pounds, was successfully launched by a *Mu* rocket on

February 16, 1971.) It was also true that the flight of *Osumi* had in fact not been a total success, since the lack of a proper guidance system had apparently left it wobbling freely in space. Out of the great Japanese postwar success story, space achievement by 1970 had been less than a brilliant chapter. The Government recognized this and decided a new policy was required.

The space program progressed, in fifteen years, from the first firing of a miniscule "pencil" rocket in 1955 to the success of the *Lambda* 4S-5 *Osumi* in 1970. Between those two dates, achievements were considerable, although the space effort was characterized by a complex and disjointed administration, shoestring budgets, and adherence in a large degree to the "do-it-yourself" philosophy. The guiding principles of the program were: (1) exclusively peaceful purposes; (2) independence: priority to Japanese technology; (3) no secrecy; and (4) international cooperation.

Research and development were carried on by two separate organizations, Tokyo University's Institute of Space and Aeronautical Science, with testing facilities in Kagoshima Prefecture in Kyushu, and the National Space Development Center of the Government's Space and Technology Agency, which tested at Tanegashima, a small island off Kyushu, famed in history as the spot where Westerners first set foot on Japanese soil and where the first Western firearm, a Portuguese arquebus, was introduced into Japan in the year 1543.

A third program, already mentioned, has been conducted by the Defense Agency, which concentrated on short-range missiles and tested on still another island, Niijima. All programs were financed by the Government (Tokyo University is a Government institution, with its space program funded through the Ministry of Education) but cooperation between and coordination of the programs has been somewhat less than effective. The scientists of Tokyo University were sensitive to charges of contributing to the defense program and shunned cooperation with the missile programs of the Defense Agency.

Fifteen principal commissions, agencies, and bureaus in eight different ministries of Government and twenty-five research institutes and observatories are listed in a Japanese Government publication as engaged in space activities of one kind or another. Besides these official agencies, twenty-two principal private industrial firms produce space equipment and facilities.[11] Efforts to unify the space effort resulted in the formation in 1968 of the Space Activities Commission, attached directly to the Prime Minister's Office and with the mandate to formulate space policies, adjust activities of the various agencies, estimate budgets, and outline training programs. In October 1969 the National Space Development Agency (NASDA) was established by law, replacing the National Space Development Center and with the purpose of developing artificial satellites, launch vehicles and tracking systems. The President of NASDA is appointed by the Prime Minister with the consent of the Space Activities Commission. Thus NASDA should enjoy a certain degree of independence. It was given funds at the time of its foundation amounting to $4.93 million. [12]

Another body, the Science Council of Japan, attached directly to the Prime Minister's Office, had attempted to assume exclusive responsibility for science policy. Some members of this Council, which included social as well as natural and physical scientists, have shown marked ideological and political predilections in their approach to scientific problems. In this they were representative of a large segment of Japanese intellectuals who still are swayed by an outdated Marxism. Council members, suspicious of "military-tainted" research, criticized scientific cooperation with the United States on grounds that it might invite American military influence and involuntary catering by Japan to American foreign policies. Fortunately, the formation of the Space Activities Commission and NASDA in effect removed policy influence over the space program from the Science Council and finally achieved a much needed coordinated policy control.

The Tokyo University Space Center and the National Space Development Center (before its conversion to NASDA) divided the tasks in the rocket and satellite programs. The Tokyo University group produced only scientific satellites, whereas NSDC confined itself to "application" satellites. The *Lambda* rocket series, one of which boosted the 84 pound satellite *Osumi* into orbit, was developed by Tokyo University. The *Mu* rocket, some four times larger than the *Lambda* and with an estimated range of from 4,000 to 5,000 miles, was also a Tokyo Universtiy product. The *Mu* rocket has been compared with the American *Minuteman* because it is similar in size and range. According to some estimates, *Mu* rockets, if provided with advanced guidance equipment, could carry nuclear warheads into Communist China and the Soviet Union. The *Mu* rocket was to have orbited a satellite on September 23, 1970, but failed at its fourth stage, which did not ignite. This launching came after six postponements. On February 16, 1971, Japan's second satellite, the 138.6 pound *Tansei* (Light Blue), was successfully launched by the *Mu* rocket. According to press reports, its orbit was not the intended one, owing to a faulty control system.

The objectives of the National Space Development Center were to develop rockets, "application" satellites, and tracking systems for them. In contrast to Tokyo University, which used solid fuels exclusively, the NSDC launched rockets functioning with both solid and liquid fuels. For example, the "Q" system, later abandoned, was to use solid fuel in the first and second stages, and liquid fuel in the third stage.

While the military implications of rocket technology are missed by no one, scientists working in this field have been reluctant to discuss such implications, insisting that the purposes of the space program must be kept strictly and exclusively peaceful. Concern over the potential military use of their rockets was said by one foreign observer to have made the professors of Tokyo University reluctant to direct their research to guidance systems. [13] More recent reports indicated that work was indeed proceeding on guidance systems. The lack of perfection in control was evidenced by the course of the two satellites put up on February 11, 1970, and on February 16, 1971.

Japanese newspapers have been less inhibited in speculating on the military uses of ventures into space than have those engaged in the projects. After the successful launching of *Osumi,* a news commentary noted that "the technical know-how certainly will feed back into the rearmament of Japan in the 1970's." The *Asahi* was quoted as saying, "The real aim of the rocket makers is to master space technology and make money in defense projects. These real aims are entwined in the cheers over launching rockets of peaceful and scientific intent." [14]

Japan's space program has in the past been characterized by the comment, "Frugality has the upper hand." The total annual space budget has been estimated as equalling roughly twelve hours of space spending by the United States. [15] The satellite finally put into orbit in February 1970 was called the "hundred million yen fireworks," calculating the combined cost, including four previous failures. Few would deny that the $278,000 price was a bargan.

Some idea of the economy of Japan's space program can be gleaned from the fact that the total budget for space research from the early 1960's through 1969 amounted to only $103 million. Costs in 1969 were $25.6 million, almost triple the 1965 expenditures.[16] Budget cuts have been frequent. A few days after the successful launching of *Osumi*, the Director General of the Science and Technology Agency, while paying his respects at the Grand Shrines at Ise, took time to tell reporters that the 1970 budget had just been cut in half, to $28 million, which was still, he noted, $8 million more than the total budget for 1968.[17] Even with remarkable ability to accomplish much at mimimum cost, the Japanese could scarcely expect a rapidly successful development of sophisticated guidance systems, powerful rockets, and heavy satellites unless more generous injections of money were to be provided.

Japan has cooperated closely with the American National Aeronautics and Space Administration (NASA) in experiments and research and since 1963 has participated in the International Telecommunications Satellite Consortium (INTELSAT); however, the scientists in charge of the advanced Tokyo University rocketry programs consistently refused to launch a satellite in a NASA rocket. As a matter of policy, the Japanese preferred to sacrifice short-term gains in speed and budgets in the interest of the "made-in-Japan" principle; the technological experience and the pride and prestige of an exclusively Japanese effort were at that time more important than the speed of the space program. Successive failures evoked successive criticisms. The fifth and finally successful try momentarily stilled the critics, but it became evident to responsible officials in the Japanese Government that the do-it-yourself principle would never win for Japan the cherished place in space in the minimum time desired.

The Japanese already had a technical cooperation agreement for space research with the United States. At their Washington meeting in November 1967, President Johnson and Prime Minister Sato announced a space accord, which was subsequently negotiated and finally signed in the summer of 1969. The agreement permitted American industry to provide to the Japanese Government or to Japanese companies under contract with the Government certain categories of technology and equipment useful in Japan's space development program. These included launch-vehicle technology up to the level of the *Thor-Delta* rocket (which the Japanese in 1970 decided to use), as well as technology applicable to construction of communications and other application satellites. In "exceptional cases," where certain components were regarded as especially sensitive, the United States Government reserved the right to provide hardware instead of design and construction information.

In signing the agreement, Japan accepted certain conditions: first, to use the technology and equipment solely for peaceful purposes; second, to exert maximum efforts to prevent the reexport of the equipment and technology to third countries except as agreed upon by both Governments; and third, to use communications satellites resulting from imported American technology in ways compatible with the objectives of INTELSAT, as it exists or may evolve.

Work was to begin on these projects through arrangements between American and Japanese companies, some contracts for which had already been drafted.

The Future of the Space Program

In the fall of 1970 the Japanese Government did an about face in its policy toward space development. No more would there be insistence on rockets made entirely in Japan. The progress in space exploration by both the United States and the Soviet Union and the successive failures in Japan's own attempts to launch scientific satellites into orbit contributed to the decision. In a report issued October 21, the Space Activities Commission set forth its policies, recommendations, and outline of the future space program. The need for importing foreign technology was openly expressed: ". . . we must strive to eliminate the technological gap with foreign countries. For this purpose, technology introduction and other means should be utilized to push space development efficiently until Japanese technologies reach a certain level." In another part of the report, the Commission stated: ". . . it is necessary for Japan to acquire as soon as possible the technology related to the medium liquid rocket engine, which could be further improved to increase its performance, in preparation for the launching of large stationary satellites in the future. This approach, moreover, is considered realistic when we take into account prospects for introduction of technology from the United States." [18]

322

One entire project, to develop the solid-and-liquid-fuel "Q" rocket, was scrapped, and in its place the construction of a rocket using liquid fuel was planned. The American *Thor-Delta*, understood to be the "workhorse" for launching miscellaneous satellites, was to be utilized by the Japanese. Their original schedule of launchings would be delayed, but the Space Activities commission believed that in the long run time would be saved and that the technological gap between Japan and the other advanced countries could be narrowed at an early date.

Plans for the future, as outlined by the Commission, called for the launching of six scientific satellites by 1976. Two "Engineering Test" satellites were scheduled for 1975 and 1976, an "Ionosphere Sounding" satellite for 1975, and an "Experimental Communications" satellite for 1977. At the same time, the Commission announced a program of research on other types of satellites: meteorological, navigational, geodetic, communications, broadcasting, and resources. Dates were not set for these later projects. The description of the "broadcasting" satellite hinted of Japan's future position in Asia: "Research on broadcasting satellites should concentrate on systems and payload instrumentation of satellites for making broadcasts to each of the Asian countries including Japan."

It was estimated that the drastic change in the space development program would delay satellite launching projects by three years, compared with the schedule previously established. Development costs for the new rockets were estimated at $275 million, almost half of the total $555 million allocated for the five-year satellite program.[19]

One science specialist, a several years' resident of Tokyo, commented that the Japanese could of course direct their space technology to military use but the costs would be heavy. Unless their present space spending grows more rapidly than past performance would suggest, progress in space, even for uniquely peaceful purposes, may be relatively slow. A shift to a military program would require reversal of the two principles that have been controlling so far: space development for peaceful purposes only and full disclosure. The political decision to embark on such a course would imply a basic change in Japan's established foreign policy and would undoubtedly be part of a decision to go the nuclear way. But before thinking about the dilemma of the weapon, it may be useful to look at the challenge that growing energy requirements will present to Japan and the part that nuclear power may play in meeting these needs.

Energy Requirements

Since no one predicts a truly serious slowdown in Japanese economic growth for the immediate future, richer sources of energy will be indispensable. Electric power demand for Japan in 1985 has been estimated, by the Japan Overall Energy Survey Council, at five times that required in 1970, or one trillion kilowatt hours. [20] The sources of energy are principally oil, coal, and water, with percentage shares in 1969 of 68, 23, and 7 respectively. The Council predicts that the share of oil, 99 percent of which must be imported, will in 1980 be even larger than today, amounting to 75 percent of primary energy sources. Coal will have diminished to 9.5 percent, water to 4.4 percent, and nuclear power will have gained an estimated 10 percent share. As we shall see later, the last is a most conservative prediction. Japan's dependence on imported energy, according to the Council's projections, will have increased from nearly 75 percent in 1967 to almost 90 percent in 1980. (See Tables 13-1 and 13-2.)

Oil

It is natural that during this decade the Japanese pursuit of oil around the world will continue intensively, even while a nuclear power industry is developed apace. According to figures of the Ministry of International Trade and Industry (MITI), oil consumption per day, which in 1969 was 3.3 million barrels, is expected to rise to 5.1 million by 1975 and to between 12 and 13.7 million barrels by 1980. In value, Japan's crude oil imports in 1969 amounted to $1.9 billion, an increase of 13.2 percent over the 1968 imports of $1.68 billion. [21]

The Japanese have been deeply concerned not only over their heavy dependence on imported oil for the power to run the wheels of industry but also over the predominant Middle Eastern origin of this oil. They have felt they were suffering an involuntary servitude to geography, too great a vulnerability to political combustion in the Middle East, and too much dependence on the Southeast Asian sea route for the continuous, moving lifeline of giant tankers. Furthermore, Middle Eastern oil has a high sulfurous

324

content, which makes it less desirable because of its polluting effect.

For all of these reasons, the Japanese have been trying to reduce the degree of their dependence on Middle East oil and have succeeded to some slight degree. In 1967, 91.9 percent of Japan's oil imports came from the Middle East; this percentage was brought down to 90.2 percent in 1968 and to 87.3 percent in 1969. At the same time, imports from Southeast Asia, largely from Indonesia, with a low sulphur content, increased from 8.1 percent in 1968 to 10.9 percent in 1969. Imports from Indonesia more than tripled in quantity between 1967 and 1969. [22]

The Japanese are searching for oil the world over. Ten companies have been pursuing twelve projects, in various parts of Indonesia and in Canada and Alaska, all in different stages of development or operation. [23] For the future, nearby supplies exist in the Soviet Union, ever anxious to improve economic relations, and possibly in the offshore areas near the Ryukyu Islands, already discussed.

The smell of oil in far-flung places has not led the Japanese to neglect the possibilities of discovering the precious fuel in their own backyard. Offshore areas along the coast of Hokkaido and parts of Honshu have been allocated and surveys undertaken. Oil has in fact been found in small quantities off the coast of Akita, Yamagata, and Niigata prefectures, in the Japan sea; but Japan's domestic production of 15,000 barrels per day is of little significance in her total consumption. A rich find in Japanese waters would be for Japan the bonanza of the century.

Coal

Coal is less important than oil as a fuel for Japan, and domestic production has accounted for as much as 15 percent of total requirements. This percentage is expected to decrease, however, and heavier reliance on imports will be unavoidable. In 1969, Japanese imports of coal amounted to about 43 million tons, valued at $713 million—more than the total two-way trade with Communist China. Oil imports in the same year were more than two and a half times this amount in value.

An example of Japan's interest in coal was announcement of the proposed construction by 1973 of a new port in British Columbia, about 500 miles north of Vancouver, to handle giant Japanese

Table 13-1

Prospect of Primary Energy Sources (in units of 10^{13} kcal)

Type of energy	1967 Quantity	1967 Percent	1975 Quantity	1975 Percent	1980 Quantity	1980 Percent
Water power	17.1	8.3	22.2	6.6	26.4	4.4
Nuclear power	.0		8.0	2.4	60.1	10.0
Coal	50.6	24.6	55.1	16.3	56.5	9.5
Domestic coal	(29.6)	(14.6)	(31.4)	(9.3)	(31.4)	(5.3)
Oil	132.8	64.7	246.2	72.8	446.9	74.8
Imported	(125.1)	(60.8)	(222.1)	(65.6)	(431.8)	(72.2)
Others (natural gas,						
charcoal, etc.)	5.0	2.4	6.9	1.9	7.8	1.3
Domestic	(4.9)	(2.3)	(5.1)	(1.4)	(4.8)	(0.8)
Totals	205.5	100.0	338.4	100.0	597.7	100.0
Domestically produced energy	52.4	25.5	59.6	17.6	63.5	10.6
Imported energy	153.1	74.5	278.8	82.4	534.2	89.4

Source: *Nihon no Anzen Hosho. 1970 e no Tenbo*, 1969 edition, Tokyo, 1969, p. 252, (Japan's Security. Outlook on 1970). Projections made by the *Overall Energy Survey Council*.

Table 13-2

Future Outlook of Japan's Power Generating Capacity (in Megawatts electric power, MWe)

	1970	1975	1980	1985	1990
Hydro	18,700	24,000	32,900	43,600	58,400
Fossil	37,000	75,000	91,200	109,900	105,800
Nuclear	1,300	9,000	27,000	60,000	119,700
Total	57,000	108,000	151,100	213,500	283,900

Sources: Japan Atomic Industrial Forum, *Atoms in Japan*, September 1970 Supplement; United States Atomic Energy Commission, American Embassy, Tokyo.

freighters, which would carry automobiles to Canada (40 percent of all cars in British Columbia in 1970 were of Japanese make) and return with cargos of high quality coking coal. Press reports speculate that after 1973 the Japanese will buy three million tons of coal a year, to be shipped through the new port of Prince Rupert. [24]

Nuclear Power

Predictions vary about the future of nuclear power. Some optimists declare that in the year 2000, 70 percent of the world's electricity will be generated by atomic energy. Others are less sure that the fossil fuels will yield such an important place to the atom. Determining factors will be technology, availability of resources, and relative costs.

Various forecasts have been made of the percentage of Japan's energy requirements that will in the future be supplied by nuclear power. The most conservative guess is 10 percent by 1980. Japan's Long Range Plan for the Development of Atomic Energy, formulated in 1967, called for a capacity of 6 million kilowatts by 1975 and from 30 to 40 million kilowatts by the end of 1985. However, the Japan Atomic Energy Commission concluded in 1970 that nuclear generating capacity would exceed the plan, reaching 8.66 million kilowatts by 1975 and easily surpassing the 30 to 40 million kilowatts goal in 1985. [25] Still later, in November 1970, the Atomic Energy Industry Forum projected 27 million kilowatts, or 17 percent of total energy requirements, by 1980; 60 million by 1985; and 120 million by 1990. [26] (See Table 13-2.) At this rate, atomic power would then reach 42 percent of the total electric power capacity in the country. In 1985, according to the U.S. Atomic Energy Commission, American capacity for production of electricity by nuclear energy will reach 280 million kilowatts.

During the first ten years of Japan's nuclear energy program, 1956 to 1965, a total of $500 million was spent, divided equally between the Government and private mining and manufacturing industries. Government budgets for nuclear research and development jumped appreciably in succeeding years, from $48 million in 1967 to $84 million in 1969 and to $109 million in 1970. Of the 1970 budget, well over half was allocated to the Power Reactor and Nuclear Fuel Development Corporation and almost a third to the

Japan Atomic Energy Research Institute. About $7.5 million was earmarked for development of the nuclear-powered ship now under construction. [27]

Like the space program, Japanese nuclear energy development must observe the principles of no military use and no secrecy. These conditions were stipulated in the Basic Atomic Energy Law, passed in 1955 at the time Japan's national nuclear effort was begun. The Law provided that "research, development, and utilization of atomic energy are limited to peaceful uses" and that programs and results must be made public.

Japan's Reactors

By 1957 a first small American research reactor went critical, and in 1962 the first Japanese-made research reactor was in operation. In 1963 the Japan Power Demonstration Reactor, of General Electric make and "Boiling Water" type, first generated electricity in Japan. The first commerical production of electricity took place at the Tokai Power Station, built in the town of Tokai, about 65 miles northeast of Tokyo, by the Japan Atomic Power Company (JAPCO). The reactor, a Calder-Hall type fueled with natural uranium, graphite moderated, and CO_2 cooled, was imported from Great Britain in 1960. The plant first went into full commerical operation in July 1967, with a generating capacity of 166,000 kilowatts. Difficulties were experienced in late 1967, and the station was shut down temporarily, first for a week and later for a period of a hundred days. [28]

JAPCO built its second power station in Tsuruga, Fukui Prefecture, on the Japan Sea coast, using an American Boiling Water reactor manufactured by the General Electric Company. With construction begun in April 1966, the station was completed and in full operation by the end of March 1970. The generating capacity was 322,000 kilowatts, subsequently increased to 357,000 kilowatts.

By April 1970 Japan's production of electric power by nuclear energy reached 488,000 kilowatts. Two additional power plants were put into operation later in the year, with a combined generating capacity of 800,000 kilowatts. One was the Fukushima Power Station No. 1 of the Tokyo Electric Power Company, located in Fukushima Prefecture, near the Pacific coast, and using a General Electric reactor; the other was the Mihama Power

Station No. 1 of the Kansai Electric Power Company, located in the Mihama area of Fukui Prefecture near the coast of the Japan Sea, and using equipment produced by the Westinghouse Electric Company and the Mitsubishi Atomic Industry Group. [29]

In addition to the four plants listed above, bringing Japan's nuclear power capacity from 178,000 kilowatts at the end of 1969 to 1.3 million kilowatts at the end of 1970 (American capacity was 2.8 million kilowatts in 1968), nine additional plants are in the process of construction or are planned, all to be completed by the end of 1975 or the beginning of 1976.

The Japanese have set out to increase as rapidly as possible the degree of domestically produced components in their nuclear power plants. The "Nuclear Power White Paper" (The Annual Report of the Japan Atomic Energy Commission) published in July 1970 described the progress in achieving *kokusan* (domestic production). In the Tokai-mura plant, which went into operation in 1967, only 35 percent of the equipment was made in Japan. This percentage increased to 55 percent in the Tsuruga plant, and was planned to reach 90 percent in two power stations now scheduled for completion in 1974. [30]

A Nuclear-Powered Ship

Plans for a nuclear-powered ship were first approved by the Japanese Government in 1963 and were revised in March 1967 to specify the construction of an experimental nuclear-powered vessel of 8,000 tons. The Japan Nuclear Ship Development Agency was formed to carry through the project, and contracts were signed with the Ishikawajima-Haruma Heavy Industry Company for the ship construction ($8 million) and with the Mitsubishi Atomic Power Industries for the reactor system ($7.4 million).

The ship, christened *Mutsu* after the city in Aomori Prefecture in northern Japan that is to be the ship's mother port, was launched June 12, 1969. The ship was expected to be ready for operation during the first half of 1972, but in October 1970 the director of the Japan Atomic Industrial Forum, after an inspection of the ship, announced that because of changes in equipment specifications and other technical reasons, completion of the ship would be delayed by approximately a year, until about March of 1973. [31]

It remains to be seen how useful Japan will judge the building of the *Mutsu* to have been. Many Americans probably wonder whether the *Savannah* was worth the cost. For Japan, however, the successful completion of a nuclear-powered vessel will mark another milestone, and like putting a satellite into space, launching *Mutsu* will be a symbol of Japan's advance to front rank position in the world of the 1970's.

The Problem of Fuel

The essential ingredients in the production of nuclear energy are uranium and plutonium. The latter is produced in the course of reactor operation, but the former is the indispensable raw material of atomic energy. Needless to say, intensive investigations of Japanese soil have been made which, as of April 1970, indicated resources of uranium (U_3O_8) amounting to 7,700 tons, but not ore of highest quality. [32] Since Japan's uranium needs are calculated to reach 100,000 tons by 1985, indigenous supplies are of little help. (The JAEC in 1970 estimated Japan's cumulative requirements of U_3O_8 in 1990 at 190,000 to 230,000 tons.) Japan is now buying enriched uranium from the United States but is at the same time conducting research on methods of enrichment and seeking sources of uranium ore in other countries.

A Japanese-American agreement signed in February 1968 guarantees a supply by the United States of 161 tons of enriched uranium for a period of 30 years from 1967, calculated on the consumption of reactors in operation by 1975 and generating by then 5.5 million kilowatts of electricity. (As noted above, present estimates are more than 8 million kilowatts by 1975.) The agreement was welcomed as ensuring the operation of the Japanese nuclear power program, but at the same time uneasiness was expressed at this "serious dependence on one nation," which so completely placed Japan's atomic energy policy under an American "umbrella." [33]

A truly independent nuclear program requires development of the enrichment process and access to ample supplies of natural uranium. Because of its application to weapons production, enrichment technology has been highly classified and not available for transfer from the United States. Although Japan has access to supplies of enriched uranium from the United States it is natural that a primary objective of the Japanese nuclear program is to achieve an independent enrichment capability.

For some years Japanese scientists have been engaged in research on the two systems for enrichment that have been used in the United States and Europe, the gaseous diffusion and centrifuge processes. According to the Japanese Atomic Energy Commission, good results have been obtained in both research programs, although apparently much work must yet be done before production of enriched uranium in industrial quantities becomes possible. An evaluation of the state of development and of the relative merits of the two systems is planned for 1972, in the expectation that a decision will then be made on which method to use. The importance attached to the problem of enrichment technology was shown by the establishment in May 1969 of a Council for the Study of Uranium Enrichment. [34]

During his visit to the United States in September 1970, Director General of Defense Nakasone produced a mild sensation in Washington and Tokyo by proposing, to Secretary of Defense Laird and publicly in a speech at the National Press Club, that the United States join with Japan and perhaps other countries to produce enriched uranium for peaceful purposes. The Director General is reported to have told the Defense Secretary that Japan was considering starting work in 1971 on a gaseous diffusion plant to produce enriched uranium. Although Nakasone reiterated that Japan would not produce nuclear weapons and insisted that his proposal for sharing the secrets of enriching uranium was made not as head of the Defense Agency but as a prominent LDP politician, the first American reaction was reported as cool and skeptical. The appropriateness of discussing the enrichment of uranium for peaceful purposes with the Secretary of Defense was puzzling and, regardless of Nakasone's assurances, officials at the time were unenthusiastic about sharing secrets which might not be protected and which could be used to make weapons. [35]

In a statement made in Tokyo after his return from the United States in September 1970, Nakasone underscored the importance to Japan of power generated from atomic energy, because of the growing demand and the necessity to reduce the consumption of oil, with its resulting pollution. He said that although research had started on uranium enrichment techniques, only 300 million yen ($833,000) had been appropriated for this purpose in 1970. Such meager funds would permit only the slowest progress. Indeed, he said, some experts calculated that even to construct a plant capable of producing only about one sixth of the demand for enriched uranium in 1985, would cost 300 billion yen ($833 million). For all of these reasons, Nakasone was appealing for a speeded up research program and calling upon the United States to supply the know-how for the enrichment process. He also suggested the establishment of an international organ for the manufacture of enriched uranium. [36]

Uranium

Access to adequate supplies of uranium is essential for Japan if an important share of future electricity needs is to be produced by nuclear energy. Some estimates conclude that as the use of nuclear power increases, natural uranium resources may be exhausted by the end of the century. The Japan Atomic Energy Commission has quoted European sources to show that world consumption of uranium will exceed production after about the year 1973. According to these sources, the production of uranium in 1970 was 38,000 short tons to meet a demand of 18,500 short tons. However, the demand in 1975 was estimated to be from 44,000 to 59,000 tons, and in 1980 between 73,000 and 103,000 tons. The conclusion from these projections was that the development of new sources of uranium ore would be essential from the mid-'seventies on. [37]

Some Americans in the power industry are much less concerned over future shortages of uranium. They see instead—for the United States—insufficient supplies of coal and oil. A senior consultant of National Economic Research Associates was quoted in the publication *Nuclear Industry* as forecasting a "supply crisis" in natural gas in a few years, uncertainty over adequate future supplies of oil, and a worsening situation as regards coal. However, he concludes, "the exception to the current problem of shortage or threatened near-term shortage in the fuels is uranium . . . the results of recent exploration efforts indicate that uranium will be in ample supply for a considerable time in the future." [38]

Facing the possibility of a future shortage of uranium, the Japanese have made and are continuing to make all-out efforts to secure sources of supply and opportunities to participate in the exploitation and development of uranium mines. In May 1970 a group of firms in the electricity and mining industries formed a special corporation for the purpose of investigating, exploring, and developing sources of nuclear materials overseas.

Thus far Canada has been the principal supplier of uranium ore to Japan, and both long- and short-term contracts have been signed by Canadian and Japanese firms. Other areas where the Japanese have sought uranium, either by purchase or by joint exploration, have been France, the United States (Colorado and Wyoming), Indonesia, Australia, and Africa (Kenya, Somalia, Niger, Gabon, and the Central African Republic). At the same time continued investigations are being carried on in various prefectures of Japan where additional uranium deposits may exist.[39]

The Fast Breeder Reactor

One solution to a uranium shortage appears to be the fast breeder reactor, which converts uranium into plutonium and over a period of time makes more plutonium than it consumes. An official of the Japanese Science and Technology Agency has described the importance for Japan of the breeder reactor: "Japan is qualified to maintain the position as an industrial country and so develop further only if she succeeds in the development of the fast breeder reactor, which is bound to occupy the main portion of power generation in the future."[40] Consequently, as is happening in the United States and European countries, Japan is energetically pursuing a program of research and development in breeder reactors.

The Japanese plan is to build an experimental fast breeder reactor, which they have picturesquely named *Joyo* (Eternal Sun), with an original electricity-generating capacity of 50,000 kilowatts, expected to increase to 100,000 kilowatts. The schedule calls for this reactor to go critical in 1973. A prototype reactor, called *Monju*, a word which suggests the saying "two heads are better than one," is projected for criticality in 1977, with a capacity of 300,000 kilowatts. Thus, the Power Reactor and Nuclear Fuel Development Corporation (PNC) hopes to have a fast breeder reactor as well as an Advanced Thermal Reactor, which utilizes heavy water, in operation in the 1980's.

Some observers are not optimistic about the rapid success of the quest for breeders. The well-known nuclear physicist Edward Teller has been quoted as saying that "the fast breeder has resisted the head-on attack of our best technological people for twenty years. I doubt it will become a success very soon." [41] The associate editor of *Electric Light and Power* suggested in April 1968 that 1985 looked like a more reasonable date for the perfection of breeders than the 1980 target date previously anticipated in the nuclear power industry. He commented that unless fast breeders were working within twenty years "the first generation of nuclear power stations may be the last." [42] Teller has also expressed some anxiety about the safety hazards of breeder reactors, which to be effective must, he says, generate at least a million kilowatts.

As we have seen, nuclear energy will probably not soon threaten the supremacy of oil among the sources of Japan's future energy requirements. Electric power generated in presently operating nuclear plants is more expensive than that produced by conventional means. Higher costs in Japan result largely from the infancy of the industry and the difficulty of finding appropriate sites for nuclear reactors because of topography, densely populated areas, objections of local inhabitants, and dangers of earthquakes. Safety standards are particularly high in Japan because of these hazards. The Japanese Government and the power companies have recognized the importance of making thorough studies of environmental problems and of winning understanding from citizens in areas where plants are to be situated.

The cost factor may in the future favor nuclear power. Westinghouse has made a projection of the "widening coal-nuclear cost gap" which shows that in 1972 the cost of nuclear fuel will be half that of delivered coal and by 1980 only a little more than a third. [43] Moreover, the polluting effect of oil used as a fuel will favor increased use of nuclear power. Nevertheless, expectations from nuclear energy may be exaggerated in Japan, as they may be in the United States and in other parts of the world where the consumption of power rises without cease. In Japan, moreover, the social and political risks of a nuclear power program loom larger: a serious nuclear accident in Japan or elsewhere would jog the memories of Hiroshima and deal a serious setback to the program.

More generally, the world's uranium supplies could prove insufficient or inaccessible, and the breeder reactors may not appear in time.

In the meantime, however, the nuclear genie having been released from his bottle, beckons powerfully. Inevitably, in an age dominated by superpower, he also holds aloft a promise of national prestige and military security. The military promise, however, requires a national political decision—for Japan, an excruciating decision.

Notes

1. Report to Participants, *Changing Japan: A Survey of Western Business Relations* (New York: McKinsey and Company, Inc., 1964), pp. 2-8, 3-4. The figures are attributed to the Japanese Ministries of Finance and of International Trade and Industry (MITI).

2. *Japan Economic Yearbook 1970* (Tokyo: The Oriental Economist, 1970), p. 78.

3. *Nihon Keizai,* December 12, 1969; *Asahi,* December 13, 1969. 1969 figures from American Embassy, Tokyo.

4. *Business Week,* May 16, 1970.

5. P. B. Stone, *Japan Surges Ahead: The Story of an Economic Miracle* (New York: Frederick A. Praeger, 1969), pp. 142-43.

6. The source for these figures and other information used in this section is the American Embassy, Tokyo.

7. Kanamori Hisao, *Keizai Taikoku "Nippon"* ("Nippon," the Great Economic Nation), (Tokyo: The Japan Economic Research Center, Nihon Keizai Shimbunsha, March 26, 1970), pp. 119-20.

8. *Ibid.,* p. 120.

9. *Nihon Keizai,* October 22, 1970.

10. Boei-cho (Defense Agency), *Gaisan Yokyo no Taiyo* (Summary of Estimated Budget Request), *FY1971* (Tokyo: Defense Agency, August 1970), p. 15.

11. *Space in Japan 1969-70* (Tokyo: Science and Technology Agency, January 1970), pp. 10-11, 20-21, 106-63.

12. *Ibid.,* p. 34.

13. F. Roy Lockheimer, *The Rising Sun in Space, Part I: The University of Tokyo,* Report Service, East Asia Series, Vol. XIV, No. 1 (Japan) (New York: American Universities Field Staff, January 1967), p. 7.

14. "Space Ventures Japanese Style," Tokyo UPI dispatch, *Hokubei Mainichi,* San Francisco, February 16, 1970.

15. F. Roy Lockheimer, *The Rising Sun in Space, Part II: International Cooperation, Organization, and the Future,* Reports Service, East Asia Series, Vol. XIV, No. 2 (Japan) (New York: American Universities Field Staff, February 1967), p. 19.

16. *Space in Japan 1969-70, op. cit.,* p. 29.

17. *Nihon Keizai,* February 16, 1970.

18. Government of Japan, Space Activities Commission, *Space Development Program (Decision for 1970),* Tokyo, October 21, 1970.

19. *Japan Times,* October 22, 1970.

20. Nakasone Yasuhiro, "Uranium Enrichment Plant Should Be Constructed Quickly." Source: American Embassy, Tokyo.

21. *Oil and Gas Journal,* June 8, 1970; Tsu-sho Sangyo-sho (Ministry of International Trade and Industry), *Tsusho Hakusho 1970, Kakuron* (Foreign Trade White Paper 1970, Detailed) (Tokyo: Min. of Int. Trade and Ind., July 10, 1970), p. 231.

22. *Foreign Trade White Paper 1970, op. cit.,* pp. 228 and 231.

23. Anzan Hosho Chosa Kai (Security Research Council), *Nihon no Anzen Hosho, 1970 e no Tembo* (Japan's Security, Outlook on 1970), 1969 edition (Tokyo: August 10, 1969), p. 214.

24. *Japan Times,* October 6, 1970.

25. Genshiryoku Iin-kai (Japan Atomic Energy Commission), *Genshiryoku Hakusho, Genshiryoku Nenpo 1969* (White Paper on Atomic Energy: Annual Report on Atomic Energy 1969) (Tokyo: July 1970), p. 3.

26. *Mainichi,* November 16, 1970.

27. JAEC, *Annual Report 1969, op. cit.,* p. 151.

28. Japan Atomic Energy Commission (JAEC), *Twelfth Annual Report 1967-1968* (in English) (Tokyo: 1968), p. 35.

29. JAEC, *Annual Report 1969, op. cit.,* pp. 30-35.

30. *Ibid.,* pp. 34-35.

31. *Japan Times,* October 30, 1970.

32. JAEC, *Annual Report 1969, op. cit.,* p. 44. Non-Communist world sources of uranium were estimated in the mid-1960's at about 575,000 tons of U_3O_8 in ore. The three leading nations were Canada (200,000 tons), United States (150,000 tons), and South Africa (140,000 tons). One ton of average ore contains from 2 to 5 lbs. of U_3O_8. (Source: Encyclopaedia Britannica).

33. *Mainichi,* February 19, 1968.

34. JAEC, *Annual Report 1968, op. cit.,* p. 6.

35. *New York Times,* September 11, 1970.

36. Nakasone, *op. cit.*

37. JAEC, *Annual Report 1968, op. cit.,* p. 14.

38. "Nuclear Power Is Often an Imperative Choice, Despite Pitfalls," *Nuclear Industry,* September 1970. The quotation is from Mr. Abraham Gerber, Senior Consultant, National Economic Research Associates.

39. JAEC, *Annual Report 1969, op. cit.,* pp. 44-45.

40. Victor Galinsky and Paul Langer, *The Japanese Civilian Nuclear Program* (Santa Monica, California: The Rand Corporation, August 1967), p. 33.

41. Richard Curtis and Elizabeth Hogan, *Perils of the Peaceful Atom; The Myth of Safe Nuclear Power Plants* (Garden City, N.Y.: Doubleday and Company, 1969), p. 206.

42. *Ibid.,* p. 208.

43. *Nuclear Industry,* September 1970, *op. cit.*

14 The Nuclear Option: The Political Question

The Conditions for Making the Weapon

In the Cabinet reshuffle at the beginning of 1970, Prime Minster Sato gave the important post of Director General of the Japan Defense Agency to the bright, dynamic, young (52) Nakasone Yasuhiro. When not a Cabinet minister, Nakasone had been severely critical of the Sato government, and he had long been known as a proponent of strong defenses for Japan. A Japanese *Who's Who* describes him as the "most radical advocate of rearmament and the man who advocated the so-called 'Atom Pile Budget'."[1] In March 1970, a few days after a meeting with foreign press correspondents in Tokyo, Nakasone told his staff at the JDA that most of the journalists seemed to assume it was only a matter of time until Japan had its own nuclear weapons. He commented that the newsmen had apparently not understood what the Prime Minister had been saying or the debates in the Diet but had probably been influenced by the views of the American writer Herman Kahn, who, as the Director General put it, "says that Japan's nuclear armament is inevitable." Nakasone explained that he had told the correspondents that, in his opinion, Japan should not now or in the future produce nuclear weapons. He said he had come to this decision in his own mind in August of 1969.[2]

Foreign "Japan watchers" may indeed worry more about whether Japan will decide to go the nuclear way than do the Japanese themselves. Still, a subject taboo for many years has now come to be discussed with increasing frequency by intellectuals, commentators, and politicians. Ishihara Shintaro, the popular novelist who won a seat in the House of Councillors in 1968 with an unprecedented popular vote—equal to the total vote for all Communist candidates—has spoken out widely and emphatically in favor of Japan's possessing nuclear weapons. Public opinion polls have shown about 20 percent favoring Japan's own weapons; in one poll, taken in April 1969 and cited by Ishihara, the percentage in favor went as high as 45 percent, with 46 percent in opposition. As to be expected, polls reveal that when given the choice, more Japanese think their country "will" have nuclear arms than believe it "should" have them.[3]

The debate will probably heat up as the decade advances. Some Americans have publicly predicted that Japan will have the bomb by 1975. Japanese seem much less certain. Recently more of them have been considered seriously the consequences of such a decision. The Liberal Democratic Party has stood on the three nuclear principles (not to possess or manufacture nuclear weapons and not to admit them into the country) which Sato has described as one of the "four nuclear pillars," the other three being (1) efforts for nuclear disarmament; (2) dependence on the American nuclear deterrant; and (3) promotion of the peaceful uses of atomic energy. Policies can always be changed, and Sato has been careful to leave nuclear options open: he has consistently opposed a Diet resolution which would make permanent a nuclear ban.

How to make the bomb is not an obstacle. Japan is high on the list of the world's potential nuclear-weapon powers, the other prominent potential producers being India, West Germany, Israel, Switzerland, Sweden, and the United Arab Republic. Specialists guess that if the political decision were made, an explosive device and a nuclear warhead could be built in less than three years. A priority project supported by heavy appropriations would, of course, materially shorten the lead time. As the ambitious program now under way to utilize nuclear energy for electric power progresses, a shift to weapons manufacture will become progressively easier.

Assuming that Japan has the technological capacity to make a bomb, other considerations besides technology and the final political decision would affect the success of the enterprise. Among these are budget, organization, personnel, public opinion, and legal restraints.

Budget. Japan's economy, with its expected continued high growth rate, can accommodate a military nuclear effort, although the president of the country's largest bank has warned that "the enormous expense involved would impair sound economic growth."[4]

A United Nations report of 1967 outlined a budget for nuclear weapons, divided into such categories as "small but meaningful" and "modest scale but good quality." After calculating various sums for plutonium war heads, medium-range missiles, and even two submarines with nuclear missiles, the report estimated a total for the "modest" program of $560 million annually for ten years. Yet, according to the report, numerous other expenses connected with delivery systems and precision instruments would bring the total far above this figure, surpassing the more than $800 million for nuclear weapons expended annually by Great Britain and by France.[5]

Japanese have estimated that appropriations of $1 billion a year for ten years would be required if the result is to be more than a "meaningless toy." Such an expenditure would constitute more than a tenfold increase in the present nuclear energy effort and more than two thirds of the present total defense budget. While Japan's economy could stand this burden, an adjustment of priorities would be required among the numerous demands facing Japanese governments in the coming years.

Organization. Japan's dramatic economic advance in the world owes much to the prodigious and spectacular achievements of private industrial organizations. However, a nuclear weapons program presents different demands. It requires a Manhattan Project-type effort involving the close cooperation, coordination, and massive concentration of many diverse individuals and organizations, including scientists, bureaucrats, and industrialists. While such a combine is far from impossible, Japan's postwar experience does not include a large-scale national enterprise of this kind. One of Japan's brilliant, well-known younger university professors told the author in Tokyo: "You Americans overestimate Japan. Our GNP is high, but the gap between the United States and Japan—sociological and in efficiency and organization—is still enormous. Japan is not good at large, coordinated organization. Our success has been in private industry. The *Apollo* moon expedition shows the kind of technology and organization required for a nuclear weapons program. Japan is far from this stage."

Personnel. Japan's politically sensitive scientists are watchful that no military dimension enters a research program. Scientific cooperation with the United States in specific instances was blocked because of the participation of American military officers in projects suggested, even though the research was not directed to military purposes. For example, the cooperative monitoring of radioactivity proved difficult to carry out because of sensitivity to participation by technically qualified members of the American military. Inasmuch as scientists holding these political views are dispersed throughout Japan's space and nuclear energy programs, their lack of cooperation in a military effort, should the Government undertake nuclear weapons production, could be a serious handicap. Their presence also militates against any attempt by the Government to carry out a clandestine program.

Public Opinion. Unquestionably, as pride in country grows, aversion to things nuclear will also diminsh. Whether it will disappear is another question. One recalls the emotion aroused in 1954 when radioactivity from hydrogen bomb tests at Eniwetok affected Japanese fishermen: the Diet unanimously passed a resolution to ban atomic and hydrogen bombs from every nation. By October 1970, American nuclear-powered submarines had visited Japan forty times, and one could say that the Japanese had become conditioned to these routine visits; however, the 1968 visit of the aircraft carrier *Enterprise* aroused demonstrations of unprecedented dimensions. By 1973, when Japan's own atomic-powered ship is scheuled to be launched, the "nuclear allergy" may well have become a forgotten disease. At least, it probably will not break out in the presence of a homemade, nonmilitary vessel. It might revive, however, should Japan's Self-Defense fleet be augmented by the addition of domestically produced nuclear-powered submarines.

To power ships, even warships, with nuclear energy and to make a nuclear weapon are very different things. The Japanese youth of today, while free of the psychological war scars of the older generations, nevertheless shares the peace idealism of students in the United States and around the world. Public opinion may well become conditioned to nuclear power—unless there should be an accident—but nuclear weapons "made in Japan" could still face strong popular opposition in the decade of the 1970's.

Legal Restrictions. Certain legal and policy restrictions, while not insuperable obstacles should a future Japanese Government decide to construct nuclear weapons, would make the decision more difficult. These problems would arise from the Constitution, the security treaty with the United States, the Atomic Energy Law,

342

the partial nuclear test ban treaty, the present Government's announced nuclear policy, and the nuclear non-proliferation treaty.

In July 1955, a year after the formation of the Self-Defense Forces, "Honest John" rockets were brought into Japan; asked about these weapons, Prime Minister Hatoyama replied that he would approve bringing in nuclear weapons if they were absolutely necessary and intended only for self-defense. In April 1957, the Government stated officially that nuclear weapons were offensive weapons and therefore unconstitutional. However, a month later, Prime Minister Kishi announced in the Diet the Government's view that the possession of "defensive" nuclear weapons was not unconstitutional. In 1958 the Government published a more detailed interpretation of what was and was not a nuclear weapon, stating that a weapon, like the Honest John, is a nuclear weapon when fitted with a nuclear warhead but a non-nuclear weapon when not so fitted. Prime Minister Kishi reiterated in 1959 his position that defensive nuclear weapons were permitted, and this has been the interpretation consistently taken by succeeding Governments.[6] This stand was confirmed by the Defense White Paper issued October 20, 1970, which reiterated that small-sized nuclear weapons, if within the limit necessary for self-defense and not an aggressive threat to another nation, would be legally and constitutionally permissible.[7]

Consequently it can be assumed that should the Government decide to build nuclear weapons, the official position would be that since they were to be used exclusively for defense, the Constitution would not be violated. It is not difficult to imagine, however, that opponents of the Government's policy would denounce the decision as contrary to the spirit of Article 9 and therefore a contravention of the Constitution. It is also possible that by the time a decision to "go nuclear" became politically feasible, the Government might decide to seek revision of the Constitution to remove all doubts as to the constitutionality of the action.

The essence of the security treaty system is the provision to Japan of the American "nuclear umbrella." As long as the security treaty exists, Japan enjoys this protection. One of the principal justifications for the prior-consultation arrangements is prevention of the introduction or storage of nuclear weapons on Japanese soil, including, after 1972, Okinawa. Termination of the security treaty

343

would in itself be a powerful incentive for Japan to rearm fully, including the production of nuclear weapons. Of course, Japanese decisions to end the treaty and to make the bomb might be taken simultaneously or in sequence, one after the other.

If a decision to produce the bomb is·made, the Atomic Energy Law would have to be revised, since it clearly restricts nuclear power production to peaceful purposes. The course of Diet action and the strengths and attitudes of the political parties at the time would be judged by the Government if it contemplated revision of the law. Even making due allowance for growing nationalism and changes in public opinion over the coming years, one can now scarcely conceive of a more divisive and disruptive parliamentary issue during the 1970's.

While Prime Minister Sato's three nuclear principles have won practically unanimous support throughout the nation, he has been the first to recognize that policies change. He has resisted attempts in the Diet to freeze the principles into a Diet resolution, on the grounds that he does not wish to tie the hands of coming generations. Thus, a future Prime Minister could change these principles; he and his party would be the judges of the political feasibility of such a step at any given time.

Japan's adherence to the partial nuclear test ban treaty would have the practical effect of limiting the testing of nuclear weapons to underground sites. Given the narrow limits of Japanese territory, testing sites would present a problem. It is possible that with the return of administrative control over the Ryukyu Islands in 1972, some of the uninhabited areas of these islands might provide the required facilities.

The nonproliferation treaty deserves special attention.

The Nuclear Non-Proliferation Treaty

When President Johnson transmitted the Treaty on the Non-Proliferation of Nuclear Weapons (NPT) to the Senate for ratification on July 9, 1968, he said he considered it to be the most important international agreement limiting nuclear arms since the nuclear age began. He called it "a triumph of sanity and of man's will to survive."[8] Although the Soviet Union, the United Kingdom, and the United States (the three Depositary Governments) and fifty-three other nations had signed the treaty on July 1, it was more than a year and a half before the Japanese Government finally affixed its signature on February 3, 1970.

The purposes of the treaty were stated by President Johnson at the White House signing ceremony on July 1, 1968, "to commit the nations of the world which do not now have nuclear weapons not to produce or receive them in the future; to assure equally that such nations have the full peaceful benefits of the atom; and to commit the nuclear powers to move forward toward effective measures of arms control and disarmament."[9] Besides the prohibition on the transfer, receipt, and manufacture of nuclear weapons and nuclear explosive devices, other important elements of the treaty are (1) the obligations imposed on the non-nuclear weapon nations to accept safeguards for the verification of treaty observation; (2) the encouragement of exchange of equipment and technology for peaceful uses of nuclear energy; (3) the undertaking that benefits from nuclear explosions will be made available by nuclear weapon powers at as low a charge as possible; and (4) commitment to pursue negotiations for the achievement of nuclear disarmament and complete disarmament. The treaty, which endures for a period of twenty-five years, provides that five years after it went into effect a conference is to be held to review its operations and to assure that its purposes and provisions are being realized. Finally, each party to the treaty is accorded the right to withdraw from the treaty "if it decides that extraordinary events, related to the subject matter of this treaty, have jeopardized the supreme interests of its country."[10]

Japan's hesitation in signing the NPT was due to a number of reasons. One was a reluctance to commit the Government publicly to a renunciation of the option to produce nuclear weapons. A Foreign Office analysis of the treaty published in October 1969 openly listed, as a disadvantage of signing the treaty, the fact that "a free hand for nuclear armament would be lost." As a corollary, it mentioned that lack of a military program would prevent the transfer of weapons technology to peaceful uses. However, the Foreign Office document emphasized that Japan's national policy is not to have nuclear weapons but to depend upon the security treaty with the United States; consequently, so long as these policies remained in effect, the disadvantage relating to weapons production would have no substance.[11]

Other concerns about the non-proliferation treaty related to its effects on the nation's security and on the development of research, production, and use of atomic energy for peaceful purposes. The treaty appeared discriminatory in imposing prohibitions and an inspection system only on countries not then possessing nuclear weapons. It was felt that in return for these sacrifices, a potential nuclear power, such as Japan, should ask for assurances of security, ideally in the form of disarmament but also in guarantees from the nuclear weapon nations.

To meet the desires of the non-nuclear weapon countries for security assurances, the Soviet Union, the United Kingdom and the United States on June 19, 1968, before the opening of the treaty to signatures, promised to assist any state threatened with nuclear aggression. The principal operative paragraph of the American declaration reads as follows:

> The United States affirms its intention, as a permanent member of the United Nations Security Council, to seek immediate Security Council action to provide assistance, in accordance with the Charter, to any non-nuclear-weapon state party to the Treaty on the Non-Proliferation of Nuclear Weapons that is a victim of an act of aggression or an object of a threat of aggression in which nuclear weapons are used. [12]

Two days later, on June 21, the Security Council passed a resolution welcoming the intention expressed by "certain States that they will provide or support immediate assistance" to a party to the treaty that becomes a victim of an act or threat of aggression in which nuclear weapons are used. [13]

At the time of signing the NPT, on February 3, 1970, the Japanese Government issued a carefully prepared formal statement explaining its point of view on the treaty and the points which would be considered before ratification. The objectives and spirit of the treaty were supported, and the treaty was termed a first step toward disarmament. The hope was expressed that both France and the People's Republic of China would sign as soon as possible and that in the meantime they would take no action contrary to the objectives of the treaty. The discriminatory character of the NPT was pointed up, with the conclusion drawn that this would not be finally removed until each possessor of nuclear weapons gave them up and total nuclear disarmament was achieved. The statement highlighted the commitments of the three

346

powers to help signatory nations attacked or threatened and expressed the hope that the three would continue to search for effective means to preserve the security of those countries without nuclear weapons. In a sentence which hinted that Japanese ratification might depend on future actions, the Government said that it would studiously observe the progress of disarmament negotiations, Security Council actions relating to the protection of non-nuclear-weapon nations, and other matters affecting the national interests of Japan. Finally, on the question of security, the Japanese statement "took note" of Article 10, which provides for withdrawal from the treaty in case of "extraordinary events jeopardizing the supreme interests of the country."[14]

The question of the NPT and its relation to Japan's security has been discussed publicly in Japan over the past three years. The obvious and principal weakness of the treaty has always been seen as the absence of France and mainland China, but particularly of China, from the signatories. Japanese see little chance that the Peking Government will join in the future. They are also skeptical about the value of both the Soviet and the United Nations guarantees. The invasion of Czechoslovakia did little to encourage any notion of a Russian "protection." Therefore, while the Japanese have sometimes pictured themselves as huddling under a joint Soviet-American nuclear non-proliferation umbrella, the Soviet side of the umbrella appears somewhat leaky and limp. As for the American side, the security treaty remains Japan's first guarantee of future safety. Indeed, some Japanese believe that signing of the NPT makes the security treaty all the more precious. As one Defense Agency official is supposed to have said, "With the NPT in our right pocket, we had better be sure the security treaty is safely in our left pocket."

Perhaps of even greater concern to the Japanese than security is the possible restrictive effect of the NPT on their nuclear energy program. Article 3 of the treaty describes arrangements for safe-guards, to be agreed upon by each country with the International Atomic Energy Agency (IAEA). On this point the Japanese Government statement rejects arrangements which might be hampering; it further warns that the character of these arrangements will be taken fully into consideration in deciding whether to ratify the treaty.

The Japanese are not satisfied with the inspection procedures of the IAEA, which would form the basis of the safeguards arrangements. To meet the complaint of discriminatory inspection, both the United States and the United Kingdom announced that they would accept IAEA inspection of American and British nuclear facilities not related to defense production. Actually, Japanese atomic facilities and materials are now being inspected by IAEA representatives, because of agreements with the United States, United Kingdom and Canada for the purchase of nuclear materials. In fact, according to Japanese sources IAEA inspectors now examine some 69 reactors in 25 countries, of which 22 are in Japan. They complain that the inspectors come too often and are too thorough and meticulous! For the future, they are concerned over the leakage of industrial secrets and the hampering of the development of their technology. The Japanese Government statement expresses the hope that safeguards requirements can be satisfied as much as possible by organs of the countries concerned and as simply as possible. The Government urges that ample precautions be taken to avoid the leakage of industrial secrets and that the methods of inspection be improved as nuclear technology advances.

The Japanese have another fear. Inspection in West Germany is to be conducted by the European organization EURATOM instead of by the IAEA. The Japanese believe that EURATOM standards and procedures are more lenient than those of IAEA. They object to this discriminatory treatment and insist that inspection of Japanese installations must be equivalent to that carried out by EURATOM. Foreign Minister Aichi stated that ratification of the NPT would be conditional on assurances of this equality of treatment.[15]

Some Japanese industrialists have been especially uneasy about the effect of the NPT on the nuclear power industry. They foresee a rapid development in the production of reactors and nuclear facilities and envision a future lucrative export market. The NPT poses a possible danger to industrial technology and to Japan's competitive potential in the future. The President of the Atomic Power Corporation has warned, "The Government should not hasten ratification of the nuclear non-proliferation treaty. Ratification should be made only after a concrete arrangement for the inspection method is made and only when it is clear that our complaints have been satisified:"[16] The Japanese are highly sensitive to the protection of technology used in the development

348

of uranium enrichment processes and fear the risk of disclosure of this technology through inspection. The ban on production of nuclear explosion devices is also troubling, since it might prevent Japanese construction companies from bidding on engineering projects such as the digging of a second Panama canal, which might require such explosives. The ability to hire this know-how as provided in the treaty, is not a satisfactory compensation.

The extent of Japanese unhappiness over the restrictions imposed by the treaty was expressed in the final sentence of the Government statement, which declared, "No peaceful application or use of nuclear energy by a non-nuclear-weapon nation should be prohibited or limited for the reason that it could also be used for the manufacture of nuclear weapons or nuclear explosive devices, nor should the transfer of information, materials, or equipment be refused for this reason." A professor of science at Tokyo Education University cited this section of the statement as proof that the Japanese Government was reserving the right to produce nuclear weapons. He opposed the NPT, but for reasons different from those of the industrialists. He insisted on certain preconditions for ratification, including undertakings by the United States and the Soviet Union to redouble their efforts for nuclear disarmament and by the non-nuclear-weapon nations not to produce nuclear weapons. He called the attitudes of both Japan and West Germany very vague on the latter point. His third condition was adherence to the treaty by the other nuclear-weapon nations, China and France.[17] Subsequently, an official of the Foreign Office replied, through the columns of the *Mainichi* newspaper, pointing out that nuclear technology, especially the processes for uranium enrichment, can be used both for peaceful purposes and for the manufacture of weapons and that the intent of the statement was to specify that the use of nuclear energy should not be prohibited just because in some cases the technology could also be used to produce weapons. He expressed particular concern that Japan not be prevented from developing a process for the enrichment of uranium. He went on to say that Japan was not claiming the right to conduct research in technology that could be used only for weapons purposes, such as techniques concerned with the manufacture of nuclear warheads. He reiterated that the "supreme national policy" of Japan is to utilize atomic energy strictly and exclusively for peaceful purposes.[18]

Another consideration affecting policy toward the treaty has been the attitude of other potential nuclear powers. The nation which Japan had watched most closely was West Germany. Consequently, when the West German Government signed the treaty on November 28, 1969, this action influenced the Japanese Government, as probably did similar subsequent actions by Sweden and Switzerland.

The Japanese Government has been in no hurry to ratify the NPT. Further discussions, clarifications, and negotiations with the IAEA in Vienna were demanded. Meanwhile, the treaty went into force on March 5, 1970, after 97 nations had signed it and 47 had deposited their ratifications.[19] Because of the importance of Japanese ratification, there seemed little doubt that extraordinary efforts would be made to meet the complaints regarding safeguards. Since Japan had taken the step of becoming a signatory, it seemed likely that ratification would follow in due and deliberate course.

Elements in the Choice

"Japan may go nuclear even if it doesn't make good sense." This reported opinion of a young but influential Japanese political scientist may reflect the attitude of a growing number of Japanese, who see many reasons why Japan should not make nuclear weapons but fatalistically feel, that the nuclear road may be inevitable.[20]

A decision to produce nuclear weapons would be the most fateful act of a Japanese Government since World War II. It would be a decision which could not be blamed on the United States, as in one way or another can most of the important postwar Japanese decisions: the Constitution, the peace treaty, the security treaty, the recognition of Nationalist China, and the establishment of the Self-Defense Forces. The decision would reverse the only element of foreign policy, the banning of nuclear weapons, that until now has been supported by a national consensus and would signify a course toward full rearmament, a goal repeatedly rejected by each succeeding head of the Japanese Government.

To arrive at such a decision would not be easy. The preconditions for the secrecy that in the United States shrouded the wartime Manhattan project and in Japan the deliberations in 1941 of the ruling group when it decided to go to war with America do

350

not exist in the free and open atmosphere of the Japan of the 1970's. In retrospect, the minutes of the imperial conferences in the critical weeks preceding Pearl Harbor now read like a script from which no actor dared to deviate, a predetermined plot which led relentlessly to the final tragedy. It taxes the imagination that decision making in Japan in the 1970's could ever unfold in similar fashion. Yet, there is the Japanese national character, and with it the possibility that prestige could well outweigh realism in a "national decision," buttressed by a "national imperative."

Let us look first at the forces which could impel Japan to become a nuclear power and then at the possible consequences of such a decision.

Prestige. By becoming third in the world in economic strength, Japan has entered the league of Big Powers. Historically and traditionally, a Big Power is an armed power. The slogan of the Meiji founders of Japan was, "Rich Country, Big Army." Until the disaster of World War II, Japan's remarkable development had been based on these two principles, the industrialization and economic modernization of the country and the construction of a strong Army and Navy. Today nuclear weapons have become the synonym of "Big Army" and the badge of a "Big Power." Of course, there are different classes of badges. Possession of a "middle-sized" A-bomb, such as that of France and China today, merits only a middle-class badge. While China may some day win more impressive nuclear credentials, no one is likely soon to break into the exclusive two member Soviet-American nuclear club.

As nationalism grows in Japan, pride in country raises the prestige and nuclear weapons gain as symbols of prestige. The few who openly advocate nuclear weapons for Japan stress the strengthened voice in international affairs which they would bring, a practical and profitable benefit of prestige. Doi Akio, a former lieutenant general and head of a research organization in Tokyo, believes that nuclear weapons will put backbone into Japan's diplomacy.[21] Ishihara Shintaro, the popular novelist and member of the House of Councillors, looks to nuclear weapons to help meet diplomatic crises in the future. He foresees that an expanding Japanese economic drive will trigger conflicts with other powers. Backed by nuclear armament, Japan could surmount these crises. Without it, submission might be the only course. He worries about Soviet interference in the Middle East and Japan's crucial "oil road," and concludes that nuclear weapons would be a better deterrent than aircraft carriers, that their existence would be a powerful assist to finding a peaceful settlement. "At such a time having nuclear weapons would be much better than not having them." [22]

Loss of Confidence in American Protection. Another reason for Japan to go nuclear could be loss of confidence in the American defense guarantee. In Henry Kissinger's phrase, the world has become militarily bipolar and politically multipolar. The mutual deterrence of the Soviet Union and the United States has so far acted to prevent a world nuclear war and will, it is hoped, continue to do so in the future. It is not surprising, however, that the Japanese question how the United States would respond to an attack on Japan if that response risked nuclear retaliation against the United States. Obviously the question is unanswerable. A Japanese defense specialist put it directly to the writer: "No one believes the United States would attack the Soviet Union or China with nuclear weapons if either attacked Japan. The security treaty guarantee is meaningful only if no attack occurs, but China and the U.S.S.R. do *not* attack because it *is* there."

Deterrence and the belief in it are psychological, and judgment in Japan as to the value of the American guarantee will be affected by American policies and actions in Asia. How the Americans extricate themselves from Vietnam, the nature of the aftermath in Southeast Asia, and the application of the Nixon Doctrine will be watched intensely by government leaders in Tokyo. Prime Minister Sato's recognition of the security interests of his own country in both the Korean peninsula and the Taiwan area suggests the very special attention that will be paid to a continuing American influence in these areas.

A breakdown of mutual trust and confidence between Japan and the United States could have incalculably dangerous consequences. It could result from conflicts of interests or from radical changes in the foreign policy outlook of the United States. A "Vietnam hangover" that deprived the word "commitment" of all practical meaning could fundamentally alter the American position in Asia. In this situation, Japan might look to rearmament, including nuclear weapons, as the only path to survival.

Independence. Related to this possible crisis of confidence yet different in motivation is the natural and growing desire for military independence from the United States. The growing popularity of the phrase *jishu boei* (autonomous defense), used without precision to mean an undetermined build-up of the Self-Defense Forces, has been previously described. Few have pursued *jishu boei* to its logical meaning of total self-reliance for defense, with the security treaty terminated and all American forces and bases removed. The Socialists and Communists call for this now, although as we have seen, only the Socialists would do away with all armed forces; even the Communists recognize the need for a military organization of some kind.

Prime Minister Sato has said that the treaty should be kept for "a few years," but he leaves the way open after that. If the treaty was terminated, unless it was replaced by some other form of security guarantee, the logical step in the minds of many conservative Japanese would be to get the bomb. With American military protection removed, Japan would be physically and psychologically open and vulnerable. The "independence" so gained might logically demand the fullest military support, to include both revision of the Constitution and the acquisition of nuclear weapons. At such a moment, there would be those to point out that independence is at best a relative thing and that a Japan living in Asia in the 1970's is peculiarly *dependent*, not only upon relationships with other Asian nations but even more so upon ties with nations of the West and around the world. Still the psychological *feel* of independence expected from admission into the circle of nuclear-weapon-nations might be the lure which would impel the choice.

Threat. Finally, the appearance of a sudden, sobering, believable threat could tip the scales to a nuclear decision. Japanese do not now live in serious fear of their neighbors. Officials with responsibilities for defense say publicly that they envisage no serious threat against their country for at least the next five or ten years. If Japan should arm herself with nuclear weapons, these would be more token than real against Russia. But with China it would be different. Should China take on a new belligerence and by deeds convince Japan that the security of the Korea-Taiwan-Okinawa-Japan area might be at stake, going nuclear might be the response evoked. One can guess that in the face of such a situation, the stimulus to public opinion would be strong enough to smother most political opposition to nuclear arms.

The Likely Consequences of a Nuclear Decision

If the circumstances described above bring about a Japanese nuclear decision, what would be its consequences? Deferential to the unpredictability of future events and their context, one can only suggest certain eventualities.

Internal Political Conflict. A decision to build the bomb would split the Japanese body politic as no issue has done since the termination of the war. Assuming that the Liberal Democratic Party, with its comfortable parliamentary majority, were to support this step—and there would be dissidents within the party—the opposition parties would most certainly be unanimously against it. As Robert Guillain, the astute French journalist and experienced Japan hand, says: "The fight against 'the Japanese bomb' could bring to the Left the unity, vigor and even the revolutionary force which it has so much lacked for more than twenty years." [23] Not only the Left and organizations affiliated with the Left but intellectuals, professional people; and certainly great numbers from the "salary-men" and middle-class groups would join in opposing this action. All of the propeace, antiwar, and antinuclear emotions and sentiments, potent and latent, would be mobilized. Some pronationalist movements would also rise, most of them directed by right-wing organizations with long histories.

Although the Government would doubtless insist that the decision did not raise a constitutional question, amendment of the Atomic Energy Law would be required, and the battle would have to be taken to the Diet. Unless public opinion had changed radically and the opposition forces had in the meantime lost heavily in influence and numbers, the struggle both inside and outside the Diet could be expected to surpass in violence the treaty riots of 1960. Certainly no issue in postwar Japan could inspire more partisanship, more emotions, and more violence than this one.

Times change, and public opinion changes with them. It is true that attitudes of the Japanese are becoming more nationalistic and the numbers of those who believe fatalistically that Japan will have nuclear weapons may be growing. How fast this change is occurring is difficult to measure, and what attitudes a younger generation moving into positions of influence will take is a matter

354

of speculation. However such a change will hardly be so rapid that acceptance of nuclear weapons by a popular majority will be achieved within this decade. Furthermore, the evaluation of the nuclear weapon as an element of security has already changed, and that change cannot help affecting the attitudes of those who, in the 1970's, will hold the power of decision.

Security. The value to Japan of nuclear weapons as a deterrent is being seriously questioned. The made-in-Japan "unusable weapon" would neither frighten the Russians nor intimidate the Chinese, who have all the advantages of geography, population, and resources on their side. Kaihara Osamu, chief of the secretariat of the National Defense Council, whom we have quoted before, has minced no words in evaluating an atomic weapon for Japan. Responding to the argument that submarines carrying MIRV's (multiple independently targetable re-entry vehicles) would be effective for Japan's security, Kaihara wrote in a recent magazine article that this was a "beautiful dream" because it was impractical, noting that it would be "impossible to match Soviet nuclear missiles." He concluded, "If we started from nothing in nuclear armament, what ever we could build up would be tiny fireworks compared with the Soviet nuclear arsenal." [24]

Japan would have little hope of achieving a second-strike capability. Nakasone Yasujiro, Director General of the Defense Agency, has made this point publicly a number of times. [25] Japan, with its small islands, its jammed industrial complexes, its ever-growing, crowded cities, and its gigantic, continuously extending Tokyo-Yokohama megalopolis, which is both the heart and nerve center of the country, could scarcely be more vulnerable to nuclear obliteration from Chinese or Soviet missiles within immediate range. Some argue that nuclear-armed submarines, safe from attack, would assure a second-strike capability. However, the chance to fire a few missiles with nuclear warheads at an enemy that had already destroyed the cities and industries of the homeland would be hollow comfort for the demoralized survivors of an all out atomic bombardment.

A nuclear power balance has prevented wars between the superpowers but has not prevented protracted conflict in Korea and in Vietnam. The best that can be said is that thus far the mutual Soviet-American nuclear deterrent has kept the wars in Asia from expanding into nuclear conflicts. A Japanese so-called deterrent would be of an entirely different dimension; it would deter neither a Big Power bent on attack nor the smaller, local, and uncontrollable wars.

Kishida Junnosuke, well-known commentator on scientific matters, has characterized the political value of possessing nuclear weapons as a myth. He describes the 1950's as the decade when the Big Powers sought security through military strength, the 1960's as the period in which nuclear weapons became symbols of national prestige and the 1970's a time of multipolarity, when nuclear weapons would cease to be the key to security. He sees the most serious threats to world peace and stability as arising out of unrest caused by the poverty of Asia, the instability and immaturity of societies around the world, and the effect of social unrest in the United States on America's world leadership and responsibilities.[26]

Rearmament and the Revival of Militarism. For months the principal theme of Peking's propaganda directed to Japan has been the "revival of Japanese militarism." During negotiations in April 1970 for the renewal of the memorandum trade agreement, Chou En-lai put special stress on this point, and reference to it was included in the joint communique issued at the end of the meetings. Ironically, a few days after the trade talks had been concluded and while the Chinese press was hurling its invectives against a purportedly revived Japanese militarism, two American congressmen who had recently visited Tokyo issued a report charging, "There is a strong effort underway by some groups in Japan toward rearmament and a seeming return to the old 'Greater East Asia Co-prosperity Sphere' . . . the study mission evidences concern over Japan's emphasis on the new militarism."[27]

As can be imagined, identical attacks from Peking and Washington on succeeding days were bombshells in Tokyo. Government officials and parliamentarians hastened to deny the charges. The Japanese Communist Party, while pointing to its own long-term struggle to block American and Japanese imperialists trying to revive militarism, vigorously denounced the "Mao Tse-tung faction" and set forth the JCP position that Japanese militarism is *not* "completely revived," since it is limited by the Constitution and by restrictions on overseas dispatch of troops, conscription, and the mobilization of political and social life for military purposes.[28]

Japan's present-day armed forces, the present policies of the

Government toward defense and nuclear weapons, and the present state of public opinion hardly add up to a "new militarism." However, a decision to build the bomb would be synonymous with rearmament, and if Japan should take this turn, militarism could in fact revive. If the so-called "military-industrial complex" is now more shadow than substance, in a Japan headed for nuclear armament, both the military and industry would quickly acquire new dimensions of power and influence in the country. The nation would be shifting to an entirely new and hazardous course.

China. Japan would not aspire to reach the nuclear capability of the two superpowers; Japan's bomb would be built with an eye always on China. Inevitably, Japan and China would become direct nuclear competitors, the Japanese measuring their own progress in terms of "superiority" or at least "sufficiency" with respect to the Chinese nuclear arsenal.

This plunge into a weapons race with neighboring China would destroy the chances for accommodation which most Japanese desire. It would run counter to the "peace diplomacy," which in spite of present limitations holds hope, for many Japanese, that the natural, mutually beneficial relation between the two leading powers in Asia can some day be brought about. Restoration of normal relations with China is destined to be a prime foreign policy objective of any Japanese Government. To ruin the chances of success in achieving this objective by making Chou's worst fears come true would be folly, and easily understood to be such by the man on any Japanese street.

The United States. Although the United States was responsible for the formation of Japan's first defense forces and in succeeding years actively encouraged increased defense spending and the expansion of the SDF, the American Government has consistently opposed Japan's acquiring nuclear weapons and has urged Japan to subscribe to the nuclear non-proliferation treaty. American technology has been transferred only on condition that it be utilized exclusively for peaceful purposes. A Japanese decision to create an independent nuclear capability, unless it occurred under radically altered circumstances in which American tacit agreement or even assistance were received, would seriously injure the Japanese-American relationship. If the security treaty were not terminated at the same time, it would rapidly lose its meaning and the American role in Japan's defense would end.

357

Instead of the power center for stability in East Asia anticipated by Americans and Asians alike, a nuclear-armed Japan would likely become a force for confusion, uncertainty, and instability, distrusted by the United States and feared by Asian neighbors.

Southeast Asia. Iwasa Yoshizane, one of Japan's most influential business leaders, president of the Fuji Bank and vice-president of the Federation of Economic Organizations, has described very clearly the consequences in Southeast Asia that would follow the nuclear arming of Japan:

> It would be interpreted as confirmation of deep-rooted suspicions of Japan, and fears of her "economic aggression," in the countries of Southeast Asia. Apprehensions and misgivings over Japan's economic advance and military strength are already rife in Asia; nuclear armament merely to placate shallow nationalism would intensify the discord with Communist China to an ominous degree and, at the same time, nullify what goodwill has been built up in Southeast Asia through painstaking efforts of the past two decades. In short, by resorting to nuclear arms Japan would run serious risk of finding herself again isolated in Asia.[29]

To anyone who has visited Southeast Asia and discussed the Japanese economic advance in these countries, Iwasa's words ring true. Suspicions and doubts are strong now; they would immeasurably increase in the face of a nuclear-armed Japan.

The hardheaded industrialists who are responsible for so much of the brilliant economic success that has brought Japan to top rank among the world powers are not likely to direct the nation deliberately to a course that led to disaster once before. Munitions-makers may yearn for the cash benefits of an expanded military establishment, including a program to manufacture nuclear weapons. But these profits are of minimal significance when compared with the totality of a rapidly growing Japanese economy. Moreover, they would risk disastrous losses of good will and trade in the places most critically important to Japan: the United States, China, and Southeast Asia. This is not to suggest that Japan's industrialists do not favor a steady expansion of defense production, including the development of a munitions export industry. But this is far different from going the nuclear way.

The power of the *zaikai*, the industrial and business leaders, is impressive, and the relationship with government is far tighter and closer than anything like it in the United States. To shift to an atomic policy is not conceivable without strong *zaikai* backing. Before such a decision would be arrived at, some very cold and careful calculations would be made about its effect on foreign trade, foreign policy, and the political and economic relations with other countries, especially those in Asia.

Uemura Kogoro, president of the most powerful economic organization in Japan, the *Keidanren* (Federation of Economic Organizations), told a French journalist that Japan would not build atomic weapons. To do so, he said, would be to help make a world of fools like the old ones—as if Japan had learned nothing from the past—and then to perish in a general nuclear catastrophe. A second choice would be to bet on a world tempered by past experience, where strength would come through economic development at home and in a country's neighboring areas. Uemura said that Japan had made the second choice and was betting on peace.[30]

The Decision and Sensitivity to History

The preceding pages have projected factors in national decision-making. There remains the possibility alluded to by the professor that "Japan may go nuclear even if it doesn't make sense." The Japanese are sometimes unpredictable and are subject to sudden shifts of mood. Foreigners have been amazed that a totally indoctrinated Japanese people, supporting loyally a militaristic, xenophobic regime, not only could overnight accept with docility and complete submission a military occupation by the enemy they had fought for four years, but could embrace democracy wholeheartedly and without reservation. If this could happen, could not the reverse occur—a sudden return to militarism? These fears are fed by reports of growing nationalism in Japan, of the seeming tolerance of nuclear weapons shown in public opinion polls, and of calls for greater defense expenditures.

Contemplating the problem of Japan and nuclear weapons, one should not discount the impact of history and the curve of historical learning. The 1970's are not the 1930's. Japan's failure to achieve economic ascendance in East Asia during those years and in the war which followed is not forgotten in Japan today. The kind of military which brought only tragedy then has little to recommend it now. And Japan's enormous economic achievements to date have come about not because Japan had military power but, to a certain degree, because Japan had no military power. While the urge for independence from American apronstrings may be great, the appreciation that *interdependence* is indispensable in a nation's life, particularly to an island nation like Japan, is fully understood by the modern leaders of this nation. Although Japan is uniquely homogeneous and somewhat insulated in habits of thought by language and culture, there are few peoples in the world more sensitive to foreign reactions and to foreign opinion. A decision to build a nuclear weapon would not, in the 1970's, be made in a vacuum, nor would it be made in the repressive, make-believe atmosphere of a 1941 imperial conference. The impact of the outside world would break through and, in the end, would probably have a determining effect.

Notes

1. *The Japan Biographical Encyclopedia and Who's Who, 1964-65,* 3rd ed. (Tokyo: The Rengo Press), p. 1014.

2. "JDA Director Nakasone's Second Broadcast to the Agency," *Asagumo* (organ of the Self-Defense Forces), March 19, 1970.

3. Murata Kiyoaki, "Straws in Nuclear Wind," *Japan Times,* November 13, 1970; *Yomiuri,* May 31, 1970. Various polls are cited in these articles.

4. Iwasa Yoshizane, "Japan-U.S. Economic Cooperation with Asia in the Seventies," *The Pacific Community,* Tokyo, April 1970, p. 389.

5. Anzen Hosho Chosa-kai (Security Research Council), *Nihon no Anzen Hosho, 1970 e no Tembo* (Japan's Security, Outlook on 1970), 1968 edition (Tokyo: July 15, 1968), p. 342.

6. *Yomiuri,* February 10, 1968.

7. Boei-cho, *Nihon no Boei* (Japan's Defense), Defense White Paper (Tokyo: Japan Defense Agency, October 20, 1970), p. 48.

8. U.S., Department of State, *Bulletin,* Vol. LIX, No. 1518 (July 29, 1968), p. 126. (Hereafter referred to as *DSB).*

9. *DSB,* Vol. LIX, No. 1517 (July 22, 1968), p. 85.

10. For text of the treaty see *DSB,* Vol. LIX, No. 1514 (July 1, 1968), pp. 8-11.

11. *Asahi,* October 13, 1969.

12. *DSB,* Vol. LIX, No. 1515 (July 8, 1968), p. 57.

13. *Ibid.*, pp. 58-59.

14. "Kaku heiki fukakusan joyaku choin no sai no Seifu Seimei" (Government Declaration on the signing of the nuclear nonproliferation treaty), *Asahi* (evening), February 3, 1970.

15. "Hijun ni tsuite Joken: Shisatsu EURATOM nami" (Condition to Ratification: Inspection Equivalent to that of EURATOM), Foreign Minister's Statement, *Asahi* (evening), February 3, 1970.

16. Quotation from Ipponmatsu Tamaki, President of the Japan Atomic Power Corporation, in *Mainichi,* September 7, 1969.

17. Miyake Yasuo, "Nuclear Nonproliferation Treaty and Scientists' Position," *Mainichi* (evening), February 10, 1970.

18. Yatabe Atsuhiko, Chief, Science Section, Foreign Ministry, "Nuclear Nonproliferation Treaty and Science and Technology," *Mainichi*, February 19, 1970.

19. *DSB,* Vol. LXII, No. 1605 (March 30, 1970), p. 410.

20. Michael Berger, "Japan Today: Talk about Rearmament." *San Francisco Chronicle,* June 2, 1970. Quoted is Kosaka Masataka, professor of political science at Kyoto Universtiy.

21. *Yomiuri,* February 29, 1968.

22. "Nihon no Kakubuso ni tsuite" (Regarding the Nuclear Armament of Japan), Symposium participants: Ishihara Shintaro, member House of Councillors; Doba Hajime, *Yomiuri* International Relations Research Council; *Kokubo* (National Defense), November 1969, pp. 16-17.

23. Robert Guillain, *Japon, Troisieme Grand* (Paris: Editions du Seuil, 1969), p. 228.

24. Kaihara's article in the magazine *Shokun,* December 1970, is quoted in Murata.

25. "Dialogue Between Nakasone Yasuhiro and Ishibashi Masashi on Japanese Militarism," *Yomiuri,* May 4, 1970.

26. Kishida Junnosuke, "Deployment of MIRV and New Nuclear Age," *Asahi,* March 17, 1970.

27. U.S., Congress, House, Committee on Foreign Affairs, *Report of Special Study Mission to Asia by Hon. Lester L. Wolff, New York and Hon. J. Herbert Burke, Florida,* 91st Cong., 2nd sess., April 22, 1970, pp. 4-5.

28. Sakaki Toshio, "Irresponsible Attack Against JCP Helps Militarist Forces," *Akahata* (Red Flag), September 19, 1970.

29. Iwasa Yoshizane, *op. cit.,* p. 389.

30. Robert Guillain, *op. cit.,* p. 229.

15 The Japanese-American Relationship

Periods in the Japanese-American Relationship

It should be clear from the preceding chapters that an American element has been a continuous part of the history of postwar Japan. To extricate it would be as impossible as to remove the grain from a piece of wood. We have already described many of the policies and actions the United States has taken with respect to Japan and have, perhaps, conveyed some impression of the enormous American influence which has been brought to bear on Japan and of the major problems confronted by the two countries in recent years.

If, for convenience sake, we should divide the postwar Japanese-American relationship into periods, the first, one of occupation and total American control, would extend from 1945-1952; the second, the post-Occupation period, would run for thirteen years, until 1965. That year opened in the still warm glow of the Olympic Games held the autumn before and saw Japan reverse the trade trend with the United States and achieve an export surplus. This third period, lasting until 1970, could be characterized as Japan's postwar coming of age. The fourth period, which began in 1970, might be described as the period of independence and cooperation. With Okinawa's return promised for 1972, with Japan's growth solid and still expanding, and with new problems looming ahead, the character of the Japanese-American relationship had changed and was changing still. Differences of view had arisen and it became clear that neither country would satisfy the other's expectations. Never had there been a time when each nation needed so much to understand the other. The decade offered great prospects but challenged both Japan and the United States with new and complex tasks and responsibilities.

In his 1970 State of the Union message, President Nixon termed Japanese-American friendship and cooperation the "linchpin for peace in the Pacific."[1]   But problems loomed as the decade opened. Ironically, the "crisis of 1970" in the Japanese-American relationship, if it could be so called, turned out to be somewhat different from what pessimists had projected for the year when the Japanese-American security treaty was to become subject to notice of termination. Rather than reflecting a political rift, the "crisis" issued from unfortunate attitudes in both countries fashioned primarily in the crucible of economic competition. In the United States, resentments over Japan's phenomenal trade successes breathed new life into old shibboleths and prejudices and threatened to blur objective appraisals of the meaning of Japan's relationship with the United States. In Japan the new spirit of independence inspired a psychological need to "stand up to the United States," while at the same time an uncomfortable unsureness about the American future and American influence in Asia spread among the people of Japan.

Security and Economics

Since 1945 the United States has been inextricably involved in the dual problems of Japanese security and economic development. As we have seen, Americans urged renunciation of war and arms in the Constitution of 1946 but four years later ordered armed forces to be established. In the security treaties of 1951 and 1960, the United States assumed obligations for Japan's security which both governments have decided to continue.

While Japan lay helpless in the aftermath of defeat, General MacArthur was authorized to bring in supplies "to prevent such widespread disease or civil unrest as would endanger the occupying forces or interfere with military operations."[2] From this cautious and carefully rationalized beginning, the United States went on to help Japan to rebuild and expand her economic strength.

The 1950's began with war in Korea and the first security treaty. The war not only motivated the creation of the nucleus of a Japanese military force but, through American spending for the war, also boosted the Japanese economy into its ever upward spiral.

The 1960's opened with violence in Tokyo over ratification of the revised treaty and witnessed America's increasing entanglement in conflict in Southeast Asia. Japanese-American trade burgeoned, and during the later years of the decade Japanese industry was again the beneficiary of American spending for yet another war in Asia. Estimates place the amounts at about a billion dollars a year in direct and indirect American procurement for the war in Vietnam.

The "Treaty Crisis of 1970"

The real crisis was expected in 1970. After June 23 the security treaty was no longer untouchable, since either Tokyo or Washington could at any moment decide to end it.

On June 23 an estimated 774,000 people gathered throughout Japan to demonstrate against the treaty. The numbers exceeded by more than 200,000 those who participated in the 1960 "struggles" at their peak. Virtually all Leftist parties and factions joined in the protest. Communists and Socialists united in a "one day joint struggle." New Left Groups held their separate rallies. A few militant young workers and students hurled Molotov cocktails and fire bombs. Members of certain industrial unions struck for brief periods, never more than a few hours. Some demonstrators or bystanders were injured, and a professionally prepared and efficiently operating police made scattered arrests. Except for traffic jams and stoppages, the general public suffered a minimum of inconvenience.[3]

Japanese Government leaders were enormously relieved when June 23 had passed into history. Although the large numbers who took to the streets seemed to attest to the unpopularity of the treaty, to responsible leaders the 1969 elections had spoken far louder than the June demonstrations. None of the excessive violence of 1960 had occurred: no forced entry into public buildings, no destruction of police vehicles, and above all, no loss of life, and no martyrs. And, contrary to threats, no general strike had paralyzed economic life.

Why did the "treaty crisis of 1970" come and go with such little trouble?

First, the Japanese Government had decided to let the treaty continue in effect "automatically"—a stratagem that avoided debate in the Diet and a repetition of the 1960 parliamentary crisis. Second, Okinawa's promised return in 1972 removed the most explosive issue in Japanese-American relations. Third, the Liberal Democratic victory at the polls in December 1969 and the disastrous defeat, in the same elections, of the principal opposition party (the JSP) reinforced the Government's claim of a mandate to keep the treaty. Fourth, both the Socialists and Communists, as well as the General Council of Trade Unions (*Sohyo*), had vigorously opposed the violent actions of the New Left militants. Finally the student movement, which in 1960 had been the moving force of violence, by 1970 had become largely quiescent, weakened as it was by factional strife, police efficiency, a new control law, and a public backlash.

Both the Japanese and American Governments confirmed in official statements that the treaty would be kept in effect. Secretary of State Rogers spoke of the "highly valued" role of the treaty "in maintaining the peace and security of the Far East, including Japan."[4] The Japanese statement confirmed the Government's intention to "firmly maintain the treaty in the interest of the maintenance of the security of Japan" and expressed the conviction that "unswerving pursuit of this policy in the 1970's is supported extensively by the people." The statement went on to assert that "the best conceivable way to secure national existence and development . . . is to build up our self-defense power in consonance with national capabilities and to ensure the peace and security of the Far East, including Japan, by the Japanese-American security system."[5]

The passing of the landmark of 1970 changed the nature of the defense relationship between Japan and the United States. The ties were loosened. The Japanese, as they themselves asserted, entered the "age of choice." Their leaders put no time limit on the further duration of the treaty. Neither did they specify any changes anticipated for the future. Government party statements spoke of keeping the treaty for a "considerably long period of time," although some party leaders foresaw the need to review the treaty and its effect as the years of the decade progressed.

Confidence in self-defense power will naturally lessen dependence on the treaty, and skillful adjustments to a changing world environment will be required. Much will depend upon events in Asia and upon American policies and responses in the Pacific region.

The Economic "Crisis"

A different Japanese-American "crisis" threatened in 1970. It was symbolized by the breakdown in textile negotiations that occurred in Washington on June 24, the day after the "day of the treaty." Few Americans knew about it at all, just as few Americans were aware of a "treaty crisis." Amazingly, three quarters of a million Japanese could demonstrate in their homeland against an American treaty and the event receive minimal news coverage in the United States.

Americans do, however, know about Japan's economic "invasion." Although American advertisers seldom emphasize the Japanese origin of their products—one company selling a Japanese automobile went to great lengths in an advertising campaign to feature *one part* of its product as American made—the average American is now convinced that the quality of Japanese goods is high. Sales prove that Americans buy Japanese automobiles, motorcycles, radios, television sets, tape recorders, cameras, binoculars, and dozens of other articles without prejudice. American consumers are used to the ubiquitous "Made in Japan" labels in the merchandise they finger in the stores.

Americans have seldom worried whether their economy could stand competition from the ambitious Japanese, and few were aware in June 1970 of growing friction with Japan. However, a combination of circumstances acted to intensify the resentments and irritations of American businessmen, already feeling the pinch of the gigantic Japanese trade drive. These feelings spread among congressmen, ever sensitive to the grievances of their constituents.

What were the elements in this economic crisis of 1970?

First, a fast-growing Japanese-American trade has tipped drastically in favor of Japan. By American statistics, total trade in 1969 was $8.4 billion, 50 percent higher than in 1966 and a 20 percent jump over 1968. (Japanese-American trade in 1970 surpassed $10 billion.) Japan's surplus reached the unprecedented figure of $1.4 billion. [6] Within the first six months of 1971 Japan's favorable trade balance with the United States was $1.38 billion. Traditionally, the United States had always sold more to Japan than it bought; in 1961 this surplus amounted to $783 million. In 1965 the balance changed, and the figures on the American side

367

have been red ever since. To make the situation more painful, Japan's total trade surplus in 1969 was more than three times our own, $3.7 billion against $1.2 billion. This contrasted with the $3 billion to $5 billion surplus to which we had been accustomed in the recent past. By 1971 our surplus had become a deficit.

Second, Japanese exports to the United States compete with American-made products. They include machinery, iron and steel, cloth, clothing, automobiles, electrical appliances and equipment, and miscellaneous manufactured articles, all of which are made in the United States. On the other hand, the United States sells to Japan agricultural commodities, raw materials such as wood and raw cotton, and specialized machinery and equipment, all sought by the Japanese because these materials are not available or locally produced in Japan. The combination of quality merchandise, aggressive selling methods, and competitive prices has been successful in the American market, as in other parts of the world. In 1969, nearly 30 percent of Japan's total foreign trade was with the United States, by far Japan's most important trading partner. In fact, the remarkable initiative, drive, and audacity of Japanese industrialists captured for them almost monopoly positions in the United States in certain highly specialized manufactures, for example, pianos and barber chairs!

Third, the most prickly economic issue has been liberalization of trade controls and of capital investment. Although committed to liberalization through membership in GATT (General Agreement on Trade and Tariffs), IMF (International Monetary Fund) and OECD (Organization for Economic Cooperation and Development), Japan has taken action with such grudging reluctance that American traders and investors have become more impatient and resentful as the years have passed.

Liberalization

Controls over imports have only slowly been relaxed. Battles have raged over particular articles of trade. Once it was lemons. Later, the items were oranges, grapefruit, bourbon whiskey, color film, glass, industrial sewing machines, computers and parts, and light aircraft. Ever prodded by American urging, the Japanese have proceeded piecemeal, issuing a list of certain liberalized articles at one date, another installment at a later date, and so on by the calendar. In September 1970, 90 commodities were still restricted.

The Government's timetable called for further reductions: to 80 items by the end of 1970, to 60 in April 1971 and to less than 40 by September 1971. In discussing their import barriers, Japanese officials do not fail to point out that West Germany restricts 40 products among Japanese exports, France 83, Italy 63, Denmark 71, and Sweden 54.[7] Finance Minister Fukuda Takeo wrote in *Pacific Community* for January 1971 that "Japan is determined . . . to remove all quantitative import restrictions."[8]

Capital liberalization has seemed to inspire a Japanese-American dialogue of the deaf. For American producers, freedom to invest is the expected response of an advanced industrial nation to the natural desires of foreign enterprise to do business in that nation and to share in its production and market. They fail to understand why the Japanese Government has been so reluctant to welcome their investment and their participation in Japan's strong, booming economy.

For years American officials and businessmen have complained, protested, and lectured to the Japanese about their restrictive practices. In each of the annual conferences between the leading Cabinet officers of the two countries, international investment has been high on the agenda. American Secretaries of State and of Commerce have each year repeated their discontent over the slowness of the Japanese program for capital liberalization. Typical was the reference to this subject in the joint communique issued September 15, 1967, after the Japanese Government had announced its five-year schedule for removing restrictions:

> The United States expressed appreciation for the effort that went into the formulation of the Japanese program as a first, although somewhat disappointing, step, and expressed the hope that liberalization be accelerated as soon as possible.[9]

Almost three years later, Under Secretary of State for Political Affairs U. Alexis Johnson, previously Ambassador to Japan, was still urging the Japanese to hasten the liberalization process:

> . . . if Japan is going to continue its spectacular economic development, Japan must be willing to grant to others that same freedom of economic enterprise within Japan as Japan is seeking and in large degree receiving in other economically developed countries, especially in the United States.[10]

In late 1970, after three stage of liberalization, the last of which was described in Japan as a "giant step" toward freeing industries for foreign participation, a former Under Secretary of State, George W. Ball, was still critical:

> Japan does not know its own strength. Why should a nation of a hundred million people, which has become the second largest industrial power in the non-Communist world, be afraid to open its markets to foreign goods, or its economy to foreign investments? [11]

From the Japanese have come repeated assurances that liberalization will be carried out. They have defended their timetable, stressing the fact that by September 1970 more than 80 percent of their industires had already been opened to foreign participation.

The Japanese program to liberalize direct investment began in 1967, when a five year schedule, to be carried out in four stages, was announced.[12] Domestic industries at that time were divided into 560 "categories," and at the first stage, in July 1967, fifty were liberalized for "automatic approval"—seventeen with foreign ownership permitted up to 100 percent and thirty-three up to 50 percent. Most of these industries had little appeal to foreigners, including, as they did, such enterprises as ice-making and silk-yarn production. Many, such as shipbuilding, and steel production, and brewing, were already so controlled by Japanese manufacturers as to offer little prospect of successful competition.

The second stage, effected in March 1969, added 155 industries to the list, twenty at 100 percent and one hundred thirty-five at 50 percent. At the same time, the powerful Federation of Economic Organizations (*Keidanren*) announced that the fifty-fifty principle would be most appropriate for Japan and that a limited number of "strategic" industries, such as those related to defense, nuclear energy, electronic computers, natural resources, and public utilities, would not be open to foreign investors for an indefinite period.

Items on this second list, too, were unattractive to foreign investors, who were also dissatisfied with the policy of limiting their ownership to 50 percent in most cases. This reaction was demonstrated by the fact that foreigners applied to invest in only seventeen of the industries designated in the first two lists.

The third stage of decontrol became effective September 1, 1970, with the addition of 320 items, which brought the total number of freed categories to 524.[13] A final and fourth stage was scheduled for the fall of 1971, which would, in the words of Finance Minister Fukuda, enable "foreign capital to invest in every type of enterprise in Japan's manufacturing industry, with the exception of a small number of enterprises carried on the negative list."[14] These were the "strategic" industries listed above.

Automobiles have constituted a special friction point because of the dramatic rise of Japanese exports to the United States and the continued barring of American cars and their makers from Japan, the former by taxes and duties and the latter by prohibition of investment.

A duty of 17.5 percent, the highest for any major country, is levied on motor vehicles imported into Japan (the U.S. tariff is 4.5 percent). In addition, a discriminatory tax system effectively keeps out most American automobiles. In 1969 the flow was 276,112 Japanese cars sold in the United States against 4,133 American vehicles entering Japan. In monetary terms, Japanese automobile exports to the United States increased tenfold in four years, from $34 million in 1965 to $340 million in 1969.[15]

Although both Ford and General Motors operated assembly plants in Japan during the 1930's, no investment by an American automobile manufacturer has been permitted since World War II. The Japanese automobile-makers fear domination of their market by the powerful American automobile producers and plead for time to build up their so-called "young, growing companies." Nevertheless, in the face of building foreign pressure, liberalization of the automobile industry to accommodate foreign investment was first announced for October 1971, then advanced to April. Negotiations quickly opened between Japanese and American companies for joint ventures, which could enter the Japanese market as soon as government approval could be obtained.

By the end of 1970, seventy-seven out of five hundred twenty-four industries were made available for 100 percent foreign ownership. The remaining four hundred forth-seven were restricted to a maximum of 50 percent. Portfolio investments, allowing no participation in company management, could be held by foreigners up to 25 percent in non-restricted industries and to 15 percent in those designated restricted. No single foreign investor could own more than 7 percent of the stock of any enterprise.[16]

Numbers were impressive, but even after the third stage the industries themselves still lacked luster for foreign eyes. What American could work up enthusiasm for investing in such "industries" as oatmeal, handkerchiefs, vacuum bottles, mashed potatoes, or bamboo shades or for producing Japanese *sake* in Japan?

Even more frustrating than the laws regulating foreign investment, exchange, and trade and the restricted categories of investment were the policies, customs, procedures, and the "network of established 'administrative practices'." [17] For the foreign investor, the intricacies of the Japanese bureaucracy are irritating and bewildering, involving the Ministries of Finance, International Trade and Industry, and Foreign Affairs, the Customs Service, and numerous bureaus and offices, which often act independently of each other and in contradiction to other agencies of government. In addition are the threatened "countermeasures," principally amendments of the antimonopoly and fair trade laws, which are designed to offset "disrupting influences" that might result from the liberalization program. [18]

The controversy over capital liberalization is essentially a conflict between a Japanese system, different in structure and outlook and conditioned by a unique culture and language, and foreigners, especially Americans, increasingly engaged in multinational operations, taking foreign investment for granted, and irked by the complexities and resistance of the Japanese. The political and industrial leaders of Japan have accepted liberalization in principle and recognize that Japan must eventually open wide her doors. They are not, however, about to change their system of operation. Moreover, they appear fearful and lacking in the assurance that should characterize leaders of a great power. A quarter of a century has not been long enough to dispel the worries over possible foreign control and bring to Japan the confidence of power. Japanese remind their foreign friends that the GNP may be third in the world but per capita income is only fourteenth.

Meanwhile, foreigners trying to enter the Japanese business system grow more frustrated. As a Japanese professor of law and commerce has written, "It is hardly to be wondered at . . . that foreign investors, perplexed by Japan's xenophobic insularity and ignorant of her language, try frantically, but with only doubtful success, to find the key that will open the door to Japanese business." [19]

At the same time, it must be recorded that many Americans and other foreigners do business successfully in Japan. Some of these are the long-established concerns, with enough knowledge and experience to adjust happily to the Japanese scene. Successful foreign businessmen are glad to join Japanese partners in whom they have confidence and who can speak and act for the firm. The uncomplaining Americans are usually those who have taken the trouble to study Japan and to learn at least some of the language, the history, and the culture of the people with whom they live and work. In the process, they acquire tolerance and an appreciation, if not a full understanding, of the values respected in Japan. They find that their willingness to work in the system and their consequent sensitivity to their surroundings create the favorable atmosphere indispensable to success.

Obviously, there must be attempts at understanding on both sides, because international business is a reality and Japan cannot and will not remain outside the mainstream. As the Tokyo correspondent of the *Economist* and *Financial Times* of London has written, "The dilemma is that Japan is, by any measure, the most insular country in the world: yet economic pressure demands that she combat this insularity and build bridges, simultaneiously, East and West, North and South."[20]

Japanese economic relations with Americans will continue to beget American frustrations and misunderstandings. It is to be hoped that this inevitable "static" will not corrode the larger Japanese-American relationship.

The Case of Textiles

Restrictions are not all on the Japanese side. While clamoring for Japanese liberalization, the United States has for years sought to restrict competitive imports by persuading the Japanese to impose "voluntary" quotas on certain categories of goods they send to America. The system has worked satisfactorily for some products, less well for others. The Japanese iron and steel industry has efficiently but not enthusiastically policed its own exports, in deference to protests from the steelmakers of the United States.

While Americans rush to protect some industry against competition from abroad and to bolster their balance of payments, other interests dictate other actions. For example, the United States has asked the Japanese to put quotas on their *imports* of lumber from the Pacific Northwest, fearful that they were buying too much. Such action is hard to justify as a defense of the American balance of payments.[21]

Textiles are a case study worth examining.

Negotiations for an agreement to set quotas on Japanese textile imports into the United States broke down in June 1970, after both Foreign Minister Aichi and MITI Minister Miyazawa had dramatically flown together to Washington, to break the deadlock. But the conclusion was collapse and not agreement. The rupture came over the time limit voluntary quotas would remain in effect; the Japanese insisted on one year, the Americans held out for three.

The failure had much more meaning than its effect on the textile trade between two Pacific neighbors. It was the first postwar occasion when the two countries had publicly failed to agree on an important issue; it was the first time Japan had decisively said "No" to the United States. The shock was severe in Washington. In Tokyo, ministers who by Japanese custom might have resigned after such a failure won praise for standing up to the Americans. The "No" was a symbolic gesture, a declaration of Japan's independence in a new age of relations with the huge American "partner."

Some interested Americans resented the "No." Some saw a new wave of anti-Japanese feeling arising among business, industrial, and banking circles and spreading to Congress. Some, with exaggerated emotion, saw the atmosphere building into tensions which recalled the 1930's. A story going the rounds in Washington was that an American businessman on his return from Honolulu jokingly remarked that he had "checked to see if Pearl Harbor was still there." Some Japanese described their textile-makers as reaching a peak of stubbornness and desperation, ready for *kami kaze* attacks risking self-destruction!

Textiles should be put in perspective. They are more important to Japan than to the United States, amounting to 14 percent of Japan's exports and about 10 percent of production, whereas they represent 10 percent of American imports and about 3 percent of American production. In dollar value only 4.2 percent of the textiles consumed in the United States are imported, and of the imports only a quarter come from Japan. Half are bought from the developing countries, such as South Korea, Taiwan, and Hongkong, and the remaining fourth from Europe. Textile imports

374

to the United States from Japan in 1969 amounted to about $500 million. More important were Japanese sales to the United States of machinery and appliances, including electronic equipment amounting to $2.2 billion and iron and steel valued at $728 million.

It is hard to prove that the American textile industry is depressed because of Japanese competition. In fact, profits of the industry as a whole increased slightly in 1969—by about $5 million over the previous year. Factories in North and South Carolina have suffered slumps and have had to lay off workers, and some have closed their doors. Sales in the textile industry dropped an estimated 1 percent in 1969, while imports of textiles increased 16 percent. Causes for these setbacks have certainly included increased automation and the general business decline, as well as competition from abroad. In any case, employment in the industry is said to have dropped in the first quarter of 1970 less than 20,000 from the record 1968 level of 990,000 workers.[22]

Whatever the economic facts may have been, everybody knew that the issue was political. Two promises, understood but not discussed, were crucial. In the Presidential campaign of 1968, Republican promises were made to Southern political leaders that support would be repaid by help for the textile industry against foreign competition, Japanese in particular. It was no secret that Southern politicians, Senator Strom Thurmond of South Carolina in particular, expected the pledge to be fulfilled. The textile industrialists of the south would no doubt have demanded the same price had the Democratic candidate been elected President.

The second promise was made by Prime Minister Sato to President Nixon during their meetings in Washington in November 1969. No one is quite sure what he said; not only is a conversation between chiefs of state a privileged communication but the nature of the Japanese language is such that a natural vagueness is compounded by the difficulties of translation. Okinawa had been returned, and the President brought up the subject of textiles. The all-knowing Japanese press speculated that Sato replied *"Nan to ka yarimasho"* ("I'll do something somehow") or *"Zensho shimasu"* ("I'll take care of it") and the translation came out "I'll try."[23] Whatever the exact words and meaning, Americans afterwards believed that at the conference in which agreement to return Okinawa was made, the Japanese Prime Minister promised to limit textile exports to the United States. Later, when the negotiations failed, it was Sato's "broken promise" which rankled most.

Minor in itself, the disagreement over textiles threatened to release a wave of protectionism that could change the direction of American trade policy, stimulate retaliation from other countries, and go far to nullify the progress made in recent decades toward greater freedom of international economic exchange. Signs began to show in the Congress as other special interests lined up behind textiles to seek their special protection. The Congressional mood grew more deeply critical of the Japanese; some observers went so far as to speculate whether the Senate, giving vent to its anger, might seek some way to obstruct the return to Japan in 1972 of the administrative rights over Okinawa.

Most observers agreed that the textile talks need not have failed. American negotiators were criticized for being insensitive, high handed, and haughty. They seem to have irritated and annoyed the Japanese by their method of approach. At the same time, the Japanese were divided; the powerful textile industry was pitted against the government, and there were differences in point of view between MITI and the Foreign Office. A Japanese correspondent in Washington commented that both governments, "bound by their respective industrial circles, were totally unable to act diplomatically." [24] This may be an exaggeration, but it represented impressions left by the event.

Japanese-American negotiations resumed later in 1970, in a second effort to reach agreement on voluntary quotas for textiles. They adjourned before Christmas, to continue again in 1971. Secretary of Commerce Stans announced at the time the meetings were suspended that the American textile manufacturers believed that no workable formula was being developed.

The Mills Bill, which included provisions for mandatory quotas, was not brought before the 91st Congress, but Mr. Stans said in a press interview, "The Japanese know as well as we do that we just ran out of time because of delays in the Senate or there would have been a trade bill." [25]

The danger lay ahead: would Japan and the United States be able to resist protectionism and retaliation? would the textile breakup become a forgotten episode or would it start a series of complications, changing the nature of trading principles and endangering the cooperation of the two nations in the far more critical tasks to confront them in Asia in the 1970's?

Japanese and American Attitudes

American traders at home and abroad have progressively experienced the stings of Japanese competition. This suddenly materializing economic giant has challenged American enterprise and expertise in a way no nation has done before. The erstwhile magnanimous, admiring, but sometimes patronizing postwar American feelings toward Japan have in some cases changed sharply to shock, resentment, and anger that remind of prewar sentiments. Some futurists tell us that the 21st Century will be Japan's century but some Americans, while outwardly congratulating the coming winner, may find little pleasure in the prospect.

Edward Seidensticker, professor and translator of Japanese literature, has astutely observed that "the American view of Japan seems to fluctuate between almost unconditional affection and unconditional antipathy." He adds that "both views are of course unrealistic and invite dangers." [26] In the prewar and World War II periods, the Chinese were heroes and the Japanese villains in American eyes. In the Occupation, Americans suddenly saw the Japanese as friendly, attractive, and hospitable people. Japan's image was transformed into a romantic combination of flowers, temples, kimono-clad beauties, Zen Buddhism, and a graceful way of life. As Seidensticker wrote in 1965, "The violent wartime dislike has given way to a sentimental fondness." [27]

Now there is danger of another drastic swing of the pendulum. The new American mood feeds on several elements. One is the American instinct to compete, which can only become more intense as Japan's drive for markets and materials musters greater power. Another is the growing American frustration over Japan's continuation of onerous restrictions on foreign investment while Japanese invest freely around the world, threaten to dominate lucrative markets, and sell more to America than America sells to them. A third and perhaps more pervasive element is the travail of the present-day United States: the nightmares over Indochina, crime, race, pollution, inflation, balance of payments, and nagging and complex responsibilities in the world. In the throes of this experience, the American is riled to see Japan enjoying the ostensible "free ride" made possible by security "made in U.S.A." but seemingly ungrateful for American largesse since the war. Thus, some Americans ask the question, "What did we get in return for Okinawa?" Others accuse Japan of thinking selfishly only of current profits and further gains while disregarding the interests of poor nations and the security and stability of East Asia. At the same time a few, such as the congressmen who made a study tour of Asia, shudder at an imagined prospect of revived militarism turning Japan in the disastrous direction taken by the prewar Empire.

Japanese attitudes have been less extreme. During the war, feelings of respect and even admiration for Americans were never fully extinguished. Since the war, Japanese have liked and imitated Americans but have freely and passionately criticized American policies and actions. Indeed, some Americans find it difficult to understand how successive Japanese governments can so completely and consistently have supported American policy in Southeast Asia while intellectuals and commentators thundered at the United States and opinion polls showed preponderant popular majority disapproval of American policies in Vietnam.

As confidence revived in the power and position of their nation, it was natural that the Japanese should see the United States in a different light. The more thoughtful among them still recognized the pivotal essentiality of their relationship with the United States, but a newly found pride in country demanded release from the overpowering American influence they had lived with since the war. Prime Minister Sato marked the end of the postwar period with the return of Okinawa, and psychologically this restoration to the homeland of territory so long lost, plus the new freedom to end the security treaty, brought welcome relaxation of a too tight and too enduring American bond.

To the foreigner, this confidence and independence does not jibe with the strict guarding of Japan's economy against entry from the outside. He asks how this first-class nation, with prospects for greater power ahead, can engage fully in the business of the international marketplace and yet remain so closed. Japanese industry and government indeed retain paternalistic and protective feelings for the enterprises they have together so carefully nurtured. This is the history of Japan's success, and it is not easy to open wide the doors to competition from the outside. Yet liberalization will come; it is official policy, and there is no turning back the clock. Ohira Masayoshi, former Minister of Foreign Affairs and of International Trade and Industry, able, broadminded, and with a lively sense of humor, described his country

378

aptly as an "international outsider." He acknowledged that many Japanese actions were not understandable to Europeans and Americans and that the country's goal should be to become an "international insider." He conceded that many of his compatriots thought this would be impossible, that the hundred million Japanese would always remain "outside." However, lacking resources and requiring imports, Japan had no choice. Ohira believed that by liberalizing and thus becoming an "international insider," the dialogue with the United States would become natural and easy.[28]

American and Japanese Expectations

In spite of Japan's newfound sense of independence from the United States, American actions in Asia will weigh heavily on Japanese decisions; and mutual expectations, whether fulfilled or unsatisfied, will significantly influence Japan's policies in the 1970's.

American expectations from Japan are on the record. President Nixon referred in his 1970 Foreign Policy Report to Congress to Japan's "unique and essential role . . . in the development of the new Asia." After identifying Okinawa as the "pivotal question concerning the future of our relations with Japan," he declared that "Japan's partnership with us will be a key to the success of the Nixon Doctrine in Asia." Later in the same document the President returned to the relationship with Japan, describing it as "crucial in our common effort to secure peace, security, and a rising living standard in the Pacific area." With a nod to Japanese constitutional and political limitations on military cooperation, Nixon added, "But we shall not ask Japan to assume responsibilities inconsistent with the deeply felt concerns of its people."[29]

Continually pressed to "play a key role in Asia," the Japanese rightfully ask what they in turn can expect from the United States in the 1970's. They will welcome the reduced American presence in Asia envisaged in the Nixon Doctrine, but judgments will be influenced by the manner, the speed, the places, and the environment of such reductions.

The two spots in Asia where Japanese eyes will rivet on American actions and reactions are Indochina and Korea.

Japanese feelings about the Vietnam War have been a combination of regret for the United States, sympathy for the Vietnamese, and the passivity of observers who watch a tragedy from afar. During the long years of conflict, the Japanese have repeatedly recalled their own desperately frustrating experiences in China and have seen no satisfying exit for the Americans, whom they pity for becoming so entangled. Mixed with this sentiment, although usually under the surface, has also been the sharp consciousness that again the white man is fighting people of a different race.

However the Japanese may have felt about the war, the nature of its outcome is of the greatest concern to them. An acknowledged American "defeat" and precipitate military withdrawal from Southeast Asia would produce despair in Japan. Japanese leaders would feel forced to reassess their security relationship with the United States and their defense policy.

Most Japanese expect no American "victory" in Vietnam, and many would view with indifference or even complacency growing Communist influence in Indochina. Responsible leaders, however, would hope, as a minimum, to see major fighting end and some stability restored. Unanimously, they would wish American forces, at least naval and air contingents, to remain in the area and would hope the British would decide to stay in Singapore. Japanese self-interest would dictate their desires for safety and stability to protect Japanese trade and investment in Southeast Asia.

Korea is nearer home than Southeast Asia, and ever since Korean security has been recognized as essential to Japanese security, the Republic of Korea has appeared to the Japanese in a new light. Therefore, when the press broke the news of a planned American removal of forces from Korea, there was dismay in Tokyo. Sato asked Secretary Rogers to consider with great care the timing of any such military reductions; Defense Director General Nakasone reminded a Diet committee that American military forces in South Korea also brought security to Japan.

Two effects were immediately forecast in Japan: (1) the ROK would look to Japan for more help, and (2) the Americans, in phasing out of Korea, would build up in Okinawa.

The first was soon confirmed. Korean government officials quickly appealed to Japan for much greater economic cooperation. One Japanese journalist hinted that the Koreans "in their hearts" probably wanted military assistance from Japan, but President Park firmly denied that his government would ever depend on Japan militarily.[30] The Japanese defense industry, already eyeing Asia as a market for arms and ammunition, would no doubt like to sell arms to the ROK and may see heightening tension between the two Koreas as opening opportunities for military aid in the future. In the meantime, Japanese economic cooperation, in the form of loans and investments, will likely go ahead at an accelerating pace.

While the Japanese feel more comfortable with an impressive American military presence in East Asia, they are less enthusiastic about a concentration of forces and installations in Okinawa. Government officials are well aware of the multitude of problems that will plague them once Okinawa returns to the fold in 1972. They have hoped that by then base problems would be more manageable and that reduction and consolidation, *not* expansion, would be in progress. These hopes are apparently shared by the Americans, who have revealed no intention to build up the military potential of the Okinawan bases.

With 1970 gone, the Left set a new target: 1972. That would now be the year not only of Okinawan reversion but of forced abandonment by the Americans of their bases in Japan and Okinawa. The "struggle of 1970" was to become the "struggles of the 1970's," with the first crisis billed for 1972. The rhetoric of the opposition elements in the country quickly adapted to this theme.

The announcement by Japan and the United States on December 21, 1970, that 12,000 American forces would be withdrawn from Japan by June 1971 and that 10,000 Japanese base workers would probably lose their jobs surprised many Japanese. The Americans were moving faster than expected; after the proposed reductions were carried out, there would be little of the American "spear" left in Japan. Japanese asked the question: could the "shield" of the Self-Defense Forces provide security without the "spear?"

Just as the Okinawans saw reversion in a new light when it was about to come upon them so thinking Japanese were disquieted at the thought of too quickly vanishing G.I.'s. The prospect of large dismissals of Japanese employees came as a shock. Three hundred restaurant owners near the Misawa air base suddenly faced an uncertain future. Press commentaries on rumors of reductions advised the Americans "not to hurry too much."

Of more consequence than the adjustments of employment and facilities was the concern of Japan's leaders over the future defense of the country. The situation long advocated by the Democratic Socialists would in fact come about: *yuji churyu* (stationing of forces only in an emergency). The spear would return when needed. The Director General of Defense was unperturbed. He assured his countrymen that the reduction of American Forces had been taken into consideration in designing the Fourth Defense Build-up Plan and expressed confidence that American supplementing of Japan's own defense capability would guarantee the security of Japan.[32] Uniformed officers in the SDF were reported to be less sanguine, grumbling that an enlarged Japanese shield could never supplant an offensive American spear.

Arguments began in the Diet over just what Japan's defense power should be, and as usual no one could satisfactorily define the elusive term "autonomous defense." One thing was clear: whatever measurement might be established for "adequate" security, the cost would be high. Most military installations would be turned over to the SDF or operated jointly, and for this, major appropriations would be required. If, as Director General Nakasone had stated, the achievement of "adequate" self-defense would be realized only after two more Build-up Plans, or by 1981, the SDF might not be able to move in as fast as the American military moved out.

Images and Feelings

At the beginning of the decade of the 1970's, Japanese-American relations were characterized on both sides by expectations that might not be fulfilled and by attitudes of diminished confidence and trust.

The Japanese expected the American commitment to the defense of Japan to be kept but wondered more and more whether, over the coming years, this promise would still be credible. They remembered American preachments about free trade and the Kennedy Round and were acutely aware of American attempts to break down Japanese restrictions, yet they viewed with alarm the trend toward protectionism in the United States. They were grateful for the promised return of Okinawa but were not sure what was expected of them. They were determined not to become the "policemen of Asia," and apparently this was not an American intention; yet they sensed that the drastic reduction of American military strength in Asia pointed to Japan, among the non-Communist powers, to fill the vacuum. Their own security was also directly involved as the Americans departed. Yet no one wanted Japan to remilitarize, least of all the Japanese themselves. Japan hoped America would stay but was no longer sure this would happen.

The Japanese image of the United States has changed. A country which had inspired admiration and respect now engendered doubt. With the blood of war in Asia and the gruesome close-ups of crime and violence in American cities and streets vividly communicated by television, radio, newspapers, and magazines, it was no wonder that America appeared torn asunder and on the brink of disaster. Many Japanese intellectuals, exuding confidence in the solid prosperity and bright future of their own country, openly worried about the stability of American society.

On the other hand, Americans with an interest in Japan were irritated at what they considered to be Japan's closed economy and were disappointed at the paucity of true aid to the developing countries. Many recognized that Japan could not send troops overseas or join military pacts, but they expected more evidence of a sense of responsibility for security in East Asia. Sato's pronouncements were not enough. They hoped Japan was planning for a greater security role in the future and they looked to the Tokyo Government for more dynamic leadership to move the nation in that direction.

Notes

1. U.S., Department of State, *The State of the Union,* Excerpts from President Nixon's Address to the Congress, *Bulletin,* Vol. LXII, No. 1598 (February 9, 1970), p. 146.

2. "Basic Initial Post-Surrender Directive to Supreme Commander for the Allied Powers for the Occupation and Control of Japan, November 3, 1945," Supreme Commander for Allied Powers, *Political Reorientation of Japan, September 1945 to September 1948,* Report of Government Section (2 vols., Washington, D.C.: U.S. Government Printing Office, 1949), II, Appendix A: 13, paragraph 29a, p. 436.

3. *The Japan Times,* June 24, 1970.

4. U.S., Department of State, *Bulletin,* Vol. LXIII, No. 1620 (July 13, 1970), p. 33.

5. *Ibid.*, p. 33.

6. Japanese-American trade statistics are confusing because each country computes them differently. Japan uses a c.i.f. basis to calculate imports; costs, insurance and freight incurred in getting the goods to the land edge in Japan are included. The United States uses the FOB basis, meaning the value of the goods at the time they are loaded aboard the vessel coming to the United States. Thus, the discrepancies in the 1969 Japanese-American trade figures are as shown in Table 15-1.

Table 15-1

Exports and Imports, 1969 (in millions of dollars)

U.S. data:

U.S. exports to Japan (FOB)	3,490
U.S. imports from Japan (FOB)	4,888
Total	7,378
U.S. deficit	1,398

Japanese data: (customs clearance basis)

Japanese exports to U.S. (FOB)	4,972
Japanese imports from U.S. (C.I.F.)	4,090
Total	9,062
Japan's surplus	882

7. Fukuda Takeo, "Japan to Promote Further Liberalization," *Pacific Community*, Vol. 2, No. 2 (January 1971), p. 246.

8. *Ibid.*, p. 246.

9. U.S.: Department of State, "Joint Communique of the Sixth Meeting of the Joint United States-Japan Committee on Trade and Economic Affairs," Washington, D.C., September 13-15, 1967. Press Release No. 199, September 15, 1967, paragraph II, 4.

10. U.S.: Department of State, "The Role of Japan and the Future of American Relations with the Far East," Address by Hon. U. Alexis Johnson, Under Secretary of State for Political Affairs, before the American Academy of Political and Social Science, Philadelphia, Pennsylvania, April 10, 1970. Press Release No. 116, April 10, 1970, p. 7.

11. George W. Ball, "Japan Urged to Reassess Its Attitude" *Pacific Community*, Vol. 2, No. 1 (October 1970), p. 13.

384

12. For an analysis of the nature and early period of the capital liberalization program, see T. F. M. Adams and N. Kobayashi, *The World of Japanese Business* (Tokyo and Palo Alto: Kodansha International, 1969), pp. 229-57.

13. "Japan's Capital Liberalization," *Fuji Bank Bulletin,* November 1970, p. 198.

14. Fukuda, *op. cit.,* p. 248.

15. Tsusho Sangyosho (Ministry of Trade and Industry MITI), *Tsusho Hakusho 1970. Kakuron* (White Paper on Foreign Trade, Detailed) (Tokyo: MITI, July 10, 1970), pp. 499 and 501.

16. *Fuji Bank Bulletin,* November 1970, *op. cit.,* p. 198.

17. Adams and Kobayashi, *op. cit.,* p. 239.

18. American Chamber of Commerce in Japan, Investments Committee, "Capital Liberalization," ACCJ Position Paper for 1970, *The Journal of the American Chamber of Commerce in Japan,* October 5, 1970, p. 11.

19. Adams and Kobayashi, *op. cit.,* p. 240.

20. Henry Scott Stokes, "Japan's Liberalization Policy," *Pacific Community,* Vol. 2, No. 2 (January 1971), p. 260.

21. Leon Hollerman, "Liberalization and Japanese Trade in the 1970's," *Asian Survey.* Vol. X, No. 5 (May 1970), p. 434n.

22. United States-Japan Trade Council, *How Much Would Textile Quotas Cost the United States?* (Washington, D.C.: United States-Japan Trade Council, Inc., May 1970), p. 4. The United States-Japan Trade Council is registered as an agent of a foreign organization, the Japan Trade Promotion Office.

23. "Hiwa Kosaku suru Nichi-Bei Sen-i Kosho no Ketsuretsu" (Complex Inside Secret Stories of the Breakup of the Japanese-American Textile Negotiations), *Asahi Journal,* Tokyo, July 12, 1970, p. 96.

24. *Nihon Keizai,* June 26, 1970.

25. *The New York Times,* December 24, 1970.

26. Edward Seidensticker, "The Image," in Herbert Passin, ed., *The American Assembly, the United States and Japan* (Englewood Cliffs, N.J.: Prentice-Hall, Inc., 1966), p. 18.

27. *Ibid.,* p. 25.

28. *Yomiuri,* July 6, 1970.

29. U.S.: Department of State, "U.S. Foreign Policy for the 1970's, A New Strategy for Peace," A Report to the Congress by Richard Nixon, President of the United States, February 18, 1970," *Bulletin,* Vol. LXII, No. 1602 (March 8, 1970), pp. 295 and 296.

30. *Asahi,* July 19, 1970.

31. *Sankei,* December 5, 1970.

32. *Nihon Keizai,* December 13, 1970.

Japan's Role
in the 1970's

Japanese Objectives

In 1962, Prime Minister Ikeda Hayato, in a speech to foreign correspondents in Tokyo, referred to the East-West conflict and commented that the "West" was supported by three pillars: Western Europe, the United States and Canada, and Japan. He said that Japan was still small, that the economy must grow, and that his problem was to double the country's GNP by the end of the 1960's.[1] When 1970 came, Japan's GNP had multiplied four and a half times in the decade.

Eight years after Ikeda's speech, his successor, Sato Eisaku, told the Japanese Diet in February 1970 that the decade of the 1970's would be "an era where Japan's national power will carry un- precedented weight in world affairs."[2] The question for the decade remained: whether this power would continue to be largely economic or whether it would translate itself into political or even military influence.

"Pillar of the West" may, in the 1970's become a less apt meta- phor for Japan than it was a decade earlier. The Japanese would like to think globally and not in terms of an East-West confrontation. While continuing to place first priority on relations with the United States, they may devote greater energies in the coming years to improving relations with the Soviet Union and, particularly, with mainland China.

Japan's vital interests are concerned with arms and yen, with security and economics. We have seen how Japan has protected these interests; let us now consider the directions in which these interests are likely to lead.

Security

Assuming political stability through the decade, Japan's primary

387

objective will naturally be the security of her own territory. This will largely depend upon good relations with the United States, security and stability in relations with her closest neighbors (Communist China, the Soviet Union, South Korea, and Taiwan) and stability in Southeast Asia.

We can expect the build-up of the Self-Defense Forces to continue, and if by the end of the decade these become at least seventh among the world's armed forces (the defense budget for 1971 is projected at $1.8 billion), they will have gone far to reach the desired "adequacy" for the defense of the homeland. In addition, the Japanese-American security treaty, although perhaps somewhat changed in character, will probably continue to protect Japan with its "nuclear umbrella." Within the decade, American bases and military personnel are likely to have almost disappeared from Japan and will be much reduced in Okinawa, if not removed entirely. A close Japanese-American military relationship will probably survive, with the principle of "stationing of forces in an emergency" maintained.

Revision of the Constitution may again become a live issue and, if so, will produce widespread political controversy in the country. The fate of Article 9 and the actions Japan might take were it repealed—sending troops abroad or joining security pacts—depend, as we have noted, to a large degree on events outside of Japan.

New dimensions into which Japan's security role may extend are the development of an export armaments industry and programs of military assistance to other countries, with priority to the defense needs of Southeast Asian developing nations. Needless to say, such steps would provoke hostile eruptions on the Left. Also possible would be the participation by Japan in United Nations peacekeeping efforts, specifically in Indochina, should military contingents be requested for such purpose. Japan's cooperation with the United Nations would necessarily be conditioned by Japanese political judgments at the time.

Korea is a special case. Japanese Governments will be highly sensitive to the threat of conflict in the Korean peninsula. Should war break out between the South and the North, Japan would hope for immediate American response and would most surely facilitate this reaction by any means short of dispatching combat forces. The South Koreans would have to be desperate indeed ever to ask or to tolerate Japanese troops on their soil. A Japanese professor recently quoted the angry response of the president of a South Korean University to the suggestion that the Self-Defense Forces might replace departing American troops in South Korea: "In that case, we would join North Korea, to fight Japan!" Another Korean answered the same question, "I would kill myself!"[3]

While Japan's leaders are inhibited by a public opinion wary of involvement, the relationship between the security of the ROK and Japan is more than a phrase out of the Nixon-Sato communique. Few other threats are recognized, but war in Korea would be too close for comfort.

As for longer term changes in Japan's defense posture, the security treaty may take on a somewhat different meaning but will probably not soon be terminated, either by Japan or by the United States. With a smaller American military presence and with the implementation of the Nixon Doctrine banning "more Vietnams," the importance of the "Far East" clause diminishes and Japanese fears of becoming entangled in American conflicts may be assuaged. Such changes in the effect of the treaty could come about, not be revision of the treaty itself, but by interpretation forced by the impact of realities in Asia.

From today's perspective, it appears unlikely that a decision to produce nuclear weapons will be made by Japan during the 1970's. We have examined the reasons which might impel the Japanese Government to such action and have discussed the consequences of such a decision. Outside events would likely be determining, and in this the United States holds more responsibility than China or any other power. An abrogation of the security treaty or the turning of the United States's back on Asia could well influence the Japanese to conclude that they must shift from the principle of collective defense with the United States to actual military independence, including an arsenal of atomic bombs. At present it seems improbable that American policy and actions in East Asia would go so far as to invite such a response and that the collective security principle would, as a consequence, be so completely broken.

Economics

The urge for growth persists, and Japan's GNP is bound to climb to greater heights. The export drive and the search for raw materials will continue, although the enormous and increasing internal and external demands will likely slow the acceleration of economic growth. Direct Japanese-American competition may sharpen and become more acrimonious.

Any ascent to the coveted rank of superstate will not be a straight, smooth, uninterrupted glide. The pursuit of resources, technology, and expanding markets will be intense but never free from obstacles. As we have seen, the internal problems which beset Japan are becoming more pressing, and Japanese Governments in this decade cannot ignore the pressures for better housing, health, sanitation, education, communications, and environment—in sum, improvement in the quality of life. The problem of accommodating the intensified industrialization of a megalopolis with liveable environment faces a geographically limited Japan with even more urgency than it does the United States.

Japan's growing economy must cope with the reactions of the world. Thus far, Japanese products have sold themselves, and many markets with many consumers seem endlessly to absorb the goods of excellent quality and attractive price which Japan's manufacturers produce. But even a flood can meet resistance. Justifiably or not, Southeast Asian countries already resent too much Japanese economic influence and rebel at high-handed methods, pressure salesmanship, arrogance, and failure to understand and sympathize with the customs, traditions, and actions of local peoples. So far, such reactions have not seemed to affect trade, which continues to leap ahead. But at some point the Japanese will suffer. Just as American businessmen need to try to gain better understanding of and sensitivity to the culture that makes the Japanese what they are, so the Japanese need to break down the alienation between themselves and other Asians. As a prominent Japanese professor has stated, "The psychological distance between Japanese and other Asians is greater than between Japanese and Western nations."[4]

The Japanese leaders know the problems that face them both at home and abroad and they appreciate that the great successes which have been prophesied for them depend in a large degree on how well they meet these challenges. The test will be whether their determination, dedication, and energy can be quickly and efficiently mobilized to solve problems of a more complex and intangible nature than the creation and operation of a mammoth producing machine.

Two Countries: The United States and China

Premier Sato, in his speech at the opening of the Diet on January 22, 1971, spoke of two countries whose relations with Japan were of major importance: the United States and China. He affirmed that what happens in Japanese-American relations has a greater influence "on our people's livelihood than relations with any other country." At the same time he underscored his desire to improve relations with Communist China by referring to that country for the first time publicly as the People's Republic of China.[5] Interestingly enough, President Nixon followed suit in his 1971 State of the World message, in which he spoke of drawing "the People's Republic of China into a constructive relationship with the world community and particularly with the rest of Asia."[6]

The United States

The economic exchange between Japan and the United States is so great and the postwar partnership so close that it is difficult to conceive of a break between the two countries. Nevertheless, as we have seen in the preceding chapter, Japanese-American problems are exasperating and are growing. It would be a mistake for either nation to take the other for granted.

In spite of the tension over voluntary quotas, trade barriers, capital liberalization, and the ever sharper competition in each other's markets and in the world at large, economic questions will probably not seriously threaten the alliance during the decade of the 1970's. Japanese Governments have set a course to break down restrictions and to liberalize trade and investment. This they will not reverse. Americans will doubtless continue to complain, however, that the pace is too slow. The Japanese system can hardly be expected to change, and Japanese methods and attitudes will probably continue to frustrate the Americans trying to exploit their opportunities in Japan. But economic issues will surely never overcome partners with so much at stake.

The problem of security will be more difficult. Much will depend upon the smoothness of the transition of the military bases from American control to SDF operation and joint use. Theoretically, this process should meet the needs of both sides. The Americans are committed to a reduction in forces by the Nixon Doctrine, and the Japanese welcome the disappearance of the American-made "base nuisances" and the resulting stimulus to more independent defense. At the same time, the change produces new problems for Japanese Governments. The inevitable dismissal of Japanese base workers incites the labor unions and opposition organizations to protests and demonstrations, which have already occurred both in Okinawa and in Japan proper. More troublesome will be the shift in targets for the Left—from the American military to the Japanese Self-Defense Forces. The agitation will be slightly altered in character, but again, as in Okinawa, the Left may well be revealed to be more anti-military than anti-American. The timing, the manner, and the readiness of the SDF to assume their added responsibilities will all be essential factors determining the smoothness of the change.

As the American forces—the "precious guests," the hostages for Japan's security, as a JDA official described them—disappear, the credibility of the American deterrent will be ever in the forefront of Japanese leaders' minds. Their observation of events in the United States will most decisively affect their judgments. Japanese intellectuals now quite openly question the reliability of the American partner.

Part of Japanese uneasiness over the dependability of the American "spear" in time of need comes from the perception of a dilemma that could face the United States in the coming years. The Nixon Doctrine, as first enunciated by the President in Guam on July 25, 1969, contained two major points: (1) that the United States would keep its treaty commitments; and (2) that except for the threat of a major power involving nuclear weapons, the United States would expect the Asian nations to handle by themselves the problems of military defense. But a plausible possibility is a threat to Japan not immediately involving the use of nuclear weapons yet too serious to be handled by the homeland-bound Self-Defense Forces. At such a moment, would the United States come to the aid of Japan and risk not only "another Vietnam" but possible war with China or the Soviet Union? Sensing the mood of the American people, the Japanese may well question the rapidity and effectiveness of an American response to such a threat. Thus, the urge to beat the shield into a spear might become irresistible.

Serious doubts about the American deterrent may be allayed during the first part of the decade, principally because the Japanese are not convinced that a real threat now exists. The coming years will probably be a period of Japanese buildup and American readjustment and the increased use of diplomacy. Short of an outbreak in the Korean peninsula or a sudden burst of Chinese belligerency, the Japanese will avoid judgments, watching the trend of events in the world, most especially and intently those in the United States of America.

China

In a broadcast on New Year's Day 1971, Prime Minister Sato told his national audience that "Japan has no diplomacy unless we come to grips with the China problem."[7] During the 1970's a basic Japanese policy will be to avoid conflict with mainland China. Most Japanese would probably agree that there is no reason for China to be a threat to Japan or Japan a threat to China. As Defense Director General Nakasone said at the beginning of 1970, "Japan must establish the major principle that 'the Japanese people and the Chinese people will never fight against each other again.'" Still, he envisaged no strong solidarity between the two. He went on to say, "In that case, Japan must turn its face toward the seas . . . . The inevitable direction will be cooperation with the United States."[8]

The successive recognition of the People's Republic by a number of nations, beginning with Canada, and the close vote in the 1970 session of the United Nations General Assembly brought a new sense of urgency to Japan's consideration of China policy. The possibility of a favorable vote in 1971 on admission of China to the United Nations and the anxiety about being left behind in competition for mainland markets were compelling factors for Japanese leaders. As always, however, Taiwan was the sticking point. Some additional Japanese industrial firms, bowing to Chou En-lai's dictate that firms trading with Taiwan could not trade with mainland China, announced that no new ventures would be initiated in Taiwan. These included Mitsubishi Shoji, which had extremely extensive investments in Taiwan.[9] Members of the pro-Peking group in the LDP openly advocated abandoning trade and investment with the Republic of China on Taiwan in order to extend full recognition to the People's Republic. More Japanese, no doubt, hoped that their government could deal profitably with the PRC without abandoning the very important political and economic interests in Taiwan.

The propaganda barrage from Peking became more virulent, as we have seen. The denunciations of Sato and his "henchmen" as "imperialist stooges" and "revivers of militarism" could be expected to become more shrill as recognition by other countries gave Mao and his associates more confidence and more arrogance. The 1971 round of negotiations for a Japanese-Chinese Memorandum Trade Agreement was, as expected, punctuated by still more violent abuse of the Sato government than had been the case in previous years.

As long as Japan's conservative LDP leadership remains in power, the Chinese dilemma is likely to continue. In spite of growing pressure from the pro-Peking group within the LDP and of increasing public interest in Japan's relations with the People's Republic, neither Sato nor a successor of similar conservative bent is likely soon to vote to eject Taiwan from the United Nations. The Japanese would doubtless be most happy if a formula could be found to permit both mainland China and Taiwan to belong to the United Nations. The membership of Byelorussia and the Ukraine in the United Nations, although both belong to the Soviet Union, could be a useful precedent. The Japanese have special reasons of their own not to reject Taiwan. Their treaty with the Republic of China ended the war between China and Japan, but the Peking government does not recognize this treaty and has insisted that Japan abrogate it as a condition of recognition. The Chinese Communists would demand that a new peace treaty be signed to end the state of war and there is no guarantee that they would not demand reparations. The Japanese are deeply grateful to Chiang Kai-shek for never imposing war reparations upon them, and they are apprehensive as to what Peking's attitude toward the subject might be.

While Japan's present interests in Taiwan are largely economic, it is reasonable to surmise that Japanese leaders see great advantages in a future independent government on the island, whether one totally cut off from the mainland or one with *de facto* independence and some nominal allegiance as a "part of China." The Japanese are aware of the generally favorable attitude of the Taiwanese people toward Japan and know how much in the

Japanese interest a close relationship with a free Taiwan would be. An island with 14 million inhabitants is hardly comparable to a land mass with 800 million, but Japan will not easily or quickly abandon this former colony, with its great potential of benefit for the long-term future.

The Japanese sense no threat from China, but they will be alert to Chinese military developments and to Chinese subversion in the parts of Southeast Asia where their country's interests loom. Tokyo Governments will try to solve the China problem, not by building up military arsenals, but by diplomacy and economics. Furthermore, Japan will be patient, recognizing that events on the Chinese mainland, in Taiwan, and in the world, will be more decisive than any policies which Japan could devise or carry out now.

Japan's Role

For several years, foreigners—and Japanese too, for that matter—have been writing incessantly about Japan's "role" in the world. Headlines suggest the themes: "Japan's Search for Its Role"; "A Bigger Role for the 'Rich Man of Asia'"; "Japan Scans Wider Asian Role"; "Japan Takes Steps to the Fore."

Visions of the future Japanese role differ. Some foresee a 21st Century superpower, ahead of the United States in GNP, fully militarized, and a full-fledged member of the nuclear "club." Others portray an "economic animal," inspired only by "my-home-ism" and the power of the yen, producing day and night, exploiting the world's resources, selling anything and everything to the world, so absorbed in the pursuit of profits and GNP that no time nor inclination is left for acts unrelated to business.

Neither of these dreams is practical, likely, or desirable, either for the Japanese or for the rest of the world.

The Japanese themselves are bewildered. They ponder their nation's destiny, but few see clearly what it ought to be. The headlines read: "Sato Foresees Major Role for Japan in 1970's," but the Prime Minister's suggestions, beyond keeping the American partnership and developing a solution to the "China problem," list only needed domestic reforms that could be taken for granted: control of violence; reform of education; remedying pollution, the housing shortage, and the stresses of urbanization;

modernizing agriculture; and stabilizing prices. Mention was made of the necessity to base economic policies on an "international outlook," but this could hardly be a "role," and furtheremore, it was confined to Japan's economic interests abroad. [10]

A Japanese professor heard Prime Minister Sato speak to the United Nations General Assembly in October 1970. He wrote that Soviet Foreign Minister Gromyko had addressed an overflowing crowd just before Sato's speech was scheduled, using cold war verbiage to attack the United States. He was given a storm of applause as he finished. Afterwards, many delegations and numerous members of the audience quickly left the meeting and Sato was left to speak to an almost empty hall. The scene was proof to the professor that Japan counted for little in international affairs: "However proud Japan may be of ranking third in terms of GNP in the world, economic power alone will not enhance its international voice." [11]

Americans seem usually to hear about Japan only when cries are raised about the threat of Japanese exports, when students and police are rioting, or when a famous author commits *seppuku* publicly. Arthur Schlesinger's account of President Kennedy's term of office, *A Thousand Days*, makes no mention of American relations with Japan; yet it was President Kennedy who called Japan the "homeland" for Okinawans and gave encouragement to their desire for reversion to Japan, and in his administration regular Cabinet-level economic conferences were instituted by Japan and the United States. For Japan, these alone were epoch-making events.

A year-end American television review in 1970 by leading commentators on international events and problems failed to discuss Japan, and it was not until the last few seconds of the broadcast that one of the participants suddenly remarked that Japan had not been mentioned once. It would be interesting to know how many Americans can identify the Prime Minister of Japan or recall the name of any leading living Japanese.

As may have become clear in these pages, the Japanese are still an insular people who, in spite of their massive international trade and increasing travel, have difficulty in breaking down barriers between themselves and peoples of the rest of the world. Communication is their most serious problem. Diplomats and businessmen sent abroad usually speak acceptable English, and many are completely fluent. Still, it is true that few Japanese politicians speak a foreign language well. The Cabinet Minister who leads a delegation to an international conference usually depends upon an interpreter. At conferences of Southeast Asian ministers, where English is commonly used, often it is only the Japanese delegate who cannot communicate in the lingua franca of the others.

The fault does not lie only with the Japanese. Americans can with little grace criticize the Japanese for lacking linguistic competence. Many of us seem to take for granted that people of other countries will learn *our* language. Japanese, of course, is especially difficult, and it requires unusual effort and persistence to gain a working knowledge of it. Recently, it was said that no more than three out of eight hundred American businessmen in Tokyo know enough Japanese to make an impromptu after-dinner speech; at one time, only two American correspondents stationed in Japan could dispense with an interpreter.

The Japanese are inward-looking, self-critical, and self-analytical. We have noted their priority interest in domestic problems, as shown in public opinion polls and in pre-election campaigns. Politicians give foreign policy credit for determining elections, but in fact it plays a relatively minor positive role. An American observer recently cited a list of ten non-fiction best sellers in 1970 to suggest the trend of popular interest. Not one was concerned with a foreign country or any aspect of foregn affairs. Exclusively devoted to Japanese subjects, these books treated Japanese ceremonies, education, business, management, cookery, and religion (a book of essays on Buddhism and "Cut Down the *Soka Gakkai*"). The one book written by a foreigner was a translation of Robert Guillain's *Japon Troisième Grand,* published as *Daisan no Taikoku Nippon (The Third Great Power, Japan).*[12]

The Japanese know that their role must be more than that of a producer, buyer and seller of goods, that they must not be considered an international orphan. As former Foreign Minister Ohira said, Japan must become an international "insider." But how? The negatives are easier to identify than the positives.

It is not likely that Japan will become the "policeman of Asia" or that during the 1970's it will move to exert military power in East Asia. As we have suggested, only the most extreme circumstances, such as the complete disappearance of an American armed presence in the Pacific (which seems highly improbable) or some new and provocative challenge from the Soviet Union or Communist China (likewise unexpected and unlikely) would impel Japan to flaunt armed might in Asia. As we have seen, Japan cannot legally join a regional security pact with military obligations or dispatch armed forces outside the country without first amending the Constitution. Although in late February 1971 certain members of the LDP formed a committee to study the Constitution with the aim of revising it during the 1970's, this issue, if actually brought forward, would spark bitter controversy within and without the party. A proposal for constitutional revision, especially of the "no-war" provisions of Article 9, would unite the opposition parties and much of the country against the Government as would no other issue except a proposal to build an atomic weapon. Prime Minister Sato has thus far wisely shown no inclination to introduce this explosive question into Japanese politics.

The failure of Mishima Yukio to inspire the Self-Defense Forces by his dramatic appeal and suicide revealed that the Japan of the 1970's is not the Japan of the 1930's. Nothing has so far been found in the attitudes or beliefs of SDF members to suggest the seeds of a coup d'etat. Nor have Rightist political movements shown signs of vigor or expansion. Some observers point to Japan's youth as unscarred by defeat in war and therefore imbued with national pride. They see them as dedicated to restoring their country's independence through military power. But young Japanese, like young Americans, are pacifists. They join anti-war movements by the thousands, and while their radicalism will mellow and many will become loyal workers for Japan's great capitalists and spare no energies to build the prosperity of their country, they show no signs of harboring a chauvinism that will break out in a revival of militarism, Chou En-lai's dark accusations notwithstanding. Such moods could change, of course, and outside events and threats, as we have noted, can have their effect. But it seems reasonable to expect that for a while to come, both in the United States and in Japan, nationalism and militarism will not be the forces that capture the hearts and minds of youth.

There could be many scenarios of what Japan *may* do and what Japan *should* do in the 1970's but no one, Japanese or American, can make such judgments with certainty. However, if one holds the dangers of projecting the future well in mind and points out that many surprises, unforeseen events and influences will condition what really happens, one may be pardoned for one's temerity in suggesting some directions that Japan might take. To summarize, the following are probabilities in the 1970's, most of which have already been discussed in the course of these chapters.

Japan will probably maintain the American alliance, interpreting the security treaty more flexibly and taking over military facilities evacuated by American forces but still depending upon the treaty guarantee as a deterrent and a last resort.

Japan's growing "independence" from the United States will appear in both security and economic policies. The SDF will gain confidence in its capabilities as added military strength develops through the Fourth and Fifth Defense Build-up Plans. Conscription appears highly unlikely, although acute shortages of manpower and expanded SDF responsibilities could conceivably make a draft feasible within the decade. Although the American military presence will be reduced to a minimum, the principle of collective security will be respected, meaning, in fact, continuation of close cooperation and coordination between the defense establishments of Japan and the United States, especially in the technological field and in the exchange and evaluation of information.

Japan will undoubtedly carry out its announced policies of trade and capital liberalization and will go far to remove barriers to the free entry of goods and investment into the country. No revolutionary change can be expected, however, in the system that controls Japan's economy, nor will the 50-50 principle in direct investment be soon abandoned. Pressures for greater internationalization of outlook and practice will result in major advances and improvement of relations with foreign entrepreneurs.

Intensified efforts will certainly be made to develop more trade and communication with mainland China. At the same time, Tokyo will search patiently and persistently for a formula that would permit diplomatic relations with Peking without complete abandonment of Taiwan. Close coordination and consultation between Tokyo and Washington will continue.

Japanese Governments will continue to press for the return of the northern territories from the Soviet Union, without, however, expecting quick gratification of the demand. Return of the

Habomais and Shikotan could become possible if the Soviet Union were to conclude that Japan's military ties with the United States had weakened and that increased Soviet influence would counteract closer Japanese-Chinese relations. Trade with the Soviet Union will continue, and projects of economic cooperation in Siberia and Sakhalin will be scrutinized closely and agreed upon if Japan concludes that a particular scheme is useful and advantageous and the terms are right. Maintaining strict neutrality in the Sino-Soviet dispute, the Japanese will try to keep satisfactory relations with both nations and will avoid arrangements that might irritate one or the other, create an imbalance, or lean to one or the other side.

Japan's perception of a threat to her security will depend upon the policies and actions of the U.S.S.R. and the People's Republic of China. At present, no serious, imminent threat from either is anticipated, although the SDF will direct its warning systems, intelligence activities, and military preparedness to the two continental Communist powers.

The Korean peninsula will be the focus of alert. The Japanese Government will continue to emphasize trade and aid with the Republic of Korea, as elements in the stability and security of that nation. It is likely that during the decade Japan may become a donor of military aid. If so, South Korea could be a recipient. In case of an outbreak of hostilities, the Japanese Government will doubtless be prepared to facilitate American action to defend the South, if that should be decided.

In the developing countries of Southeast Asia, Japan will carry ongrowing programs of economic and technical aid. Her objectives will be the betterment of Japan's economy and also the improvement of stability and security of the area, which will increasingly concern Japanese leaders as the years advance. Added emphasis will be placed on regional and multilateral assistance, and Japan, as the only Asian donor nation, will feel the necessity of taking a leading part in these arrangements. The Japanese Government will attempt to improve the image of Japan in the Southeast Asian nations by urging private companies to pay greater attention to the selection of qualified, adaptable personnel with understanding and sympathy for the countries in which they serve. Governmental programs of cultural and educational exchange will no doubt be stressed and expanded. The manner in which the increasing aid programs are administered will be of major significance. Whether foresight and skill will change the Japanese image in Southeast Asia is uncertain, especially if Japanese trade and aid attain such magnitude that Southeast Asians believe they have traded their economic independence for domination by Japan.

Japan will recognize an identity of interests with the advanced nations in the Pacific and will be inclined to cooperate with them in regional activities or arrangements. It is problematical whether a formalized "Pacific Community," to include Australia, Canada, Japan, New Zealand, and the United States, or a Pacific free trade area will emerge.

Japan will seek with greater urgency opportunities for political leadership in international arenas. Efforts to secure a seat in the United Nations Security Council will not abate but will probably be successful only when an expansion of Security Council membership becomes feasible. This could happen at the time the People's Republic of China is admitted to the world body. Japan's leaders will watch continually for chances to play a part in the settlement of international disputes, peacekeeping in Indochina, disarmament, and other problems which may arise, especially in Asia. Japan's ability to assume such responsibilities is, of course, first dependent on the opportunity. So far, no real challenge has presented itself: attempts to solve the Malaysia-Indonesia dispute during Sukarno's regime were abortive, and the 1970 Djakarta conference on the problems of Indochina offered little real hope of peace-making. If the occasion develops, how successfully will Japan respond? Here not only the solidarity and determination of the government in power but the diplomatic finesse, personality, and sensitivity of the chosen individuals will come into play. Thus far, no Japanese has figured prominently on an international stage.

Economic growth has brought Japan international prestige but has also brought the same battery of problems that face the United States, only in a more concentrated and brutal form. While Japan's leaders cast their eyes about in search of a world role, the populace demands priorities for removing the ills they see immediately before them. We have already described them: *kogai*, including pollution, congestion, and all the outgrowths of frenetic urbanization, and the outrageous inadequacies in the social infrastructure. The threat of death through destruction of the environment has brought the Japanese up short to insist at long last that the quality of life is more precious than a whopping GNP. The

Japanese have demonstrated their genius for directing energies and resources to the achievement of a decided goal. After neglecting the problems of environment for years, they could attack them with a success that might surprise the world. The Japanese public will be more excited over this battle than over the complex relations of their country with the rest of the world.

The problem of Okinawa will not disappear with reversion in 1972. The agitation for complete American abandonment of the military bases will intensify and, coupled with the problems of labor and land adjustment and of the take-over of administration, will present the Governments of Japan and the United States with hard choices. The dissatisfactions and fears of the Okinawan people, real or imagined, and their resentment of continued military controls and influence—directed at the United States command but also increasingly at the Japanese Self-Defense Forces—will encourage and strengthen the political Left. In future elections, the opposition parties may continue to gain. When a reversion agreement is presented for ratification by the Japanese Diet and the United States Senate, the power of the Left and instability in Okinawa could affect its smooth passage in both bodies. The U.S. Government would be concerned for the security of the Okinawan bases against a Left determined to close them. This could be the "crisis of 1972," already proclaimed by the opposition forces in Japan. Probably the cooperation of the Japanese and American Governments will be close, and it is to be hoped that trouble can be avoided. To postpone reversion would seriously disturb relations between the United States and Japan. On the other hand, any precipitate withdrawal of American forces from Okinawa and a too rapid turnover to the Japanese SDF would aggravate conditions of instability.

The Nixon Doctrine's effect on the American position in East Asia will influence Japanese-American relations. In spite of official American assurances to the contrary, some responsible Japanese fear an American return to isolationism. They ponder the future consequences of a spreading flow of Soviet naval power into the Pacific and a potential creeping Chinese Communist influence in East and Southeast Asia. Observing the disturbed political atmosphere in the United States produced by the Indochina war and foreseeing a substantial reduction of American military power in the western Pacific, these Japanese worry about the speed and certainty of an American response should Japan be truly threatened. It is this fear which, if not dispelled, could in the future encourage Japanese leaders to decide that the safest alternative for them would be a totally independent defense, meaning full rearmament including nuclear weapons. At such a turning point for Japan, the Left would profit by the Government's dilemma and exert all-out efforts for a policy of so-called "neutrality" and full accommodation with the Soviet Union and Communist China. Such a policy, if set in opposition to the alternative of full rearmament, would win some support among the Japanese public. If ever adopted, it would bring disaster to the Japanese-American relationship.

President Nixon recognized the crux of the issue in his 1971 State of the World message: "We need to head off possible overreactions in the new era: a feeling on our part that we need not help others, and a conclusion on their part that they cannot count on America at all." [13] There is a vast difference between American interests in Indochina and in Japan. The security of Japan is pre-eminent among the national interests of the United States in Asia. No other country—including China—in Asia is as important to the United States, at least through the 1970's, if not beyond. Unless we are to isolate ourselves from Asia, an unthinkable course for a leading power in the world and in the Pacific, the essentiality of our relationship with Japan is absolute. The American task is to convince both Americans and Japanese that this is true. For it is in the selfish interest of the United States—as well as in the interest of Japan—that Japan not become again a militaristic nation or shrink into a "neturality" that looks to the continent and not to the ocean.

Japan in the 1970's has the rare opportunity to demonstrate to the world that in spite of Mao Tse-tung's dictum, power does not necessarily come out of the barrel of a gun; that a great power does not have to be a great military power. As the GNP mounts and aid to the developing countries grows, Japan's influence in Asia will also increase. This influence will be better accepted and will be far more effective if it comes from a Japan that continues to renounce the use of nuclear weapons and maintains armed forces exclusively for self-defense. Japan's role will then be played mainly through economics and diplomacy, and as Japan wins deeper respect and confidence from the world, new opportunities will arise for the quiet, constructive tasks that the Japanese can so efficiently accomplish.

The modernization of Japan should be the shining example to all nations, above all, to those in Asia. If in this century Japan's arms are strong enough to protect the nation but never powerful enough to threaten others, if Japan's yen are used both for the welfare of her own citizens and generously for the common good of mankind, then prestige and respect will be forthcoming and Japan's role will be constructive, effective, and worthy of the Great Power Japan will have become.

Notes

1. The Foreign Correspondents Club of Japan, "Remarks by Prime Minister Hayato Ikeda at the Foreign Correspondents Club Luncheon," December 6, 1962, Press Release No. 191.

2. *New York Times,* February 15, 1970.

3. Eto Shinkichi, "Structure of Anti-Japanese Arguments," *Jiyu,* December 1970.

4. *Japan Times,* June 24, 1970.

5. *New York Times,* January 23, 1971.

6. *U.S. Foreign Policy for the 1970's, Building for Peace,* A Report to the Congress by Richard Nixon, President of the United States, February 25, 1971 (Washington, D.C.: U.S. Government Printing Office, 1971), p. 106.

7. *New York Times,* January 8, 1971.

8. *Nihon Keizai,* January 1, 1970.

9. *Sankei,* December 10, 1970.

10. *New York Times,* February 15, 1970.

11. *Sankei,* Evening ed., November 13, 1970.

12. F. Roy Lockheimer, "A Note on Japan in 1970," American Universities Field Staff, East Asia Series, Vol. XVII, No. 4 (Japan), July 1970, p. 2.

13. *U.S. Foreign Policy for the 1970's, Building the Peace, op. cit.,* p. 10.

Index

Index

410

413

John K. Emmerson, U.S. Minister and Deputy Chief of Mission in Tokyo from 1962 to 1967, began a lifetime of experience in Japan in 1936, as a Language Officer in Tokyo. He subsequently became Vice-Consul in Osaka, and in 1940 he was appointed Third Secretary at the Embassy in Tokyo. In 1941 he was assigned to the Division of Far Eastern Affairs of the Department of State, and during World War II he was political advisor to General Joseph W. Stilwell in the China-Burma-India theater and also served with the American Observers Mission in Yenan, China, then under Communist control. In 1946 he returned to Japan as Assistant Chief of the Division of Japanese Affairs in the Department of State. A veteran of 33 years with the Foreign Service, Mr. Emmerson has also held high-ranking posts in Moscow, Taipei, Lima, Karachi, Paris, Lagos, and Salisbury. In 1954, he was awarded the Meritorious Service Award of the Department of State, and in 1968 he received the honorary degree of LL.D. from Colorado College. He retired from the Foreign Service in 1968 and is currently Senior Research Fellow at the Hoover Institution, Stanford University, and Research Associate at the Center for Strategic and International Studies, Georgetown University.

DATE DUE

APR 2 6 '77			
MAY 2 5 '77			
APR 2 0 '82			
APR 2 0 1982			
DEC 1 8 1990			
MAY 6 1992			
MAY 1 0 1995			
GAYLORD			PRINTED IN U.S.A.